Advances in Computer Vision and Pattern Recognition

More information about this series at http://www.springer.com/series/4205

Thomas B. Moeslund · Graham Thomas
Adrian Hilton
Editors

Computer Vision in Sports

Springer

Editors
Thomas B. Moeslund
Aalborg University
Aalborg
Denmark

Adrian Hilton
University of Surrey
Guildford, Surrey
UK

Graham Thomas
BBC R&D
London
UK

ISSN 2191-6586 ISSN 2191-6594 (electronic)
Advances in Computer Vision and Pattern Recognition
ISBN 978-3-319-09395-6 ISBN 978-3-319-09396-3 (eBook)
DOI 10.1007/978-3-319-09396-3

Library of Congress Control Number: 2014956904

Springer Cham Heidelberg New York Dordrecht London

Printed on acid-free paper

Springer International Publishing AG Switzerland is part of Springer Science+Business Media (www.springer.com)

Preface

Sports is said to be the social glue of society. It allows people to interact irrespective of their social status or age. With the rise of the mass media, a significant quantity of resources has been channeled into sports in order to improve understanding, performance and presentation. For example, areas like performance assessment, which were previously mainly of interest to coaches and sports scientists, are now finding applications in broadcast and other media, driven by the increasing use of online sports viewing which provides a way of making all sorts of performance statistics available to viewers. Manual creation of data describing details in sports events is tiresome and in many cases simply unrealistic. Technology is therefore becoming more and more crucial as the demand for improved understanding, performance and presentation increases. Moreover, since the nature of most sports means that monitoring by the use of sensors or other devices fixed to players or equipment is generally not possible, a rich set of opportunities exist for the application of computer vision techniques to help the competitors, trainers and audience.

The purpose of this book is to present the state-of-the-art as well as current research challenges in applying computer vision to problems in sports. The book was inspired by the CVPR'13 workshop titled *Computer Vision in Sports*. The workshop was well received and therefore led to the idea of this book. About half of the 14 chapters in this book are extended workshop papers, whereas the rest are invited papers from research groups active within this field. The book is organized into four parts focused on answering the following four research questions:

Where is the Ball?
Where are the Players?
What are they Playing?
What's Going on?

These four parts are preceded by an introductory chapter that outlines the opportunities for applying computer vision in sports, using examples of some current commercial products. It also explains how the different chapters in this book extend the state of the art and fit into the bigger picture.

The editors would first of all like to thank the authors for contributing to this book. Without you there wouldn't be a book! Second, we also like to thank the reviewers for providing constructive feedback helping to sharpen each chapter. Lastly, we would like to thank Wayne Wheeler from Springer for taking the initiative to organize this book and for guidance during the entire process of putting this book together.

Aalborg, Denmark, June 2014	Thomas B. Moeslund
London, UK	Graham Thomas
Guildford, UK	Adrian Hilton

Contents

Contributors

Narendra Ahuja University of Illinois at Urbana-Champaign, Urbana, Champaign, IL, USA

Indriyati Atmosukarto Advanced Digital Sciences Center (ADSC), Singapore, Singapore

Alina Bialkowski Queensland University of Technology, Brisbane, QLD, Australia; Disney Research, Pittsburgh, PA, USA

Peter Carr Disney Research, Pittsburgh, PA, USA

William Christmas Centre for Vision, Speech and Signal Processing, University of Surrey, Guildford, UK

Arcangelo Distante CNR-ISSIA, Bari, Italy

Mykyta Fastovets University of Surrey, Guildford, UK

Rikke Gade Visual Analysis of People Lab, Aalborg University, Aalborg, Denmark

Marcel Germann ETH Zurich, Zurich, Switzerland

Bernard Ghanem King Abdullah University of Science and Technology (KAUST), Thuwal, Saudi Arabia

Markus Gross ETH Zurich, Zurich, Switzerland

Jean-Yves Guillemaut University of Surrey, Guildford, UK

Adrian Hilton Centre for Vision Speech and Signal Processing (CVSSP), University of Surrey, Guildford, Surrey, UK

Rafal Kapela Faculty of Computing, Poznan, Poland

Richard Keiser Vizrt Switzerland, Nyon, Switzerland

Josef Kittler Centre for Vision, Speech and Signal Processing, University of Surrey, Guildford, UK

Marco Leo CNR-INO, Arnesano, Italy

Jingchen Liu Microsoft, Sunnyvale, CA, USA

Patrick Lucey Disney Research, Pittsburgh, PA, USA

Iain Matthews Disney Research, Pittsburgh, PA, USA

Pier Luigi Mazzeo CNR-INO, Arnesano, Italy

Kevin McGuinness Insight Centre for Data Analytics, Dublin City University, Dublin 9, Ireland

Thomas B. Moeslund Visual Analysis of People Lab, Aalborg University, Aalborg, Denmark

C. Krishna Mohan Indian Institute of Technology Hyderabad, Hyderabad, India

K. Srirama Murthy Indian Institute of Technology Hyderabad, Hyderabad, India

Massimiliano Nitti CNR-ISSIA, Bari, Italy

Noel E. O'Connor Insight Centre for Data Analytics, Dublin City University, Dublin 9, Ireland

Tiberiu Popa Concordia University, Montreal, Canada

Mohamed Saadalla King Abdullah University of Science and Technology (KAUST), Thuwal, Saudi Arabia

Hideo Saito Graduate School of Science and Technology, Keio University, Kohoku-ku, Yokohama, Kanagawa, Japan

Khurram Soomro Center for Research in Computer Vision, University of Central Florida, Orlando, FL, USA

Paolo Spagnolo CNR-INO, Arnesano, Italy

Sridha Sridharan Queensland University of Technology, Brisbane, QLD, Australia

Ettore Stella CNR-ISSIA, Bari, Italy

Aleksandra Swietlicka Faculty of Computing, Poznan, Poland

Sho Tamaki Graduate School of Science and Technology, Keio University, Kohoku-ku, Yokohama, Kanagawa, Japan

Graham Thomas BBC Research and Development, Salford, MediaCity UK

Shyju Wilson Indian Institute of Technology Hyderabad, Hyderabad, India

Changsheng Xu Institute of Automation, Chinese Academy of Sciences, CSIDM, People's Republic of China

Fei Yan Centre for Vision, Speech and Signal Processing, University of Surrey, Guildford, UK

Amir R. Zamir Gates Computer Science, #130, Stanford University, Stanford, CA, USA

Tianzhu Zhang Advanced Digital Sciences Center of Illinois, Singapore, Singapore

Remo Ziegler Vizrt Switzerland, Nyon, Switzerland

Chapter 1
Introduction to the Use of Computer Vision in Sports

Graham Thomas, Thomas B. Moeslund and Adrian Hilton

Abstract Computer vision has a lot to offer the world of sports, for the competitors, organizers and viewers. This chapter sets the scene for this book, by outlining some of these applications, giving examples of what is already being used, and referring to the relevant chapters later in the book where current research is presented. It then goes on to discuss the main themes covered by these chapters, and how they relate to each other.

1.1 Introduction

The world of sports intrinsically involves fast and accurate motion that is not only challenging for competitors to master, but can also be difficult for coaches and trainers to analyse, and for audiences to follow. The nature of most sports means that monitoring by the use of sensors or other devices fixed to players or equipment is generally not possible. This provides a rich set of opportunities for the application of computer vision techniques to help the competitors, trainers and audience.

This book presents a picture of some of the current research challenges in applying computer vision to problems in sports. To set the scene for rest of the book, this chapter looks at possible application areas for computer vision through the life cycle of a sports event, from training and coaching in the run-up to an event, through to the event itself, and in analysing what happened afterwards (which often feeds

---

G. Thomas (✉)
BBC Research and Development, 5th Floor, Dock House, MediaCity, Salford M50 2LH, UK
e-mail: graham.thomas@bbc.co.uk

T.B. Moeslund
Visual Analysis of People Lab, Aalborg University, Rendsburggade 14,
9000 Aalborg, Denmark
e-mail: tbm@create.aau.dk

A. Hilton
Centre for Vision Speech and Signal Processing (CVSSP), University of Surrey,
Guildford, Surrey GU2 7XH, UK
e-mail: a.hilton@surrey.ac.uk

T.B. Moeslund et al. (eds.), *Computer Vision in Sports*,
Advances in Computer Vision and Pattern Recognition,
DOI 10.1007/978-3-319-09396-3_1

back into further training and coaching). This chapter concludes with an overview of the remainder of the book, introducing the main chapter groupings: 'Where is the ball?' (Chaps. 2–4), 'Where are the players?' (Chaps. 5–8), 'What are they playing?' (Chaps. 9–11) and 'What's going on?' (Chaps. 12–14).

1.2 Computer Vision in Training and Coaching

To the average sports viewer or amateur sports player, the use of technology in training may not be particularly apparent when compared to more obvious uses such as analysis of performance in TV coverage. However, technology plays a major role in training, both at the professional level, and for many amateurs. This section outlines some applications in training and coaching where computer vision can play an important role.

1.2.1 Training Individual Athletes

Getting the optimum performance from an athlete involves understanding and applying the principles of biomechanics [1], relating the underlying physics of forces and motion to the way that people move. Various techniques exist for measuring the forces and motion of people [2], such as force plates to measure ground reaction forces for jumping and running sports. To measure the detailed motion of athletes in training, commercially available motion capture systems based on optical markers on the athlete and multiple calibrated fixed cameras around the sides of the 'capture volume' can be used. For sports such as skiing where the large area covered and uncontrollable lighting make optical systems impractical, approaches based on inertial sensors [3] can be used.

In some situations, it is not practical to attach any kind of marker or transducer to the athletes or the equipment that they are using, and pure vision-based approaches using the natural appearance of the person or object are the only methods available. One example of this is in training table tennis players, where knowledge of the ball trajectory can be very useful but any modifications to the ball to help measure this would not be feasible. Chapter 3 presents an approach to estimating ball trajectories from video analysis, using two cameras or a single RGB+depth camera. Another example is analysing the performance of athletes in a competition environment, where the only source of data may be a single video feed; approaches to tracking the positions of an athlete's limbs in this situation are discussed in Chap. 8.

1.2.2 Coaching in Team Sports

To help improve the performance of teams in sports such as football, analysing the ways in which both individual players move, and the overall formation of the team, can provide very valuable insights for the team coach. Ideally, the coach would have access to a complete recording of the positions of all players many times per second throughout an entire training session or actual game.

Commercial multi-camera player tracking systems tend to rely on a mixture of automated and manual tracking and player labelling. One such system [4] uses 8–10 cameras positioned at the corners of the pitch (see Fig. 1.1), connected via an IP link to a central control room, where the images are recorded. Events such as tackles and passes can be identified and logged manually live, and after the match the images are analysed semiautomatically to produce player positions at a rate of 10 Hz. The live data tend to be of most value to broadcasters, to provide statistics for live broadcast or web streaming, while the player position data can be analysed in-depth off-line to provide insight into player performance for team coaches. Another system is the SportVU system from STATS [5] which uses one or two clusters of three cameras, and can currently be used for football and basketball, with systems for Hockey, American Football and Cricket reportedly being in development.

For some applications such as identifying particular stages of a game through identifying team formations, knowledge of the positions of individual players is not necessary, and fully automated approaches may be possible. Chapter 12 describes research into recognizing game states through occupancy maps derived from static cameras covering the whole area of play, which could be used to quickly find key parts of a recorded match. Where key player formations can be determined from the field-of-view typically covered by a moving broadcast camera, analysing the image from this one camera can provide an automated way of identifying incidents of interest, as described in the context of American Football in Chap. 13.

Fig. 1.1 Cameras installed at a football ground for player tracking (picture courtesy of Prozone)

1.3 Computer Vision During Sports Events

When a sporting event is taking place, there are opportunities for computer vision to help both the referee and other officials to keep track of exactly what is happening, and also to help provide full coverage and detailed analysis of the event for TV viewers. This section looks at several applications in this area, which tend to be characterized by the need for real-time performance.

1.3.1 Help for the Referee

One of the first commercially available multi-camera systems based on computer vision [6] was developed for tracking cricket balls in 3D, and was first used in 2001. It was subsequently applied to tennis; although broadcast cameras were initially used to provide the images [7], the system is generally now deployed with a number of dedicated high-frame-rate synchronized cameras viewing the tennis court [8], as there is no need to register the resulting 3D tracks to the images from the main broadcast cameras, and space is available around the court (often on the roof of the stands) to install them. Being static, they are easier to calibrate, and short shutter times and higher frame rates can be used. There is a lot of prior knowledge about tennis that the system can use, including the size and appearance of the ball, its motion (once it is hit, its motion can be predicted using the laws of physics), and the area over which it needs to be tracked. The cameras and the geometry of the court can be accurately calibrated in advance. The system first identifies possible balls in each camera image, by identifying elliptical regions in the expected size range. Candidates for balls are linked with tracks across multiple frames, and plausible tracks are then matched between multiple cameras to generate a trajectory in 3D. The system is sufficiently accurate that it can be used by the referee to determine whether a ball lands in or out, being first used for this in 2005. When applied to cricket, it can be used to predict the path that the ball would have taken if the batsman had not hit it, or if it had not turned when bouncing, as shown in Fig. 1.2.

More recently, various systems to determine whether a football has crossed the goal line have been developed. At the time of writing, FIFA has certified goal-line technology (GLT) installations at 29 football grounds [9]. Of these, 22 are based on a multi-camera computer vision system developed by Hawk-Eye, 6 use a similar vision system developed by GoalControl, and one uses GoalRef, an RF system (with a transponder in the ball) developed by Fraunhofer IIS. The system from GoalControl was also used for the 2014 World Cup in Brazil. Some insights into the development and testing of a vision-based GLT system are given in Chap. 4.

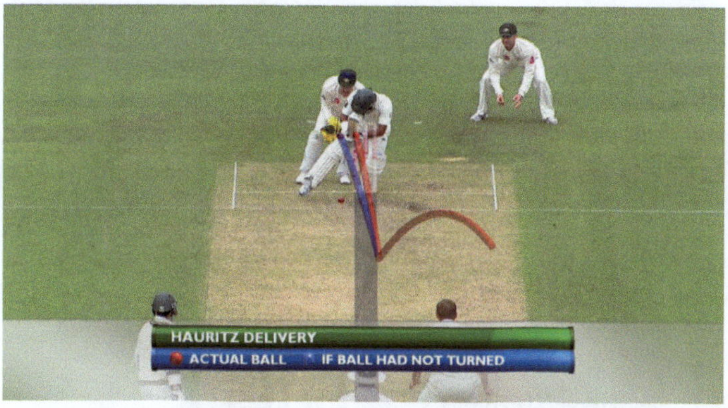

Fig. 1.2 Analysis and prediction of cricket ball motion (picture courtesy of Hawk-Eye Innovations)

1.3.2 Sports Analysis for TV

Computer vision plays an important role in many sports graphics systems, helping sports presenters on TV explain events to viewers. These systems are one of the more 'visible' uses of computer vision, being commonly used for sports such as football and thus seen by many millions of people.

Any system that draws graphics so as to appear registered to the real world requires some form of camera calibration. The first systems relied on mechanical sensors to measure the pan and tilt of the camera on a fixed mount, and sensors on the lens to measure zoom and focus settings. Calibration data for the lens are needed to relate the 'raw' values from these lens encoders to focal length. Ideally, lens distortion and 'nodal shift' (movement of the notional position of the pinhole in a simple camera model, principally along the direction-of-view) should also be measured by the calibration process and accounted for when images are rendered. The position of the camera mounting in the reference frame of the sports pitch also needs to be measured, for example by using surveying tools such as a theodolite or range-finder. An example of a camera and lens equipped with sensors, for placing virtual graphics on athletics coverage, is shown in Fig. 1.3. However, this approach is costly and not always practical, for example if the cameras are installed and operated by another broadcaster and only the video feed itself is made available. The sensor data have to be carried through the programme production chain, including the cabling from the camera to the outside broadcast truck, recording on tape or disk, and transmission to the studio. Also, any system that relies on sensor data cannot be used on archive recordings for which no data are available.

Most current sports graphics systems that require camera calibration achieve this using computer vision, using features at known positions in the scene. This avoids the need for specially equipped lenses and camera mounts, and the problems with getting sensor data back from the camera. In sports such as football where there are prominent line markings on the pitch at well-defined positions, a line-based tracker

Fig. 1.3 Camera with sensors on lens and pan/tilt mount for virtual graphics overlay

is often used [10]. In other sports such as ice hockey or athletics, where lines are less useful, a more general feature point tracker can be used [11]. However, for live use in applications where there are very few reliable static features in view (such as swimming), sensor-based systems are still used.

The addition of some relatively simple image processing can allow graphics to appear as if drawn on the ground, and not on top of people or other foreground objects or players, if the background is of a relatively uniform colour. For example, for football, a colour-based segmentation algorithm (referred to as a 'chromakeyer' by broadcast engineers) tuned to detect green can be used to inhibit the drawing of graphics in areas that are not grass-coloured, so that they appear behind the players. The fact that the chromakeyer will not generate a key for areas such as mud can actually be an advantage, as long as such areas are not large, as this adds to the realism that the graphics are 'painted' on the grass. Figure 1.4 shows an example of graphics applied to rugby; other examples of this kind of system applied to American Football include the '1st and Ten™' line [12] and the 'First Down Line' [13].

An extension of this approach can be used to overlay the performance of several contestants during successive heats of an event, such as a downhill ski race [14]. This requires the calibration of the moving camera in a repeatable way, so that the background can be aligned from one heat to the next, and may also require the video timing to be synchronized so that competitors are shown at the same time from the start of the heat. More advanced segmentation techniques are required than for overlay of graphics on grass, as a colour-based key is unlikely to be sufficient on more general scenes. However, the segmentation need not always be pixel-accurate as the background should be the same in both images if the alignment is good, meaning that segmentation errors will only be visible where one competitor overlaps another. Figure 1.5 shows an example of such a technique being used.

Fig. 1.4 Example of virtual graphics overlaid on a rugby pitch (picture courtesy of Red Bee Media)

Fig. 1.5 Overlay of successive heats of a ski competition (picture courtesy of Dartfish)

The approaches discussed above provide visual enhancements in an existing camera image. However, in some situations, the best point-of-view to use when analysing the event may not correspond to where a camera was actually placed. This applies particularly when presenting an analysis of a team sport such as football, where understanding the relative locations of the players is important. Cameras that can move around (as distinct from just panning/tilting/zooming) are sometimes used at such events; these include shoulder-mounted cameras used by a cameraman who can run along the side of the pitch, or cameras suspended on wires over the pitch. However, even these may not provide images that give the best explanation of critical moments in the game.

Synthesising a camera image from a new ('virtual') viewpoint can be a useful tool for the sports presenter, and is a classic problem in computer vision. A combination of foreground object segmentation and camera calibration can allow the approximate 3D positions of players to be inferred from a single camera view, if some simple assumptions can be made. For players standing on a pitch, it is reasonable to infer their 3D position by assuming that the lowest point of each silhouette (usually the feet) is in contact with they ground (usually assumed to be planar). This simple approach can be used to create a crude 3D model of the scene [15], by placing the segmented players into a 3D model of a stadium, as textures on flat planes positioned at the estimated locations. An example of this approach is shown in Fig. 1.6 [16]. This allows the generation of virtual views of the game from locations other than those at which real cameras are placed, for example to present a view of the scene that a linesman may have had when making an offside decision, or to provide a seamless 'fly' between an image from a real camera and a fully virtual top-down view more suitable for presenting an analysis of tactics.

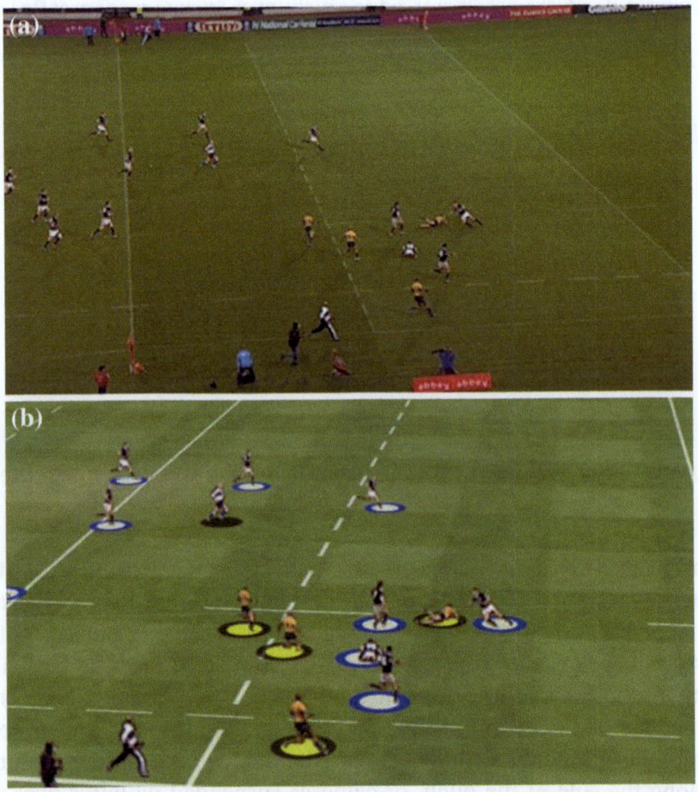

Fig. 1.6 Generation of a virtual view from a single camera image (picture courtesy of Red Bee Media). **a** Original image. **b** Virtual view

This simple player modelling approach works well in many situations, but the use of a single camera for creating the models restricts the range of virtual camera movement, with the planar nature of the players becoming apparent when the viewing direction changes by more than about 15 degrees from that of the original camera. Furthermore, overlapping players cannot easily be resolved. One solution to these problems is to use pre-generated 3D player models, manually selected and positioned to match the view from the camera. It can take a skilled operator several minutes to model such a scene, which is acceptable for a post-match analysis programme but too slow for use in an instant replay. The player models also lack realism. Approaches using two or more cameras, either to create a '2.5D' model that allows smooth blending between multiple billboarded images, or to infer the player pose in 3D by matching player silhouettes to a library of pre-generated poses, are described in Chap. 7. This chapter also includes a discussion of techniques for creating full 3D models from camera images [17].

In addition to determining the 3D location and appearance of players, information about their pose and their interactions with their immediate environment or sports equipment can be obtained using computer vision techniques and used to provide data that can help the commentator. Examples of this include estimating the stride length or centre-of-gravity of athletes, the pedalling speed of a cyclist or the angle-of-entry and splash size of a diver [18]. In a typical live sports situation, there may be only be one camera view available of an event; some of the challenges this presents and approaches that can be taken to deducing details about an athlete's motion from a single image are discussed in Chap. 8.

1.3.3 Automating the Coverage of Sports Events on TV

An area of current research in sports TV production is the automating of the camera control using computer vision. This is a very challenging task, as it involves both the tracking of fast action, and framing an aesthetically pleasing shot that helps to 'tell the story' of what is happening in the event. It is unlikely that fully automated systems will replace cameramen in the foreseeable future for high-profile events such as major football matches, although there may be opportunities for automating the coverage of minority-interest events where a large production budget cannot be justified, particularly with ever-increasing capacity to deliver video to niche audience sectors via the internet.

One approach to the automatic control of cameras is to use a cameraman to control one main camera that is equipped with sensors or a computer vision system to determine its pose. The pose data from this camera are then used to control a number of 'slave' robotic cameras in different locations, so that they all show the same area of the action but from different viewpoints. One example of such a system is described in [19].

A more ambitious approach is to identify the area of interest using computer vision techniques, and automatically frame a shot to cover this. One inherent problem to solve is that of latency: even with very low-latency vision algorithms and robotic cameras, it is hard to match the performance of a human who can anticipate what might happen. One solution to this is to use fixed wide-angle high-resolution cameras, and crop a portion of the image out that shows the main action [20]. This allows a delay to be applied to the video to compensate for the processing time, and could also allow some element of look-ahead in the tracking and shot framing algorithms. Even with an ultra-high-definition camera system, this approach can reduce the resolution available significantly compared to a conventional pan/tilt/zoom broadcast camera; a hybrid approach that combines some degree of reframing and video delay with a robotic camera is one potential solution to this [21]. Some approaches to tracking players that could be used to control shot framing are discussed in Chaps. 5 and 6.

1.4 Computer Vision for Analysis After the Event

Once a sports event has finished, there may be a significant amount of video material that can be used, both for TV-type applications (viewing past events in a video-on-demand system, or watching key highlights in particular events) and to help coaches and competitors learn from previous events. This section highlights some examples of how computer vision algorithms can help with these tasks.

1.4.1 Identification of Sports in Large Video Collections

Sports programmes produced by broadcasters and other professional media production companies are likely to be accompanied by metadata created during the production process, that should identify the kind of sport being covered, as well as giving additional details such as date, location, name of the competition and names of the teams or competitors. However, in unstructured video databases, or recordings of TV programmes that cover a wide range of sports within one programme, there may be little or no metadata available to identify the sport. Computer vision techniques have been developed to help in these situations, with details of some approaches being described in Chaps. 9 and 11. A related application is to identify the kind of sports that were played in a sports hall over a long period of time to provide feedback to those running the facility; details of a solution to this problem that makes use of locked-off thermal cameras viewing the sports hall are given in Chap. 10.

1.4.2 Identification of Key Events Within a Sports Recording

The identification of key moments in a recording of a sports event is a prerequisite for a number of applications, including editing a ‘highlights video’ of the event, or placing markers on a timeline to allow viewers to quickly scroll to interesting incidents. Current practice in broadcast TV production involves logging events as they happen, either by someone in the production team, or by a third-party supplier such as Opta [22], who use a large number of people to manually enter data on events such as kicks and tackles in football. Where such data are not available, computer vision techniques can be used to process recordings of events to obtain some useful information. Chapter 2 describes an approach for tracking the ball from a single wide shot of a tennis court, for applications including determining the state of play. Chapter 14 describes two approaches that effectively 'reverse engineer' decisions made while an event was being covered, by detecting interesting events from the pattern of camerawork, and reading overlaid scoreboard graphics in a broadcast programme.

1.5 Introduction to the Remainder of the Book

The following chapters give deeper insights into some of the techniques at the forefront of computer vision research for sports applications. Various application areas have already been mentioned in this chapter, with some techniques having applications in several stages in the life cycle of a sports event. The chapters have therefore been grouped by the kind of information that the techniques they describe are trying to produce: 'Where is the ball?' (Chaps. 2–4), 'Where are the players?' (Chaps. 5–8), 'What are they playing?' (Chaps. 9–11) and 'What's going on?' (Chaps. 12–14).

1.5.1 Where Is the Ball?

Many of the different sports activities performed at both a professional and amateur level involve a ball. Indeed, seen from the outside, many sports are rather simple and can be described as a matter of placing a ball in a certain location more times than the opponent. Looking closer, each sport is of course much more complicated with multiple layers being revealed as the skills of the players/team/viewer increase. Across many sports, when computer vision methods are applied to enhance the different stages in the life cycle of sport events, a crucial ability is to be able to keep track of where the ball is. This will help to resolve critical situations by for example objectively assessing whether a ball in football has crossed the goal line or not, see Fig. 1.7. Furthermore, it will also aid the process of automatic understanding of the different events that have occurred in a particular game, which in turn opens up possibilities for automatic generation of statistics as well as automatic annotation for post-event search.

At a first glance, the notion of ball tracking may appear relatively simple compared to for example player tracking. However, one needs to remember that failure to track the ball accurately is normally much more critical. The exact location of the ball

Fig. 1.7 World Cup 1966. Goal? No-goal? We are still arguing...

can essentially define the result of a game whereas inaccurate player tracking and even loss of track is often acceptable. Moreover, the ball is normally small and fast-moving compared to the size of the playing field and hence limited spatio-temporal resolution as well as significant occlusion can further complicate matters.

In the first part of this book, three different chapters (2, 3 and 4) will provide insights into state-of-the-art ball tracking within three different sports types: tennis, football, and table tennis.

In Chap. 2, Yan et al. present work on ball tracking for tennis. The motivation is that the trajectory of the ball carries significant semantic information and can thus provide a better understanding of the play as opposed to current research based on analysing the audio and the actions of the players. The aim is to produce a generic system that can handle video sequences from non-specialist data capture systems. Besides occlusion and other obvious issues, this ambition also leads to significant detection problems due to motion blur, resolution and colour coding. Yan et al. follow a multilayered data association approach. First, a sliding window is used to analyse each detection and its spatio-temporal neighbours. From this, tracklets are built and defined as nodes in a graphical model. Some of these nodes originate from the trajectory of the real ball, while others are by-products of false positives and/or incorrect associations. Temporal optimization across the entire graphical network results in the most likely trajectory of the ball in an entire rally. The algorithm is evaluated on broadcast videos from three tennis tournaments and found to work robustly even in difficult scenarios.

In Chap. 3, Tamaki et al. present work on ball tracking for table tennis. The motivation is the need for an automatic data collection tool that is used to understand and later improve the performances of players. Currently, such data are collected manually, which is of course very time-consuming and hence difficult to deploy. In table tennis, the 3D trajectory of the ball is of interest and this work therefore aims at first estimating the 3D positions of the ball and from this reconstructing the 3D trajectory. The approach is based on the notion that due to the low weight of the ball and the fact that it is spinning, the ball will follow a 3D trajectory located on a tilted plane. During runtime, the 3D detections are filtered and then fitted to a trajectory located on such a plane. The method is evaluated using two different data capturing devices: a stereo setup using two RGB cameras, and a RGB-D camera. Tests show that using the stereo setup allows for accurate tracking of the 3D trajectory of the ball, but is perhaps too impractical for use due to the required setup and calibration. Using the RGB-D camera, on the other hand, allows for a less cumbersome setup, but unfortunately the frame rate of the camera is too low compared to the speed of the table tennis ball and hence too few 3D detections can be extracted. A better 3D sensor may circumvent this issue opening up possibilities for a useful and practical solution to the problem of automatic data collection in table tennis.

In Chap. 4, Spagnolo et al. present work on tracking a football with the purpose of assessing whether or not the ball has crossed the goal line. Goal-line technologies have been a hot topic in modern football for a long time, with notable incidents including questionable decisions in high-profile games such as the two England versus Germany World Cup matches in 1966 and 2010. The approach in this work is to continuously estimate the 3D position of the ball when it is close to the goal and estimate whether it has crossed the line. This is achieved by using three cameras focused on the goal area. In each camera, the ball is detected and triangulation (using two or three views) is used to find the 3D position. The detection of the ball is carried out as a combination of dynamic background subtraction, circle detection, appearance modelling and temporal consistency. Since the required accuracy of goal-line technology is a few centimetres and as the speed of the ball can reach 120 km/h, the choice of methods in this work is made with hard real-time constrains in mind. The system is evaluated on both controlled scenarios and a significant number of real football matches. The tests indicate that the system has the potential for assisting the referee in making better decisions.

1.5.2 Where Are the Players?

Although the position of the ball is of key interest in critical situations, like goal/no-goal, for many other aspects in the life cycle of sports events, the whereabouts of the players (and their limbs) also carry significant information. This ranges from understanding the team dynamics, to extracting statistics of individuals in team sports, and understanding the detailed pose of athletes in for example running or high-jump. Clearly such data can provide valuable insights both when it comes to optimizing the training and performances of individuals and teams, and for automatically annotating video sequences for post-event search. But equally importantly, such data can also be used on-the-fly by producers to enhance the viewing experience, for example, to generate a novel viewpoint as illustrated in Fig. 1.8. With strong competition between different sports broadcasters, the need to innovate is high and hence more advanced

Fig. 1.8 Virtual view generation using the approach described in Chap. 7. **a** Two input images. **b** Novel view

methods for providing compelling viewing experiences can be expected. Computer vision will definitely be one of the enabling technologies as it uses data that has been captured non-invasively.

Detection and tracking of players via computer vision is complicated by issues like occlusion, motion blur, low resolution and image compression. Furthermore, when detecting and tracking players in a team, algorithms are further challenged by the fact that team members often wear very similar clothing. One aspect that may ease detection and tracking is that in many situations sports are performed in a highly controlled environment, meaning that background clutter is almost non-existent and hence the players tend to stand out from the background.

In the second part of this book, four chapters will provide state-of-the-art insights into how to obtain the whereabouts and pose of the players. The first two (5 and 6) aim at tracking the individual positions, while the latter two (7 and 8) aim at estimating the pose of the players.

In Chap. 5, Zhang et al. present a tracking framework focused on tracking one object. The framework is not limited to sports data, but is general enough to be applied to most tracking problems within computer vision. The approach followed in this work is based on the notion that one of the main difficulties in tracking is to be able to handle occlusion. While occlusion may be hard to predict, it can be assumed that an occlusion event in one frame can be propagated to the next frame. Moreover, the pixel errors that are common in tracking due to occlusions are not randomly distributed, but rather form a contiguous region. In this chapter, these two ideas are merged into a sparse learning framework. The developed system is evaluated on both sports videos and other types of video data. The system is found to outperform six state-of-the-art trackers especially during occlusion.

In Chap. 6, Liu and Carr also present a tracking framework. This work, as opposed to the work described in the previous chapter, is aimed at tracking multiple team players simultaneously. Since players on the same team tend to look similar in terms of appearance, a tracker will have to rely on predictions when inferring trajectories from detections. To this end a motion model is required. In sports, however, player movements are highly complex and hence very hard to model in practice. The novelty in this work is to estimate the current motion model for each player based on the current game context. In team sports, players follow certain movement patterns based on the overall game context (defence, offence, etc.) as well as the local context, where a player from one team often has the same trajectory (for a short interval) as a player from the opposite team. In this work, these game contexts are found from occupancy maps and correlation of nearby tracklets. The tracking framework developed is evaluated on both field hockey and basketball. The main findings are that the use of game context in motion models improves tracking accuracy by more than 10 %, and that the importance of the different game contexts depends on the sport.

In Chap. 7, Popa et al. present work on pose estimation of players. The motivation behind this work is to have a method that allows a sports broadcast producer to generate novel views of the scene. Such capability allows an enhanced viewer experience as the state of play can be visualized from the viewpoint of individual players, coaches, referees, linesmen, etc. The viewer is likely to be even more immersed in the broadcast as commentators can provide further in-depth insights into the game. Current methods for virtual view generation are costly and hence only used in post-event analysis. In this chapter, the goal is a real-time method and two rather different approaches are followed. The first matches the silhouettes of a player in multiple views with a database of different poses. The resulting 3D pose will be coarse and is therefore corrected using local optical flow as well as temporal consistency. The second method does not explicitly extract the skeleton of a player, but rather learns the local 3D geometry. This is done by approximating the 3D shape of a player by triangles, each aiming at modelling a rigid part of the body. Both methods provide impressive results on real broadcast sequences of football and offer two interesting ways forward for automatic generation of virtual views in sports broadcasts.

In the last chapter in this part of the book, Fastovets et al. present work on accurate pose estimation. In most team sports, semantic data can often be inferred from location information alone. However, in more individual sports like athletics much of the semantic information is carried in the actual pose and movements of the different body parts, e.g., the number of steps during a sprint or the body pose on impact with the water in diving. The human body has a high number of degrees-of-freedom and finding the correct pose in each frame is therefore extremely challenging due to self-occlusion and local minima in the search space. The approach in this chapter is a semiautomatic method whereby the pose is manually annotated in a number of keyframes. These then serve as anchor points in a graphical optimization scheme as well as seeds for learning the appearances of the different body parts. While this method is not fully automatic, it still provides a significant speed-up compared to manually annotating all frames and at the same time an evaluation demonstrates that the method is much more robust than state-of-the-art pose estimation methods, especially when dealing with challenging pose variations as seen in sports.

1.5.3 What Are They Playing?

The chapters in this part address the problem of identifying the sports type from video footage. This can be an important problem for automatic labelling of datasets, as the starting point for subsequent play analysis or monitoring of sports play activities in public facilities, as in Chap. 10. A variety of approaches have been developed which are each evaluated on a substantial corpus of data achieving promising results and demonstrating the potential for automatic visual classification of sports.

Chapter 9 presents a comprehensive review of action recognition in sports and in particular the use of the UCF Sports dataset that has been widely used as a benchmark for performance evaluation. The UCF dataset comprises real sports broadcast footage of 10 actions with 150 clips in total. The review breaks the problem down into the sub-tasks of action localization and recognition. A chronology of research progress and different approaches to address each of these sub-tasks is presented together with their performance benchmarked on the UCF dataset. Action recognition is decomposed into three main stages: feature extraction; learning; and classification. The contribution of different approaches to each of these steps is reviewed. This provides useful insights into existing approaches drawing on experience with the evolution and benchmarking of techniques on the UCF dataset leading to conclusions about the requirements for future action recognition frameworks to operate on real sports footage.

The classification of sports types in indoor arenas using infrared thermal imaging is presented in Chap. 10. Thermal imaging resolves the issue of individual privacy for video capture of public spaces and has the advantage of distinguishing individuals based on heat characteristics rather than colour or grey scale which are often ambiguous for imaging under poor illumination conditions. The chapter considers the classification of five common indoor sports: badminton; basketball; indoor soccer; volleyball; and handball. The thermal image gives a clear separation of the players from the background sports arena as illustrated in Fig. 1.9. The player locations are then used to classify the sports type. An end-to-end system system for sport classification is presented including acquisition, camera calibration, player segmentation, player-to-player occlusion handling and player localization. Classification of sports type is based on the temporal occupancy distribution of player location in the arena integrated over a 10 min period. This is demonstrated to give 90 % overall true positive classification rate across a comprehensive dataset spanning almost two weeks of footage from a public sports arena. This work demonstrates a practical approach to reliable classification of indoor sports that is robust to errors in player detection and segmentation.

Fig. 1.9 Example of thermal imagery of indoor stadium sports (Chap. 10)

1.5.4 What's Going On?

In the final part of this book, three chapters present systems for the automatic analysis and classification of sports play. These contributions demonstrate that substantial progress has been made towards automatic game play analysis that is an essential tool for teams to monitor player performance and team interaction for coaching together with tactical analysis of opposing teams. The first chapter in this part (Chap. 12) proposes a representation to improve the analysis of game play that is robust to errors in visual tracking. The approach is evaluated on field hockey but has wider applicability. Chapter 13 addresses the detection and analysis of play formation in American football. Finally, Chap. 14 uses audio-visual features together with on-screen scoreboard analysis to detect key events in broadcast footage with reliable performance across a wide range of sports.

Chapter 12 addresses the representation of team activities to cope with errors in the individual player tracks due to the inherent ambiguity in visual tracking. To achieve a compact representation a bilinear spatio-temporal basis model using role representation is proposed to clean up the errors in the player detections. The role representation provides a low-dimensional description of the team play that is not dependent on individual player identity. The approach is evaluated across a dataset comprising seven complete field hockey matches, employing a state-of-the-art player tracker as input. This representation is compared to previously proposed occupancy maps where the playing field is discretized into a set of cells and the number of player detections is stored for each cell. Team activity is then encoded as the cell occupancy over time. This representation is less sensitive to missing or erroneous tracks for individual players; however, the resulting feature space is high dimensional due to the variability in the occupancy and noise in individual player tracks. Results (Fig. 1.10) demonstrate that occupancy maps provide a good representation of global behaviour allowing recognition of team play activities but require a high-dimensional space. The proposed spatio-temporal model based on player roles is demonstrated to provide a compact representation of team behaviour that allows identification of individual activities.

Chapter 13 addresses the automatic recognition of team play formation in American football, a sport that has a high level of structured play. The chapter proposes an approach to automatically identify the formation of key plays at the frame level. This is then used as the starting point for automatic classification of the type of offensive team formation. Labelling and analysis of offensive formation is a manual process required for performance and tactical analysis of teams and their opponents. Formation frame detection is performed by identifying the frame with least motion. Line of scrimmage is then detected based on player density at the formation frame. The offensive team are then identified based on the player formation shape and classified into one of five formation types using a multiclass support vector machine. Evaluation on a large corpus with over 800 play clips of American football games demonstrates a performance of 95 % in detecting the play formation and 98 % in identifying the line of scrimmage and 67 % in the more ambiguous task of classifying the formation of the offensive team.

The final chapter in this volume (Chap. 14) presents a real-time system for event detection in broadcast footage of field sports. The system presented detects key events such as scores, near misses and other dramatic action in the game play. Two independent approaches are employed for event detection using audio-visual feature and on-screen scoreboard-based analysis. To allow application across a wide range of sports the system avoids the use of sports-specific visual cues such as pitch colour commonly used in field sport analysis. In the first approach, audio-visual features are trained for different events such as goals and other exciting game play. Different learning approaches for event detection are evaluated and it is found that artificial neural networks and decision trees achieve good results with event detection accuracy of around 90 %. The score-based approach analyses the on-screen score through numeral detection achieving a 100 % performance. This approach is complementary to the audio-visual feature-based event detection method as it is only capable of

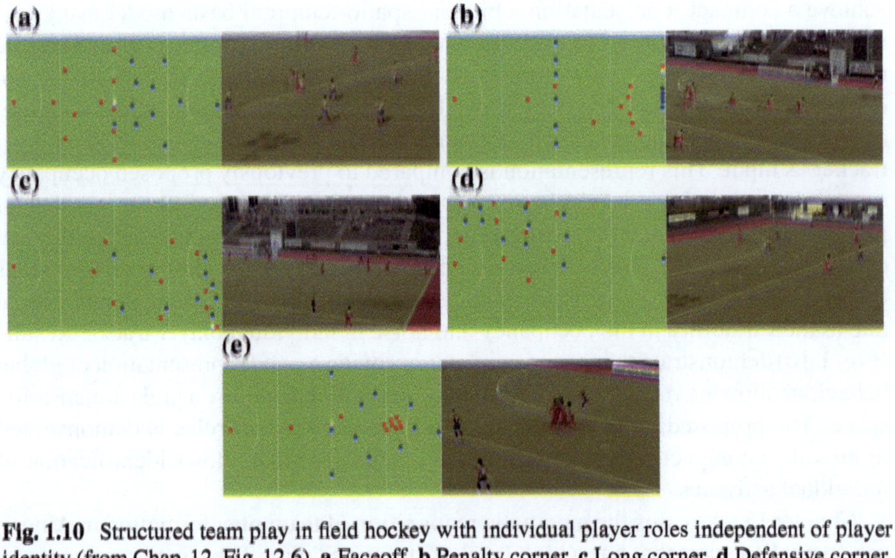

Fig. 1.10 Structured team play in field hockey with individual player roles independent of player identity (from Chap. 12, Fig. 12.6). **a** Faceoff. **b** Penalty corner. **c** Long corner. **d** Defensive corner. **e** Goal

detecting events which result in a score and thus cannot identify other events of interest such as near misses. The system is evaluated on a diverse range of field sports including soccer, rugby, American football, hockey and basketball.

1.6 Conclusion

Sports are big business, with the European football market alone being worth 19.4 billion Euro in 2011–2012 [23], and marketing revenue from the Olympics in the period 2009–2012 exceeding $8bn [24]. This provides a rich market for anything that can improve the experience of sports for participants or viewers.

This chapter has set the scene for the rest of the book, by looking at opportunities for applying computer vision to solve problems at all stages of a sports event, from training and coaching before an event, though to the event itself, and analysis of captured video after the event. Examples of commercial products that use computer vision for sports were discussed; those currently used to analyse performance to help in training include systems from Prozone [4], Dartfish [25], and STATS [5]. Others provide graphical enhancements, including graphics systems for broadcasters such as Sportvision [12], Orad [13] and Red Bee Media [16], and systems for generating virtual fly-arounds of events including Replay Technologies [26] and Viz Libero [27]. Some systems are currently used to help with refereeing games, such as the Hawk-eye system for tennis [6], and the goal-line technology systems that are currently certified by FIFA [9]. This is by no means an exhaustive list.

Despite the current availability of computer vision systems for various sports applications, there is ample scope to improve upon the performance of these systems and to take computer vision into more challenging areas. This is the motivation for the work described in the remainder of this book, which is divided into four parts: 'Where is the ball?' (Chaps. 2–4), 'Where are the players?' (Chaps. 5–8), 'What are they playing?' (Chaps. 9–11) and 'What's going on?' (Chaps. 12–14). Each of these parts was briefly summarized.

Ball tracking is a fundamental part of many applications yet remains challenging, particularly in the presence of occlusions or when a small number of cameras are being used, as will be discussed in Chaps. 2–4. Fully automated player tracking and pose estimation is difficult, but if solved would open the door to applications such as automated camera control and in-depth analysis of sports such as athletics, as well as better generation of statistics or synthesis of virtual views; some new approaches for this will be explored in Chaps. 5–8.

An area that is currently not well covered by commercial products is the 'higher level' analysis of sports, where multiple event or motion detections are used to infer things like the type of sport being played, or to detect kinds of events within a sport, for example for automatic highlights generation or searching of video archives. Approaches to identifying types of sports will be discussed in Chaps. 9–11, while Chaps. 12–14 conclude the book by looking at recognizing particular team behaviours or formations and detecting specific kinds of events.

References

1. Blazevich A (2007) Sports biomechanics: the basics. A & C Black, London
2. Robertson G, Caldwell G, Hamill J, Kamen G, Whittlesey S (2014) Research methods in biomechanics, 2nd edn. Human Kinetics, Champaign
3. Brodie M, Walmsley A, Page W (2008) Fusion motion capture: a prototype system using inertial measurement units and GPS for the biomechanical analysis of Ski racing. Sports Technol 1(1):17–28
4. Prozone Sports Ltd. (2014) Prozone post-match analysis. http://www.prozonesports.com. Cited 23rd March 2014
5. Stats (2014) SportVU Player Tracking Technology. http://www.stats.com/sportvu/sportvu.asp. Cited 5th May 2014
6. Hawk-Eye Innovations (2011) Hawk-Eye Tennis Officiating System. http://www.hawkeyeinnovations.co.uk. Cited 23rd March 2014
7. Owens N (2003) Hawk-Eye tennis system. In: International conference on visual information engineering (VIE2003), pp 182–185. IEE conference publication no. 495, July 2003
8. McIlroy P (2008) Hawk-Eye: augmented reality in sports broadcasting and officiating. In: Proceedings of the 7th IEEE/ACM international symposium on mixed and augmented reality ISMAR 08, Washington, DC, USA. IEEE Computer Society
9. FIFA Certified GLT Installations (2014). http://quality.fifa.com/en/Goal-Line-Technology/FIFA-certified-GLT-installations. Cited 23rd March 2014
10. Thomas G (2007) Real-time camera tracking using sports pitch markings. J Real Time Image Proc 2(2–3):117–132. Available as BBC R&D white paper 168. http://www.bbc.co.uk/rd/publications/whitepaper168.shtml
11. Dawes R, Chandaria J, Thomas G (2009) Image-based camera tracking for athletics. In: Proceedings of the IEEE international symposium on broadband multimedia systems and broadcasting (BMSB 2009), May 2009. Available as BBC R&D white paper 181. http://www.bbc.co.uk/rd/publications/whitepaper181.shtml
12. Sportvision (2014) 1st and Ten™Line System. http://www.sportvision.com/foot-1st-and-ten-linesystem. Cited 6th April 2014
13. Orad (2014) Trackvision First Down Line System. http://www.orad.tv/fdl. Cited 6th April 2014
14. Reusens M, Vetterli M, Ayer S, Bergnozoli V (2007) Coordination and combination of video sequences with spatial and temporal normalization. European patent specification EP1247255A4, 2007
15. Grau O, Price M, Thomas G (2001) Use of 3-D techniques for virtual production. In: SPIE conference on videometrics and optical methods for 3D shape measurement, San Jose, USA, January 2001. Available as BBC R&D white paper 033. http://www.bbc.co.uk/rd/publications/whitepaper033.shtml
16. Red Bee Media (2014) The Piero™Sports Graphics System. http://www.redbeemedia.com/piero. Cited 6th April 2014
17. Hilton A, Guillemaut J, Kilner J, Grau O, Thomas G (2011) 3D-TV production from conventional cameras for sports broadcast. IEEE Trans Broadcast 57(2):462–476
18. Dawes R, Weir B, Pike C, Golds P, Mann M, Nicholson M (2012) Enhancing viewer engagement using biomechanical analysis of sport. In: Proceedings of the NEM summit, Istanbul, 16–18 October 2012, pp 121–126. Available as BBC R&D white paper 234. http://www.bbc.co.uk/rd/publications/whitepaper234
19. Sports Video Group (2013) Hybrid aims to cut costs for live sports with automated sport track system. http://sportsvideo.org/main/blog/2013/06/hybrid-aims-to-cut-costs-for-live-sports-with-automated-sport-track-system. Cited 6th April 2014
20. Kaiser R, Thler M, Kriechbaum A, Fassold H, Bailer W, Rosner J (2011) Real-time person tracking in high-resolution panoramic video for automated broadcast production. In: Proceedings of 8th European conference on visual media production, 16th November 2011, London, UK

21. Carr P, Mistry M, Matthews I (2013) Hybrid Robotic/virtual Pan-Tilt-Zoom cameras for autonomous event recording. In: Proceedings of ACM multimedia 2013, October 2125, 2013, Barcelona, Spain
22. Opta Sports Data Company (2014) http://www.optasports.com. Cited 6th April 2014
23. Deloitte (2013) Deloitte Football Money League 2013—Highlights. http://www.deloitte.com/view/en_GB/uk/industries/sportsbusinessgroup. Cited 5th May 2014
24. International Olympic Committee (2013) Olympic Marketing Factfile 2013. http://www.olympic.org/Documents/IOC_Marketing/Olympic_Marketing_Fact_File_2013.pdf. Cited 5th May 2014
25. Dartfish (2014) Video software solutions. http://www.dartfish.com/en/. Cited 5th May 2014
26. Replay Technologies (2014) Free Dimensional Video Technology. http://replay-technologies.com/technology. Cited 5th May 2014
27. Vizrt (2014) The Viz Libero System. http://www.vizrt.com/products/viz_libero/. Cited 5th May 2014

Part I
Where Is the Ball?

Chapter 2
Ball Tracking for Tennis Video Annotation

Fei Yan, William Christmas and Josef Kittler

Abstract Tennis game annotation using broadcast video is a task with a wide range of applications. In particular, ball trajectories carry rich semantic information for the annotation. However, tracking a ball in broadcast tennis video is extremely challenging. In this chapter, we explicitly address the challenges, and propose a layered data association algorithm for tracking multiple tennis balls fully automatically. The effectiveness of the proposed algorithm is demonstrated on two data sets with more than 100 sequences from real-world tennis videos, where other data association methods perform poorly or fail completely.

2.1 Introduction

Effective and efficient sports video annotation systems have wide applications in, e.g. content-based video retrieval, enhanced broadcast, summarisation, object-based video encoding, automatic analysis of player tactics, to name a few. Owing to advances in computer vision and machine learning, building such tools has become possible [10, 13, 15].

Much of the effort in sports video annotation has been devoted to court games such as tennis and badminton, not only due to their popularity, but also to the fact that court games have well- structured rules. In court games, ball trajectories carry rich semantic information for the annotation. However, tracking a ball in broadcast video is an extremely challenging task. In broadcast videos, the ball can occupy as few as only 5 pixels; it can travel at very high speed and blur into the background; the

F. Yan (✉) · W. Christmas · J. Kittler
Centre for Vision, Speech and Signal Processing, University of Surrey,
Guildford GU2 7XH, UK
e-mail: f.yan@surrey.ac.uk

W. Christmas
e-mail: w.christmas@surrey.ac.uk

J. Kittler
e-mail: j.kittler@surrey.ac.uk

T.B. Moeslund et al. (eds.), *Computer Vision in Sports*,
Advances in Computer Vision and Pattern Recognition,
DOI 10.1007/978-3-319-09396-3_2

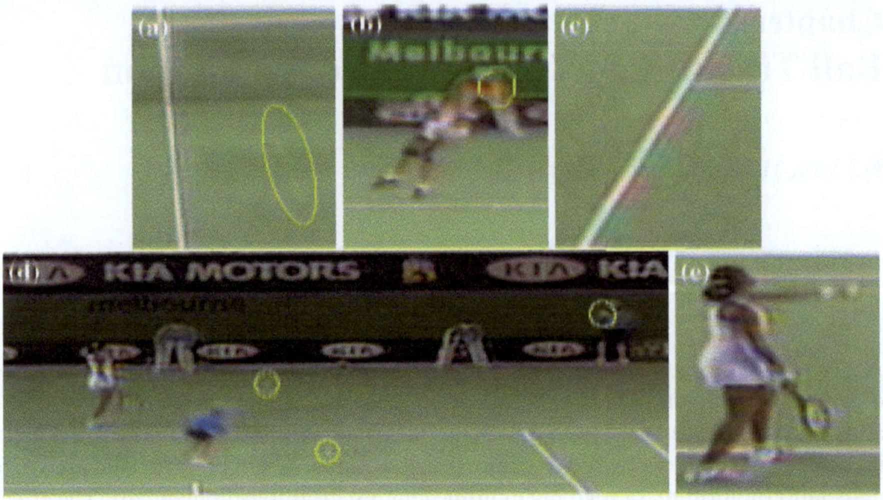

Fig. 2.1 Image patches cropped from frames demonstrating the challenges of tennis ball tracking. **a** Ball travels at high speed and blurs into background, making it very hard to detect. **b** Far player serves. The ball region contains only a few pixels, and due to low bandwidth of colour channel, its colour is strongly affected by the background colour. **c** Chroma noise caused by PAL cross-colour effect. This may introduce false ball candidates along the *court lines*. **d** Multiple balls in one frame. A new ball (*left*) is thrown in by a ball boy, while the ball used for play (*middle*) is still in the scene. There is another ball (*right*) in the ball boy's hand. **e** A wristband can look very similar to the ball, and can form a smooth trajectory as the player strikes the ball

ball is also subject to occlusion and sudden change of motion direction. Furthermore, motion blur, occlusion, and abrupt motion change tend to occur together, when the ball is close to one of the players. Example images demonstrating the challenges in tennis ball tracking are shown in Fig. 2.1.

As a result of these challenges, many existing tennis annotation systems avoid ball tracking and rely only on audio and player information [6, 10, 12, 15, 31]. As a result, they can only annotate at a crude level, e.g. highlight detection [10], shot type classification [13], action recognition [31]. In this chapter, we explicitly address the challenges, and propose a fully automatic tennis ball tracking algorithm. Before presenting the algorithm, in the following we briefly review related work in the literature.

2.1.1 Related Work

Object tracking is one of the key topics of computer vision. Briefly speaking, object tracking is concerned with finding and following the object of interest in a video sequence. Two pieces of information are essential for any object tracking problem: object appearance and object dynamics. Depending on the way, these two pieces of information are combined, tracking algorithms can be broadly categorised into track-after-detection (TAD) type of approach and track-before-detection (TBD) type.[1]

In the TAD approach, object candidates are first detected in each frame. After this step, only the candidates are used for the tracking, the rest of the image is discarded. The tracking problem then involves two elements: data association and estimation. While data association deals with measurement origin uncertainty, i.e. which candidates are object-originated and which are clutter-originated (which candidates are which-object-originated in a multiple object tracking scenario); estimation deals with measurement inaccuracy, i.e. what is the "true state" of the object, assuming the object-originated candidate has been identified. The TAD type of approach is suitable for tracking small and fast-moving objects with simple representations. Typical examples can be found in aerospace and defence applications [1, 2, 17, 19, 24], where scans of radar signal are equivalent to frames in a video, and an object candidate is simply a point in a scan with no resolvable features.

The TBD approach, on the other hand, is suitable for tracking large and slowly moving objects with complex representations. In a TBD approach, hypotheses about the object's position in a state space are generated, and then evaluated using the image. Depending on the features used for evaluating the hypotheses, this type of approach can be further categorised into contour-based tracking, colour-based tracking, etc. The TBD approach is often used together with a particle filter, since a particle filter provides a nice probabilistic framework for combining the hypotheses. Example applications of the TBD approach include people tracking, face tracking [11, 21, 28]

A tennis ball is a small and fast-moving object with few features. We therefore believe the TAD approach is more suitable for tracking a tennis ball. We first generate ball candidates in each frame using image processing techniques. Each candidate is then treated as a two-dimensional point in the image plane without resolvable features. We then try to solve a pure data association problem using only the positions of these candidates. Once the data association problem is solved, the estimation problem becomes trivial. For example a Kalman smoother can give a Minimum Mean Square Estimate (MMSE) of the object state.

Several tennis ball tracking algorithms have been reported in the literature [16, 18, 22, 23, 25, 30]. All these algorithms adopt the TAD approach. Some of the existing algorithms have been successfully applied in practice for enhanced broadcast [23, 25]. In [23, 25], multiple cameras are used. This allows tracking the ball in the 3D real world space, which significantly simplifies the data association problem.

Techniques in [16, 18, 22, 30], on the other hand, rely on a single camera. In this sense, they are more closely related to the scope of this chapter. In [18, 22, 30], the focus is on ball candidate generation rather than data association. Typically, foreground moving objects are extracted by frame differencing. The resulting blobs are then tested using visual features such as size, shape and colour. Among the blobs that have passed the test, the one that is closest to a predicted position is used to update the trajectory. In other words, the data association problem is implicitly addressed

[1] Note that TBD is short for track-before-detection instead of track-by-detection, which is in fact TAD (track-after-detection).

with a nearest neighbour type of single hypothesis scheme. This implicitly imposes the assumption that the false candidate rate is very low, and the true ball detection rate is reasonably high.

In [16], the authors propose a data association algorithm under the name of Robust Data Association (RDA), and use RDA to track a tennis ball in monocular sequences. RDA does not use the naive single hypothesis data association scheme. The key idea of RDA is to treat data association as a motion model fitting problem. First, ball candidates in each frame are detected. A sliding window containing several frames is then moved over the sequence. A RANSAC-like algorithm is used to find the motion model that is best at explaining the candidates inside the window. An estimate of the ball position in one frame, e.g. the middle frame in the sliding window, is then given by this model. As the sliding window moves, eventually ball positions in all frames are estimated.

The remainder of this chapter is organised as follows. In Sect. 2.2 we propose a layered data association (LDA) algorithm for tennis ball tracking. Experimental evaluation is presented and discussed in Sect. 2.3. Finally, Sect. 2.4 concludes the chapter.

2.2 Layered Data Association

In this section, we present our three-layered data association scheme for tracking the tennis ball. From bottom to top, the three layers are: candidate level association, tracklet level association and path level analysis (Fig. 2.2).

1. Assume ball candidates in each frame have been generated. Also, assume a temporal sliding window is moved over the sequence. At the **candidate level**, we exhaustively evaluate for each candidate in the middle frame of the sliding window whether a small ellipsoid around it in the column-row-time space contains one candidate from the previous frame and one candidate from the next frame. If it does, we fit a dynamic model to the three candidates. The fitted model is then optimised recursively using candidates in the sliding window that are consistent with it. This process is repeated until convergence, forming a "tracklet".
2. As the sliding window moves, a sequence of tracklets is generated. These tracklets may have originated from tennis balls or from clutter. We formulate **tracklet level** association as a shortest path problem. We construct a weighted and directed graph, where each node is a tracklet, and the edge weight between two nodes is defined according to the "compatibility" of the two tracklets. If we were to assume that there was only one ball to track, and that the first and last tracklets of

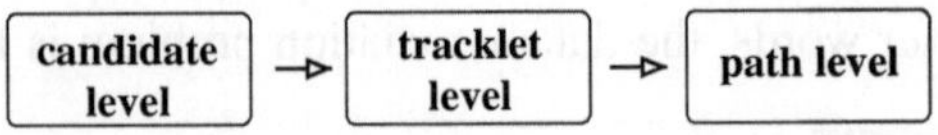

Fig. 2.2 The three layers of the proposed data association scheme

this ball were already known, the shortest path between the two tracklets (nodes) in the graph would then correspond to the trajectory of the ball.

3. We relax above assumptions by looking for shortest paths between all pairs of nodes in the graph, instead of the shortest path between a given pair of nodes. By analysing the all-pairs shortest paths at the **path level**, the first and last tracklets of each ball can be identified. Track initiation/termination of this multiple object tracking problem is then automatically dealt with.

2.2.1 Candidate Level Association

Assume a tennis sequence is composed of K frames numbered from 1 to K. Let us denote the set of candidates in frame k by $\mathscr{C}_k = \{c_k^j\}_{j=1}^{m_k}$, where m_k is the number of candidates in frame k, c_k^j is the jth of them, and $k = 1, \ldots, K$. Assume a temporal sliding window containing $2V + 1$ frames is moved over the sequence. At time i, the interval I_i spans frame $i - V$ to frame $i + V$. We project all the candidates inside interval I_i, i.e. all the candidates in $\mathscr{C}^{(i)} = \{\mathscr{C}_{i-V}, \ldots, \mathscr{C}_{i+V}\}$ onto the row-column image plane. In this image plane, centred at each $c_i^j \in \mathscr{C}_i$ and with radius R, a circular area A_i^j is considered, where R is the maximum distance the ball can travel between two successive frames. We examine if at least one candidate from $\mathscr{C}_{i-1}$ and at least one candidate from $\mathscr{C}_{i+1}$ fall into A_i^j (see Fig. 2.3). Assume $c_{i-1}^{j'} \in \mathscr{C}_{i-1}$ and $c_{i+1}^{j''} \in \mathscr{C}_{i+1}$ are found inside A_i^j, throughout the rest of this chapter, we call the three candidates $c_{i-1}^{j'}$, c_i^j and $c_{i+1}^{j''}$ a seed triplet.

The acceleration of a tennis ball in the 3D world space is constant if the air resistance is ignored, since the ball is subject only to gravity. According to perspective geometry [9], after the projective transformation to the 2D image plane, the motion of the ball is approximately constant acceleration, as long as ΔZ is negligible compared

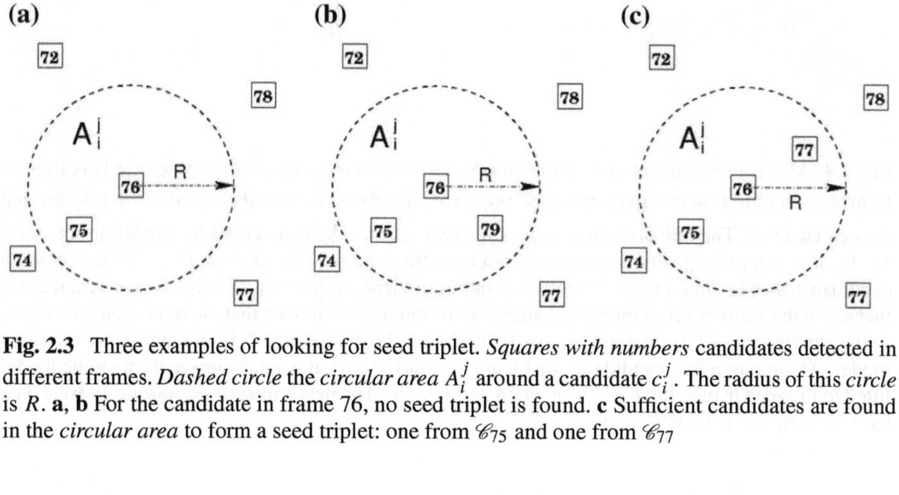

Fig. 2.3 Three examples of looking for seed triplet. *Squares with numbers* candidates detected in different frames. *Dashed circle* the *circular area* A_i^j around a candidate c_i^j. The radius of this *circle* is R. **a, b** For the candidate in frame 76, no seed triplet is found. **c** Sufficient candidates are found in the *circular area* to form a seed triplet: one from $\mathscr{C}_{75}$ and one from $\mathscr{C}_{77}$

to Z, where ΔZ is the distance the ball moves in the world space between two frames along the direction perpendicular to the image plane, and Z is the distance from the ball to the camera along the same direction.

Consider any three candidates detected in frames k_1, k_2 and k_3, where $k_1 < k_2 < k_3$. Let the positions of the candidates in the image plane be $\mathbf{p_1}$, $\mathbf{p_2}$ and $\mathbf{p_3}$, respectively. A constant acceleration model M can be solved as:

$$\mathbf{v_1} = \frac{\mathbf{p_2} - \mathbf{p_1}}{\Delta k_{21}} - \frac{\Delta k_{21} \times \mathbf{a}}{2} \tag{2.1}$$

$$\mathbf{a} = 2 \times \frac{\Delta k_{21} \times (\mathbf{p_3} - \mathbf{p_2}) - \Delta k_{32} \times (\mathbf{p_2} - \mathbf{p_1})}{\Delta k_{21} \times \Delta k_{32} \times (\Delta k_{21} + \Delta k_{32})} \tag{2.2}$$

where $\Delta k_{21} = k_2 - k_1$, $\Delta k_{32} = k_3 - k_2$, $\mathbf{a}$ is the constant acceleration, $\mathbf{v_1}$ is the velocity at time k_1, and $\mathbf{p_1}, \mathbf{p_2}, \mathbf{p_3}, \mathbf{a}, \mathbf{v_1} \in \mathbb{R}^2$. An estimate of the ball position in any frame k is then given by

$$\hat{\mathbf{p}}_{\mathbf{k}} = \mathbf{p_1} + \Delta k \times \mathbf{v_1} + \frac{(\Delta k)^2}{2} \times \mathbf{a} \tag{2.3}$$

where $\Delta k = k - k_1$. Such a model can be fitted to any three candidates detected in different frames. We apply it to the seed triplet found inside A_i^j, as illustrated in Fig. 2.4a. In this special case, $k_1 = i - 1$, $k_2 = i$ and $k_3 = i + 1$.

Compared to the random sampling scheme in Robust Data Association (RDA) [16], the advantage of using seed triplets for model fitting is that a seed triplet

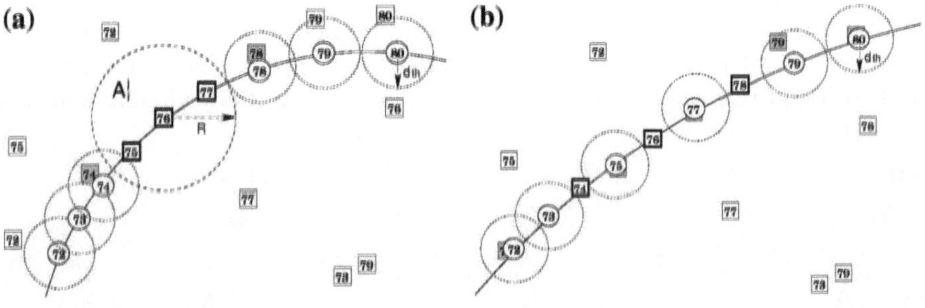

Fig. 2.4 Model fitting and model optimising. *Squares with numbers* candidates detected in different frames, including true positives and false positives. *Big dashed circle* the *circular area* A_i^j around the candidate c_i^j. The radius of this *circle* is R. *Bold squares* the triplet used for model fitting. *Solid circles with numbers* positions estimated with the fitted model. *Small dashed circles* the region a candidate has to fall into to be a support. The radius of these *circles* is d_{th}. *Shaded squares* candidates that are in the support set of the model after the current iteration. Note that the bold squares are also in the support set. **a** Fitting a motion model to the seed triplet in Fig. 2.3c. **b** Optimising the fitted model. Assume in **a** two candidates, one from $\mathscr{C}_{74}$ and one from $\mathscr{C}_{78}$ are consistent with the model fitted to the seed triplet, i.e. $\dot{k} = 74$, $\ddot{k} = 78$ and $\dddot{k} = 76$. The new triplet (*bold squares* in **b**) is then used to compute a "better" model

has a higher probability of containing only true positives than a sample set that is drawn randomly from all candidates in the sliding window [20]. However, even if a seed triplet is free of false positives, the model computed with it is usually poor, as estimates are given by extrapolation. This can be seen in Fig. 2.4a. As the estimates get further away from the seed triplet on the time axis, they depart from the detected ball positions in row-column plane rapidly.

We remedy this by recursively optimising the model using supports found in the previous iteration [4]. First, we define the support of a model as a candidate that is consistent with the model. More precisely, a candidate $c_k^j \in \mathscr{C}^{(i)}$ located at $\mathbf{p}_\mathbf{k}^\mathbf{j}$ is said to be a support if $d(\hat{\mathbf{p}}_\mathbf{k}, \mathbf{p}_\mathbf{k}^\mathbf{j}) < d_{\text{th}}$, where $d(\cdot, \cdot)$ is the Euclidean distance between two points; $\hat{\mathbf{p}}_\mathbf{k}$ is the estimated ball position at time k as given by the model; and d_{th} is a predefined threshold. In the rare case where more than one candidate satisfies this condition at time k, only the one with the smallest $d(\hat{\mathbf{p}}_\mathbf{k}, \mathbf{p}_\mathbf{k}^\mathbf{j})$ is selected as a support.

Let $\mathscr{S}$ be the set of supports of a model. Also, let

$$\begin{aligned} \dot{k} &= \min k \quad \forall c_k^j \in \mathscr{S} \\ \dddot{k} &= \max k \quad \forall c_k^j \in \mathscr{S} \\ \ddot{k} &= \arg\min_k \left| |\dddot{k} - k| - |k - \dot{k}| \right| \quad \forall c_k^j \in \mathscr{S} \end{aligned} \tag{2.4}$$

We use the three candidates in $\mathscr{S}$ from frame $\dot{k}$, $\ddot{k}$ and $\dddot{k}$ as a new triplet to fit another model. Since the candidates in the new triplet are further apart from each other, more estimates are interpolated. The resulting model is usually "better" than the one computed with the seed triplet. One iteration of the optimisation is thus complete (Fig. 2.4b).

Now, we need a measure of the quality of a model. RANSAC-like algorithms normally use the number of supports a model gets. In [27], a maximum likelihood version of RANSAC, MLESAC, is proposed as a more accurate measure. However, MLESAC involves estimation of mixture parameters of a likelihood function [16, 26], which can be complicated and computationally expensive. In our implementation, the following cost function [27] is adopted:

$$C = \sum_{k=i-V}^{i+V} \sum_j \rho(\mathbf{p}_\mathbf{k}^\mathbf{j}) \tag{2.5}$$

where

$$\rho(\mathbf{p}_\mathbf{k}^\mathbf{j}) = \begin{cases} d^2(\hat{\mathbf{p}}_\mathbf{k}, \mathbf{p}_\mathbf{k}^\mathbf{j}) & \text{if } d(\hat{\mathbf{p}}_\mathbf{k}, \mathbf{p}_\mathbf{k}^\mathbf{j}) < d_{\text{th}} \\ d_{\text{th}}^2 & \text{if } d(\hat{\mathbf{p}}_\mathbf{k}, \mathbf{p}_\mathbf{k}^\mathbf{j}) \geq d_{\text{th}} \end{cases} \tag{2.6}$$

and a smaller C indicates a better model.

Having defined C, the optimisation loop terminates when the support set $\mathscr{S}$ stops expanding, or when C increases. More specifically, let $M^{(z)}$ be the model after the zth iteration, $C^{(z)}$ be its cost, $\dot{k}^{(z)}$ and $\dddot{k}^{(z)}$ be defined as in Eq. (2.4). The optimisation loop terminates if

$$(\dot{k}^{(z+1)} = \dot{k}^{(z)} \wedge \dddot{k}^{(z+1)} = \dddot{k}^{(z)}) \vee (C^{(z+1)} > C^{(z)}) \tag{2.7}$$

and $M^{(z)}$ is retained as the final fitted model to the current seed triplet.

A tracklet T is defined as the combination of a parameterised model M and its support set $\mathscr{S}$, i.e. $T = \{M, \mathscr{S}\}$. For interval I_i, the above model-fitting process is applied to each seed triplet that contains each c_i^j in $\mathscr{C}_i$. We then retain only tracklets that have more than m_{th} supports, and denote the lth retained tracklet in I_i by $T_i^l = \{M_i^l, \mathscr{S}_i^l\}$. As the sliding window moves, a sequence of tracklets is generated. Figure 2.5 plots all 672 tracklets generated in an example sequence in the row-column-time 3D space. In the figure, a tracklet T_i^l is plotted as its dynamic model M_i^l, and is bounded by $\dot{k}_i^l$ and $\dddot{k}_i^l$.

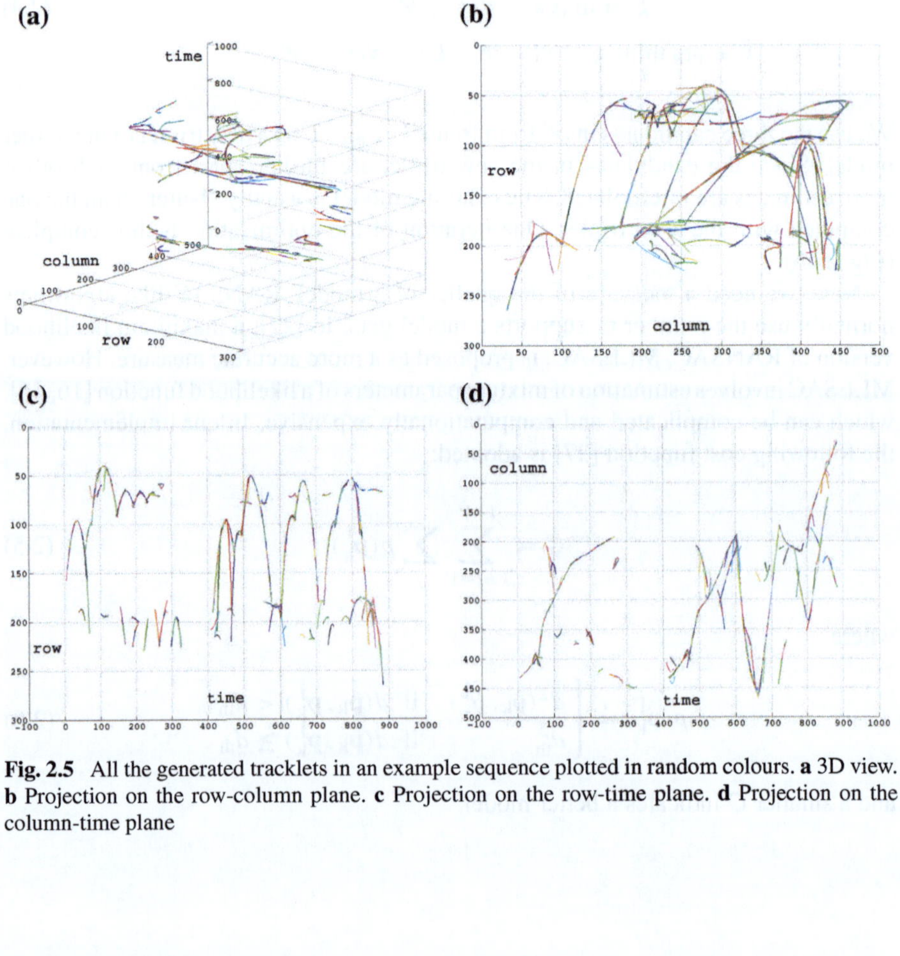

Fig. 2.5 All the generated tracklets in an example sequence plotted in random colours. **a** 3D view. **b** Projection on the row-column plane. **c** Projection on the row-time plane. **d** Projection on the column-time plane

2.2.2 Tracklet Level Association

The tracklet level association problem is mapped onto a graph. We construct a weighted and directed graph $\mathscr{G} = \{\mathscr{N}, \mathscr{E}\}$, where $\mathscr{N}$ is the set of nodes, and $\mathscr{E}$ is the set of edges. Each node in $\mathscr{N}$ is a tracklet, and the node corresponding to tracklet T_i^l is denoted by n_i^l. Clearly, $\mathscr{N}$ is composed of stages as

$$\mathscr{N} = \{\mathscr{N}_{1+V}, \mathscr{N}_{2+V}, \ldots, \mathscr{N}_{K-V-1}, \mathscr{N}_{K-V}\} \tag{2.8}$$

where the ith stage $\mathscr{N}_i$ is the set of nodes (tracklets) generated in interval I_i, I_i centres on frame i and spans frame $i - V$ to frame $i + V$, and K is the number of frames in the sequence. A directed edge from node n_u^p to node n_v^q, $e_{u,v}^{p,q}$, exists in $\mathscr{E}$, if

$$u < v \ \wedge \ \dot{k}_v^q - \dddot{k}_u^p \le k_{\text{th}} \tag{2.9}$$

where $\dot{k}_v^q$ is the $\dot{k}$ of tracklet T_v^q, $\dddot{k}_u^p$ is the $\dddot{k}$ of tracklet T_u^p, and $u, v \in [1 + V, K - V]$. The assumption here is that misdetection of the ball can happen in at most k_{th} successive frames, where $k_{\text{th}} \in \mathscr{N}^+$. An example of graph topology is given in Fig. 2.6.

Both M and $\mathscr{S}$ of the tracklets are used to define the edge weight between two nodes. First, two nodes n_u^p and n_v^q are said to be "overlapping" if

$$u < v \ \wedge \ \dot{k}_v^q - \dddot{k}_u^p \le 0 \tag{2.10}$$

For overlapping nodes, their support sets are used. Two overlapping nodes are "conflicting" (not compatible) if for $\dot{k}_v^q \le k \le \dddot{k}_u^p$, $\exists k$ such that

$$(\exists c_k^{j'} \in \mathscr{S}_u^p \ \wedge \ \nexists c_k^{j''} \in \mathscr{S}_v^q) \ \vee \ (\nexists c_k^{j'} \in \mathscr{S}_u^p \ \wedge \ \exists c_k^{j''} \in \mathscr{S}_v^q)$$
$$\vee \ (\exists c_k^{j'} \in \mathscr{S}_u^p \ \wedge \ \exists c_k^{j''} \in \mathscr{S}_v^q \ \wedge \ \mathbf{p}_k^{j'} \ne \mathbf{p}_k^{j''}) \tag{2.11}$$

In other words, two compatible tracklets should agree on the support in every frame in the overlapping region: either both having the same support, or both having no support. The edge weight between two overlapping nodes is then given by

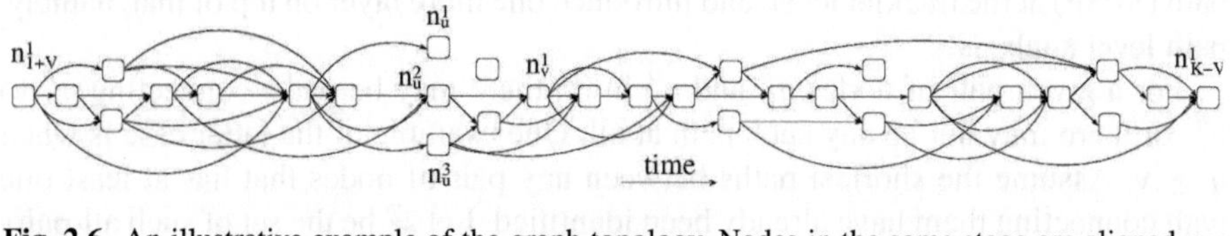

Fig. 2.6 An illustrative example of the graph topology. Nodes in the same stage are aligned *vertically*. Note that the number of nodes in a typical sequence is of the order of 10^2–10^3. Far fewer nodes are plotted in this figure for ease of visualisation

$$w_{u,v}^{p,q} = \begin{cases} \infty & \text{if } n_u^p \text{ and } n_v^q \text{ are conflicting} \\ 0 & \text{otherwise} \end{cases} \tag{2.12}$$

For non-overlapping nodes, their parameterised models are used. Ball positions from frame $\ddot{k}_u^p$ to frame $\dot{k}_v^q$ are estimated. The edge weight is then defined as

$$w_{u,v}^{p,q} = \min d(\hat{\mathbf{p}}^{\mathbf{p}}_{\mathbf{u,k}}, \hat{\mathbf{p}}^{\mathbf{q}}_{\mathbf{v,k}}), \quad \forall k \in [\ddot{k}_u^p, \dot{k}_v^q] \tag{2.13}$$

A path in a directed graph is a sequence of nodes such that from each node (except the last one), there is an edge going to the next node in the sequence. In an edge-weighted graph, the weight of a path is defined as the sum of the weights of all the edges it goes through. The shortest path between two nodes is the path with the smallest weight among all possible paths.

The edge weight defined in Eq. (2.12) and Eq. (2.13) can be thought of as a compatibility measure. For now, we assume that there is only one ball to track, and the first and last nodes that have originated from this ball are already known. The Dijkstra's algorithm [8] can then be applied to find the shortest path between the pair of nodes. We manually specify the first and last ball-originated nodes in the third play of the example sequence as source node and destination node. The result of applying Dijkstra's algorithm is illustrated in Fig. 2.7: a shortest path that corresponds to the ball trajectory. According to the definition of edge weight, the shortest path found is guaranteed to be non-conflicting: at any time k, there is at most one candidate in the support sets of the shortest path. The data association problem is thus solved.

In tennis ball tracking, the points at which the ball changes its motion abruptly correspond to key events such as hit and bounce, and provide important information for high-level annotation. We use the algorithm of generalised edge-preserving signal smoothing to detect these key events. A more detailed description can be found in our previous work [29].

2.2.3 Path Level Analysis

In this section, we relax the assumptions made in the previous section, and show how this relaxation can lead to a fully automatic algorithm for tracking multiple balls. The key idea is to use all-pairs shortest path (APSP) instead of single-pair shortest path (SPSP) at the tracklet level, and introduce one more layer on top of that, namely, path level analysis.

For a given pair of nodes n_u^p and n_v^q in $\mathcal{G}$, there may be paths connecting n_u^p to n_v^q, or there may not be any such path at all. One example of the latter case is when $u \geq v$. Assume the shortest paths between any pair of nodes that has at least one path connecting them have already been identified. Let $\mathcal{Q}$ be the set of such all-pairs shortest paths, and Q is the number of paths in $\mathcal{Q}$. Q is in the order of N^2, where N is the number of nodes in the graph. Now, observe that the paths that correspond to ball trajectories form a subset of $\mathcal{Q}$. Our goal is to reduce the original set of APSP $\mathcal{Q}$ to its subset that contains only paths that correspond to the ball trajectories (Fig. 2.8).

(a)

(b)

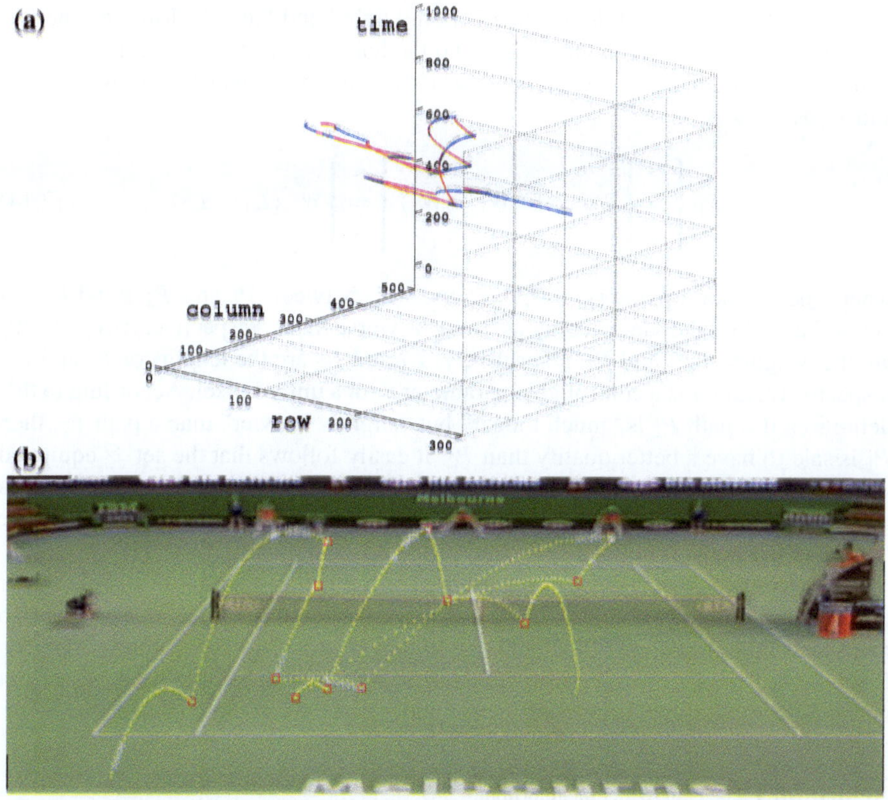

Fig. 2.7 **a** *Shortest* path given by Dijkstra's algorithm. Adjacent nodes in the *shortest* path are plotted alternatively in *blue* and *red*. 3D view. **b** Ball trajectory superimposed on the mosaic image. *Yellow circles* positions of the candidates in the support sets of the nodes in the *shortest* path. *White crosses* interpolated tennis ball positions. *Red squares* detected key events

Fig. 2.8 An illustration of the *shortest* path in Fig. 2.7 in the graph. *Striped red squares* the manually specified source node and destination node. *Red squares* the *shortest* path between the source node and the destination node

To this end, we need to define the relative quality and compatibility of the paths. Recall that the weight of a path is the sum of the weights of all edges the path goes through. We then define the length of a path to be the size of the union of the support sets in all its nodes. It should be noted that according to the definitions of weight and length of a path, the term "shortest path" used in the previous sections should have been "lightest path". However, we chose to use "shortest path" for the sake of consistency with the terminology used in the literature.

Intuitively, a good path is one that is both "light" and "long". However, there is usually a trade-off between the weight and the length of a path: a longer path tends to be heavier. Taking this into account, we define the relative quality of two path P_1 and P_2 as follows:

$$P_1 \left\{ \begin{array}{c} > \\ = \\ < \end{array} \right\} P_2 \quad \text{if } (W_1 - W_2) \left\{ \begin{array}{c} < \\ = \\ > \end{array} \right\} \alpha \cdot (L_1 - L_2) \tag{2.14}$$

where the relation operators ">", "=" and "<" between P_1 and P_2 stand for "is better than", "has the same quality as", and "is worse than", respectively; W_1 and W_2 are the weights of P_1 and P_2, respectively; L_1 and L_2 are the lengths of P_1 and P_2, respectively; and α is a controllable parameter with a unit of pixel. According to this definition, if a path P_1 is "much longer" but "slightly heavier" than a path P_2, then P_1 is said to have a better quality than P_2. It easily follows that the set $\mathscr{Q}$ equipped with an operator "$\geq$" satisfies transitivity, antisymmetry and totality. According to order theory [7], $\mathscr{Q}$ associated with operator "$\geq$" is a totally ordered set. The relative quality of the paths is defined.

The definition of pair-wise compatibility of the paths is straightforward. Under the assumption that two objects cannot produce the same candidate in a frame, two paths are said to be compatible if and only if they do not share any common support. It should be noted, however, two paths that do not share any common node are not necessarily compatible, because different nodes can have common supports.

Algorithm 1 The path reduction algorithm

Input: Set $\mathscr{P}$ with p paths, and empty set $\mathscr{B}$.
Output: A reduced set $\mathscr{P}$.

```
while 𝒫 is not empty do
    Remove the best path P* in 𝒫 from 𝒫
    if P* is compatible with all paths in ℬ then
        add P* to ℬ
    end if
end while
```

We propose a simple path reduction algorithm (see Algorithm 1) to prune the APSP set. According to the definition of relative quality and pair-wise compatibility of the paths, the paths in the resulting subset are mutually compatible, and are optimal in the sense that the best remaining path in $\mathscr{P}$ was always considered first. We call the output of the path reduction algorithm $\mathscr{B}$ the Best Set of Compatible Paths (BSCP).

Now, we have a complete data association algorithm for tracking multiple objects fully automatically. We apply the complete algorithm to the example sequence. With path level analysis, track initiation and track termination is automated, and multiple plays can be handled. By looking for all-pairs shortest paths, a set $\mathscr{Q}$ with $Q = 87{,}961$ paths is obtained. The path reduction algorithm is then applied, which gives a BSCP $\mathscr{B}$ containing 11 paths. In descending order, the numbers of supports (lengths) of

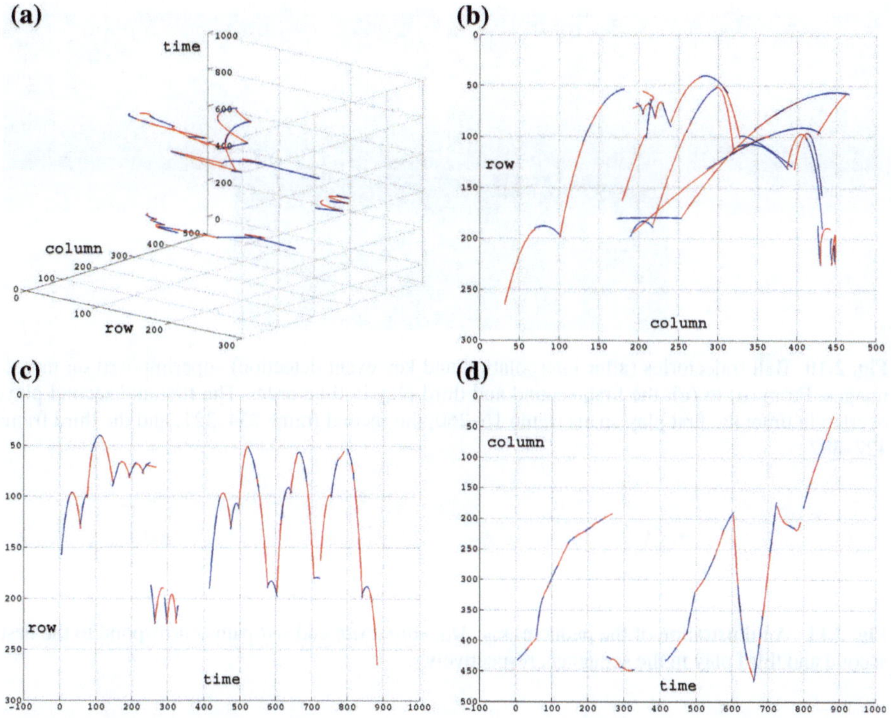

Fig. 2.9 Results of applying the complete algorithm to the example sequence: three paths in the thresholded BSCP $\mathscr{B}_{\text{th}}$. Adjacent nodes in each path are plotted alternatively in *blue* and *red*. **a** 3D view. **b** Projection on the row-column plane. **c** Projection on the row-time plane. **d** Projection on the column-time plane

the paths in $\mathscr{B}$ are: 411, 247, 62, 23, 20, 17, 17, 16, 15, 10, 9. It is a reasonable assumption that a path corresponding to a ball trajectory has more supports than a path corresponding to the motion of a non-ball object, e.g. a wristband. We set a threshold L_{th} and keep only the paths that have more supports than L_{th}. This results in a thresholded BSCP $\mathscr{B}_{\text{th}}$ with three paths, where each path corresponds to a play in the sequence. The paths in $\mathscr{B}_{\text{th}}$ are plotted in the 3D space in Fig. 2.9. In Fig. 2.10, the three reconstructed trajectories are superimposed on mosaic images. An illustration of the three paths in the graph is shown in Fig. 2.11.

2.3 Experiments

In this section, we first introduce data sets used in our evaluation and tracking algorithms under comparison. We then define performance metrics. Finally, experimental results are presented, including a study of sensitivity of the proposed method to parameters.

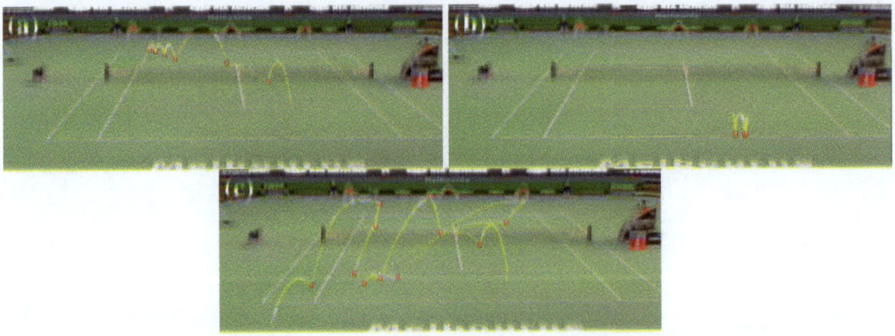

Fig. 2.10 Ball trajectories (after interpolation and key event detection) superimposed on mosaic images. From (**a**) to (**c**): the first, second and third play in time order. The first and second plays overlap in time: the first play spans frame 16–260; the second frame 254–321; and the third frame 427–887

Fig. 2.11 An illustration of the paths in $\mathscr{B}_{\text{th}}$. *Magenta*, *cyan* and *red* paths correspond to the first, second and third play in the sequence, respectively

2.3.1 Experimental Data

Experiments were carried out on broadcast tennis videos from three tennis tournaments. A broadcast tennis video is composed of shots, such as play, close-up, crowd, advertisement. A play shot is a shot in which the ball is in play. In a play shot, the camera is usually from behind one of the players, and has small pan, tilt and zoom (PTZ) motion. Tennis ball tracking is performed only on play shots. In this chapter, we also refer to a play shot as a "sequence".

The three data sets used contain 165 sequences in total. A set with 25 sequences was used as training set, and the other two with 70 sequences each as test sets. Some statistics of the three data sets are shown in Table 2.1. In Table 2.1, $\bar{N}$ is the average number of false candidates in each frame, and r_d is the probability that a ball is detected as a candidate (ball detection rate). In our experiments, the parameters of the proposed method were assumed independent of each other, and were tuned

Table 2.1 Statistics of experimental data

	Game	Court type	No. of seq	No. of frames	Length (min)	$\bar{N}$	r_d (%)
Training set	Australian'03 Women's	Artificial	25	15,716	5.2	12.1	90.3
Test set 1	Australian'06 Men's	Artificial	70	60,094	20.0	10.6	91.6
Test set 2	Wimbledon'05 Men's	Grass	70	43,706	14.6	16.5	88.2

separately on the training set to maximise the F-measure of event detection. The definition of F-measure which will be given shortly in Sect. 2.3.3. The optimal set of parameters obtained during the training was: $V = 10$, $R = 20.0$, $d_{\mathrm{th}} = 5.0$, $m_{\mathrm{th}} = 6$, $k_{\mathrm{th}} = 20$, $L_{\mathrm{th}} = 45$, and $\alpha = 1.0$.

The proposed data association algorithm takes as input the tennis ball candidates in each frame. In each sequence, image frames were first de-interlaced into fields. For the sake of consistency with the terminology used in the literature, we have used "frame" to refer to "field". After de-interlacing, homographies between frames were calculated by tracking corresponding corners that are automatically detected, and were used to compensate the global motion (camera PTZ) between frames [3, 14]. Foreground moving objects were then extracted by differencing nearby frames and thresholding the differences. Finally, a simple filter was applied to keep only foreground blobs with an appropriate size. These blobs were used as tennis ball candidates for tracking algorithms.

2.3.2 Algorithms Under Comparison

For comparison with the proposed algorithm, PDA [1] and RDA [16] were also implemented. Due to the abrupt motion changes, PDA lost track in most sequences. We will therefore focus on the comparison between the proposed method and RDA. In RDA, the number of trials, n, is chosen so that the probability of finding a set consisting entirely of true positives, P, is greater than a threshold P_0. It has been shown [5] that

$$n \geq \log(1 - P_0)/\log(1 - \varepsilon^s) \tag{2.15}$$

where ε is the ratio of the number of true positives to the number of all candidates, and s is the size of each sample set. In our experiments, P_0 was set to 0.95, and the interval size was set to 15, both as suggested in [16]. According to Eq. (2.15), at least 8,161 trials were needed. The mixture parameters of the likelihood function in RDA were estimated recursively until convergence, also as suggested in [16]. As to dynamic model, the same constant acceleration model as defined in Eq. (2.1) and Eq. (2.2) was used. Since RDA cannot deal with track initiation and track termination, we manually specified the frames in which it was applied.

2.3.3 Evaluation Methods

2.3.3.1 Matching the Tracked Trajectories and the Ground Truth Trajectories Automatically

For each sequence, let $\mathscr{T}_{\mathrm{gt}}$ be the set of trajectories in the ground truth, and $\mathscr{T}_{\mathrm{tr}}$ be the set of trajectories given by the tracker. Each trajectory is a sequence of points in the row-column-time 3D space. Define an assignment scheme as a correspondence between the two sets of trajectories that satisfies: each trajectory in $\mathcal{T}_{\mathrm{gt}}$ corresponds to at most one trajectory in $\mathcal{T}_{\mathrm{tr}}$, and vice versa.

Observe that an assignment scheme consists of correspondence pairs. For a given pair, let $\mathcal{I}^*$ be the time interval where the two trajectories overlap. For each frame in $\mathcal{I}^*$, two ball positions are given, one by the tracker and one by the ground truth. The two positions are compared. If the distance between them is smaller than a threshold, the two trajectories are said to be "matched" in this frame. The match score of a pair of trajectories is defined as the total number of frames where the two trajectories are matched. Finally, the quality of an assignment scheme is defined as the sum of match scores of all its correspondence pairs. Among all possible assignment schemes, the one with highest quality is chosen.

2.3.3.2 Quality of Track Initiation and Track Termination

Having obtained the correspondence between $\mathcal{T}_{\mathrm{gt}}$ and $\mathcal{T}_{\mathrm{tr}}$, we can measure the performance of the tracker from several aspects. Let $T^i_{\mathrm{gt}} \in \mathcal{T}_{\mathrm{gt}}$ and $T^i_{\mathrm{tr}} \in \mathcal{T}_{\mathrm{tr}}$ be the trajectories in the ith pair, and $\mathcal{I}^i_{\mathrm{gt}}$ and $\mathcal{I}^i_{\mathrm{tr}}$ be the time interval of T^i_{gt} and T^i_{tr}, respectively. Moreover, let T'^j_{gt} be the jth trajectory in $\mathcal{T}_{\mathrm{gt}}$ that is not in any correspondence pair, and $\mathcal{I}'^j_{\mathrm{gt}}$ be its time interval; and let T'^k_{tr} be the kth trajectory in $\mathcal{T}_{\mathrm{tr}}$ that is not in any correspondence pair, and $\mathcal{I}'^k_{\mathrm{tr}}$ be its time interval. Now, define

$$I^{\cap} = \sum_i |\mathcal{I}^i_{\mathrm{gt}} \cap \mathcal{I}^i_{\mathrm{tr}}| \tag{2.16}$$

and

$$I^{\cup} = \sum_i |\mathcal{I}^i_{\mathrm{gt}} \cup \mathcal{I}^i_{\mathrm{tr}}| + \sum_j |\mathcal{I}'^j_{\mathrm{gt}}| + \sum_k |\mathcal{I}'^k_{\mathrm{tr}}| \tag{2.17}$$

The quality of track initiation and track termination on this sequence is then:

$$\beta = I^{\cap}/I^{\cup} \tag{2.18}$$

where β ranges between 0 an 1. When $\beta = 1$, track initiation/termination is said to be perfect.

2.3.3.3 Proportion of LOT

In addition to the quality of track initiation and termination, we would also like to know how close the positions given by the tracker are to the ground truth. Consider the ith pair of trajectories in the best assignment scheme. Two ball positions are given in each frame in $\mathscr{I}^i_{\text{tr}} \cap \mathscr{I}^i_{\text{gt}}$, one by the tracker and the other by the ground truth. We define tracking error as the Euclidean distance between the two positions. For a given sequence, the number of such errors is $I^{\cap}$. A loss-of-track (LOT) is then defined as when tracking error is greater than 6 pixels. Let the number of LOTs in the given sequence be I^L_m. The proportion of LOT is then defined as:

$$\gamma = I^L / I^{\cap} \tag{2.19}$$

2.3.3.4 Quality of Event Detection

We also measure the performance of the proposed algorithm in terms of quality of event detection. For each trajectory in $\mathscr{T}_{\text{gt}}$, points that correspond to motion discontinuities are marked up as ground truth events. These events correspond to racket hitting the ball, the ball bouncing on the ground and the ball touching the net. We then compare the events detected by an event detection algorithm against the ones in ground truth. A detected event in a tracked trajectory T^i_{tr} is regarded as "matched" if it is within 3 frames and 5 pixels of a ground truth event in the corresponding ground truth trajectory T^i_{gt}. We report the F-measure of event detection, which is the harmonic mean of the precision and the recall. The F-measure ranges from 0 to 1, and a larger value indicates a better performance.

The quality of event detection is obviously affected by the event detection algorithm used, and thus not a direct quality measure of the ball tracking algorithm. However, event detection plays a crucial role in high-level annotation. We present the quality of event detection to give an idea of the performance of the ball tracking algorithm in the context of tennis video annotation.

2.3.4 Results and Discussion

Experimental results on the two test sets are shown in Table 2.2. The quality of track initiation/termination of the two methods is not comparable, since in RDA this was manually dealt with. In terms of proportion of LOT and F-measure of event detection, the proposed method outperforms RDA significantly on both test sets. In RDA, estimates are given by the best models in corresponding intervals independently of

Table 2.2 Experimental results on the test sets

		β	γ (%)	F-measure	Frames/s
Test set 1	Proposed	**83.7 %**	**3.51**	**0.758**	**98.4**
	RDA	–	11.74	0.423	3.6
Test set 2	Proposed	**82.2 %**	**3.66**	**0.729**	**109.3**
	RDA	–	13.23	0.411	3.2

each other, and the concept of "tracklet" does not exist. This significantly limits RDA's ability to deal with complexities in broadcast tennis video. In fact, RDA works only under a strong assumption: a model fitted to three candidates that have all originated from the ball being tracked is always "better" than that fitted to candidates that have not. This assumption is not true in broadcast tennis sequences because:

1. Ball trajectories can overlap in time, i.e. there may be multiple balls in the same part of a sequence;
2. Clutter-originated candidates can also form smooth trajectories that can be explained by constant acceleration models;
3. A ball can change its motion drastically. As a result, even a model fitted to three ball-originated candidates can have a poor quality.

By contrast, the proposed method slices the data association problem into layers, and each layer is designed to solve the data association problem at its own level. It is therefore more flexible in dealing with the complexities in broadcast tennis video. (see Fig. 2.12 for an example).

The proposed algorithm also has the advantage of being more efficient. The fact that it always starts model fitting from a seed triplet allows it to eliminate false

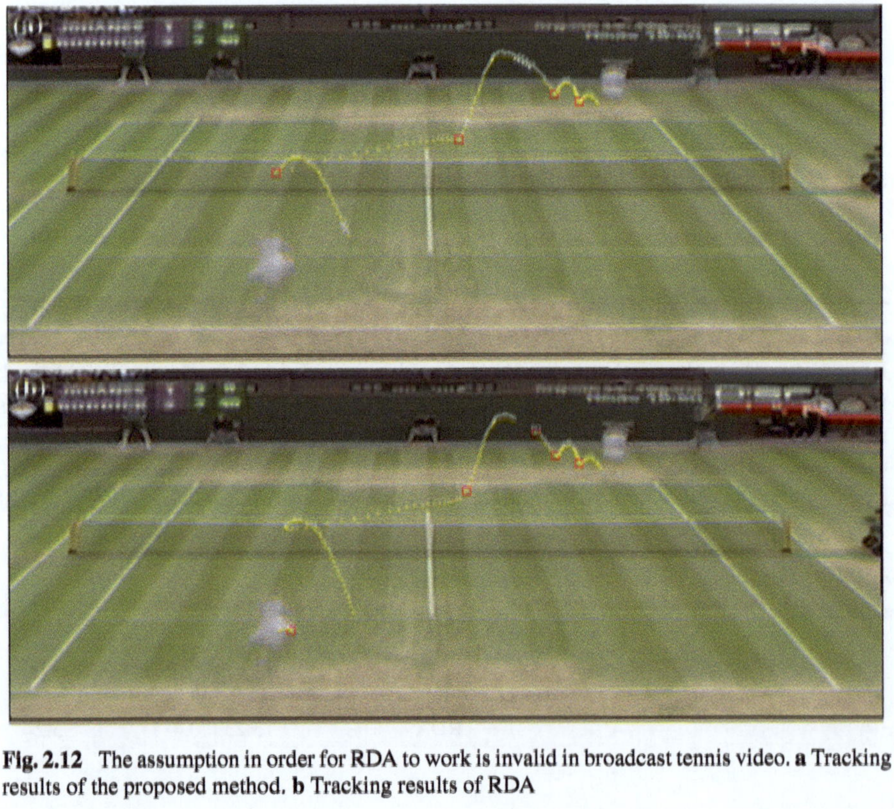

Fig. 2.12 The assumption in order for RDA to work is invalid in broadcast tennis video. **a** Tracking results of the proposed method. **b** Tracking results of RDA

Table 2.3 Sensitivity to parameters

	Opt. param.	RDA	V		R		d_{th}		m_{th}	
			7	13	15.0	25.0	4.0	6.0	4	8
β	83.7 %	=	82.8 %	82.9 %	83.6 %	83.7 %	82.9 %	83.0 %	83.0 %	75.9 %
γ	3.51 %	11.74 %	3.94 %	3.78 %	3.58 %	3.50 %	3.87 %	3.29 %	3.82 %	3.75 %
F-measure	0.758	0.423	0.725	0.770	0.754	0.759	0.732	0.768	0.763	0.696
Frames/s	98.4	3.6	102.2	93.8	100.3	96.6	128.4	81.4	55.7	152.9
	k_{th}		L_{th}		α					
	15	25	30	60	0.001	0.01	0.1	10.0	100.0	1,000.0
β	76.5 %	85.1 %	80.0 %	84.0 %	42.5 %	49.3 %	78.1 %	76.8 %	75.2 %	75.1 %
γ	2.78 %	4.46 %	2.89 %	3.29 %	2.10 %	2.14 %	2.64 %	5.78 %	7.48 %	7.60 %
F-measure	0.740	0.747	0.747	0.759	0.538	0.584	0.738	0.700	0.668	0.667
Frames/s	105.6	89.4	92.9	102.4	88.8	91.3	96.0	98.5	100.0	100.2

candidates very quickly. Taking test set 1, for example at each time step, on average 10.6 candidates are evaluated. On average, there are 1.02 seed triplets containing each candidate, and it takes 3.7 iterations for model optimisation to converge. The effective number of models evaluated is then $10.6 \times 1.02 \times 3.7 \approx 40$. On the other hand, according to Eq. (2.15), at least 8161 models are needed in RDA. The estimation of mixture parameters of the likelihood function in RDA is also time-consuming. Time in Table 2.2 was measured on a single thread of an Intel Xeon 3.0G computer running Linux, and overhead of disk I/O was included. Both algorithms were implemented in C++.

Finally in Table 2.3 we show the sensitivity of the proposed algorithm to parameters using test set 1. It is evident from the table that the proposed algorithm is not sensitive to small changes of most parameters. However, when the parameter for determining the relative quality of two paths, α, varies over a large range, paths can be inappropriately merged or broken, severely degrading track initiation/termination and event detection. We can also see that the proposed method is sensitive to the increase of the tracklet threshold m_{th}. This is because when m_{th} is too high, ball-originated tracklets are discarded, and the shortest path algorithm is forced to take a wrong path. On the other hand, when m_{th} is low, false tracklets are allowed. However, the shortest path algorithm can remove them effectively.

2.4 Conclusions

In this chapter, we have presented a layered data association algorithm with graph-theoretic formulation for tracking multiple objects that undergo switching dynamics in clutter. At the object candidate level, tracklets are grown from sets of candidates that have high probabilities of containing only true positives. The tracklet association problem is then mapped onto a graph, and solved with an all-pairs shortest path formulation and path level analysis. This results in a fully automatic data association algorithm which can handle multiple object scenarios. The proposed data association algorithm has been applied to tennis sequences from several tennis tournaments to track tennis balls. Comparative experiments show that it works well on sequences where other data association methods perform poorly or fail completely.

References

1. Bar-Shalom Y, Fortmanm TE (1988) Tracking and data association. Academic Press Inc, Boston
2. Bar-Shalom Y, Kirubarajan T (2001) Estimation with applications to tracking and navigation. Wiley, New York
3. Christmas W, Kostin A, Yan F, Kolonias I, Kittler J (2005) A system for the automatic annotation of tennis matches. In: Fourth international workshop on content-based multimedia indexing
4. Chum O, Matas J, Kittler J (2003) Locally optimized Ransac. In: DAGM-symposium, pp 236–243
5. Chum O, Matas J, Obdrzalek S (2004) Enhancing Ransac by generalized model optimization. Asian Conf Comput Vis 2:812–817
6. Coldefy F, Bouthemy P, Betser M, Gravier G (2004) Tennis video abstraction from audio and visual cues. In: IEEE international workshop on multimedia signal processing
7. Davey B, Priestley H (2002) Introduction to lattices and order. Cambridge University Press, Cambridge
8. Dijkstra E (1959) A note on two problems in connexion with graphs. Numer Math 1:269–271
9. Hartley R, Zisserman A (2004) Multiple view geometry in computer vision, 2nd edn. Cambridge University Press, Cambridge
10. Huang Y, Chiou C, Sandnes F (2009) An intelligent strategy for the automatic detection of highlights in tennis video recordings. Expert Syst Appl 36:9907–9918
11. Isard M, Blake A (1998) Condensation—conditional density propagation for visual tracking. Int J Comput Vis 1(29):5–28
12. Kijak E, Gravier G, Oisel L, Gros P (2003) Audiovisual integration for tennis broadcast structuring. In: International workshop on content-based multimedia indexing
13. Kijak E, Gravier G, Gros P, Oisel L, Bimbot F (2003) Hmm based structuring of tennis videos using visual and audio cues. IEEE Int Conf Multimed Expo 3:309–312
14. Kittler J, Christmas W, Kostin A, Yan F, Kolonias I, Windridge D (2005) A memory architecture and contextual reasoning framework for cognitive vision. In: 14th Scandinavian conference on image analysis
15. Lai J, Chen C, Kao C, Chien S (2011) Tennis video 2.0: a new presentation of sports videos with content separation and rendering. J Vis Commun Image Represent 22:271–283
16. Lepetit V, Shahrokni A, Fua P (2003) Robust data association for online applications. CVPR 1:281–288
17. Mazor E, Averbuch A, Bar-Shalom Y, Dayan J (1998) Interacting multiple model methods in target tracking: a survey. IEEE Trans Aerosp Electron Syst 34(1):103–122
18. Miyamori H, Iisaku S (2000) Video annotation for content-based retrieval using human behavior analysis and domain knowledge. In: International conference on automatic face and gesture recognition, pp 320–325
19. Musicki D, La Scala BF, Evans RJ (2004) Integrated track splitting filter for manoeuvring targets. In: IEEE international conference on information fusion
20. Myatt DR, Torr PHS, Nasuto SJ, Bishop JM, Craddock R (2002) NAPSAC: high noise, high dimensional Robust estimation—it's in the bag. In: British machine vision conference, pp 458–467

21. Nummiaro K, Merier E, van Gool L (2003) An adaptive color-based particle filter. J Image Vis Comput 21(1):99–110
22. Pingali GS, Jean Y, Carlbom I (1998) Real time tracking for enhanced tennis broadcasts. In: CVPR, pp 260–265
23. Pingali GS, Opalach A, Jean Y (2000) Ball tracking and virtual replays for innovative tennis broadcasts. In: ICPR, pp 4152–4156
24. Streit R, Luginbuhl T (1995) Probabilistic multi-hypothesis tracking. Technical Report
25. The Hawkeye Tennis System (2014) http://www.hawkeyeinnovations.co.uk
26. Tordoff BJ, Murray DW (2005) Guided-MLESAC: faster image transform estimation by using matching priors. PAMI 27(10):1523–1535
27. Torr PHS, Zisserman A (2000) MLESAC: a new robust estimator with application to estimating image geometry. Comput Vis Image Underst 78:138–156
28. Viola P, Jones M (2004) Robust real-time object detection. IJCV 57(2):137–154
29. Yan F, Kostin A, Christmas W, Kittler J (2006) A novel data association algorithm for object tracking in clutter with application to tennis video analysis. In: CVPR
30. Yu X, Sim C, Wang JR, Cheong L (2004) A trajectory-based ball detection and tracking algorithm in broadcast tennis video. ICIP 2:1049–1052
31. Zhu G, Huang Q, Xu C, Xing L (2007) Human behavior analysis for highlight ranking in broadcast racket sports video. IEEE Trans Multimed 9(6):1167–1182

Chapter 3
Plane Approximation-Based Approach for 3D Reconstruction of Ball Trajectory for Performance Analysis in Table Tennis

Sho Tamaki and Hideo Saito

Abstract A plane approximation-based approach for 3D reconstruction of ball trajectory is introduced, which was developed as a solution to the problem with conventional analysis in table tennis. There are methods of reconstructing 2D ball trajectories or 3D trajectories of balls heavier than those in table tennis. However, these methods cannot be adopted to reconstruct the 3D trajectories of table tennis balls, because there are problems that are attributed to the dimensions of the trajectories and weight of the balls. The method proposed in this chapter could reconstruct the 3D trajectories of a table tennis ball. The key feature of the method is that it approximates that a ball is traveling on tilted planes. This approximation makes reconstruction robust against failure to measure 3D ball positions. Two systems were developed based on the new method. A system using two RGB cameras experimentally demonstrated that it could provide accurate information for match analysis. A system using an RGB-D camera was experimentally demonstrated that the system could provide accurate information for service analysis.

3.1 Introduction

There has recently been increasing interest in statistical analysis in sports sciences [1–3]. The analysis has been called "performance analysis" and described as "an objective way of recording performance so that key elements of that performance can be quantified in a valid and consistent manner" by International Society of

S. Tamaki (✉) · H. Saito
Graduate School of Science and Technology, Keio University,
3-14-1, Hiyoshi, Kohoku-ku, Yokohama, Kanagawa, Japan
e-mail: tamaki@hvrl.ics.keio.ac.jp

H. Saito
e-mail: saito@hvrl.ics.keio.ac.jp

T.B. Moeslund et al. (eds.), *Computer Vision in Sports*,
Advances in Computer Vision and Pattern Recognition,
DOI 10.1007/978-3-319-09396-3_3

Performance Analysis of Sports in [4]. Coaches can use the results of performance analysis to optimize decision making. There has been some research that has aimed at applying methods of performance analysis to table tennis [5, 6].

However, table tennis coaches and players have rarely conducted performance analysis because this analysis in table tennis requires enormous amounts of time or huge budgets due to the heavy workload imposed by data collection. It is not currently available for many practitioners to carry out analysis because of the inefficiency of data collection methods.

A system without computer vision technologies was developed to solve this problem. It made data collection more efficient by supporting input operations by just using a graphical user interface (GUI). This system certainly advanced solutions to the problem. For example, the system enabled performance analysis at the London Olympics in 2012. While the system achieved advances, it still had a major problem in that they required a lot of time to collect shot data, such as the positions where the ball was hit and where it bounced. We call the analysis with the software "conventional analysis" in this chapter. The main problem of the conventional analysis originated from its dependence on the operation of manual input. Automated data collection is therefore urgently required. If we could obtain the 3D trajectories of table tennis balls automatically, this problem would be solved.

Here, we propose a vision-based approach for reconstructing the 3D trajectories of table tennis balls. There are several methods of reconstructing 2D ball trajectories or 3D trajectories of balls that are heavier than table tennis balls. However, they cannot be adopted to reconstruct the 3D trajectories of table tennis balls because there are problems that are attributed to the dimensions of the trajectories and weights of balls. The proposed approach in this chapter can be used to reconstruct the 3D trajectories of table tennis balls. The key feature of the proposed method is approximation where the ball is traveling on tilted planes. This approximation makes the reconstruction robust against failures to measure 3D ball positions in various frames. In addition, the proposed approach can successfully be used to reconstruct trajectories with ball candidates including false positives. The method of dealing with false positives is based on the method proposed by Yan et al. [7]. We developed a system using two RGB cameras based on the new method. The system obtains shot data for match analysis and is expected to solve the problem with conventional analysis. We then developed a system using an RGB-D camera to optimize usability for practitioners. Although the system using the RGB-D camera cannot reconstruct the trajectories of fast-moving or rotating balls due to functional issues with the RGB-D camera, the system is still useful for analyzing services. Moreover, we expect that the system would be able to reconstruct the positions of any balls in the future when the frame rates and the measurement range of depths of RGB-D cameras were enhanced. The proposed method experimentally demonstrates that it made performance analysis more useful for table tennis practitioners through these developments in the systems.

This chapter consists of eight sections. Section 3.2 briefly describes conventional analysis. Section 3.3 considers technical issues in reconstructing the 3D trajectories of table tennis balls with usable photographic devices for performance analysis.

Section 3.4 introduces related work. Section 3.5 describes proposing method that overcame several technical issues. Section 3.6 introduces the system that uses two RGB cameras, which we experimentally evaluated. Section 3.7 introduces the system using an RGB-D camera, which we also experimentally evaluated. Finally, we conclude the chapter in Sect. 3.8.

3.2 Conventional Analysis

We developed a GUI computer software to conduct performance analysis efficiently. Table tennis matches were analyzed with conventional analysis in two steps with the software : (1) analysis that provided brief results based on data related to rallies and (2) analysis that provided detailed results, based on data collected at (1) and data related to shots. We collected data related to rallies in analysis (1), such as those from the server, the scoring player, and the shot number of the scoring shot.[1] After the data were collected, we computed statistics that could be used as indicators of (a) the scoring possibility depending on serves or returns, (b) transitions in scores, and (c) the scoring possibility depending on the shot number. Many data were obtained automatically with this software, based on the assumption that a shot was played alternately by players. Input operation was therefore just to record the times of shots and the shot number of the scoring shots, and we could conduct this analysis in real time. We collected data related to shots in analysis (2), such as the types of shots and the direction (position from which the ball bounced and the direction in which it moved) of a shot. After the data were collected, we computed the statistics that could be used as indicators of (a) the scoring possibility depending on the type of shot and (b) the scoring possibility depending on the direction of the shot. We mainly analyzed the spatial factor of tactics in this analysis. It was difficult to manually record the precise coordinates of shots, but it was possible to record the data on a scale according to a 3×3 divided area of a half court. Spatial tactics in table tennis are generally considered based on the 3×3 divided area. We could therefore use the direction data if they were obtained on a 3×3 scale of accuracy.

The conventional analysis using the developed system was conducted by Japanese national team at the London Olympics in 2012 for performance analysis at the competition venue. We analyzed 136 matches based on (1) and 59 matches based on (2) as a result of this analysis, which provided advanced performance analysis in table tennis. However, the problem where we needed a great deal of time to collect shot data remained because this could not be solved by manually collecting data conventionally, and a method of automatically collecting data was needed urgently.

[1] Shot number denotes the ordinal number of shots in a rally. For example, making the serve is the first, and receiving it is the second.

3.3 Technical Issues

The enormous workload imposed by collecting shot data is the most important problem with conventional analysis. We propose a method of reconstructing the 3D trajectories of table tennis balls to solve this problem. 3D trajectories provide the spatial features of shots (e.g. the positions from which balls bounced, their maximum height, and the direction and velocity of movements). However, because we cannot set up optimal environments for performance analysis in practice, it is difficult to reconstruct the 3D trajectories of table tennis balls.

Let us consider usable devices in practical scenario (e.g. competition venues and training rooms). The setup to operate devices for performance analysis would be difficult to achieve if it required many devices. Therefore, the smaller the number of devices, the better. We can minimize the number of devices by using only one device that can detect depth, like an RGB-D camera. However, since RGB-D cameras cannot be set to have either high frame rate or short exposure times, we cannot target fast-moving balls with them. We can target fast-moving balls by using two RGB cameras, although usability would decrease. We therefore used two RGB cameras or an RGB-D camera to reconstruct trajectories for this reason.

We then considered the technical issues we faced in reconstructing the 3D trajectories of a table tennis ball. First, it is difficult to detect a table tennis ball. We took a video far from the court at a competition venue. We could therefore not take images of the ball at high resolution. We would encounter the same problem when we used an RGB-D camera even in a training room because the resolution of standard RGB-D cameras is around 640×480 pixels. The diameter of a table tennis ball is less than 10 pixels in this situation and it is difficult to discriminate this from many other objects. Second, the 3D position of balls cannot be measured robustly because of the restrictions with usable devices. We cannot measure the 3D coordinates of balls with two RGB cameras when ball-to-objects, usually ball-to-player, occlusion occurs at one viewpoint. We encountered more difficult situations using an RGB-D camera because there were many missing values in the depth images we took with it. The ratio, expressed as a percentage, where we successfully measured the 3D positions of a ball was about 20 % in all frames including the ball in our experiments. We needed a method that could reconstruct the 3D trajectories of table tennis balls from a few 3D positions of the balls.

3.4 Related Work

Huang et al. [8] tried to compute a ball position in a frame by integrating segmentation-based detection and particle filter-based tracking. First, an image is segmented as foreground and background based on the color, the background is assumed to be grass field and the color is green. Ball-like objects are then extracted from the extracted foreground blobs based on the circularity and the color. The particle filter-based tracking is applied after segmentation-based detection succeeded. In their experiment, ball detection and tracking was successfully done at many frames. However, detection was sometimes failed and then false positive was tracked in successive about 40 frames. This is a common issue of ball tracking. Imaged balls cannot be differentiated from other objects robustly based only on its appearance because of their size and the poor features. Although many other researches employed same framework [9–12], they showed no effective way to avoid this problem.

Yu et al. [13] mentioned a ball in low resolution as "object-indistinguishable". In order to solve the problem of ball detection, they estimate hitting points based on the players position and the hitting sound. The ratio of the ball position which successfully computed was nearly 100 % in their experiment, even if the ratio of successfully tracked ball was 60–90 %. This method, however, is not always applicable. Many matches might be played in one competition venue or one training room at the same time. It is really a difficult problem to extract the sound generated from the targeted match.

Poliakov et al. [14] exploited the knowledge that the ball was traveling from a racket to track a tennis ball. Balls can be interpolated robustly when they know the hitting points. Their method avoided the difficulty of ball detection using racket positions. However, it was also difficult to detect rackets, especially in table tennis, because they were small and were often occluded by the players. We would have faced other difficult issues if we had used their method.

"Hawk-Eye" [15] is one of the leading system for ball detection and tracking. Balls are detected based on the size and the shape. Noise filtering is done in 3-space based on epipolar constraint. The reliability and accuracy of the system are undoubtable. It is officially used in cricket as a broadcast tool and in tennis as a line calling system. This system, however, assumes the number of cameras are sufficient for detecting a ball during a rally. We cannot take this assumption because of our constraint of the number of usable devises as we discussed in Sect. 3.3.

Yan et al. [7] reconstructed the 2D trajectories of a tennis ball from cluttered data. They approximated a motion model of balls with constant acceleration over short periods of time and linked short trajectories by solving the shortest path problem. Their experimental results indicated that this method could reconstruct a trajectory even if the detection results include many false positives. However, if we failed to measure ball positions in successive frames, the approximation used in their method would be inappropriate because the actual acceleration of the ball is not constant. We often encountered such situations in 3-space because of restrictions with usable devices, as we mentioned in Sect. 3.3. Therefore, we could not deal with the problem by using only their method.

Ren et al. [16] reconstructed the 3D trajectory of a soccer ball. They approximated the trajectory of a soccer ball with planar curves on vertical planes. Because they could obtain the 3D positions of the ball by projecting its 2D position, this method could be used to reconstruct the 3D trajectories of the ball when there were few 3D positions of balls. However, when a ball is spinning fast and changes direction after being affected by lift force, the approximation that the ball will travel on a vertical plane is inappropriate. We could not use this method because table tennis balls are light and can be severely affected by lift force. We will demonstrate that in the next section.

We could conclude that there were technical problems that related work could not solve. The problems were attributed to the dimensions of trajectories and the weights of the balls. We therefore needed a new method of reconstructing the 3D trajectories of table tennis balls.

3.5 Method for Trajectory Reconstruction

Figure 3.1 shows a flowchart for our method. The proposed method requires the following information: camera parameters, table corners in world and image space, ball candidates in world and image space, bounce time, impact time, and the start and end times of rallies. We assume the impact times, and start and end times of rallies would be recorded with the conventional method. As it is not a problem to record data with the conventional method, these assumptions are appropriate.

We will first validate the key idea behind our method, approximating a ball traveling on tilted planes, in Sect. 3.5.1. We will then describe methods of reconstructing the 3D trajectories of table tennis balls in Sects. 3.5.2 and 3.5.3. Methods of obtaining other information are described in Sects. 3.6 and 3.7 because they depend on devices.

3.5.1 Validity of Planar Approximation

First, let us consider an approximation where a ball traveling on a vertical plane is valid, which is the approximation used by Ren et al. [16]. The force that influences traveling balls is the resulting force of gravity force, drag force, and lift force. The directions of gravity force, drag force, and lift force are vertically downward, opposite to the direction of travel, and perpendicular to the velocity vector and rotation axis of

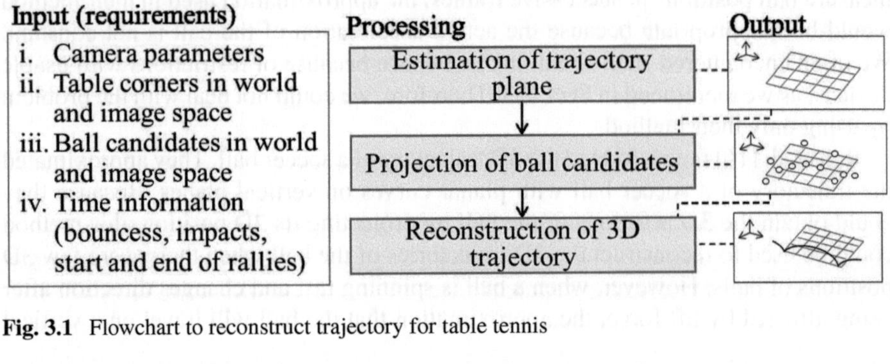

Fig. 3.1 Flowchart to reconstruct trajectory for table tennis

the ball, respectively. When balls do not rotate, only gravity and drag force influence them and they travel on the vertical plane. Even if balls rotate, they still travel on the vertical plane because the direction of lift force is the same to the direction of gravity force when the rotation axis is perpendicular to the velocity vector and parallel to the ground. We can therefore assume that balls traveling on the vertical plane when their rotation is very slow or in the direction of the rotation axis are nearly perpendicular to the velocity vector and parallel to the ground.

This condition, however, is not always the case in actual table tennis matches where the rotation of the ball can be fast and the rotation axis can head in various directions. We conducted a simulated experiment to find how far a ball could be away from the vertical plane. The trajectory of a rotating ball whose rotation axis was vertical to the ground was computed in this simulation. The travel distance on the horizontal plane was 2.74 m, which is the same length as that of a table tennis court. The rotation speed was 70 fps, which is about half that of an elite player's top spin. The motion model of the ball used the model proposed by Okada et al. [17]. Let us denote the mass of a ball as m kg, the radius of a ball as r m, and the velocity of a ball as $\dot{\boldsymbol{r}}$ m/s. Let us also denote the angular velocity as $\boldsymbol{\omega}$ rad/s, the air density as ρ kg/m^3, the drag coefficient as C_D, and the lift coefficient(or Magnus coefficient) as C_M. The motion model is defined as

$$\frac{d\dot{\boldsymbol{r}}}{dr} = \frac{1}{m}(\boldsymbol{F}_G + \boldsymbol{F}_D + \boldsymbol{F}_L) \tag{3.1}$$

$$\boldsymbol{F}_G = m\boldsymbol{g} \tag{3.2}$$

$$\boldsymbol{F}_D = -\frac{1}{2}C_D\pi a^2\rho|\dot{\boldsymbol{r}}|\dot{\boldsymbol{r}} \tag{3.3}$$

$$\boldsymbol{F}_L = \frac{4}{3}C_M\pi a^3\rho\boldsymbol{\omega}\times\dot{\boldsymbol{r}} \tag{3.4}$$

The accumulation of infinitesimal change was simulated by using this model and the difference equation below by using the classical Runge–Kutta method to prevent large errors from accumulating.

$$(\boldsymbol{r}', \dot{\boldsymbol{r}}', \boldsymbol{\omega}')^{\mathrm{t}} = (\boldsymbol{r}, \dot{\boldsymbol{r}}, \boldsymbol{\omega}^{\mathrm{t}}) + \Delta r(\dot{\boldsymbol{r}}, \frac{d\dot{\boldsymbol{r}}}{dr}, \boldsymbol{0}^{\mathrm{t}}) \tag{3.5}$$

Air density ρ was set to 1.28, drag coefficient C_D was set to 0.75, and the lift coefficient was set to 0.45 in the experiment by referring to the experimental results reported by Seydel [18]. In addition, the initial position[m] of the ball was set to (0, 0, 0), and the initial velocity[m/s] of the ball was set to (0, 10, 0), where the end and side lines of the court were defined as the X–Y plane and the vertical direction of the court was defined as the Z axis in world space. The vertical plane that provides the least mean square distance from simulated balls was computed. The average distance from the simulated balls to the plane was 291 mm and the maximum distance was 452 mm. The data in conventional analysis are recorded on a scale according to a 3×3 divided area of a half court (see Sect. 3.2). The approximation where a ball is

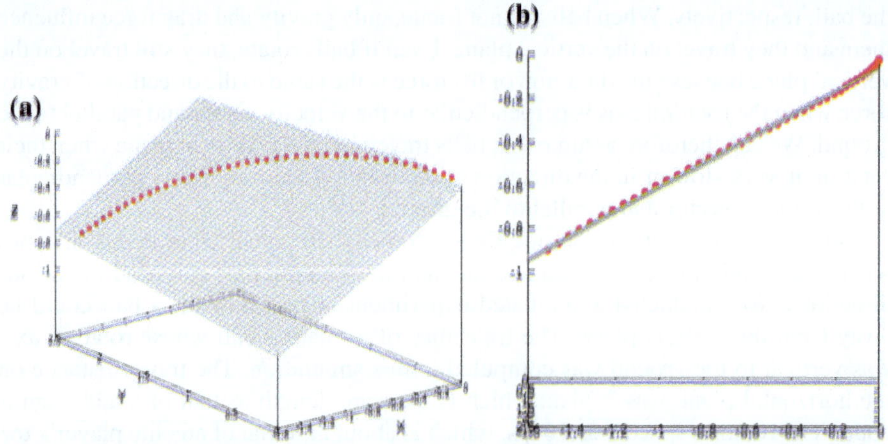

Fig. 3.2 The simulated ball trajectory and the plane that provides the least mean square distance to the trajectory. **a** Overview of the trajectory. **b** Side view of the trajectory and the plane for the comparison

traveling on the vertical plane can be too inaccurate to analyze performance and is not practical in table tennis.

A tilted plane that provided the least mean square distance from the simulated balls was then computed. The simulated balls and the plane are outlined in Fig. 3.2. The average distance from the simulated balls was 5 mm and the maximum distance was 29 mm. The error in approximation using the tilted plane is much smaller than that of approximation using the vertical plane. The error, up to 29 mm, is sufficiently small to be used in performance analysis. We can conclude at the end of validation experiment that the approximation where a table tennis ball is traveling on a tilted plane is reasonable.

3.5.2 Estimating Trajectory Planes

We approximate that ball trajectories are planar trajectories between ball-to-racket or ball-to-court collisions. We assume the bounce times and impact times were obtained. We therefore separately take each period of time between collisions into consideration after this.

Outliers are detected and eliminated by fitting the planar model to ball candidates in world space at first. Next, three optimal ball candidates are chosen. Let us denote the number of ball candidates in world space as n_c, the jth candidates as c_j, the plane constructed by three chosen ball candidates as P, and the Euclidean distance between plane P_l and candidate c_j as $D(P_l, c_j)$. The planar model that minimizes the following cost function are chosen as:

$$C = \sum_{j=0}^{n_e} D(P, c_j) \tag{3.6}$$

This computation may provide poor results when we have so few candidates because of the errors included in true positives. The trajectory plane is robustly estimated using bounce points as anchors. The number of candidates in a period can be too small to reconstruct a plane even using a bounce position. We set the threshold for the number of candidates required to reconstruct a trajectory plane with the method. The candidates in the time trajectory plane that are not reconstructed are projected to another plane, which is in the closest planes in the future or past and provides smaller C.

3.5.3 Reconstruction of Trajectory Model

First, we obtain ball candidates in world space by projecting ball candidates in image space to a trajectory plane. Let us denote the normal of a trajectory plane as $\boldsymbol{n}$, the model of the trajectory plane as $ax + by + cz + d = 0$, the imaged position of the ball as x_{image}, and the physical position of the ball on the image as X_{image}. A ball position in world space X_{world} is computed as:

$$\boldsymbol{X}_{\mathrm{world}} = -\left(\frac{d}{\boldsymbol{n} \cdot \boldsymbol{X}_{\mathrm{image}}}\right)\boldsymbol{X}_{\mathrm{image}} \tag{3.7}$$

$$\text{where } \boldsymbol{X}_{\mathrm{image}} = \boldsymbol{K}^{-1}\underline{\mathbf{x}}_{\mathrm{image}} \tag{3.8}$$

where the optical center of the camera that takes the projected ball candidate is defined as the origin of world space. The physical position of the ball on the image is computed based on Eqs. (3.7) and (3.8).

We then reconstruct the 3D trajectory model from the 3D positions of balls obtained before processes. We use the method proposed by Yan et al. [7] to estimate the trajectory model with extensions for 3D. First, false positives are eliminated based on the consecutive candidates in adjacent frames, as described in Fig. 3.3. Every

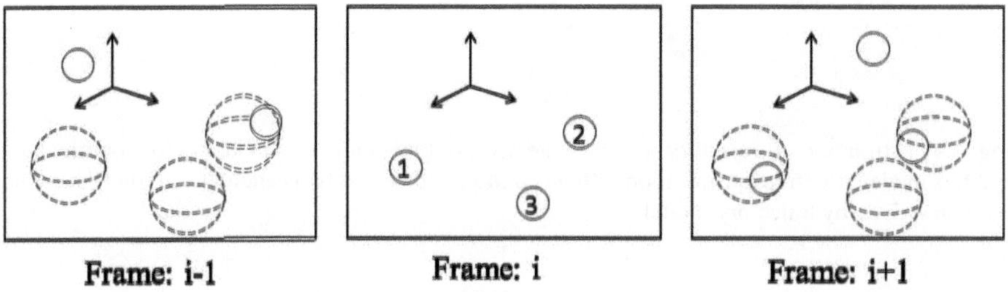

Fig. 3.3 Elimination of false positives. Candidates 1 and 3 are eliminated in frame i, because they have no consecutive candidates within the threshold range (*dashed sphere*) in frame i − 1 and/or frame i + 1. Candidate 2 is not eliminated, because it has consecutive candidates in both adjacent frames

candidate is examined in the process to check whether it has consecutive candidates, which is defined by the distance from the candidate, in adjacent frames. The distance that defines successive candidates is the maximum distance the ball can travel between frames. A candidate is eliminated when no other candidates are detected in either or both adjacent frames. If there is more than one candidate in a frame, all candidates in the frame are eliminated. Most of the false positives are eliminated after the process.

Next, trajectory models are estimated. We approximate that the motion model of the ball has constant acceleration in the specific period of time, n_c. Let us denote the positions of candidates as $\boldsymbol{p}_1$, $\boldsymbol{p}_2$, and $\boldsymbol{p}_3$, their time as t_1, t_2, and t_3 ($t_1 < t_2 < t_3$), $t_2 - t_1$ as Δt_{21}, $t_3 - t_1$ as Δt_{31}, constant acceleration as $\boldsymbol{a}$, and velocity at time t_1 as $\boldsymbol{v}_1$. The constant acceleration model can be solved as:

$$\boldsymbol{v}_1 = \frac{\boldsymbol{p}_2 - \boldsymbol{p}_1}{\Delta t_{21}} - \frac{\Delta t_{21}\boldsymbol{a}}{2} \tag{3.9}$$

$$\boldsymbol{a} = 2\frac{\Delta t_{21}(\boldsymbol{p}_3 - \boldsymbol{p}_2) - \Delta t_{32}(\boldsymbol{p}_2 - \boldsymbol{p}_1)}{\Delta t_{21}\Delta t_{32}(\Delta t_{21} + \Delta t_{32})} \tag{3.10}$$

Models could be inaccurate when they are reconstructed from successive candidates in close frames. The problem is solved with the trajectory model by using three points, i.e., the earliest, the latest, and the middle ones in inliers, which were consistent with the trajectory. This iterative optimization stops when the three points do not change or the sum of errors starts to increase. As we can see from Fig. 3.4, the distance between the trajectory model that is estimated from the three successive points (Fig. 3.4a) is longer than that of the trajectory model that is estimated after three iterations of the optimization process (Fig. 3.4b). Next, we link reconstructed trajectories in time-series order. We then smooth the trajectories with a Savitzky-Golay filter [19]. As a result, the 3D trajectories of a table tennis ball can finally be reconstructed.

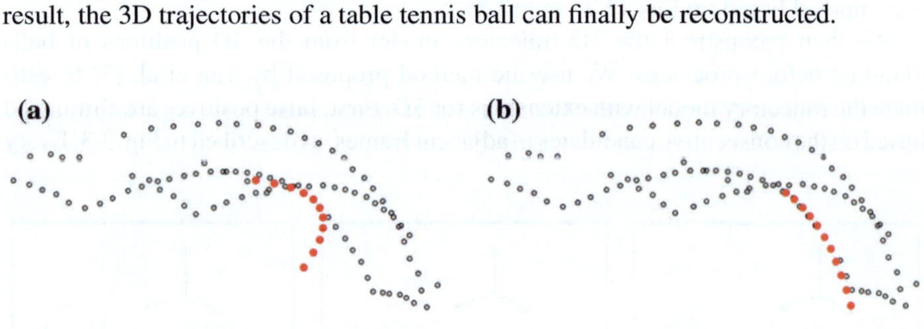

Fig. 3.4 Estimation of trajectory model by iterative optimization. **a** is model before optimization and **b** is model after tree optimizations. *Open circles* are detected ball candidates. *Filled circles* are estimates given by trajectory model

3.6 System Using Two RGB Cameras

We developed two different sensing settings of the system, two RGB cameras and an RGB-D camera, based on the proposed method. Although it is optimal to use an RGB-D camera from the aspect of usability, we have to use two RGB cameras when we need to track a fast-moving ball. The details of the system using two RGB cameras is described in this section.

3.6.1 System Architecture

Figure 3.5 has the flowchart to obtain data with the system. The steps are described in detail in the following subsections.

3.6.2 Camera Calibration

At first, camera calibration, namely obtaining intrinsic and extrinsic camera parameters, is done. We use the method proposed by Zhang [20] to compute intrinsic camera parameters. Extrinsic camera parameters are obtained from planar transformation matrix (Homography) $\boldsymbol{H}$[21]. Let us define the end lines and side lines of the court as the X–Y plane, the vertical direction of the court as the Z axis in world space, and the position[m] of the four corners as (0, 0, 0), (1.525, 0, 0), (0, 2.74, 0), and (1.525, 2.74, 0). Based on this definition, $\boldsymbol{H}$ can be computed [22]. The four corners were manually recorded. Optimal extrinsic parameters cannot be expected with this method because we only use four points on the same plane and independently calibrated each of the cameras. However, this method is easy to operate and

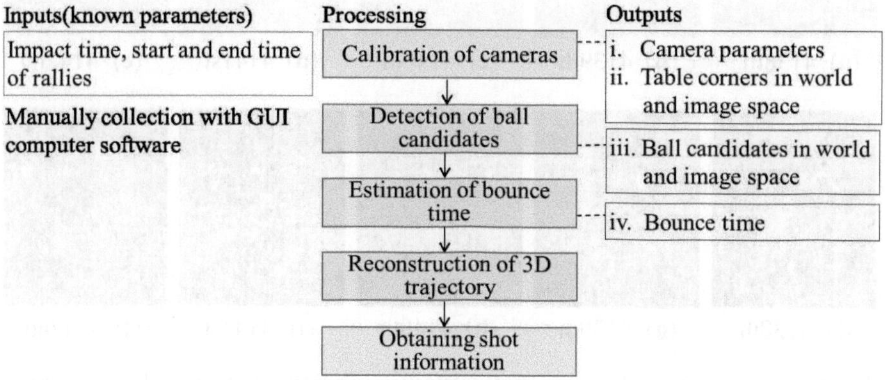

Fig. 3.5 Flowchart to obtain data using multiple camera system

can be used in many cases. Its results are also sufficiently accurate to be used for performance analysis. This is experimentally demonstrated in Sect. 3.6.5.

3.6.3 Detection of Ball Candidates

First, large segments are eliminated by using contour-based segmentation and area-based elimination. We use findContours, which is an OpenCV function, to obtain contours. Ball candidates are then detected by extracting moving objects through interframe subtraction, and extracting high-intensity segments and those that are circular.

The main aim of the elimination of the large segments is to eliminate player segments. Figure 3.6 shows some results of interframe subtraction. Player contains segments that have a similar appearance to balls and they can generate false positives. Let us denote l as boundary length, S as area. Circularity of a segment is defined as:

$$C = 4\pi s/l^2. \tag{3.11}$$

Segments are regarded as circular when their circularity is higher than the threshold. Candidates without consecutive candidates in adjacent frames were eliminated (the same as the algorithm in Fig. 3.3) after this process. Next, we computed the 3D positions of the ball by triangulation. If there are multiple candidates in a frame, no

(a) 4138th (b) 4139th (c) 4140th (d) 4141st (e) 4142nd

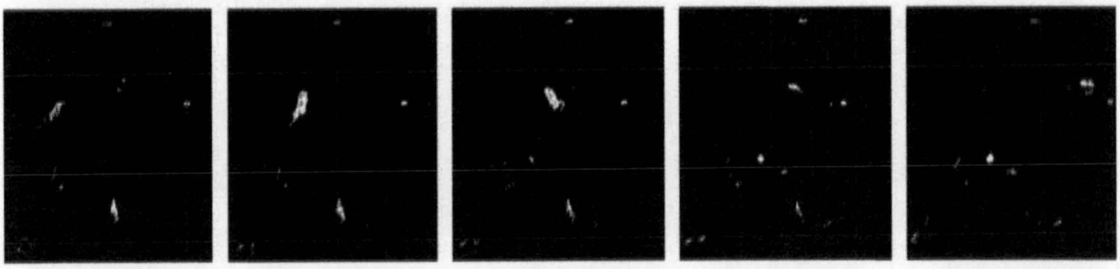

(f) 4138th (g) 4139th (h) 4140th (i) 4141st (j) 4142nd

Fig. 3.6 Samples of the results of interframe subtraction. **a**–**e** are input images, and **f**–**j** are extracted foreground candidates are computed in the frame. Finally, ball candidates in the world space can be obtained.

3.6.4 Estimation of Bounce Time

First, we reconstruct the trajectories by using the method proposed by Yan et al. [7] and smooth them with a Savitzky-Golay filter [19]. Next, we look for the time when the vertical component of the direction of movement changed from going downward to going horizontally or upward. This method cannot detect bounces when a player hit a ball right after it bounced and the ball was occluded by a racket or a player. However, this does not influence reconstructing the trajectories, since the period of time between bounces and shots is short.

3.6.5 Experiments

Experiments were performed to verify whether our method could reconstruct 3D trajectories and provide performance indicators. The subjects were experienced table tennis players who executed ten rallies. The resolution of the video was 640 × 480 pixels, and the frame rate was 60 fps. RGB cameras and a table tennis court were setup as shown in Fig. 3.7.

The reconstructed trajectory of a table tennis ball is shown in Fig. 3.8. The results for estimating the bounce positions are summarized in Table 3.1 where manually measured data were used as the reference data.

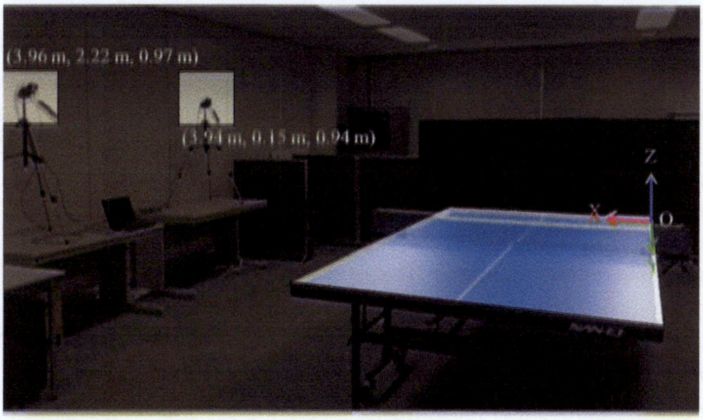

Fig. 3.7 The experimental environment and world coordinate system of the system using two RGB cameras. A *corner* denoted O in this figure is defined as the origin of world space. The plane comprised of *end lines* and *sidelines* of the court is defined as X–Y plane. *Vertical direction* of a court is defined as *Z axis*

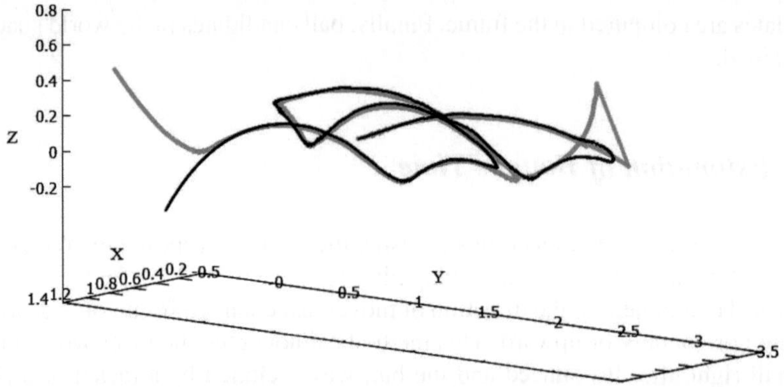

Fig. 3.8 Reconstructed trajectories with the system using two RGB cameras. *Black line* and *gray line* indicate the curves reconstructed using trajectory plane, and without using trajectory plane, respectively

Table 3.1 Results for estimating bounces

Indicator	Value
Minimum error (mm)	7.3
Maximum error (mm)	298.3
Average error (mm)	56.5
Standard deviation (mm)	50.4
Recall (%)	91.9
Precision (%)	97.1

Errors are differences from ground truth recorded manually

If we do not use planar approximation, the shape of the trajectory could be unnatural around impact due to the occlusion between players and the ball (the gray curve in Fig. 3.8). Since our method is robust against occlusion by one viewpoint, the shape of the trajectory is natural (the black curve in Fig. 3.8). The average error in bounce positions, i.e., 56.5 ± 50.4 mm (Table 3.1), is attributed to inaccuracy in calibration because ball detection and the trajectory plane were accurately estimated according to the shape of the trajectory. This error was acceptable in actual practical use of performance analysis. As we discussed in Sect. 3.2, coaches and players who consider bounce positions generally refer to a 3×3 separated area of the half court and conventional analysis provides accurate data. The short side of the separated area is 460 mm, which is much greater than the error in our method. All the bounce positions were correctly predicted in this experiment on the 3×3 scale. We could conclude that the results using the system are sufficiently accurate to solve the problem with conventional analysis.

However, we should note that we are required to setup the two RGB cameras, synchronize them, and calibrate them. Although it could be acceptable and effective in many cases, the usability is not optimal. The next section describes a system that makes it possible to solve the issue of usability.

3.7 System Using RGB-D Camera

3.7.1 System Architecture

As we mentioned in the Sect. 3.3, it is optimal to use an RGB-D camera from the aspect of usability. Although current RGB-D cameras cannot track fast-moving balls because of functional issues(e.g. low frame rates and long exposure times), these would not be problems if we only targeted services.[2] Moreover, developing the skill of service is regarded as an important issue in table tennis. It would be useful for players if there were a system to reconstruct the trajectory of services and provide their quantitative features. In addition, there is the possibility that the capabilities of RGB-D cameras will be improved and they will be able to track fast-moving balls in the future.

We developed a system that provides the features of service trajectory using an RGB-D camera. Fewer devices are required and it is easy to use. The flowchart for the system is nearly the same as the one that uses two RGB cameras (Fig. 3.5). However, the algorithms that are adopted in each process were different. The steps are described in detail in the following subsections.

3.7.2 Detection of Table Corners

First, a planar model of a court are reconstructed by using the 3D positions of all pixels in the depth images. The RGB-D camera is placed above the table, and the major part of the image is a court. We can reconstruct the planar model using the random sample consensus (RANSAC) algorithm for this reason. We then detect white lines on the reconstructed plane by using a Hough transform. Finally, four optimal points are selected from the intersections of the white lines based on the area of the quadrangle that is comprised of selected points.

3.7.3 Detection of Ball Candidates

The ball's position in depth images are required to compute its 3D positions. However, it is difficult to detect the table tennis ball in depth images because there are many missing values and there is a great deal of noise in the depth images taken with the RGB-D camera. We therefore detect the ball in the RGB images, define the range of positions where it could be in a depth images, and detect it. The position in a

[2] Players making serves in table tennis need to bounce the ball in their own court before they bounce it in the opposite court. It is therefore difficult to score by increasing the velocity of the ball. This is why many players mainly consider tactics with rotation and direction when serving.

depth image calculated from the position in an RGB image using known geometric relations could be inaccurate because the exposure of the RGB camera and the depth camera are not synchronized. We therefore needed to detect the ball in RGB images and depth images.

The method of detecting balls in RGB images is the same as that used in the system using two RGB cameras: the elimination of large segments, the extraction of moving objects, the extraction of high-intensity segments, and extraction based on circularity.

A 2D trajectory in RGB images is then reconstructed by using the method proposed by Yan et al. [7]. As we can see from Fig. 3.9, the trajectory defines the range of positions where the ball can be in a depth image. For example, when we look for ball candidates in the ith frame of depth images, the range is defined as the circumscribed rectangle of the 2D trajectory from the $i-1$th to the $i+1$ frames, which include specific size margins. Ball candidates are detected based on the area and the circularity of segments. The closest one in the detected candidates is chosen. The ball positions in the depth images provide the 3D coordinates of balls [23].

However, the ratio, expressed as a percentage, of successfully measured 3D positional data was about 20 % in all frames that included the ball (Table 3.2) in our experiment. The ratio was low because there were many missing values in the depth images taken with the RGB-D camera and the table tennis ball is small. The results indicates that the RGB-D camera cannot robustly obtain the depth values of moving table tennis balls.

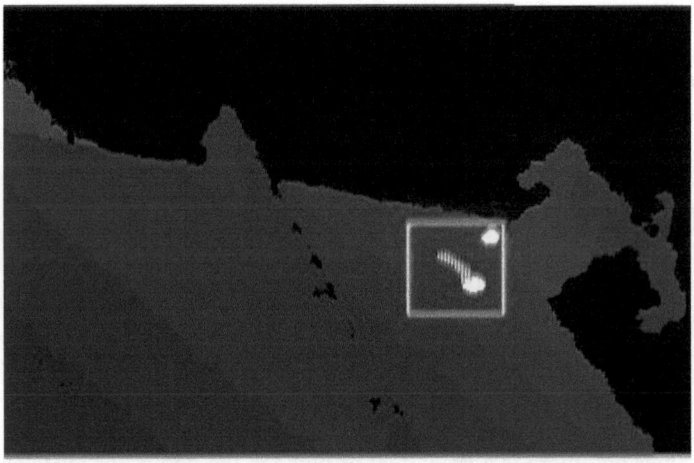

Fig. 3.9 Detection of ball candidates in a depth image. *Dotted curve* is a 2D trajectory reconstructed based on RGB images. *Rectangle* is the range of positions where ball can be, which was defined with the trajectory. While segments were candidates, and the closest one was selected as ball

Table 3.2 Results of recall ratio (%) of successfully measured 3D positional data for balls with RGB-D camera

Indicator (%)	Value
Minimum	10.3 (4/39)
Maximum	24.4 (10/41)
Average	20.7 (7.8/37.8)
Standard deviation	6.4

This table indicates RGB-D camera could not robustly obtain data from moving balls

3.7.4 Estimation of Bounce Time

We cannot use 3D positions of the ball for detecting bounces because there are too few 3D positional data as we mentioned in the previous subsection. We therefore detect bounces based on the 2D trajectory of the ball in RGB images, which have already been obtained when we detected the ball in depth images. The field of view can be assumed to be almost fixed. The bounce positions are the minimal values vertical to the direction of movement in the trajectories. The direction of movement in trajectories is determined according to the direction of movement of the ball when it bounces or peeks. The temporal differentiation of the inner product of the successive directions of movement of the ball takes a minimal value at peaks and bounces in the trajectory. We detect peaks and bounces in the 2D trajectory of the ball using this fact, and calculate the direction of movement in the trajectory by computing the average direction of movement by the ball at bounces and peaks. Let us denote the direction vector of the ball at i as $\boldsymbol{v}_i$, and the second order differential of the inner product of adjacent directions of movement by the ball as $\boldsymbol{c}_{i,i-1}$, $\boldsymbol{c}_{i-1,i-2}$. The direction of movement in 2D trajectory $\boldsymbol{d}$ is calculated as:

$$\boldsymbol{d} = \frac{\Sigma \boldsymbol{s}_i}{|\Sigma \boldsymbol{s}_i|} \tag{3.12}$$

$$\text{where } \boldsymbol{s}_i = \begin{cases} \boldsymbol{0} & \text{if } c''_{i-1,i-2} = 0 \\ \boldsymbol{0} & \text{if } c''_{i,i-1} c''_{i-1,i-2} \geq 0 \\ \boldsymbol{v}_i & \text{otherwise} \end{cases} \tag{3.13}$$

We rotate the trajectory to fit the direction of movement in the trajectory on the X axis. We can then detect bounces by seeking the minimal value for the Y components in the rotated trajectory. The service in table tennis bounces two times, i.e. first in the serving player's own court and then in the receiver's court. The second bounce position is used to estimate the trajectory plane because it is more important than the first one in tactical analysis.

3.7.5 Experiments

Experiments were carried out to verify whether the system could reconstruct the 3D trajectory of a service and provide information. The subjects were experienced table tennis players who made six services. The resolution of the RGB and the depth images were 640 × 480 pixels, and the frame rate was 30 fps. Microsoft Kinect was placed 2.3 m above the ground, opposite to the server, and used to capture videos.

The 3D trajectory of two services are shown in Fig. 3.10. The recall rates to measure the 3D positions of balls with the RGB-D camera are listed in Table 3.2. Five out of six trial shots were successfully reconstructed, the same as in Fig. 3.10a, c. The trajectory could not be reconstructed from measured positions without planar approximation because too few 3D positions were measured with the RGB-D camera (white spheres) as we can see from Fig. 3.10. Unfortunately, the accuracy of results cannot be quantitatively evaluated in these experiments, but we expect the trajectory to provide information that could be used for training purposes. However, one of the reconstructed trajectories could not be successfully reconstructed, as we can see from Fig. 3.10b, d. There were too few 3D positions of balls in the experiments. Therefore, all the ball positions in the trajectory were projected onto one trajectory plane. The projection is inappropriate for the service shown in Fig. 3.10b, d because

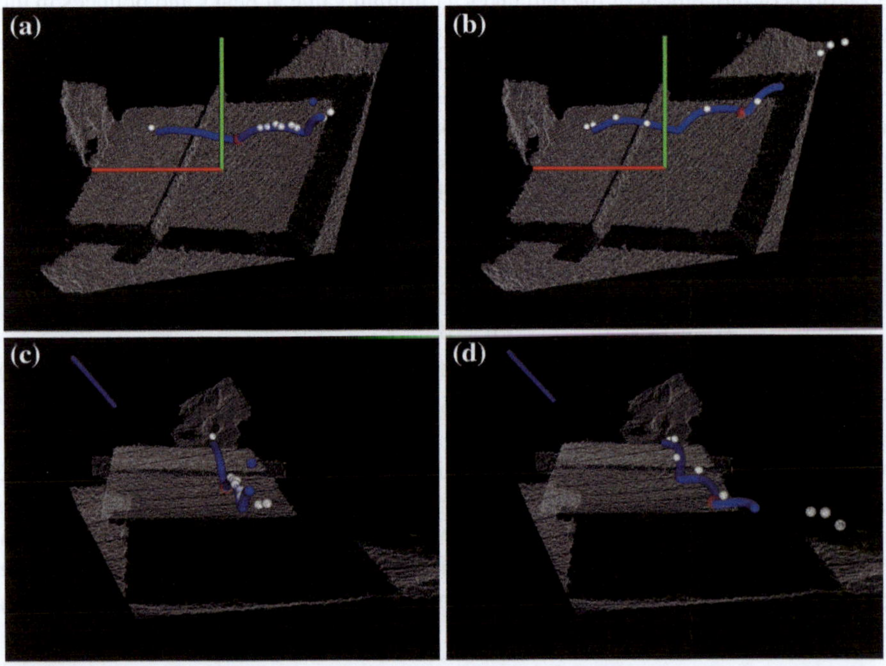

Fig. 3.10 Reconstructed 3D trajectory. This figure indicates trajectory 1 was *successful* and trajectory 2 *failed*. **a** Trajectory 1. **b** Trajectory 2. **c** Trajectory 1. **d** Trajectory 2

it rotated quickly and rapidly changed the direction of movement when it bounced. We may be able to solve the problem by using RGB-D cameras whose frame rates are higher than that of the Kinect because the problem just involves the amount of 3D positional data. Other RGB-D cameras should be considered for future systems.

3.8 Conclusion

We introduced an plane approximation-based approach of reconstructing the 3D trajectories of a table tennis ball. The key feature of the proposed method was that it was robust against failures in measuring 3D ball positions in some frames. A system using two RGB cameras was developed based on the new method and it was experimentally verified that it could provide accurate information for match analysis. We also developed a system using an RGB-D camera to optimize usability for practitioners. The system experimentally verified that it could provide accurate information for service analysis. Although the system using the RGB-D camera cannot currently track fast-moving or rotating balls, this will probably not be a problem in the future because this issue depends on the capability of current RGB-D cameras. In conclusion, it was possible to collect shot data from table tennis matches without imposing heavy workloads by using the systems. Future issues involve using the systems in practical scenarios that will contribute to make performance analysis more useful for table tennis practitioners.

Acknowledgments This work is supported by National Institute of Information and Communications Technology (NICT), Japan. We would also like to express our gratitude to Jun Nakamura for his contribution in developing and experiments of the system using an RGB-D camera.

References

1. Hughes MD, Bartlett RM (2002) J Sports Sci 20(10):739
2. Lees A (2003) J Sports Sci 21(9):707
3. Nevill A, Atkinson G, Hughes M (2008) J Sports Sci 26(4):413
4. I.S. of Performance Analysis of Sports. ISPAS home. http://www.ispas.org/index.html
5. Hui Z, Lijuan Y, Jinju H (2010) Int J Comput Sci Sport 9(3):53
6. Ivan ML, Rocco DM, Franco M (2011) In: Proceedings of the 12th ITTF sports science congress, pp 71–75
7. Yan F, Kostin A, Christmas W, Kittler J (2006) In: Proceedings of the CVPR, vol 1. IEEE Computer Society, pp 634–641
8. Huang Y, Llach J, Zhang C (2008) In: Proceedings of the ICPR. IEEE, pp 1–4
9. Ariki Y, Takiguchi T (2008) In: Proceedings of the multimedia and expo, pp 889–892
10. Liang D, Liu Y, Huang Q, Gao W (2005) In: Advances in multimedia information processing-PCM 2005, pp 864–875
11. Misu MNMFT, Matsui A, Yagi N (2007) In: Proceedings of the ICASSP, pp III937–940
12. Kim JY, Kim TY (2009) In: Proceedings of the CGIV
13. Yu X, Sim CH, Wang JR, Cheong LF (2004) In: Proceedings of the ICIP, vol 2. IEEE, pp 1049–1052

14. Poliakov A, Marraud D, Reithler L, Chatain C (2010) In: Proceedings of the CBMI. IEEE, pp 1–6
15. Hawk-eye Tennis System (2014). http://www.hawkeyeinnovations.co.uk/page/sports-officiating/tennis
16. Ren J, Orwell J, Jones GA, Xu M (2004) In: Proceedings of the ICIP, vol 3. IEEE, pp 1935–1938
17. Okada N, Yabuuchi T, Funatomi T, Kakusho K, Minoh M (2008) IEICE Trans Inf Syst J91-D(12):2950
18. Seydel R (1992) Int J Table Tennis Sci 1:1
19. Savitzky A, Golay MJE (1964) Anal Chem 36(8):1627
20. Zhang Z (2000) PAMI 22(11):1330
21. Simon G, Fitzgibbon AW, Zisserman A (2000) In: Proceedings of the ISMAR, IEEE, pp 120–128
22. Hartley R, Zisserman A (2004) Multiple view geometry in computer vision, vol 2. Cambridge University Press, Cambridge
23. Khoshelham K, Elberink SO (2012) Sensors 12(2):1437

Chapter 4
On-Field Testing and Evaluation of a Goal-Line Technology System

Paolo Spagnolo, Pier Luigi Mazzeo, Marco Leo, Massimiliano Nitti, Ettore Stella and Arcangelo Distante

Abstract Goal-Line Technology (GLT) is a system used in football game to establish if the ball has completely crossed the goal line and contextually assisting referee in awarding a goal or not. The first aim of GLT is not to replace the institutional role of the officials, but rather to help them in highly critical situations where making the correct decision is difficult. This work is focused on a real case study on a Goal-Line Technology system. The chapter details the ball detection algorithm that analyzes candidate ball regions in order to recognize the ball pattern. In order to decide about the goal event occurrence, a decision-making approach by means of camera calibration is developed. Differently from other GLT systems present in the literature, this one has two main strengths: (i) it gives, as unquestionable proof, the image video sequence that records the goal event when it occurs; (ii) it is noninvasive: it does not require any change in the typical football devices (ball, goal posts, and so on). Extensive sessions of experiments were performed on both real matches acquired during the Italian *Serie A* championship, and specific evaluation tests by using an artificial impact wall and a shooting machine for shot simulation. The obtained experimental results are encouraging and confirm that the system could help humans in ambiguous goal-line event detection.

4.1 Introduction

Soccer is the world's most popular sport and an enormous business, and every match is currently refereed by a single person who 'has full authority to enforce the Laws of the Game'. Therefore, each match is strongly influenced by referee calls and a large number of controversies may arise. In most cases, these controversies are inevitable since the rules of the game leave room for personal interpretations. However, the most glaring controversies are usually about referee calls for which no

P. Spagnolo (✉) · P.L. Mazzeo · M. Leo
CNR-INO, Via Della Liberta, 3-73010 Arnesano, Italy
e-mail: paolo.spagnolo@ino.it

M. Nitti, · E. Stella · A. Distante
CNR-ISSIA, Via Amendola, 122/DO, 70126 Bari, Italy

T.B. Moeslund et al. (eds.), *Computer Vision in Sports*,
Advances in Computer Vision and Pattern Recognition,
DOI 10.1007/978-3-319-09396-3_4

interpretation is required and about whether the ball has completely crossed goal line or not (commonly referred to as "phantom goals"). History of soccer is full of mistakes, starting from the most famous one (during World Cup 1966 a very doubtful goal was allowed to England against Germany Fig. 4.1a), and other very important ones (World Cup 2010, again England versus Germany, a goal of England's midfield Lampard was disallowed Fig. 4.1b, as well as a goal of Ukraine's Marko Devic in Eurocup 2012 against England Fig. 4.1c, and Milan's player Muntari against Juventus in a relevant match in the Italian Serie A Championship Fig. 4.1d, just to cite some examples). These 'bad calls' are shown in Fig. 4.1.

In cases like these, the referee's call is influenced by, among other things, three ineluctable factors:

- the referee's position on the field: he is not aligned with the goal line and then a parallax error affects his decision;
- the high speed of the ball that can reach up to 120 km/h. It is impossible for human visual and cognitive systems to estimate the position of such a moving object continuously. In other words, since a human being can process up to 25 images

(a) Goal? No-Goal? We are still arguing...

(b) World Cup 2010: disallowed goal

(c) Eurocup 2012: again a disallowed goal

(d) Italian Serie A: another important disallowed goal

Fig. 4.1 Examples of different controversial goals: **a** The most famous, England–Germany in the world cup 1966; **b** Again England–Germany, World Cup 2010; **c** England–Ukraine, Euro cup 2012; **d** Milan-Juventus (Italy), Serie A 2011–2012

per second, the position of the ball between two consecutive observations can significatively change (even more than a meter) and then intermediate positions of the ball can only be inferred.
- the considerable distance (about 35–40 m.) between the linemen and the goal post: this makes it very hard to evaluate goal events with a resolution of about 1–2 cm.

The only way to definitively avoid these kinds of controversies is to introduce a "goal-line technology", i.e., an automatic system to assist the referee in decisions concerning goal events.

For this purpose, different technologies have been proposed. The earliest ones were based on instant replay: in case of a controversial call about a goal event, the referee (or an assistant) could stop the game and watch the images (acquired from broadcast or dedicated cameras). This would slow down the game taking away possible plays and annoying the audience. Thus, attention has recently turned to technologies that are able to decide autonomously whether or not the ball has crossed the goal line. One of the most promising approaches uses a magnetic field to track a ball with a sensor suspended inside [9]. Thin cables with electrical current running through them are buried in the penalty box and behind the goal line to make a grid. The sensor in the ball measures the magnetic grids and relays the data to a computer which determines if the ball has crossed the line or not. The main drawbacks of this kind of technology are:

1. it cannot provide unquestionable proof of detected events;
2. it requires substantial modifications to the infrastructure of the stadium and game component (ball, playing field, goalposts, ...).

For these reasons, the efforts of several companies and research institutes are currently focused on the development of noninvasive goal-line technologies. In particular, vision-based systems appear to be very promising considering their capability to provide a posteriori verification of the system's operations [10].

In this chapter, a visual system is able to detect the goal event through real-time processing of the acquired images and immediately provide the image sequence that records the goal event under consideration is presented. The system was implemented at the Friuli Stadium in Udine, Italy. It was tested both during real matches of the Italian Serie A championship, and specific simulation sessions: in this case, the ball was shot by a shooting machine in different contexts, as explained in detail in the experimental results' section, in order to validate the system in terms of both spatial and temporal accuracy.

4.2 Related Works

In this section a brief overview of related work is presented. Firstly, some papers facing ball detection and tracking issues are reported, then some pioneering systems performing real-time analysis of soccer events are briefly outlined and discussed.

The problem of ball detection in soccer images is very difficult since the ball is represented by a small number of pixels and, moreover, it can have different scales, textures, and colors. For this reason, most ball detection approaches are based on an evaluation of the ball's trajectory. The underlying idea is that the analysis of kinematic parameters can point out the ball among a set of ball candidates [15, 17, 20]. Trajectory-based approaches are generally off-line since the evaluation of the kinematic parameters for all ball candidates requires a long period of observation. In [20], a trajectory based detection and tracking algorithm for locating the ball is presented. In the first phase, a set of ball candidates is selected according to ball size, color, and shape, and consequently a set of ball trajectories is extracted. Then, studying the trajectory information, it is relatively easy to recognize the ball as the most active object among the candidates in the soccer video. Possible false positives, such as parts of players' t-shirt or socks, do not move significantly during the game. As well, in [13], several features such as the color, the size, the ratio of the length, and the width of the ball shape are considered to extract ball candidates in each frame, then a Viterbi decoding algorithm is applied to extract the optimal path which is most likely to be the balls path in consecutive frames. Once the ball is detected, the Kalman filter and template matching tracking procedure is started using the ball location to update the template and to guide possible ball redirection.

In [15], hybrid techniques are used to identify the ball in medium and long shots. Candidate ball positions are first extracted using shape and size, then motion information is used to filter candidates in medium shots, whereas dynamic programming is applied to search for the longest path of weighted graphs constructed for ball candidates in long shots. In [17], multiple fixed cameras are used for real-time modeling of 3D ball trajectories. A motion-based thresholding process detects the candidate balls, while a probability measure calculates the likelihood of which moving object could represent a ball. Then, the 3D ball motion is modeled as a series of planar curves. Reliable estimates are obtained by triangulating multiple views. Finally, the ball trajectory is modeled as one type of ball movement: rolling, flying, in-possession, and out of play.

Direct detection algorithms based on pattern recognition approaches have also been proposed: they require zoomed images (the ball texture must be clearly visible) and have to be reinitialized if the appearance of the ball varies greatly.

For this purpose, a neural network approach is used in [2] on video images acquired by fixed cameras. A set of ball candidates is generated by using a Circular Hough Transform; then different neural networks, trained under different light conditions, are used to select the best candidate who contains the ball. The appropriate preprocessing of the ball candidate images is selected in order to guarantee the best performances of the ball recognition routine. Two opposite views of the ball are used to evaluate the 3D ball trajectory and solve occlusion problems.

In recent years, few research groups have started working on visual frameworks with the aim of recognizing real-time events.

This is a really challenging field of research for a number of reasons. First of all, these systems also have to address problems associated with the time spent on image acquisition, transmission, and processing (often the frame rate is even higher than for standard TV cameras). Furthermore, the ability to work autonomously for several hours and under all environmental conditions are additional characteristics required by these kinds of systems. In [3], the authors present a real-time visual system for goal detection which can be used as a decision support by the referee committee. Four fixed high-resolution cameras acquire 200 f/s that are elaborated by four parallel processes to track the ball and reconstruct the 3D trajectory in order to detect the frame in which the ball passes the goal mouth plane. Objects having features such as circular contour and ball texture are searched for in the image and are considered ball candidates. A set of neural networks, trained to recognize the ball in different parts of the image and in different light conditions, are used to select the most probable candidate who contains the ball. A system for automatic judgment of offside events is presented in [7]. The authors propose the use of 16 cameras located along both sides of the soccer field to cover the whole area. Player tracking and team classification are used for offside line calculation; 3D ball trajectory reconstruction allows play recognition; the integration of results from multiple cameras is used for offside judgment. In [14], preliminary results on a small number of images for offside analysis were presented; a method for ball, player and referee detection, team identification, and field extraction is proposed. The differentiation between the players of the two teams and the referee is based on the colors of the player uniforms which are compared to three sets of colors manually selected by the user clicking on the jersey of a single player from each team. Projecting the lines from each object onto the global reference point obtained during the field extraction process, the system evaluates the position of all players relative to one another. Six fixed cameras were used in [4] to cover the whole field and to acquire image sequences from both sides of the stadium. Player and ball tracking processes run parallel on the six image sequences and extract the player and ball positions in real time. All the information is projected onto a virtual field by a central supervisor. The players' poses, extracted from opposite views, are related to the ball trajectory in order to detect the player who kicked the ball.

By considering the state of the art of goal-line monitoring systems, it is evident that both research groups and commercial enterprises are working in the assembly of a real useful system. It means that the problem is very complex and difficult to be solved. Moreover, some parameters need to be considered, for example the noninvasiveness of them on both the structures of the play field and the temporal flow of the game. So, our effort is to propose a solution that respects these constraints, providing acceptable results. In the following, firstly, a brief overview of the overall system and the calibration procedure are presented (Sects. 4.3 and 4.4); then, the motion segmentation approach for moving region selection is proposed (Sect. 4.5), followed by the candidate ball procedure (Sect. 4.6) and the data fusion subsystem (Sect. 4.7). Finally, experiments obtained on real tests performed both in real games and simulation sessions are proposed (Sect. 4.8).

4.3 Overview of the System

In Fig. 4.2a, the visual system is outlined. Six synchronized cameras are placed on the stands of the stadium. For each side of the pitch, two of the three cameras have their optical axes parallel to the goal frame, the remaining one is placed behind the goal with its optical axis perpendicular to the goal frame. Each camera is connected to a processor (node) that records and analyzes the acquired images. In Fig. 4.2b, a schematic diagram of the processing steps executed by each node is shown.

The six processors are connected to a main node, which has the supervisor function. The supervisor node has a decision-making function by combining the

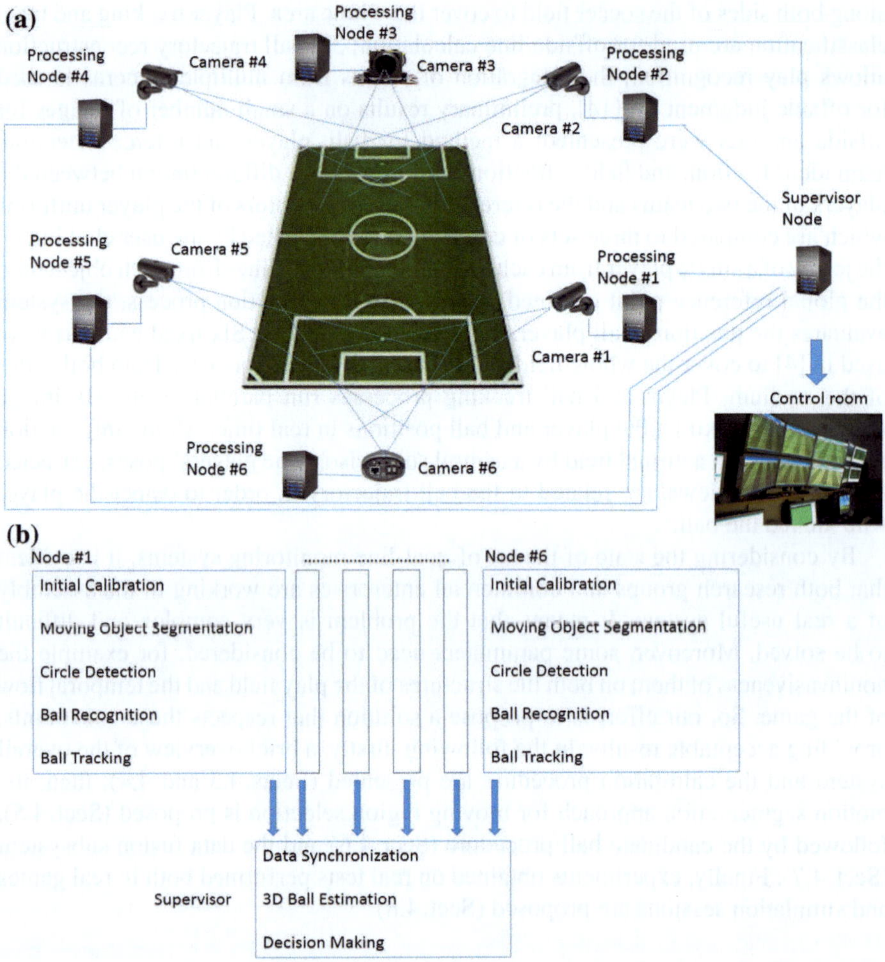

Fig. 4.2 The scheme of the visual system (**a**), and a schematic diagram of the processing steps executed by each Node (**b**)

processing results coming from the cameras. The strategy is based on some heuristics that perform data fusion evaluating the time space coherence of the ball's 3D trajectory. The processing results of the three corresponding nodes are compared and a goal event probability function is evaluated.

4.4 System Calibration

First of all, it is necessary to do a calibration step for each node in which the correspondences between the image plane and a plane in the 3D world are assessed. This step is fundamental in determining the 3D position of the ball. In other words, the homography transformation matrix is estimated by using Random Sample Consensus for each node [5] in this step. Each homography transformation matrix $\mathbf{M_i}$ relates the points on the image plane to the corresponding points on the 3D plane. The only constraint to be considered when choosing the planes is that they must not be perpendicular to the image plane of the associated camera. This calibration needs to be done only once, after camera installation, and if the cameras remain in place these measures are still valid for any subsequent matches. For the experiments reported in this chapter, the calibration phase was carried out using nondeformable steel structures: each structure defines a plane in the 3D world and specific markers were used for the identification of the control points (see Fig. 4.3).

Fig. 4.3 The calibration phase was performed using nondeformable steel structures with specific markers (*black dots*) for the identification of the control points

4.5 Moving Object Segmentation

The segmentation of the image to extract moving objects is the first processing step executed by each node. It is fundamental as it limits the ball detection to moving areas and reduces computational time.

For this purpose a background subtraction-based segmentation algorithm was implemented. The procedure consists of a number of steps. Firstly, a background model has to be generated and then continuously updated to include lighting variations in the model. Then, a background subtraction algorithm distinguishes moving points from static ones. The implemented algorithm uses the mean and standard deviation to provide a statistical model of the background. Detection is then performed by comparing the pixel's current intensity value with its statistical parameters, as explained in several works on this topic (a good review can be found in [16]). The particular context of the application imposes some constraints: first of all, players are continuously on the pitch, so it is necessary to develop a background modeling procedure that is able to handle this situation. Moreover, it is necessary to adapt the model quickly to the variations in lighting conditions, which can rapidly and significantly modify the reference image, especially in cases of natural illumination (or when artificial lights are turned on). In addition, it is necessary to avoid including players in the background model who remain in the same position for a certain period of time (goalkeepers are a particular problem for goal detection as they can remain relatively still when play is elsewhere on the pitch).

Starting from these remarks, it is evident that the first step of each background-based algorithm is background modeling. This procedure, along with the updating algorithm, is the core of a reliable segmentation procedure. Thus, here we focus our attention on this phase; after the creation of a statistical model (in terms of mean and standard deviation), the popular background subtraction approach suggested in [1] is used for segmentation. The implemented modeling algorithm evaluates the energy content for each point in a small temporal window: slow energy points contribute to the statistical background model creation, while high energy points are discarded. In the current temporal window, a point with a small amount of energy is a static point; otherwise it corresponds to a nonstatic point, in particular it could be a foreground point belonging to a foreground object present in the scene, or a background point corresponding to a moving background object. A coarse-to-fine approach for background modeling is applied in a size W (number of frames) sliding window. The first image of each window is the coarse background model $B_C(x, y)$. In order to have an algorithm able to create the required model at runtime, the mean and standard deviation are evaluated at each frame, instead of building the model at the end of a training period; then, the energy content of each point is evaluated over the whole sliding window, to distinguish real background points from others. Formally, for each frame the algorithm evaluates runtime approximations of mean (μ) and standard deviation (σ) (this approximation allows a simpler and faster incremental algorithm which works in real time—α is the learning rate that balances the updating of statistical parameters, it varies in the range [0,1] and needs to be tuned according to the light conditions):

$$\overline{\mu^t(x,y)} = \alpha\mu^t(x,y) + (1-\alpha)\overline{\mu^{t-1}(x,y)} \tag{4.1}$$

$$\overline{\sigma^t(x,y)} = \alpha|\mu^t(x,y) - \overline{\mu^t(x,y)}| + (1-\alpha)\overline{\sigma^{t-1}(x,y)} \tag{4.2}$$

only if the intensity value of that point is substantially unchanged with respect to the coarse background model, that is:

$$|I^t(x,y) - B_C(x,y)| < \text{th} \tag{4.3}$$

where th is a threshold experimentally selected. It depends strictly on the spectral content of the image, which is related to the noise level, the gain, and the black level of the sensor. The hardware used (the sensor and its thermoregulated case), jointly with the trick of turning on the system some minutes before the game (to allow the sensor to get up to the proper working conditions), permit this value to be considered as static. This way, at the end of the first W frames, the algorithm evaluates the energy content for each point as:

$$E(x,y) = \int_{t\in W} |I^t(x,y) - B_C(x,y)|^2 \tag{4.4}$$

The first fine model of background B_F is generated as:

$$B_F(x,y) = \begin{cases} (\mu(x,y), \sigma(x,y)) & \text{if } E(x,y) < \text{th}(x,y) \\ \emptyset & \text{if } E(x,y) >= \text{th}(x,y) \end{cases} \tag{4.5}$$

A low-energy content means that the considered point is a static one and the corresponding statistics are included in the background model, whereas high-energy points, corresponding to foreground or moving background objects will not contribute to the model. In all our experiments, the threshold $\text{th}(x,y)$ was set to a level of 10 % of the mean energy content for a static point (a point is considered ad static if its energy content in the examined window can be considered stable) in a window of W frames, that is:

$$\text{th}(x,y) = 0.1 * \overline{E(x,y)} \tag{4.6}$$

The whole procedure is iterated on another sequence of W frames, starting from the frame $W+1$. The coarse model of the background is now the frame $W+1$, and the new statistical values (Eqs. 4.1 and 4.2) are evaluated for each point, like the new energy content (Eq. 4.4). The relevant difference with (Eq. 4.5) is that now the new statistical parameters are averaged with the previous values, if they are present; so, the new formulation of Eq. 4.5 becomes:

$$B_F(x,y) = \begin{cases} (\mu(x,y), \sigma(x,y)) \\ \text{if } E(x,y) < \text{th}(x,y) \wedge B_F(x,y) = \emptyset \\ \\ \beta * B_F(x,y) + (1-\beta) * (\mu(x,y), \sigma(x,y)) \\ \text{if } E(x,y) < \text{th}(x,y) \wedge B_F(x,y) \neq \emptyset \\ \\ \emptyset \quad \text{if } E(x,y) > \text{th}(x,y) \end{cases} \tag{4.7}$$

The parameter β is the classic updating parameter introduced in several works on background subtraction [1, 18]. It allows the existent background model values to be updated to the new light conditions in the scene. The modeling procedure stops when a great number of background points have meaningful values:

$$\#(B_F(x,y) = \emptyset) \cong 0 \tag{4.8}$$

As mentioned above, this complex procedure allows the system to detect only moving points. This is very important for both limiting computational time and reducing false alarms. Starting from this observation, it should be noted that a low number of false positives is admitted (they influence only the computational time), while false negatives have to be mandatorily avoided (they could be a miss-detection of the ball!). For this reason, the sliding window-based modeling approach was also used for the updating procedure, allowing the system to adapt itself to variation in light conditions, but avoiding including players (and ball) in the reference model.

The temporal window W is correlated with the frame rate of the acquiring devices: in our experiments, at a frame rate of 200 fps, we set this value to 1,000, which corresponds to a sliding window of 5 s. This time interval is long enough to avoid including the ball in the model, but short enough to be sensitive to both temporal (for example, cloud effects) and permanent (artificial lights turning on/off) variations in light conditions.

Finally, a connected components analysis detects the blobs in the image. A connectivity analysis was implemented which scans the entire image, and then groups and labels neighboring pixels into regions. For each pixel, the 8-neighboring pixels are considered and put together into a list until no more connected points are found. The search is repeated until all the moving points have been considered. After this step, the position in the image and the number of points belonging to each moving region, are known. This way, regions with an area less than a given threshold are considered as noise and removed, whilst remaining regions are evaluated in the following steps.

The proposed segmentation model is general-purpose and can be used in other contexts, with the only expedient to properly set the value of W (according to the frame rate, as explained above). For example, we have also used this model in an indoor surveillance system for the detection of intruders.

4.6 Ball Detection and Tracking

An automatic method that detects ball position in each image is the central step to building the vision system. In the soccer world, a great number of problems have to be managed, including occlusions, shadowing, misdetection (the incorrect detection of objects similar to the ball), and, last but not least, real-time processing constraints. The ball detection method has to be very simple, fast, and effective as a great number of images per second must be processed. This kind of problem can be addressed by considering two different detection systems: geometric approaches that can be applied to match a model of the object of interest to different parts of the image in order to find the best fit; or example-based techniques that can be applied to learn the salient features of a class of objects from sets of positive and negative examples.

This method uses two different techniques together in order to take advantage of their peculiarities: first of all, a fast circle detection (and/or circle portion detection) algorithm, based only on edge information, is applied to the segmented image (the motion image that is the output of the previous step) to limit the image area to the best candidate containing the ball; second, an appearance based distance measure is used to validate ball hypothesis.

In Fig. 4.4, a schematic representation of the implemented procedures and reasonings aiming at detecting the ball in the acquired image is reported.

The Circle Hough Transform (CHT) aims to find circular patterns of a given radius R within an image. Each edge point contributes a circle of radius R to an output accumulator space. The peak in the output accumulator space is detected where these contributed circles overlap at the center of the original circle. In order to reduce the computational burden and the number of false positives typical of the CHT, a number of modifications have been widely implemented in the last decade. The use of edge orientation information limits the possible positions of the center for each edge point. This way only an arc perpendicular to the edge orientation at a distance R from the edge point needs to be plotted. The CHT, as well as its modifications, can be formulated as convolutions applied to an edge magnitude image (after suitable edge detection). We have defined a circle detection operator that is applied over all the image pixels, which produces a maximal value when a circle is detected with a radius in the range $[R_{\min}, R_{\max}]$:

$$u(x, y) = \frac{\int\int_{D(x,y)} \mathbf{e}(\alpha, \beta) \cdot \mathbf{O}(\alpha - x, \beta - y) d\alpha d\beta}{2\pi (R_{\max} - R_{\min})} \tag{4.9}$$

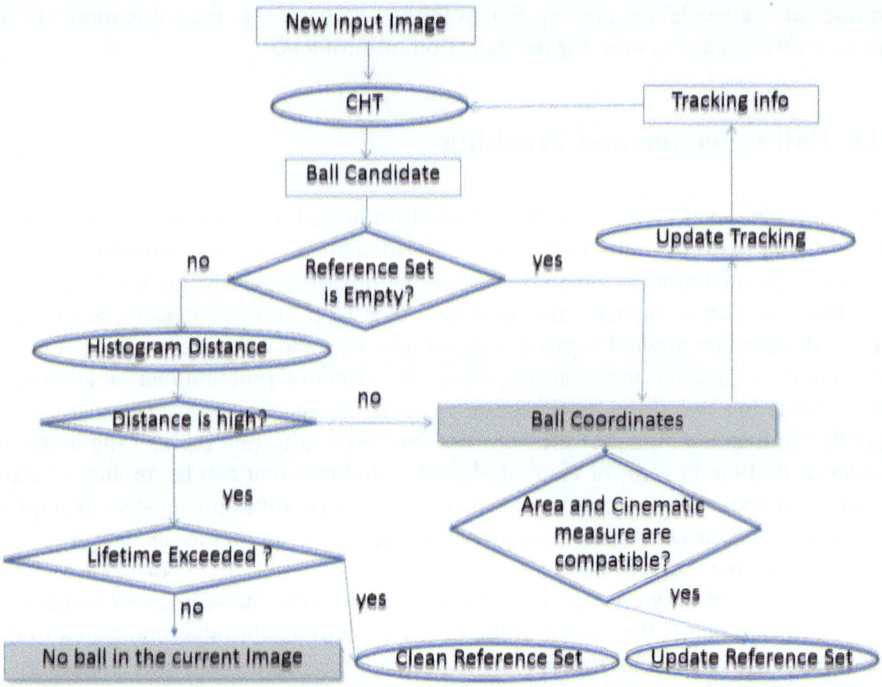

Fig. 4.4 A schematic representation of the implemented procedures and reasonings aiming at detecting the ball in the acquired image. Each new image is investigated to detect the ball; if the ball candidate is very close to existing ball models then it is validated and used for the updating of the reference set. Otherwise, it is discarded. The reference set is: built by means of cinematic evaluations on ball candidates; updated after each reliable ball detection; cleaned if no ball is detected for a long period of time

where the domain $D(x, y)$ is defined as:

$$D(x, y) = \{(\alpha, \beta) \in \Re^2 | R^2_{\min} \leq (\alpha - x)^2 + (\beta - y)^2 \leq R^2_{\max}\} \tag{4.10}$$

e is the normalized gradient vector:

$$\mathbf{e}(x, y) = \left[\frac{E_x(x, y)}{|E|}, \frac{E_y(x, y)}{|E|}\right]^T \tag{4.11}$$

and **O** is the kernel vector

$$\mathbf{O}(x, y) = \left[\frac{\cos(\tan^{-1}(y/x))}{\sqrt{x^2 + y^2}}, \frac{\sin(\tan^{-1}(y/x))}{\sqrt{x^2 + y^2}}\right]^T \tag{4.12}$$

The use of the normalized gradient vector in (4.9) is necessary in order to have an operator whose results are independent from the intensity of the gradient in each point: we want to be sure that the circle detected in the image is the most complete in terms of contours and not the most contrasted in the image. Indeed, it is possible that a circle that is not well contrasted in the image gives a convolution result lower than another object that is not exactly circular but has a greater gradient. The kernel vector contains a normalization factor (the division by the distance of each point from the center of the kernel), which is fundamental to ensuring that we have the same values in the accumulation space when circles with different radii in the admissible range are found. Moreover, normalization ensures that the peak in the convolution result is obtained for the most complete circle and not for the greatest in the annulus. As a final consideration, in Eq. 4.1 the division by $(2\pi(R_{max} - R_{min}))$ guarantees the final result of our operator in the range [−1,1] regardless of the radius value considered in the procedure. The masks implementing the kernel vector have a dimension of $(2R_{max} + 1)(2R_{max} + 1)$ and they represent the direction of the radial vector scaled by the distance from the center in each point. The convolution between the gradient versor images and these masks evaluates how many points in the image have a gradient direction concordant with the gradient direction of a range of circles. Then the peak in the accumulator array provides the center of the subimage with higher circularity that is finally passed to the validation step. Examples of subimages given as input to the ball recognition process are shown in Fig. 4.5.

The validation step assesses the similarity of appearance between the candidate region and a set of positive examples stored previously. The similarity is evaluated by computing the Bhattacharyya distance among histograms (reduced to 64 bins): this

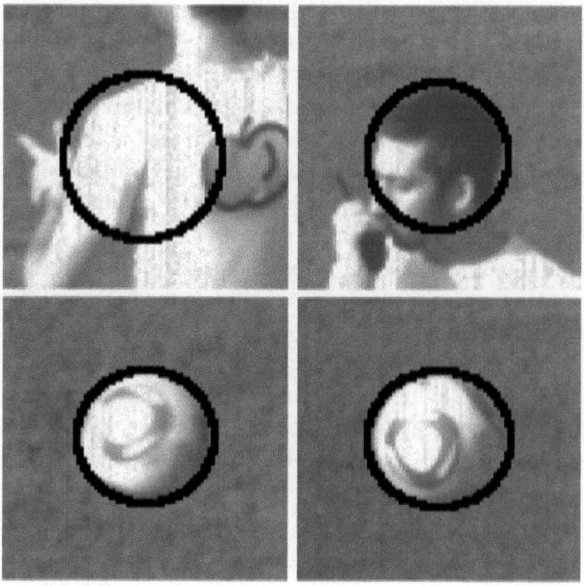

Fig. 4.5 Some images of the training set: in the *first row* there are some negative examples of the ball, in the *second row* some positive examples

measure is not computationally time-consuming but at the same time it is sufficiently robust as it is invariant to the rotation of the target (textured balls are considered) and also to slight changes in scale. One of the strengths of the proposed system is that the construction and updating of the set of reference examples for validation takes place automatically.

Initially, the set of reference examples is empty and all the moving objects with the highest value of circularity (greater than a weak threshold) and with an area compatible with that of the ball are taken into account. Their displacement on the image plane frame after frame is then evaluated in order to estimate some motion parameters (specifically direction and velocity). The candidate regions are then included in the reference set if the associated motion parameters are compatible with those that only a ball can have in case of a shot on goal (direction toward the goal and plausible number of pixel displacement between frames). At the same time, the relative distance into the image plane between the candidate regions and the other moving object in the scene is evaluated: if the relative distance is low and almost consistent, the ball candidate is discarded since it has likely been produced by incorrect segmentation of players' bodies.

The same criteria are used to add new examples to the reference set, additionally considering the value of the measurement of similarity with the preexisting examples. The maximum number of examples in the reference set is 100 and it is managed as a circular buffer.

The reference set is reinitialized when circular objects with peculiar motion parameters and low similarity (i.e., higher distances in the space of histograms) to the examples in the reference set appear in a number of consecutive frames. This way the introduction of a new type of ball or sudden and substantial changes in lighting conditions (due to clouds or floodlights) can be handled automatically. This procedure is graphically exploited in Fig. 4.4.

This way, we are able to automatically build a reference set by considering only cinematic evaluations. This set is then used for the ball validation procedure by means of the evaluation of the Bhattacharyya distance between candidates and the reference set. However, the evaluation of cinematic parameters cannot be used as a stand-alone procedure for the ball detection: the ball is often very close to other objects (players and goalposts) and the evaluation of its cinematic parameters can be unreliable. So, we build the reference set (that is very very important) only if we are almost sure that the object is a ball (no false positives are admissible at this step), and then we use these reference images to validate the ball candidates in more ambiguous images (that are typical near the goal line).

The ball has to be detected in more consecutive images in order to be sure that a true positive has been found. In this case, a different and more reliable procedure for selecting candidate moving regions is used (tracking phase). A ball position probability map, covering all the points of the processing image, is created as follows:

$$P(x, y) = \frac{e^{\left(-\frac{|(x-|\tilde{x}+V_x \operatorname{sign}(\cos\theta)|)+(y-|\tilde{y}+V_y \operatorname{sign}(\sin\theta)|)|^2}{2\sigma^2}\right)}}{\sigma\sqrt{2\pi}} \tag{4.13}$$

where $(\tilde{x}, \tilde{y})$ is the last known ball position and

$$\sigma = \frac{R_p V_{\max} n}{R_{\mathrm{cm}} T} \tag{4.14}$$

where V and θ are the local velocity and the direction of the ball in the image plane, respectively, R_p is the Ball radius in pixels, R_{cm} is the Ball radius in centimeters, $V_{\max}$ is the maximum admissible velocity of the ball (in cm/sec), T is the camera frame rate, and n is the number of frames between the past and actual ball detection (1 if, in this case, the two frames are consecutive). Thus, the maximum probability value is related to the point where, on the basis of past information about the ball's movement, the ball should be found (predicted point). The probability value decreases exponentially as the distance from the predicted point becomes close to 0 for points far from the last known ball position that cannot be reached considering the maximum speed limits (usually 120 km/h). In the following frames, the probability map is used to select candidate moving regions (like those with a probability greater than zero). This way, the ball can be detected both in case of merging with players and in case of partial occlusions. The ball's velocity, direction, and probability map are always updated using the proper value for n (i.e., the number of frames between the actual frame and the last ball detection). If the ball is not detected for three consecutive seconds (i.e., n becomes greater than T*3), past information is considered outdated and the ball detection procedure starts again considering all the candidate ball regions in the whole image.

4.7 Supervisor Node

The supervisor node has a decision-making function according to the processing results coming from the nodes. For each frame the processing units send several items of information to the supervisor, including the last frame number processed, the position of the ball (if detected), and the number of consecutive frames in which the ball has been correctly tracked. It should be noted that even if the images are synchronized in the acquisition process, the processing results are not necessarily synchronized, since each node works independently from the others. Moreover, a node may jump some frames having accumulated a significant delay during the processing. When the supervisor receives the results of three nodes for a given frame, or when it detects that synchronized data obtained cannot be retrieved for a given frame, the supervisor processes the obtained information to evaluate the occurrence of a goal event.

For this purpose, it is necessary to provide an accurate evaluation of the 3D position of the ball, and this requires a calibration procedure (described in Sect. 4.4). The 3D position is necessary because only the 2D information is not sufficient to evaluate if the ball crossed the goal line inside the goal posts or not. It can be overcome by considering the 3D ball position and its trajectory before crossing the goal line.

If the ball position is evaluated in the image plane, we project the ball onto the ground plane by means of the homographic transformation. Then we can build the line connecting this point on the ground with the corresponding one in the 2D image. This is done for all cameras, so we can find the 3D position of the ball by finding the intersection between these lines. This intersection provides the estimate of the ball position in the real-world coordinate system. In practice, this process entails uncertainty, so corresponding lines of sight may not meet in the scene. Furthermore, it is likely that in certain moments it is not possible to see the ball by one or more cameras because of occlusions, for example created by the players, the goalkeeper, or the goalposts. For these reasons, a special procedure for estimating the 3D position of the ball was introduced. If the ball is visible in only 2 cameras, the 3D distance between the two projection lines is firstly computed. Then, if this distance is smaller than a selected threshold (typically about the size of the diameter of the ball, i.e., 22 cm), the two projection lines are considered as referring to the same object (dealing with possible errors of the detection algorithms of the ball which are described in Sect. 4.6) and then the midpoint of the common perpendicular to the two projection lines is chosen as an estimate of the 3D position of the ball. If the ball is visible in all three cameras, the mutual 3D distance among the three projection lines is calculated. The two projection lines with shorter distance are then considered the most reliable and this leads the calculation to the previous case. We are aware that different approaches have been proposed in literature to handle the 3D position estimation issue by triangulation [6, 11, 12] but we have not considered using them because of the difficulties of their implementation and their high computational costs that make them unsuitable for a real-time system that must process a large number of frames per second.

Finally, if the ball is only in a single camera, its 3D position can be estimated if some previous temporally close 3D positions are available. In this case, a linear filter is used to predict the next 3D position and then to estimate the projection lines of the missing views. In other words, when possible, the 3D trajectory of the ball is evaluated and it is used for the estimation of the 3D position of the ball also when only one view is available.

4.8 Experimental Results

A prototypal system was installed at the Friuli Stadium in Udine. The system uses Mikrotron MC1362 cameras with a spatial resolution of 1024×768 pixels at 504 fps and Xeon QuadCore E5606 2,13 Ghz as the processing node. Each node is equipped with a X64-CL iPro PCI frame grabber capable of acquiring images from one Medium Camera Link™ camera and performing image transfers at rates of up to 528 MB/s.

The calibration has been done by means of a thedolite during the installation of the system, and periodically checked to avoid alterations and interference. The error introduced by the calibration step has been carefully evaluated: it is negligible along the most important direction (orthogonal to the plane of the goal), while it is about

10 cm in the other two directions (the one orthogonal to the ground plane, and the one orthogonal to the camera image plane). By considering the size of the goal posts (12 cm), the calibration error may generate uncertainty in the decision only in case of shots very close to the goal posts.

The system was extensively tested during real "Serie A" championship matches and specific experimental sessions (making use of the impact wall, slide, ball shooting machine, etc.) were conceived to evaluate goal event detection accuracy. Thus, both the system's reliability in the real context of a soccer match and its performance in very stressful sessions of shots executed using a ball shooting machine (which also allows repeatable results to be obtained) were tested. Specifically, a (portable) replica of the described system has also been installed in a Stadium in Zurich for additional massive tests, in totally different conditions (in terms of both natural and artificial light conditions, at different weather conditions, in presence of a different turf—artificial instead of natural grass).

An observation about experimental tests is mandatory: a comparison with other approaches is unfeasible, due to the complexity of the whole system. It could be interesting a comparison with commercial/industrial systems [8, 10, 19], but it is practically impossible: commercial companies do not release technical details about their systems, so they cannot be replicated. Moreover, the complexity of both hardware and software solutions make the replication of the systems practically impossible. A real comparison of the performance of several systems (including the proposed one) has been done by an external evaluation authority, but each competitor received only the results it obtained, ignoring the results of the other ones.

4.8.1 Benchmark Results

Here, we focus our attention on benchmark sessions performed outside the match (in two different stadiums, as described above). In detail, four different experiments were carried out:

- Impact Wall shots (Fig. 4.6a, b): during this test, an artificial wall was placed behind the goal line in two different positions: in the first, the ball position at the moment of impact is "No Goal", while in the second it is "Goal" (ground truth). The ball was shot by a shooting machine at different speeds. This way the accuracy of the system to detect the goal event in terms of both spatial resolution and mostly temporal resolution (at high ball speed, even at 200 fps, there are just 1–2 frames to correctly detect the goal event) can be tested.
- Sled (Fig. 4.6c): in this test, the ball is positioned on a mobile sled, and slowly moved from a nongoal to a goal position. The system's precision to detect the exact ball position (in terms of cm over the goal line) was tested.
- Free Shots: during these experiments, several shots were performed by means of the shooting machine, in different positions with respect to the goal: left, right, middle, just under the horizontal crossbar, and just over the ground; each of them at different ball speeds. We tested whether the system fails to detect a specific portion

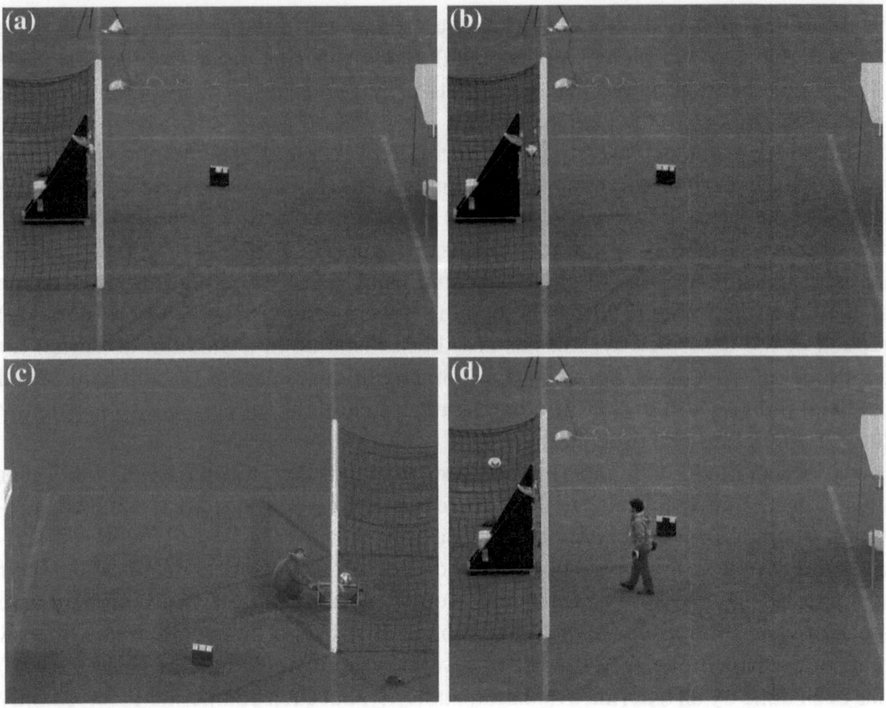

Fig. 4.6 Example of different tests. **a** Impact wall position for no goal simulation. **b** Impact wall position for goal simulation. **c** Sled. **d** Outer net (note that the ball is over the net)

of the goal area. Moreover, the reliability of the 3D reconstruction procedure (to separate shots inside and outside the goal posts) was tested.

- Outer Net (Fig. 4.6d): in this session, specific shots on the outer net were performed with the final position of the ball inside the volumetric area of the goal, but arriving from outside the goal posts. We tested the system's capability of tracking the ball accurately (even in 3D), by separating balls that arrived in the goal volumetric area from a "goal trajectory" (inside the goal posts) from balls that arrived from an external trajectory.

In order to show the weak impact of light conditions, some tests were also performed at night, in the presence of artificial stadium light. In Table 4.1 the final results are reported. The *Impact Wall* sessions gave good results, with an overall success rate of more than 91 %. The evaluation authority gave us specific values about performance, and they considered acceptable a success rate greater than or equal to 90 %. The experiments were carried out by shooting the ball at different speeds, impacting the wall in different positions.

All shots in the *Outer Net* session were correctly detected; for the *Sled session*, we reported the mean distance over the goal line detected by the system, while a more detailed analysis of this data, to emphasize that the system mostly detected the event within 2 cm, is reported in Table 4.2.

Table 4.1 Overall performance of the GLT system during extensive experimental sessions

Test	Results
Impact wall— daylight	374/398—93.97 %
Outer net—daylight	153/155—98.71 %
Free shots—daylight	310/324—95.68 %
Impact wall—night	153/168—91.07 %
Free shots—night	177/202—87.62 %
Sled—daylight	Average of 3.3 cm

Table 4.2 Sensibility evaluation of the system in the sled test

Distance (cm)	Results (%)
0–2	34/60—56.66
2–3	14/60—23.33
3–5	7/60—11.66
>5	5/60—8.33

The *Free Shots* session realized different results according to test lighting conditions: in the daylight test a success rate of over 95 % was obtained. On the contrary, in the night test, an 87.62 % success rate was obtained, in the same test. This was due to the different performances of the algorithms. First of all, the background subtraction together with computational aspects: if the segmentation algorithm, due to artificial light flickering, detects a number of moving points greater than reality, the following algorithms have to process more points causing a growing computational load, which leads to problems with memory buffers, and subsequently some frames are discarded (it should be noted that all our experiments were performed in real time). To confirm this, this test session was off-line processed again, obtaining results comparable to those in daylight. It can be concluded that this drawback can easily be overcome, by simply optimizing the code and/or improving hardware with more performing components. The same observations are valid for the night session of the *Impact Wall* test.

Figure 4.7 reports images acquired during the experimental phase and corresponding to goal events in an *Impact Wall* session (just 2 cameras are reported for this experiment, the third one is evidently occluded and cannot help in any way).

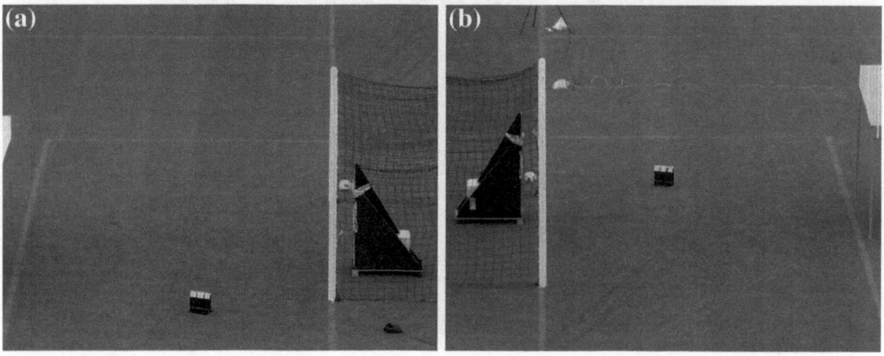

Fig. 4.7 Some images acquired during the experimental phase. **a** Camera 1. **b** Camera 2

Table 4.3 Performance in real conditions

Goal events	True positives	False negatives	False positives
72 goals	72	0	3

4.8.2 Real Match Results

In order to evaluate the system's robustness in real uncontrolled conditions, tests were conducted during real matches of the Italian Serie A Championship; in particular, the system was tested during 38 matches played at the Friuli Stadium in Udine (Italy) in two different Championships. Table 4.3 reports the goal detection results. In a real context, the important events (goals) are limited in number so the benchmark sessions reported in the previous section are mandatory in order to test the system exhaustively. On the other hand, in a benchmark session, it is really hard to introduce and simulate all possible events that could happen during a real match: the presence of players in the scene that could alter the detection of the ball (some body parts, like legs and shoulders, could be erroneously detected as the ball); the presence of logos and/or particular combinations of colors on the players' uniforms that can influence the ball detection procedure; the possibility that players randomly cross the goal line (goalkeepers often do); the presence of objects in the goal area (towels, bottles, etc.) that could lead to misclassifications.

As it can be noted, during the 38 matches there were 72 goal events that were correctly detected (no misdetections) and just 3 false positive occurrences.

In Fig. 4.8, one of the goal events correctly detected (even if the ball was occluded by one camera and the ball appearance is not very different from the player's jersey) is shown. During this experimental phase, in addition to goal events, a very controversial situation occurred: the goalkeeper saved a shot when the ball was on the goal line (see Fig. 4.9). The system evaluated that situation as No goal and the image clearly evidences that it was right.

Fig. 4.8 One of the 72 goal events occurred during the test on real matches

Fig. 4.9 A controversial situation occurred during a real match and rightly evaluated by the system as no goal

Fig. 4.10 A situation in which the system erroneously detected a goal

One of the three false positives also occurred during a complex defensive action: four defenders were close to the goal line, trying to protect the goal and one of them kicked the ball away clearly before it crossed the line (see Fig. 4.10). Afterward, a defender crossed the goal line and, unfortunately, the system recognized the pattern of the ball on his shorts (whose position was also consistent with the trajectory predicted by the ball tracking procedure). Cases like this (although rare) could happen again, and certainly need further investigation.

4.8.3 Computational Evaluations

An important aspect of this system is the real-time implementation: a quick response is mandatory for the system actually to be used. For this reason, we evaluated the delay in response for each test. In Fig. 4.11, a summary of the response time is reported. Each angular section refers to a time interval of the delay in response (yellow for a delay less than 1 s, brown for a delay between 1 and 1.5 s, and so on) with the relative percentage. As evidenced, considering the realistic threshold of 2 s for the system's response (that correspond to yellow + brown + blue sectors), it can be noted that in about 80 % of the total number of experiments the response time was acceptable.

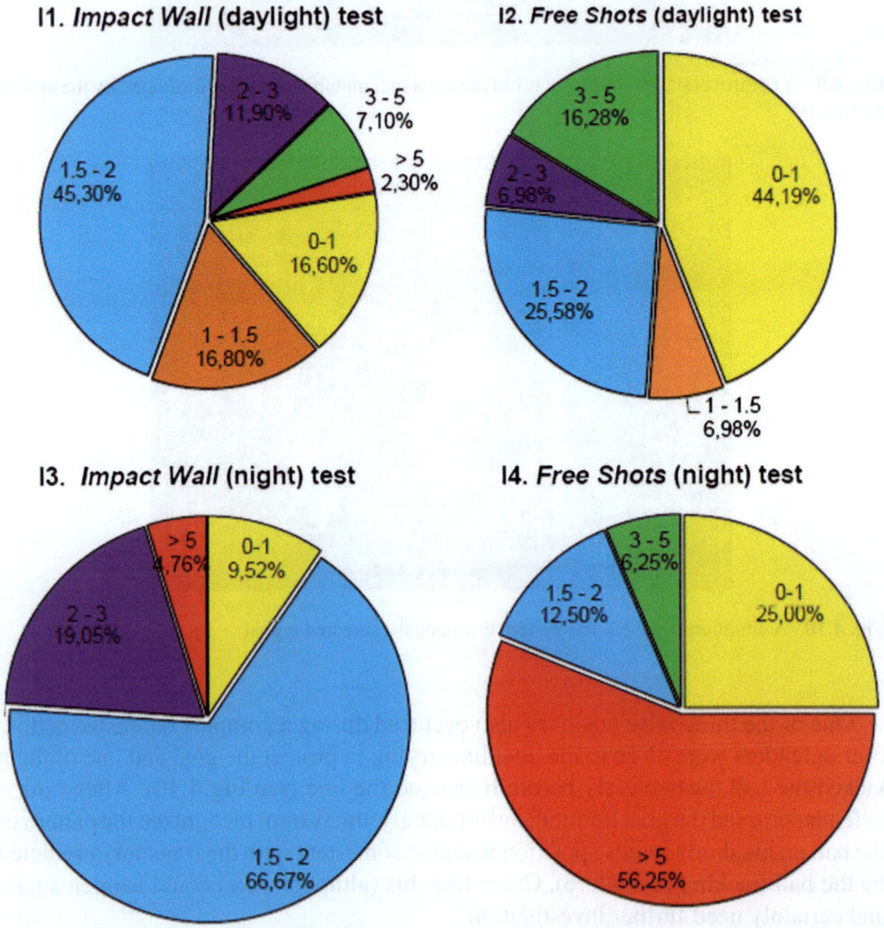

Fig. 4.11 Plot of the response time. The same colors have been used for the same time intervals (*yellow* for a delay less than 1 s, *blue* for a delay between 1.5 and 2 s, *purple* for a delay between 2 and 3 s, *green* for a delay between 3 and 5 s, and *red* for a delay over 5 s)

The only exception, as remarked previously (see Sect. 4.8.1), is for the nightly Free Shots test.

It should be noted that just minor code optimizations were made, without any kind of hardware ones. So, considering that algorithms can be further improved and optimized, it can be concluded that the real-time constraint can be achieved with a reasonable effort.

4.9 Conclusions

In this chapter, we explain our efforts in the realization of a real-time system for goal-line monitoring. We demonstrate that the use of technology to support referees in football matches is possible. The system we propose is very complex and requires several steps to work properly: the hardware installation, the calibration of cameras, the real-time processing of the image stream, the fusion and interpretation of data coming from each processing node.

We tested our system both in real matches and specific simulation sessions, with the intention of simulating all possible situations that can occur during a match. The obtained results are encouraging, and confirm that this system can be used for referee assistance. However, some issues need to be further investigated. In particular, the calibration procedure can be refined to reduce error in 3D position of the ball. The algorithms of motion segmentation and ball detection gave reliable results, but they need to be intensively tested in real contexts, because troubles can occur is a specific game (due to light conditions, ball appearance, uniform of players, and so on) even if the system worked properly in all precedent matches.

Acknowledgments The authors thank Liborio Capozzo and Arturo Argentieri for technical support in the setup of the hardware used for data acquisition and processing.

References

1. Collins RT, Lipton AJ, Fujiyoshi H, Kanade T (2001) Algorithms for cooperative multisensor surveillance. In: Proceedings of the IEEE 89(10):1456–1477
2. D'Orazio T, Guaragnella C, Leo M, Distante A (2004) A new algorithm for ball recognition using circle Hough transform and neural classifier. Pattern Recognit 37(3):393–408
3. D'Orazio T, Leo M, Spagnolo P, Nitti M, Mosca N, Distante A (2009) A visual system for real time detection of goal events during Soccer matches. Comput Vis Image Underst 113(5): 622–632
4. D'Orazio T, Leo M, Spagnolo P, Mazzeo P, Nitti M, Mosca N, Distante A (2009) An investigation into the feasibility of real-time soccer offside detection from a multiple camera system. IEEE Trans Circuits Syst Video Technol 19(12):1804–1817
5. Fischler MA, Bolles RC (1981) Random sample consensus: a paradigm for model fitting with applications to image analysis and automated cartography. Commun ACM 24(6):381–395
6. Hartley RI, Sturm P (1997) Triangulation. Comput Vis Image Underst 68(2):146–157

7. Hashimoto S, Ozawa S (2006) A system for automatic judgment of offsides in Soccer games. In: IEEE international conference on multimedia and expo, pp 1889–1892
8. http://goalcontrol.de/gc4d.html
9. http://www.cairos.com/unternehmen/gltsystem.php
10. http://www.hawkeyeinnovations.co.uk/
11. Kanatani K, Sugaya Y, Niitsuma H (2008) Triangulation from two views revisited: Hartley-sturm vs. optimal correction. In: practice, vol 4, p 5
12. Lindstrom P (2010) Triangulation made easy. In: IEEE conference on computer vision and pattern recognition (CVPR), pp 1554–1561
13. Liu Y, Liang D, Huang Q, Gao W (2006) Extracting 3d information from broadcast soccervideo. Image Vis Comput 24(10):1146–1162
14. Naidoo W, Tapamo J (2006) Soccer video analysis by ball, player and referee tracking. In: Annual research conference of the South African institute of computer scientists and information technologists on IT research in developing countries SAICSIT '06, pp 51–60
15. Pallavi V, Mukherjee J, Majumdar A, Sural S (2008) Ball detection from broadcast Soccervideos using static and dynamic features. J Vis Commun Image Represent 19(7):426–436
16. Piccardi M (2004) Background subtraction techniques: a review. In: IEEE international conference on systems, man and cybernetics, vol. 4
17. Ren J, Orwell J, Jones G, Xu M (2008) Real-time modeling of 3-d soccer ball trajectories from multiple fixed cameras. IEEE Trans Circuits Syst Video Technol 18(3):350–362
18. Toyama K, Krumm J, Brumitt B, Meyers B (1999) Wallflower: principles and practice of background maintenance. Seventh international conference on computer vision, vol 1, 255+
19. www.iis.fraunhofer.de/en/bf/ln/referenzprojekte/goalref.html
20. Yu X, Leong H, Xu C, Tian Q (2006) Trajectory-based ball detection and tracking in broadcast Soccervideo. IEEE Trans Multimed 8(6):1164–1178

Part II
Where are the Players?

Chapter 5
Occlusion Detection via Structured Sparse Learning for Robust Object Tracking

Tianzhu Zhang, Bernard Ghanem, Changsheng Xu and Narendra Ahuja

Abstract Sparse representation based methods have recently drawn much attention in visual tracking due to good performance against illumination variation and occlusion. They assume the errors caused by image variations can be modeled as pixel-wise sparse. However, in many practical scenarios, these errors are not truly pixel-wise sparse but rather sparsely distributed in a structured way. In fact, pixels in error constitute contiguous regions within the object's track. This is the case when significant occlusion occurs. To accommodate for nonsparse occlusion in a given frame, we assume that occlusion detected in previous frames can be propagated to the current one. This propagated information determines which pixels will contribute to the sparse representation of the current track. In other words, pixels that were detected as part of an occlusion in the previous frame will be removed from the target representation process. As such, this paper proposes a novel tracking algorithm that models and detects occlusion through structured sparse learning. We test our tracker on challenging benchmark sequences, such as sports videos, which involve heavy occlusion, drastic illumination changes, and large pose variations. Extensive experimental results show that our proposed tracker consistently outperforms the state-of-the-art trackers.

T. Zhang (✉)
Advanced Digital Sciences Center of Illinois, Singapore, Singapore
e-mail: tzzhang10@gmail.com

B. Ghanem
King Abdullah University of Science and Technology, Thuwal, Saudi Arabia
e-mail: bernard.ghanem@kaust.edu.sa

C. Xu
Institute of Automation, Chinese Academy of Sciences, CSIDM, People's Republic of China
e-mail: csxu@nlpr.ia.ac.cn

N. Ahuja
University of Illinois at Urbana-Champaign, Urbana, IL, USA
e-mail: n-ahuja@illinois.edu

T.B. Moeslund et al. (eds.), *Computer Vision in Sports*,
Advances in Computer Vision and Pattern Recognition,
DOI 10.1007/978-3-319-09396-3_5

5.1 Introduction

For sports video analysis, knowing the location of each player on the field at each point of the game is crucial for sports experts (e.g., coaches, trainers, and sports analysts) to better understand complex player formations and trajectory patterns, which ultimately depict the effectiveness of their teams 'strategies as well as their opponents.' Being able to effectively track players can enable the development of reliable activity recognition and higher level processing modules for sports video analysis. Such a tracking building block will have a positive impact on how sports experts analyze game footage, how content providers identify/display particular sports events and highlights accompanied with relevant advertisements, and how end users browse and query large collections of sports video. Moreover, visual tracking is a classical problem in computer vision; it is a core task for many applications [44, 48, 50] e.g., automatic surveillance, robotics, human computer interaction, action recognition, etc. It is also very challenging due to appearance variations such as occlusion, illumination change, significant motion, background clutter, etc. Over the years, a significant amount of effort has been made to overcome these challenges. To survey many of these algorithms, we refer the reader to [32, 41].

A truly robust tracking method must be able to handle occlusion. However, modeling occlusion is not straightforward. There exists a significant amount of work that addresses this issue through statistical analysis [16, 34], robust statistics [1, 7], patch matching [39], the use of multiple cameras [12, 31], context information [40], model analysis [13], and learning occlusion with likelihoods [20]. Recently, sparse representation has been successfully applied to visual tracking [29, 46, 47, 49] under the particle filter framework as an attempt to alleviate the occlusion problem in tracking. In these methods, particles are randomly sampled around the states of the tracked object according to a zero-mean Gaussian distribution. At time t, n particles are sampled. The observation (pixel color values) of each particle in the frame is denoted as: $\mathbf{x} \in \mathbb{R}^d$. In the noiseless case, each particle $\mathbf{x}$ is represented as a linear combination $\mathbf{z}$ of templates that form a dictionary $\mathbf{D} = [\mathbf{d}_1, \mathbf{d}_2, \ldots, \mathbf{d}_m]$, such that $\mathbf{x} = \mathbf{Dz}$. $\mathbf{D}$ can be constructed from an overcomplete sampling of the target object, based on an initial bounding box at the start of tracking, and dynamically updated to maintain an up-to-date target appearance model.

In many visual tracking scenarios, targets are often partially occluded or corrupted by noise. Occlusion is unpredictable as it may affect any part, or occlude any amount, of the target. The occluded object can be either a connected region or a number of randomly scattered pixels, though the former is more likely in natural images. In addition, only a sparse number of these templates is required to reliably represent each particle, which encourages $\mathbf{z}$ to be sparse. To incorporate these two pieces of information, each particle $\mathbf{x}$ should be represented as a sparse linear combination, while allowing for sparse error $\mathbf{e}$ to encode occlusion: $\mathbf{x} = \mathbf{Dz} + \mathbf{e}$. The sparse coefficients $\mathbf{z}$ and sparse error $\mathbf{e}$ are recovered by solving the following ℓ_1 minimization problem. The current tracking result is usually chosen to be the particle $\mathbf{x}$ with minimum reconstruction error w.r.t. dictionary $\mathbf{D}$.

$$\min \|\mathbf{z}\|_1 + \|\mathbf{e}\|_1 \quad \text{s.t.} \quad \mathbf{x} = \mathbf{D}\mathbf{z} + \mathbf{e} \tag{5.1}$$

This approach has demonstrated to be robust against partial occlusions, which improves tracking performance. However, it suffers from the following drawbacks: (1) The error (due to occlusion) is not sparse for many tracking scenarios, as exemplified in Fig. 5.1. Because a portion of the target is significantly occluded, we need to discard that portion for the sparsity assumption to still hold. (2) This kind of algorithm does not exploit any prior information about the occlusion, especially the important property that occlusion is spatially contiguous. By modeling error pixels as structured and sparse, the representation is made more accurate to model occlusion and better defined.

To deal with the above drawbacks, we propose a new particle filter tracker that involves tracking by occlusion detection, thus appropriately named the TOD tracker. In each frame, particles are represented in a structured sparse learning framework, which exploits prior information about the location of occlusion and its spatial contiguity. This prior is propagated from previous frames in the form of an occlusion mask. The main goal is to show how this prior information can be effectively incorporated into the sparse representation framework, thus improving its robustness against more types of realistic occlusions. Compared with existing methods, the contributions of this work are twofold: (1) We propose a structured sparse learning method for occlusion detection in object tracking. It exploits structure information to make occlusion both sparse and spatially continuous for more robust performance. To the best of our knowledge, this is the first work to use occlusion prior information through structured sparsity in object tracking. (2) Compared to the popular L_1 tracker [29] that does not model occlusion explicitly, our method is generic. In fact, it yields the L_1 tracker as a special case.

The chapter is organized as follows. In Sect. 5.2, we summarize work most related to ours. The particle filter algorithm is reviewed in Sect. 5.3. The proposed tracking approach and optimization methodology are presented in Sects. 5.4 and 5.5, respectively. In Sect. 5.6, we report and analyze extensive experimental results.

Fig. 5.1 Frames from two different video sequences portraying significant occlusion. The ground truth track of each object is designated in *green*. Clearly, occlusion renders the tracking problem very difficult. However, certain assumptions about the structuredness of occlusion (e.g., spatial contiguity) can be exploited to alleviate its effect on tracking performance

5.2 Related Work

Visual tracking is an important topic in computer vision and it has been studied for several decades. There is extensive literature, and we refer to [36, 37, 41] for a more extensive review. In this section, we review and focus on previous work, from which our proposed tracking method borrows some ideas. In fact, we provide a brief overview of visual tracking and sparse representation for object tracking.

5.2.1 Visual Tracking

In general, visual tracking methods can be categorized into two groups: generative and discriminative.

5.2.1.1 Generative Visual Tracking

Generative tracking methods adopt an appearance model to describe the target observations, and the aim is to search for the target location that has the most similar appearance to this model. Examples of generative methods include eigen-tracker [5], mean shift tracker [9], appearance model based tracker [17], context-aware tracker [38], incremental tracker (IVT) [35], fragment-based tracker (Frag) [1], and VTD tracker [21]. In [5], a view-based representation is used for tracking rigid and articulated objects. The approach builds on and extends work on eigenspace representations, robust estimation techniques, and parametrized optical flow estimation. The mean shift tracker [9] is a traditional and popular method, which successfully copes with camera motion, partial occlusions, clutter, and target scale variations. In [17], a robust and adaptive appearance model is learned for motion-based tracking of natural objects. The model adapts to slowly changing appearance, and it maintains a natural measure of the stability of the observed image structure during tracking. The context-aware tracker [38] considers the context of the tracked object for robust visual tracking. Specifically, this method integrates into the tracking process a set of auxiliary objects that are automatically discovered in the video on the fly by data mining. The IVT tracker [35] seeks an adaptive appearance model that accounts for appearance variation of rigid or limited deformable motion. Although it has been shown to perform well when the target object undergoes lighting and pose variation, this method is less effective in handling heavy occlusion or nonrigid distortion as a result of the adopted holistic appearance model. The Frag tracker [1] aims to solve the partial occlusion problem by using a representation that is based on histograms of local patches. The tracking task is carried out by combining votes of matching local patches using an object template. However, this template is not updated and therefore it is not expected to handle appearance changes due to large variations in scale and/or shape deformation. The VTD tracker [21] effectively extends the conventional particle filter framework with multiple motion and observation models to account for appearance variation caused by change of pose, lighting, and scale as well as partial occlusion. However, as a result of its adopted generative representation scheme that is not equipped to distinguish between target and background patches, it is prone to drift.

5.2.1.2 Discriminative Visual Tracking

Discriminative tracking methods formulate object tracking as a binary classification problem, which aims to find the target location that can best distinguish the target from the background. Examples of discriminative methods are online boosting (OAB) [14], semi-online boosting [15], ensemble tracking [2], co-training tracking [25], online multiview forests for tracking [22], adaptive metric differential tracking [18], and online multiple instance learning tracking [3]. In the OAB tracker [14], online AdaBoost is adopted to select discriminative features for object tracking. Its performance is affected by background clutter and can easily drift. The ensemble tracker [2] formulates the task as a pixel-based binary classification problem. Although this method is able to differentiate between target and background, the pixel-based representation is rather limited and thereby limits its ability to handle occlusion and clutter. Moreover, the MIL tracker [3] extends multiple instance learning to an online setting for object tracking. Although it is able to address the problem of tracker drift, this method does not handle large nonrigid shape deformations well. In [8], a target confidence map is built by finding the most discriminative RGB color combination in each frame. Furthermore, a hybrid approach that combines a generative model and a discriminative classifier is proposed in [43] to capture appearance changes and allow the reacquisition of an object after total occlusion. Also, global mode seeking can be used to detect and reinitialize the tracked object after total occlusion [42]. Another approach uses image fusion to determine the best appearance model for discrimination and then a generative approach for dynamic target updates [6].

5.2.2 Sparse Representation for Object Tracking

Recently, sparse linear representation based on the particle filter framework has been introduced to object tracking and has been shown to achieve significant tracking performance [4, 23, 26, 29, 30, 45, 47, 51]. In the L_1 tracker [29], a tracking candidate is represented as a sparse linear combination of object templates and trivial templates. Sparse representation is computed by solving a constrained ℓ_1 minimization problem with nonnegativity constraints to solve the inverse intensity pattern problem during tracking. The results show good performance at a high computational expense due to the ℓ_1 minimization. In fact, the computational cost grows proportionally with the number of particle samples. In [30], an efficient L_1 tracker with minimum error bound and occlusion detection is proposed. The minimum error bound is quickly calculated from a linear least squares equation, and serves as a guide for particle resampling in a particle filter framework. Without loss of precision during resampling, the most insignificant samples are removed before solving the computationally expensive ℓ_1 minimization problem. In [26], dynamic group sparsity is integrated into the tracking problem and high-dimensional image features are used to improve tracking robustness. In [23], dimensionality reduction and a customized orthogonal matching pursuit algorithm are adopted to accelerate the L_1 tracker [29]. However, this method may reduce the tracking performance sometimes [23]. In [4], a very fast numerical solver based on the accelerated proximal gradient approach is developed to solve the ℓ_1 norm minimization problem with guaranteed quadratic convergence. In [45], compressive sensing theory is adopted for real-time tracking. In [51], a sparsity-based discriminative classifier and a sparsity-based generative model are designed for tracking. Zhang et al. [47, 49] propose a multitask learning approach to jointly learn the particle representations for robust object tracking. Our proposed method is inspired by the success of these ℓ_1 minimization based trackers, and we will also adopt the sparsity property for robust tracking.

5.3 Particle Filter

A particle filter [11] is a Bayesian sequential importance sampling technique for estimating the posterior distribution of state variables characterizing a dynamic system. It provides a convenient framework for estimating and propagating the posterior probability density function of state variables regardless of the underlying distribution through a sequence of prediction and update steps. Let $\mathbf{s}_t$ and $\mathbf{y}_t^*$ denote the state variable describing the parameters of an object at time t (e.g., motion features) and its observation, respectively. In the particle filter framework, the posterior $p(\mathbf{s}_t|\mathbf{y}_{1:t}^*)$ is approximated by a finite set of n samples $\{\mathbf{s}_t^i\}_{i=1}^n$ (called particles) with importance weights w_i. The particle samples $\mathbf{s}_t^i$ are independently drawn from an importance distribution $q(\mathbf{s}_t|\mathbf{s}_{1:t-1}, \mathbf{y}_{1:t}^*)$, which is set to the state transitional probability $p(\mathbf{s}_t|\mathbf{s}_{t-1})$ for simplicity. In this case, the importance weight of particle i is updated by the observation likelihood as: $w_t^i = w_{t-1}^i p(\mathbf{y}_t^*|\mathbf{s}_t^i)$.

Particle filters have been extensively used in object tracking [41], and we also employ particle filters to track the target object. Similar to [29], we assume an affine motion model between consecutive frames. Therefore, the state variable $\mathbf{s}_t$ consists of the six affine transformation parameters (2D linear transformation and translation). By applying an affine transformation using $\mathbf{s}_t$ as parameters, we crop the region of interest $\mathbf{y}_t^*$ from the image and normalize it to the same size as the target templates in our dictionary. The state transition distribution $p(\mathbf{s}_t|\mathbf{s}_{t-1})$ is modeled to be Gaussian, with the dimensions of $\mathbf{s}_t$ assumed independent. The observation model $p(\mathbf{y}_t^*|\mathbf{s}_t)$ reflects the similarity between a target candidate and target templates in the dictionary. In this work, $p(\mathbf{y}_t^*|\mathbf{s}_t)$ is inversely proportional to the reconstruction error obtained by linearly representing $\mathbf{y}_t^*$ using the template dictionary.

5.4 Tracking by Occlusion Detection (TOD)

Occlusion is one of the most important challenges for visual tracking. In this section, we give a detailed description of our particle filter based tracking method, which makes use of occlusion prior information in a structured sparse learning framework to represent particle samples.

5.4.1 Occlusion Detection via Structured Sparsity

Occlusion detection is very important and difficult for tracking. In this section, we show how we incorporate a sparsity-inducing norm that also encodes prior structural information (spatial contiguity) regarding the support of the error incurred when sparse linear representation is used to describe particles. We expect that such structural information renders a more accurate and robust representation model that can handle occlusions in object tracking. In our particle filter based tracking method, particles are randomly sampled around the states of the tracked object according to a zero-mean Gaussian distribution. Similar to [29], we assume an affine motion model between consecutive frames. Therefore, the state of a particle $\mathbf{s}_t$ consists of the six affine transformation parameters (2D linear transformation and translation). By applying an affine transformation based on $\mathbf{s}_t$, we crop the region of interest $\mathbf{y}_t^*$ from the image and normalize it to the same size as the target templates in our dictionary. The state transition distribution $p(\mathbf{s}_t|\mathbf{s}_{t-1})$ is modeled to be a zero-mean Gaussian, with the dimensions of $\mathbf{s}_t$ independent. The observation model $p(\mathbf{y}_t^*|\mathbf{s}_t)$ reflects the similarity between a particle and target templates in the dictionary. In this chapter, $p(\mathbf{y}_t^*|\mathbf{s}_t)$ is inversely proportional to the reconstruction error obtained by linearly representing $\mathbf{y}_t^*$ using the template dictionary.

We sample n particles at each frame, and the observation (pixel color values) of the ith particle is denoted in vector form as: $\mathbf{x} \in \mathbb{R}^d$ (for simplicity, we ignore the subscript i). The observation $\mathbf{x}$ of a particle is represented as a sparse linear combination $\mathbf{z}$ of m dictionary templates $\mathbf{D} \in \mathbb{R}^{d\times m}$, as shown in Eq. (5.1). $\mathbf{D}$ is updated dynamically to handle frame-to-frame changes in target appearance (The dictionary update issue is addressed later). The popular L1 tracking work [29], which represents each particle by solving an ℓ_1 LASSO problem, can be generalized as shown in Eq. (5.1).

$$\min_{\mathbf{z},\mathbf{e}} \|\mathbf{z}\|_1 + \varphi(\mathbf{e}) \quad \text{s.t.} \quad \mathbf{x} = \mathbf{D}\mathbf{z} + \mathbf{e}, \tag{5.2}$$

In the L1 tracker, the regularizer $\varphi(\bullet)$ on $\mathbf{e}$ is chosen to be $\|\mathbf{e}\|_1$. This regularization scheme encourages the error (e.g., occlusion) to be pixel-wise sparse. This assumption fails in many tracking scenarios as exemplified in Fig. 5.1. It also does not incorporate the structural information inherent to occlusion, namely spatial contiguity. Basically, the ℓ_1-norm regularization treats each entry (pixel) in $\mathbf{e}$ independently.

It does not take into account any specific structures or possible relations among subsets of the entries. To encode this structured prior information, we assume that the spatial support of the error is contiguous. This can be enforced by modeling the error as spatially smooth. Also, this error can be assumed to be sparse, if any significant occlusion is detected and removed beforehand. Note that we assume that some pixels in a particle are occluded and those are determined by an occlusion mask that is propagated from frame-to-frame. At every frame, this mask is used to determine the pixels, from which the particle representation $\mathbf{z}$ is computed. This representation is used to estimate the error at *each* pixel. By thresholding this error with a predefined threshold, the occlusion mask is updated and propagated to the next frame.

To incorporate pairwise relationships between pixels in the particle, we adopt a graph-guided fused LASSO framework that explicitly takes into account the complex dependency structure represented as a graph, whose nodes are pixels in the particle. We assume that the d pixels in each particle are organized in a graph G with a set of nodes V and edges E. In this chapter, we adopt a simple strategy for constructing such a graph, whereby an edge exists between any pair of neighboring pixels and its weight is proportional to the correlation of their intensity values and inversely proportional to the Euclidean distance between them. More sophisticated methods can be employed, but they are not the focus of this chapter. Let $\mathbf{w}_{ml}$ denote the weight of an edge $(m, l) \in E$ that represents the strength of correlation between pixels m and l. Therefore, to encourage spatial contiguity between particle pixels, we employ a graph-guided fusion penalty, which extends the standard LASSO by fusing the $\mathbf{e}_m$ and $\mathbf{e}_l$ if $(m, l) \in E$. With the above notation, we formulate the representation problem as a structured sparse ℓ_1 problem as follows.

$$\begin{aligned} &\min_{\mathbf{z},\mathbf{e}} \|\mathbf{z}\|_1 + \lambda\|\mathbf{e}\|_1 + \gamma \sum_{(m,l)\in E} \mathbf{w}_{ml}\|\mathbf{e}_m - \mathbf{e}_l\|_1 \\ &\text{s.t.} \quad \mathbf{x} = \mathbf{D}\mathbf{z} + \mathbf{e}, \end{aligned} \tag{5.3}$$

where λ and γ are trade-off parameters that control the complexity of the model. A larger value for γ leads to a greater fusion effect. The $\mathbf{w}_{ml}$ weighs the fusion penalty for each edge such that $\mathbf{e}_m$ and $\mathbf{e}_l$ for highly correlated pixels have a large $\mathbf{w}_{ml}$. Details of solving this problem are provided in Sect. 5.5.

Discussion: In this chapter, we propose a generic formulation for robust object tracking using structured sparse learning as shown in Eq. (5.3). By defining γ differently, different object trackers are obtained. When $\gamma = 0$, TOD becomes the popular L_1 tracker [29]. In this way, the popular L_1 tracker [29] is a special case of our formulation. To the best of our knowledge, introducing the structured information in occlusion detection for tracking has not been proposed in any of the previous works. In Fig. 5.2, we present an example of how our TOD tracker works as compared to the L1 tracker. In the top row, we show a result of representing particle $\mathbf{x}$ using structured sparse learning instead of traditional sparse learning (used in L1 tracking), whose result is shown in the bottom row. Clearly, the error generated by TOD leads to a high response at the actual location of the occlusion, while it is missed by traditional

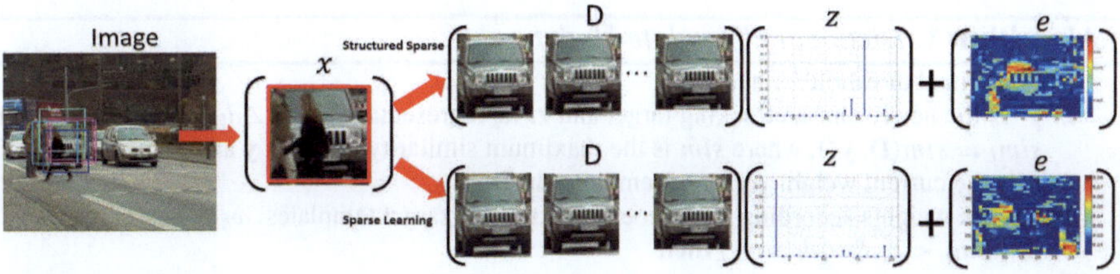

Fig. 5.2 Schematic example of TOD. The representation $\mathbf{z}$ of particle $\mathbf{x}$ w.r.t. dictionary $\mathbf{D}$ is learned by solving Eq. (5.3). Notice that $\mathbf{z}$ is sparse in general, i.e., a few dictionary templates are used to represent $\mathbf{x}$. The *first row* is our TOD, and the *second row* is the popular L_1 tracker. Compared with the L_1 tracker, our methods can obtain much more continuous occlusion detection result

sparse learning. It is evident that by enforcing spatial contiguity on the error values, the occlusion can be better localized. This error is thresholded to produce an occlusion mask that is propagated to the next frame.

5.4.2 Dictionary Template Update

In the literature, a large body of work has been proposed to use object templates for visual tracking [27]. Target appearance remains the same only for a certain period of time, but eventually the object templates are no longer an accurate representation of its appearance. A fixed appearance template is not sufficient to handle changes in appearance due to occlusion or changes in illumination and pose. Also, if the templates are updated too often, small errors are introduced each time a template is updated, errors accumulate, and the tracker may drift from the target. Many approaches have been proposed over the years to address the drift problem [19, 28]. In this chapter, we do so by dynamically updating templates in $\mathbf{D}$.

In order to initialize the object and background dictionaries, we sample equal-sized patches at and around the initial position of the object. In our experiments, we shift the initial bounding box by 1–3 pixels in each direction, thus resulting in $m = 20$ object templates as in [29]. Note that m is a user-defined parameter. All templates are normalized. To each object template, we allocate a weight ω_i that is indicative of how representative the template is. In fact, the more a template is used to represent tracking results, the higher is its weight. Next, we describe how we use these weights to update $\mathbf{D}$. As mentioned earlier, the tracking result at instance t is the particle $\mathbf{z}_i$ that is best represented by $\mathbf{D}$ such that $i = \arg\min_{k=1,\ldots,n} (\|\mathbf{x}_k - \mathbf{D}\mathbf{z}_k\|_2)$. The weight of an object template in $\mathbf{D}$ is updated depending on how much that template is used in representing $\mathbf{z}_i$. If $\mathbf{z}_i$ is sufficiently represented (up to a predefined threshold) by the dictionary, then there is no need to update it. Otherwise, the current tracking result replaces the object template that has the smallest weight. The weight of this new template is set to the median of the current normalized weight vector $\boldsymbol{\omega}$. This template update scheme is summarized in Algorithm 1. We have two criteria: (1) The

Algorithm 1: *Dictionary Template Update*

1: Predefined threshold ε_1 and ε_2
2: $\mathbf{y}^*$ is the newly chosen tracking target and $\mathbf{z}_l$ its representation. Set $\Delta d_l = \|\mathbf{x}_l - \mathbf{D}\mathbf{z}_l\|_2$ and $sim_l = sim(\mathbf{D}, \mathbf{y}^*)$, where sim is the maximum similarity between $\mathbf{y}$ and all elements in $\mathbf{D}$.
3: $\boldsymbol{\omega}$ is the current weight vector of templates in $\mathbf{D}$
4: Update weights according to the coefficients of the target templates: $\omega_k \leftarrow \omega_k \exp(\mathbf{z}_l(k))$
5: **if** $(sim_l < \varepsilon_1$ & $\Delta d_l > \varepsilon_2)$ **then**
6: $r \leftarrow \arg\min_{k=1,\ldots,m_O} \omega_k$
7: $\mathbf{D}(:, r) \leftarrow \mathbf{y}^*$, /*replace template with $\mathbf{y}^*$ */
8: $\omega_r \leftarrow \text{median}(\boldsymbol{\omega})$, /*replace weight*/
9: **end if**
10: Normalize $\boldsymbol{\omega}$ such that $\|\boldsymbol{\omega}\|_1 = 1$

similarity sim_l between the current tracking result and template should be smaller than ε_1, which avoids updating templates frequently and thus avoids tracker drift; Once the current tracking result leads to a big variance, we add it to the dictionary by replacing it with the 'least' used dictionary template; (2) The error Δd_l should be smaller than ε_2, which means we update the dictionary template if only if there is no occlusion; In our experiments, ε_1 and ε_2 are set to be 0.6, and 0.7, respectively.

5.5 Optimization

In this section, we provide a detailed description of how Eq. (5.3) is solved efficiently. First, we rewrite the graph-guided fusion LASSO problem in Eq. (5.3), using a vertex-edge incident matrix $\mathbf{W} \in \mathbb{R}^{|E|\times d}$, as follows:

$$\sum_{(m,l)\in E} \mathbf{w}_{ml} \|\mathbf{e_m} - \mathbf{e_l}\|_1 = \|\mathbf{W}\mathbf{e}\|_1$$

where each row in $\mathbf{W}$ corresponds to an edge in the graph. If we label each edge with a linear index, we can define $\mathbf{W}$ formally as below:

$$\mathbf{W}_{j,k} = \begin{cases} \mathbf{w}_{ml} & if \;\; j = (m,l) \;\; \text{and} \;\; k = m \\ -\mathbf{w}_{ml} & if \;\; j = (m,l) \;\; \text{and} \;\; k = l \\ 0 & \quad \text{otherwise} \end{cases}$$

Therefore, the overall penalty in Eq. (5.3) including both LASSO and graph-guided fusion penalty functions can be written as $\|\mathbf{B}\mathbf{e}\|_1$, where $\mathbf{B} = \left[\lambda\mathbf{W}; \gamma\mathbf{I}\right]$ and $\mathbf{I} \in \mathbb{R}^{d\times d}$ denotes an identity matrix. Then, the structured sparsity problem in Eq. (5.3) is converted into the following problem:

$$\min_{\mathbf{z},\mathbf{e}} \|\mathbf{z}\|_1 + \|\mathbf{B}\mathbf{e}\|_1 \quad s.t. \;\; \mathbf{x} = \mathbf{D}\mathbf{z} + \mathbf{e} \tag{5.4}$$

To solve Eq. 5.4, we introduce two slack variables and add two equality constraints, thus converting it into Eq. (5.5).

$$\min_{z,e} \ \|\mathbf{z}_1\|_1 + \|\mathbf{f}\|_1 \quad \text{such that: } \mathbf{x} = \mathbf{D}\mathbf{z}_2 + \mathbf{e};\ \mathbf{z}_2 = \mathbf{z}_1;\ \mathbf{f} = \mathbf{B}\mathbf{e} \tag{5.5}$$

This transformed problem can be minimized using the conventional Inexact Augmented Lagrange Multiplier (IALM) method that has attractive quadratic convergence properties and is extensively used in matrix rank minimization problems [33]. IALM is an iterative method that augments the traditional Lagrangian function with quadratic penalty terms. This allows closed form updates for each of the unknown variables. By introducing augmented lagrange multipliers (ALM) to incorporate the equality constraints into the cost function, we obtain the Lagrangian function in Eq. (5.6) that we show, in what follows, can be optimized through a sequence of simple closed form update operations (refer to Eq. (5.7)).

$$\begin{aligned}
&L(\mathbf{z}_{1-2}, \mathbf{y}_{1-3}, u_{1-3}) \\
&= \|\mathbf{z}_1\|_* + \|\mathbf{f}\|_1 \\
&\quad + tr\left[\mathbf{y}_1^T (\mathbf{x} - \mathbf{D}\mathbf{z}_2 - \mathbf{e})\right] + \frac{u_1}{2} \|\mathbf{x} - \mathbf{D}\mathbf{z}_2 - \mathbf{e}\|_F^2 \\
&\quad + tr\left[\mathbf{y}_2^T (\mathbf{z}_2 - \mathbf{z}_1)\right] + \frac{u_2}{2} \|\mathbf{z}_2 - \mathbf{z}_1\|_F^2 \\
&\quad + tr\left[\mathbf{y}_3^T (\mathbf{f} - \mathbf{B}\mathbf{e})\right] + \frac{u_3}{2} \|\mathbf{f} - \mathbf{B}\mathbf{e}\|_F^2 && (5.6) \\
&\Rightarrow \min_{\mathbf{z}_{1-2}, \mathbf{y}_{1-3}, u_{1-3}} L(\mathbf{z}_{1-2}, \mathbf{y}_{1-3}, u_{1-3}) && (5.7)
\end{aligned}$$

$\mathbf{y}_1$, $\mathbf{y}_2$, and $\mathbf{y}_3$ are lagrange multipliers, and $u_1 > 0$, $u_2 > 0$, and $u_3 > 0$ are three penalty parameters. The above problem can be solved by either exact or inexact ALM algorithms [24]. For efficiency, we choose the inexact ALM, whose details we outline in Algorithm (2). Its convergence properties can be proven similar to those in [24]. In fact, both IALM is an iterative algorithm that solves for each variable in a coordinate descent manner. In other words, each iteration of IALM involves the updating of each variable, with the other variables fixed to their most recent values. Consequently, we obtain five update steps corresponding to the five sets of variables we need to optimize for. Note that Steps 1–5 all have closed form solutions.

Step 1: [Update $\mathbf{z}_1$] Updating $\mathbf{z}_1$ requires the solution to the optimization problem in Eq. (5.8). This solution can be computed in closed form in Eq. (5.9), where $\mathcal{S}_\lambda(\mathbf{z}_{ij}) = sign(\mathbf{z}_{ij}) \max(0, |\mathbf{z}_{ij}| - \lambda)$ is the soft-thresholding operator, and $\mathbf{z}_{ij}$ is the jth element of vector $\mathbf{z}$.

$$\mathbf{z}_1^* = \arg\min_{\mathbf{z}_1} \frac{1}{u_1} \|\mathbf{z}_1\|_* + \frac{1}{2} \left\| \mathbf{z}_1 - \left(\mathbf{z}_2 + \frac{1}{u_2} \mathbf{y}_2 \right) \right\|_F^2 \tag{5.8}$$

$$\Rightarrow \boxed{\mathbf{z}_1^* = \mathscr{S}_{\frac{1}{u_1}}\left(\mathbf{z}_2 + \tfrac{1}{u_2}\mathbf{y}_2\right)} \tag{5.9}$$

Step 2: [Update f] f is updated by solving the optimization problem in Eq. (5.10) with the closed form solution shown in Eq. (5.11).

$$\mathbf{f}^* = \arg\min_{\mathbf{f}} \frac{1}{u_3} \|\mathbf{f}\|_1 + \frac{1}{2}\left\|\mathbf{f} - \left(\mathbf{Be} + \frac{1}{u_3}\mathbf{y}_3\right)\right\|_F^2 \tag{5.10}$$

$$\Rightarrow \boxed{\mathbf{f}^* = \mathscr{S}_{\frac{1}{u_3}}\left(\mathbf{Be} + \tfrac{1}{u_3}\mathbf{y}_3\right)} \tag{5.11}$$

Step 3: [Update e] e is updated by solving the optimization problem in Eq. (5.12) with the closed form solution shown in Eq. (5.13).

$$\begin{aligned}\mathbf{e}^* = \arg\min_{\mathbf{e}} \ & tr[\mathbf{y}_1^t(\mathbf{x} - \mathbf{Dz}_2 - \mathbf{e})] + \frac{u_1}{2}\|\mathbf{x} - \mathbf{Dz}_2 - \mathbf{e}\|_F^2 \\ & + tr[\mathbf{y}_3^t(\mathbf{Be} - \mathbf{f})] + \frac{u_3}{2}\|\mathbf{Be} - \mathbf{f}\|_F^2\end{aligned} \tag{5.12}$$

$$\Rightarrow \boxed{\mathbf{e}^* = \left(\mathbf{B}^T\mathbf{B} + \mathbf{I}\right)^{-1}\mathbf{G}}, \tag{5.13}$$

where $\mathbf{G} = \mathbf{x} - \mathbf{Dz}_2 + \frac{1}{u_1}\mathbf{y}_1 - \mathbf{B}^T\left(\frac{1}{u_3}\mathbf{y}_3 - \mathbf{f}\right)$.

Step 4: [Update $\mathbf{z}_2$] $\mathbf{z}_2$ is updated by solving the optimization problem in Eq. (5.14) with the closed form solution shown in Eq. (5.15).

$$\begin{aligned}\mathbf{z}_2{}^* = \arg\min_{\mathbf{z}_2} \ & tr[\mathbf{y}_1^t(\mathbf{x} - \mathbf{Dz}_2 - \mathbf{e})] + \frac{u_1}{2}\|\mathbf{x} - \mathbf{Dz}_2 - \mathbf{e}\|_F^2 \\ & + tr[\mathbf{y}_2^t(\mathbf{z}_2 - \mathbf{z}_1)] + \frac{u_2}{2}\|\mathbf{z}_2 - \mathbf{z}_1\|_F^2\end{aligned} \tag{5.14}$$

$$\Rightarrow \boxed{\mathbf{z}_2{}^* = \left(\mathbf{D}^T\mathbf{D} + \mathbf{I}\right)^{-1}\mathbf{G}}, \tag{5.15}$$

where $\mathbf{G} = \mathbf{D}^T(\mathbf{x} - \mathbf{e} + \frac{1}{u_1}\mathbf{y}_1) + \mathbf{z}_1 - \frac{1}{u_2}\mathbf{y}_2$.

Step 5: Update Multipliers $\mathbf{y}_1, \mathbf{y}_2$: We update the Lagrange multipliers in Eq. (5.16), where $\rho > 1$.

$$\begin{cases}\mathbf{y}_1 = \mathbf{y}_1 + u_1(\mathbf{x} - \mathbf{Dz}_2 - \mathbf{e}) \\ \mathbf{y}_2 = \mathbf{y}_2 + u_2(\mathbf{z}_2 - \mathbf{z}_1) \\ \mathbf{y}_3 = \mathbf{y}_3 + u_3(\mathbf{f} - \mathbf{Be}) \\ u_1 = \rho u_1;\ u_2 = \rho u_2;\ u_3 = \rho u_3\end{cases} \tag{5.16}$$

Algorithm 2: *Structured sparse learning for occlusion detection (Solving Eq (5))*

Input : data $\mathbf{x}$, parameters λ, γ, and ρ
Output: $\mathbf{z}$

Initialize $\mathbf{z}_2 = \mathbf{0}, \mathbf{y}_1 = 0, \mathbf{y}_2 = 0, \mathbf{y}_3 = 0$
while *not converged* **do**
    fix other variables and update $\mathbf{z}_1$ [Eq (9)]
    fix other variables and update $\mathbf{f}$ [Eq (11)]
    fix other variables and update $\mathbf{e}$ [Eq (13)]
    fix other variables and update $\mathbf{z}_2$ [Eq (15)]
    update multipliers and parameters [Eq (16)]
    Update final solution $\mathbf{z} \leftarrow \mathbf{z}_2$
end

The IALM algorithm that solves Eq. (5.5) is shown in Algorithm (2), where convergence is reached when the change in objective function or solution $\mathbf{z}$ is below a user-defined threshold $\varepsilon = 10^{-3}$. Empirically, we find that our IALM algorithm is insensitive to a large range of ε values. In our implementation, $u_1 = u_2 = u_3$.

Computational Complexity: For the proposed TOD, it just uses the soft-thresholding operator, and is also very fast. This complexity is on par with that of other fast particle-based tracking algorithms. In comparison, the computational complexity of the L_1 tracker [29], which uses a sparse linear representation similar to our proposed tracker, is at least $\mathcal{O}(nd^2)$, since the number of dictionary templates (object and trivial) is $(m + 2d)$ and n Lasso problems are solved independently. Clearly, our method is more computationally attractive than L_1 tracker. When $m = 21, n = 400$, and $d = 32 \times 32$, the average per-frame run-time for TOD and L_1 trackers are about 5 s and 6 min, respectively.

5.6 Experimental Results

In this section, we do experimental results that validate the effectiveness and efficiency of our TOD method. We also make a thorough comparison between TOD and state-of-the-art tracking methods where applicable. We compile a set of 10 challenging tracking sequences to evaluate TOD. The sequences are sports videos and general videos include challenging appearance variations due to changes in pose, illumination, scale, and occlusion. Most of them involve various types of partial occlusions or multiple occlusions. We compare our TOD method to 6 recent and state-of-the-art trackers denoted as: L_1 [29], RCT [45], MIL [3], IVT [35], Frag [1], and OAB [14]. We implemented them using publicly available source codes or binaries provided by the authors. They were initialized using their default parameters. In our implementation, the initial position of the target is selected manually, and we shift the initial bounding box by 1–3 pixels in each dimension, thus resulting in $m = 21$ target templates $\mathbf{D}$ (similar to L_1 tracker [29]). All our experiments are done using MATLAB on a 2.66GHZ Intel Core2 Duo PC with 18 GB RAM. For all experiments, we model $p(\mathbf{s}_t|\mathbf{s}_{t-1}) \sim \mathcal{N}(\mathbf{0}, \text{diag}(\boldsymbol{\sigma}))$, where $\boldsymbol{\sigma} = [0.005, 0.0005, 0.0005, 0.005, 3, 3]^T$. We set the number of particles $n = 400$. In Algorithm 2, we set $\lambda = 1$ and $\gamma = 5$. Next, we give a qualitative and quantitative analysis of TOD, and compare it against the 6 baseline methods. Our experiments show that TOD produces more robust and accurate tracks.

5.6.1 Qualitative Comparison

The qualitative comparison results are shown in Figs. 5.3 and 5.4, which show tracking results of the 7 trackers on a subset of the videos. The details are introduced as follows. In the *AF1* sequence, a player is tracked with appearance changes due to camera motion. Tracking results for frames {10, 162, 300, 400} are presented in Fig. 5.3a. IVT and MIL start to drift around frame 162. Due to changes in appearance, OAB and L_1 start to undergo target drift from frame 300. Frag starts to fail after frame 400. RCT can track the target through the whole sequence; however, this tracker is not as robust or accurate as the TOD tracker. For the *AF2* sequence, the player is subject to changes in illumination and pose. Based on the results in Fig. 5.3b, OAB, RCT, and L_1 start to drift from the target at frame 200, while MIL and Frag drift at frame 277 and finally lose the target. IVT tracks the target quite well with a little drift. However, the target is successfully tracked throughout the entire sequence by TOD. In *So1* shown in Fig. 5.3c, a player with white color is tracked. The results at 4 frames are shown in Fig. 5.3c. Because there is only minor occlusion by other players, most of the methods can track the face accurately except Frag, which drifts around frame 170. The *So2* sequence contains abrupt object and camera motion with significant scale changes, which cause most of the trackers to drift as shown in Fig. 5.3d. TOD, L_1, and RCT handle these changes well. Compared with L_1, TOD obtains much better performance, which shows that harnessing local structure between pixels is useful for object tracking. In the *So3* sequence, tracking results for frames {1, 27, 92, 230} are presented in Fig. 5.3e. Frag and IVT start to drift around frame 27 and 92, respectively. Due to changes in lighting and camera motion, most of the trackers drift including L_1 and OAB. TOD, MTT, and RCT can track the target through the whole sequence; however, the proposed TOD tracker shows the best performance.

On the *faceocc2* sequence, the results are shown in Fig. 5.4a. Most trackers start drifting from the man's face when it is almost fully occluded by the book. Because the L_1 and TOD methods explicitly handle partial occlusions, and update the object dictionary progressively, they handle the appearance changes in this sequence very well. Fig. 5.4b shows tracking results for the *girl* sequence. Performance on this sequence exemplifies the robustness of TOD to occlusion (complete occlusion of the girl's face as she swivels in the chair) and large pose change (the face undergoes significant 3D rotation). TOD and L_1 are capable of tracking the target during the

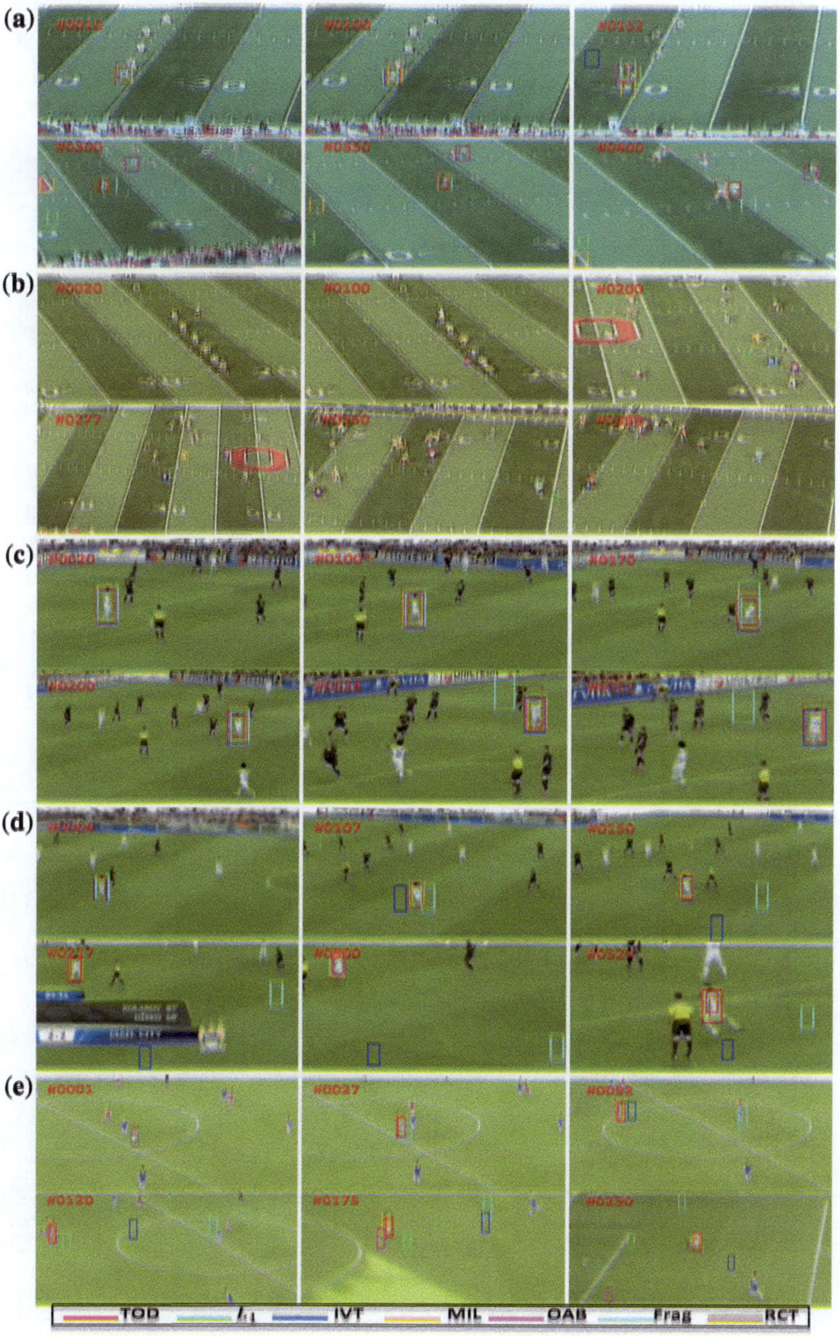

Fig. 5.3 Tracking results of 7 methods on 5 sports video sequences. Frame numbers are denoted in *red* and the 7 tracking results (bounding boxes) are color-coded in each frame **a** AF1 **b** AF2 **c** So1 **d** So2 **e** So3

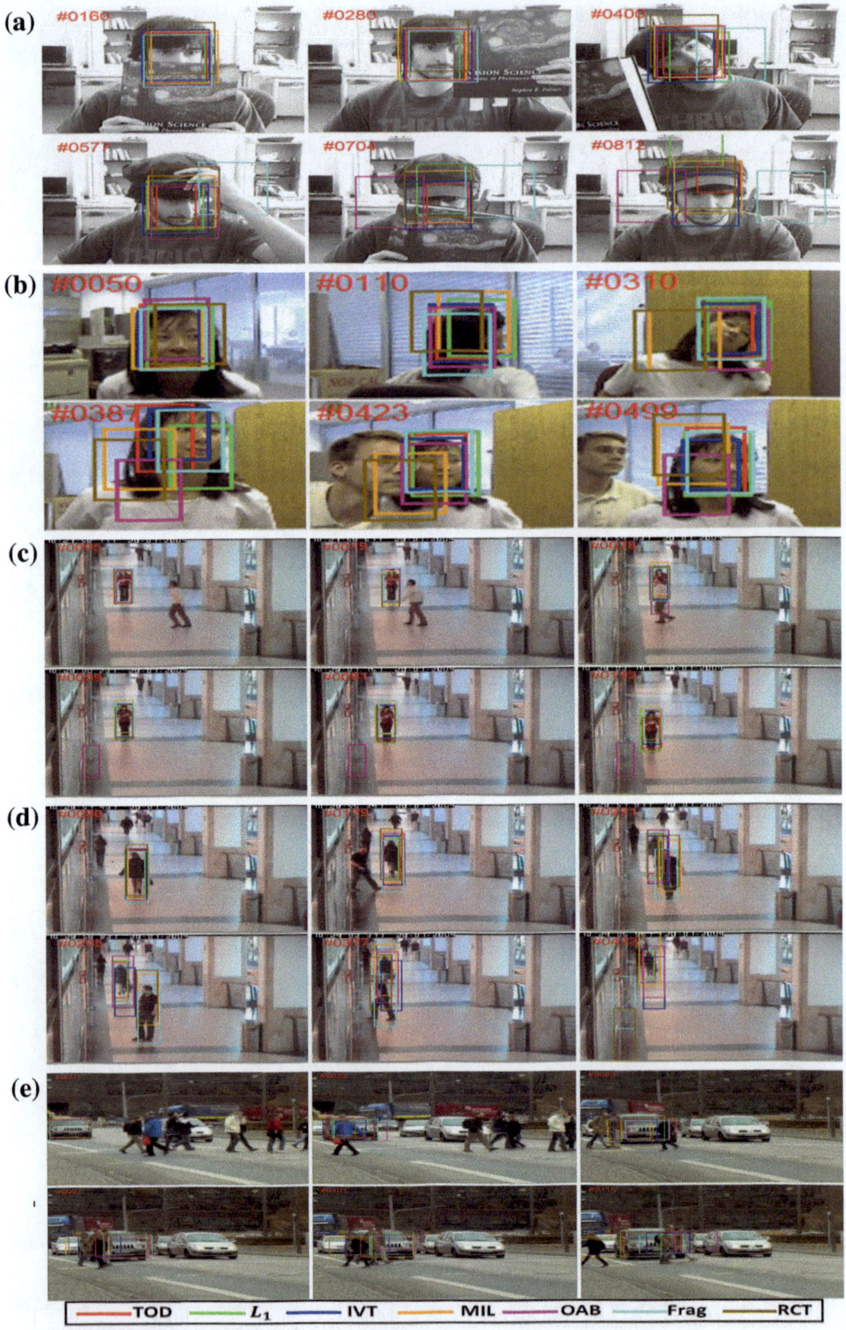

Fig. 5.4 Tracking results of 7 methods on 5 general video sequences. Frame numbers are denoted in *red* and the 7 tracking results (bounding boxes) are color-coded in each frame **a** faceocc2 **b** girl **c** onelsr1 **d** onelsr1 **e** tud_crossing

entire sequence. Other trackers experience drift at different time instances. Fig. 5.4c shows tracking results for the *onelsr1* sequence. In this sequence, partial occlusion happens, and it is much more easier. Therefore, many trackers (except OAB) can track the target through the whole video sequence. In the *onelsr2* sequence (refer to Fig. 5.4d), the walking woman is partially occluded by a walking man. IVT, MIL, Frag, OAB, and RCT lose the target woman, start tracking the man when partial occlusion occurs around frame 200, and are unable to recover from this failure. TOD and L_1 track the woman quite well. In the *tud_crossing* sequence, the target is severely occluded by multiple humans as shown in Fig. 5.4e. RCT and MIL start to drift around frame 32. Due to multiple occlusions, IVT starts to undergo target drift from frame 83. Other trackers, TOD, L_1, and Frag can track the target through the whole video; however, among all of the trackers, the TOD shows the best performance.

5.6.2 Quantitative Comparison

To give a fair quantitative comparison among the 7 trackers, we obtain manually labeled ground truth tracks for all the sequences. Most of the ground truth can be downloaded with the sequences. Tracking performance is evaluated according to the average per-frame distance (in pixels) between the center of the tracking result and that of ground truth as used in [3, 10, 29]. Clearly, this distance should be small. In Fig. 5.5, the average center distance for each tracker over the 10 sequences is plotted. TOD consistently outperform the other trackers in all sequences except for *AF2* and *onelsr1*, where they obtain very similar results to IVT. OAB is effected by background clutter and easily drifts from the target. MIL performs well except under severe illumination changes. RCT is not stable on several video sequences, especially those that contain occlusion and illumination variations. Frag and L_1 handle partial occlusion well, but tend to fail under severe illumination and pose changes. IVT is hardly affected by parameter settings and obtains good results in the absence of severe illumination changes. TOD can consistently produce a smaller distance than other trackers. This implies that TOD can accurately track the target despite severe occlusions and pose variations.

To demonstrate the effectiveness of our TOD, we compare it with the L_1 and RCT trackers, which are the most related trackers to ours based on sparse learning and have shown state-of-the-art performance [29, 45]. Based on the results in Fig. 5.5, TOD outperform the L_1 tracker and RCT. This is primarily due to the use of structure information for occlusion modeling, which makes TOD robust to occlusion problem. In addition, about the computational cost, TOD is much more efficient than L_1 as discussed in Sect. 5.5.

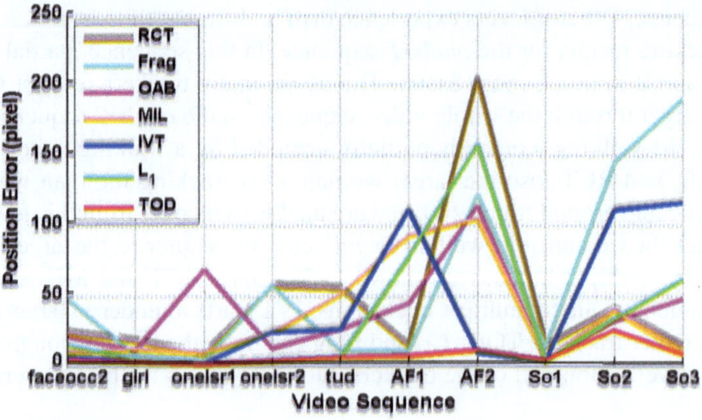

Fig. 5.5 Average distance of 7 trackers applied to 10 sequences

5.7 Conclusion

In this chapter, we propose a novel tracking method that allows for occlusion modeling and detection via structured sparse learning. By considering the structural information inherent to occlusion (e.g., spatial contiguity), the proposed TOD is much more robust for tracking under occlusion. The structured sparse learning problem is solved using an efficient IALM method. We show that the popular L_1 tracker [29] is a special case of our formulation. Also, we extensively analyze the performance of our tracker on challenging real-world video sequences and show that it outperforms 6 state-of-the-art trackers. In the future, we will do research on how to embed the temporal information to model occlusion in our framework.

Acknowledgments This study is supported by the research grant for the Human Sixth Sense Programme at the Advanced Digital Sciences Center from Singapore's Agency for Science, Technology, and Research (A*STAR).

References

1. Adam A, Rivlin E, Shimshoni I (2006) Robust fragments-based tracking using the integral histogram. In: Proceedings of IEEE conference on computer vision and pattern recognition, pp 798–805
2. Avidan, S (2005) Ensemble tracking. In: Proceedings of IEEE conference on computer vision and pattern recognition, pp 494–501
3. Babenko B, Yang M-H, Belongie S (2009) Visual tracking with online multiple instance learning. In: Proceedings of IEEE conference on computer vision and pattern recognition, pp 983–990
4. Bao C, Wu Y, Ling H, Ji H (2012) Real time robust l_1 tracker using accelerated proximal gradient approach. In: Proceedings of IEEE conference on computer vision and pattern recognition

5. Black MJ, Jepson AD (1998) Eigentracking: Robust matching and tracking of articulated objects using a view-based representation. Int J Comput Vis 26(1):63–84
6. Blasch E, Kahler B (2005) Multiresolution eoir target tracking and identification. In: International conference on information fusion, vol 8, pp 1–8
7. Chockalingam P, Pradeep N, Birchfield S (2009) Adaptive fragmentsbased tracking of non-rigid objects using level sets. In: ICCV
8. Collins RT, Liu Y (2003) On-line selection of discriminative tracking features. In: Proceedings of the IEEE international conference on computer vision, pp 346–352
9. Comaniciu D, Ramesh V, Meer P (2003) Kernel-based object tracking. IEEE Trans Pattern Anal Mach Intell 25(5):564–575
10. Dinh TB, Vo N, Medioni G (2011) Context tracker: exploring supporters and distracters in unconstrained environments. In: Conference on computer vision and pattern recognition
11. Doucet A, De Freitas N, Gordon N (eds) (2001) Sequential Monte Carlo methods in practice. Springer, New York
12. Fleuret F, Berclaz J, Lengagne R, Fua P (2008) Multicamera people tracking with a probabilistic occupancy map. IEEE Trans PAMI 30(2):267–282
13. Gay-Bellile V, Bartoli A, Sayd P (2010) Direct estimation of nonrigid registrations with image-based self-occlusion reasoning. IEEE Trans PAMI 32(1):87–104
14. Grabner H, Grabner M, Bischof H (2006) Real-time tracking via on-line boosting. In: Proceedings of British machine vision conference, pp 1–10
15. Grabner H, Leistner C, Bischof H (2008) Semi-supervised on-line boosting for Robust tracking. In: Proceedings of European conference on computer vision, pp 234–247
16. Han B, Davis L (2005) On-line density-based appearance modeling for object tracking. In: ICCV
17. Jepson A, Fleet D, El-Maraghi T (2003) Robust on-line appearance models for visual tracking. IEEE Trans Pattern Anal Mach Intell 25(10):1296–1311
18. Jiang N, Liu W, Wu Y (2011) Adaptive and discriminative metric differential tracking. In: Proceedings of IEEE conference on computer vision and pattern recognition, pp 1161–1168
19. Kaneko T, Hori O (2003) Feature selection for reliable tracking using template matching. In: Proceedings of IEEE conference on computer vision and pattern recognition, pp 796–802
20. Kwak S, Nam W, Han B, Han JH (2011) Learning occlusion with likelihoods for visual tracking. In: ICCV
21. Kwon J, Lee KM (2010) Visual tracking decomposition. In: Proceedings of IEEE conference on computer vision and pattern recognition, pp 1269–1276
22. Leistner C, Godec M, Saffari A, Bischof H (2010) Online multi-view forests for tracking. In: DAGM, pp 493–502
23. Li H, Shen C, Shi Q (2011) Real-time visual tracking with compressed sensing. In: Proceedings of IEEE conference on computer vision and pattern recognition, pp 1305–1312
24. Lin Z, Ganesh A, Wright J, Wu L, Chen M, Ma Y (2009) Fast convex optimization algorithms for exact recovery of a corrupted low-rank matrix. In: Technical Report UILU-ENG-09-2214, UIUC
25. Liu R, Cheng J, Lu H (2009) A Robust boosting tracker with minimum error bound in a co-training framework. In: Proceedings of the IEEE international conference on computer vision, pp 1459–1466
26. Liu B, Yang L, Huang J, Meer P, Gong L, Kulikowski C (2010) Robust and fast collaborative tracking with two stage sparse optimization. In: Proceedings of European conference on computer vision, pp 1–14
27. Lucas BD, Kanade T (1981) An iterative image registration technique with an application to stereo vision (DARPA). In: DARPA image understanding workshop, pp 121–130
28. Matthews I, Ishikawa T, Baker S (2004) The template update problem. IEEE Trans Pattern Anal Mach Intell 26:810–815
29. Mei X, Ling H (2011) Robust visual tracking and vehicle classification via sparse representation. IEEE Trans Pattern Anal Mach Intell 33(11):2259–2272

30. Mei X, Ling H, Wu Y, Blasch E, Bai L (2011) Minimum error bounded efficient l_1 tracker with occlusion detection. In: Proceedings of IEEE conference on computer vision and pattern recognition, pp 1257–1264
31. Mittal A, Davis LS (2003) M2tracker: a multi-view approach to segmenting and tracking people in a cluttered scene. Int J Comput Vis 51(3):189–203
32. Moeslund TB, Hilton A, Kruger V, Sigal L (2011) Visual analysis of humans
33. Peng Y, Ganesh A, Wright J, Xu W, Ma Y (2011) RASL: Robust alignment by sparse and low-rank decomposition for linearly correlated images. IEEE Trans Pattern Anal Mach Intell 34(11):2233–2246
34. Ross D, Lim J, Yang M (2004) Adaptive probabilistic visual tracking with incremental subspace update. In: European conference on computer vision
35. Ross D, Lim J, Lin R-S, Yang M-H (2008) Incremental learning for Robust visual tracking. Int J Comput Vis 77(1):125–141
36. Salti S, Cavallaro A, Stefano LD (2012) Adaptive appearance modeling for video tracking: survey and evaluation. IEEE Trans Image Process 21(10):4334–4348
37. Wu Y, Lim J, M-H Yang (2013) Online object tracking: a benchmark. In: Proceedings of IEEE conference on computer vision and pattern recognition
38. Yang M, Wu Y, Hua G (2009) Context-aware visual tracking. IEEE Trans Pattern Anal Mach Intell 31(7):1195–1209
39. Yang M, Yuan J, Wu Y (2007) Spatial selection for attentional visual tracking. In: Conference on computer vision and pattern recognition
40. Yang M, Wu Y, Hua G (2009) Context-aware visual tracking. PAMI 31(1):1195–1209
41. Yilmaz A, Javed O, Shah M (2006) Object tracking: a survey. ACM Comput Surv 38(4):13+
42. Yin Z, Collins R (2008) Object tracking and detection after occlusion via numerical hybrid local and global mode-seeking. In: Proceedings of IEEE conference on computer vision and pattern recognition, pp 1–8
43. Yu Q, Dinh TB, Medioni G (2008) Online tracking and reacquistion using co-trained generative and discriminative trackers. In: Proceedings of European conference on computer vision, pp 78–691 (2008)
44. Zhang T, Lu H, Li SZ (2009) Learning semantic scene models by object classification and trajectory clustering. In: CVPR
45. Zhang K, Zhang L, M-H Yang (2012) Real-time compressive tracking. In: Proceedings of European conference on computer vision
46. Zhang T, Ghanem B, Liu S, Ahuja N (2012) Low-rank sparse learning for robust visual tracking. In: European conference on computer vision
47. Zhang T, Ghanem B, Liu S, Ahuja N (2012) Robust visual tracking via multi-task sparse learning. In: Proceedings of IEEE conference on computer vision and pattern recognition
48. Zhang T, Liu J, Liu S, Xu C, Lu H (2011) Boosted exemplar learning for action recognition and annotation. IEEE Trans Circuits Syst Video Technol 21(7):853–866
49. Zhang T, Ghanem B, Liu S, Ahuja N (2013) Robust visual tracking via structured multi-task sparse learning. Int J Comput Vis 101(2):367–383
50. Zhang T, Liu S, Xu C, Lu H (2013) Mining semantic context information for intelligent video surveillance of traffic scenes. IEEE Trans Ind Inform 9(1):149–160
51. Zhong W, Lu H, M-H Y (2012) Robust object tracking via sparsity-based collaborative model. In: Proceedings of IEEE conference on computer vision and pattern recognition

Chapter 6
Detecting and Tracking Sports Players with Random Forests and Context-Conditioned Motion Models

Jingchen Liu and Peter Carr

Abstract Player movements in team sports are often complex and highly correlated with both nearby and distant players. A single motion model would require many degrees of freedom to represent the full motion diversity of each player and could be difficult to use in practice. Instead, we introduce a set of *Game Context Features* extracted from noisy detection data to describe the current state of the match, such as how the players are spatially distributed. Our assumption is that players react to the current game situation in only a finite number of ways. As a result, we are able to select an appropriate simplified motion model for each player and at each time instant using a random decision forest which examines characteristics of individual trajectories and broad game context features derived from all current trajectories. Our context-conditioned motion models implicitly incorporate complex interobject correlations while remaining tractable. We demonstrate significant performance improvements over existing multitarget tracking algorithms on basketball and field hockey sequences of several minutes in duration containing 10 and 20 players, respectively.

6.1 Introduction

Multitarget tracking has been a difficult problem of broad interest for years in computer vision. Surveillance is perhaps the most common scenario for multitarget tracking, but team sports is another popular domain that has a wide range of applications in strategy analysis, automated broadcasting, and content-based retrieval. Recent work in pedestrian tracking has demonstrated promising results by formulating multitarget tracking in terms of data association [1, 5, 8, 20, 25, 28, 30, 32]. A set of potential target locations are estimated in each frame using

J. Liu (✉)
Microsoft, 1020 Enterprise Way, Sunnyvale,
CA 94089, USA
e-mail: jingcli@microsoft.com

P. Carr
Disney Research Pittsburgh, 4720 Forbes Ave., Suite 110, Pittsburgh,
PA 15213, USA
e-mail: carr@disneyresearch.com

T.B. Moeslund et al. (eds.), *Computer Vision in Sports*,
Advances in Computer Vision and Pattern Recognition,
DOI 10.1007/978-3-319-09396-3_6

an object detector, and target trajectories are inferred by linking similar detections (or tracklets) across frames. However, if complex intertracklet affinity models are used, the association problem becomes NP-hard.

Tracking players in team sports has three significant differences compared to pedestrians in surveillance. First, the appearance features of detections are less discriminative because players on the same team will be visually similar. As a result, the distinguishing characteristics of detections in team sports are primarily position and velocity. Second, sports players move in more erratic fashions, whereas pedestrians tend to move along straight lines at a constant speed. Third, although pedestrians deviate to avoid colliding with each other, the motions between pedestrians are rarely correlated in complex ways (some scenarios, like sidewalks, may contain a finite number of common global motions). The movements of sports players, on the other hand, are strongly correlated both locally and globally. For example, opposing players may exhibit strong local correlations when 'marking' each other (such as one-on-one defensive assignments). Similarly, players who are far away from each other move in globally correlated ways because they are reacting to the same ball (Fig. 6.1).

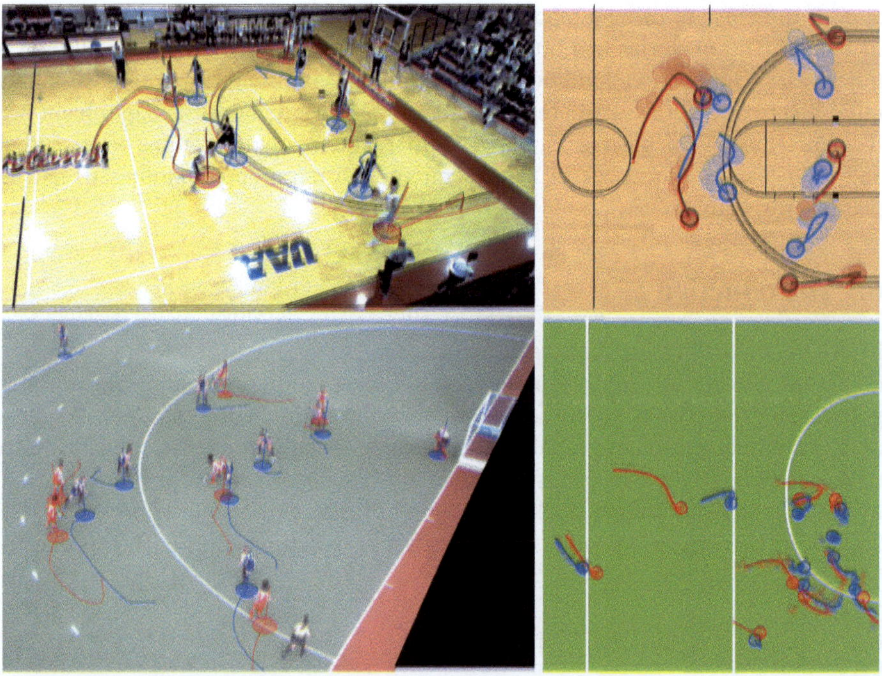

Fig. 6.1 Motion Models. A player's future motion is contingent on the current game situation. The global distribution of players often indicates which team is attacking, and local distributions denote when opposing players are closely following each other. We use contextual information such as this to create a more accurate motion affinity model for tracking players. The overhead views of basketball and field hockey show the input detections and corresponding ground truth annotations. Player trajectories are strongly correlated with both nearby and distant players

Simple, independent motion models have been popular for pedestrian tracking because they limit the complexity of the underlying inference problem [8]. However, the models may not always characterize the motion affinity between a pair of tracklets accurately. Brendel et al. [5] modeled intertarget correlations between pedestrians using *context*, which consisted of additional terms in the data association affinity measure based on the spatiotemporal properties of tracklet pairs. Following this convention, we will describe correlations between player movements in terms of *game context*. Much like the differences between the individual target motions in surveillance and team sports, game context is more complex and dynamic compared to context in surveillance. For example, teams will frequently gain and lose possession of the ball, and the motions of all players will change drastically at each turnover.

Because a player's movement is influenced by multiple factors, the traditional multitarget tracking formulation using a set of independent autoregressive motion models is a poor representation of how sports players actually move. However, motion affinity models conditioned on multiple targets (and that do not decompose into a product of pairwise terms) make the data association problem NP-hard [8]. In this work, we show how data association is an effective solution for sports player tracking by devising an accurate model of player movements that remains tractable by conditioning on features describing the current state of the game, such as which team has possession of the ball. One of our key contributions is a new set of broad *game context features* (GCF) for team sports, and a methodology to estimate them from noisy detections. Using game context features, we can better assess the affinity between trajectory segments by implicitly modeling complex interactions through a random decision forest involving a combination of kinematic and game context features. We demonstrate the ability to track 20 players in over 30 min of international field hockey matches, and 10 players in 5 min of college basketball.

6.2 Related Work

Recent success in pedestrian tracking has posed multitarget tracking as hierarchical data association: long object trajectories are found by linking together a series of detections or short tracklets. The problem of associating tracklets across time has been investigated using a variety of methods, such as the Hungarian algorithm [10, 21], linear programming [11], cost flow networks [30], maximum weight independent sets [5], continuous-discrete optimization [4], and higher order motion models [8]. Data association is often formulated as a linear assignment problem where the cost of linking one tracklet to another is some function of extracted features (typically motion and appearance). More recent work (discussed shortly) considers more complex association costs.

Crowds are an extreme case of pedestrian tracking where it is often not possible to see each individual in their entirety. Because of congestion, pedestrian motions are often quite similar and crowd tracking algorithms typically estimate a finite set of global motions. Often, the affinity for linking two tracklets together depends on how well the hypothesized motion agrees with one of the global motions. References [1, 32] solve tracking in crowded structured scenes with floor fields estimation and Motion Structure Tracker, respectively. Reference [23] uses a Correlated Topic Model for crowded, unstructured scenes.

Team sports is another relevant domain for multitarget tracking [24], with algorithms based on particle filters being extremely popular [6, 9, 14, 16, 18, 27]. However, results are quite often demonstrated only on short sequences (typically less than two minutes). In contrast, only a small amount of work has investigated long-term sports player tracking. Nillius et al. [19] generated a Bayes network of splitting and merging tracklets for a long 10-minute soccer sequence, and found the most probable assignment of player identities using max-margin message passing. Kumar and Vleeschouer proposed discriminative label propagation [2] and Shitrit et al. use multicommodity network flow for tracking multiple people [26].

In both pedestrian and player tracking, object motions are often assumed to be independent and modeled as zero displacement (for erratic motion) and/or constant velocity (for smooth motion governed by inertia). In reality, the locations and motions of sports players are strongly correlated. Pairwise repulsive forces have been used in multitarget tracking to enforce separability between objects [3–5, 12, 29]. Recently, multiobject motion models have been used in pedestrian tracking to anticipate how people will change their trajectories to avoid collisions [20], or for estimating whether a pair of trajectories have correlated motions [5]. In team sports, Kim et al. [13] estimated motion fields using the velocities of tracklets to anticipate how the play would evolve, but did not use the motion fields to track players over long sequences. Zhang et al. [31] augmented the standard independent autoregressive motion model with a database of a priori trajectories manually annotated from other games.

6.3 Hierarchical Data Association Tracking

Our tracking formulation (see Fig. 6.2) employs an object detector to generate a set $\mathscr{O}$ of hypothesized sports player locations through the duration of the video. Each detection $\mathscr{O}_i = [t_i, \mathbf{x}_i, \mathbf{a}_i]$ contains a time stamp, the player's location on the ground plane, and the player's appearance information, respectively. The goal is to find the most probable set $\mathscr{T}^\star = \{\mathscr{T}_1, \mathscr{T}_2, \ldots, \mathscr{T}_N\}$ of player trajectories where each trajectory is a temporal sequence of detections $\mathscr{T}_n = \{\mathscr{O}_a, \mathscr{O}_b, \ldots\}$

$$\mathscr{T}^\star = \arg\max_{\mathscr{T}} P(\mathscr{O}|\mathscr{T})P(\mathscr{T}). \tag{6.1}$$

The likelihood $P(\mathscr{O}|\mathscr{T})$ indicates how well a set of trajectories $\mathscr{T}$ matches the observations, and the prior $P(\mathscr{T})$ describes, in the case of sports tracking, how realistic the set of estimated player trajectories $\mathscr{T}$ is. In multitarget tracking, the prior is often simplified to consider each trajectory as an independent Markov chain

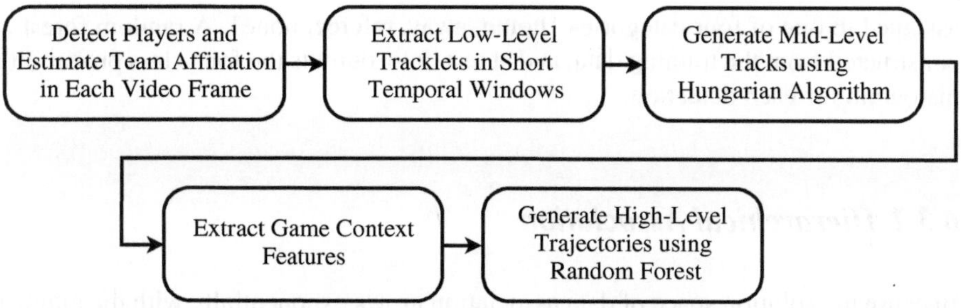

Fig. 6.2 Algorithm. Our tracking algorithm has five distinct phases: detection, low-level tracklets, mid-level tracks, game context features, and high-level trajectories

$$P(\mathscr{T}) \sim \prod_n P(\mathscr{T}_n) \tag{6.2}$$

$$\sim \prod_n \prod_t P(\mathscr{T}_n^t | \mathscr{T}_n^{t-1}), \tag{6.3}$$

where $\mathscr{T}_n^t$ indicates the trajectory of the nth player at time interval t.

In team sports, the prior is a highly complex function and is not well approximated by a series of independent trajectory assessments. We maintain the formulation of conditional independence between trajectories, but condition each individual trajectory prior on a set of game context features θ which describe the current state of the match

$$P(\mathscr{T}) \stackrel{\text{def}}{=} \prod_{n,t} P(\mathscr{T}_n^{t-1} \rightarrow \mathscr{T}_n^t | \theta). \tag{6.4}$$

Conditioning the individual motion models on game context implicitly encodes higher order intertrajectory relationships and long-term intratrajectory information without sacrificing tractability.

6.3.1 Detection

We use the method of Carr et al. [7] to generate possible (x, y) positions of players in all video frames. The technique requires a calibrated camera, and uses background subtraction to generate foreground masks. Player locations are estimated by evaluating how well a set of hypothesized 0.5-m-wide cylinders 1.8 m tall can explain each observed foreground mask. The method is tuned to only detect high confidence situations, such as when a player is fully visible and well separated from other players. For each detected position, a rectified patch is extracted from the image and a coarse RGB histogram (4 bins per channel) is computed as an appearance feature. The first few seconds of video are accompanied by user supplied labels: each detection is assigned to one of four categories {home, away, referee, none}. A random forest is constructed from the training data, and at test time, outputs the four-class probability histogram for each detection.

6.3.2 *Hierarchical Association*

Because the solution space of data association grows exponentially with the number of frames, we adopt a hierarchical approach to handle sequences that are several minutes long (see Fig. 6.3).

6.3.2.1 Low-Level Tracklets

A set Υ of low-level trackletsis extracted from the detections by fitting constant velocity models to clusters of detections in 0.5 s long temporal windows using RANSAC. Each Υ_l represents an estimate of a player's instantaneous position and velocity (see Fig. 6.4).

6.3.2.2 Mid-Level Tracks

Similar to [10], the Hungarian algorithm is used to combine subsequent low-level trajectories into a set Γ of mid-level tracks up to 60 s in duration. The method automatically determines the appropriate number of mid-level tracks, but is tuned

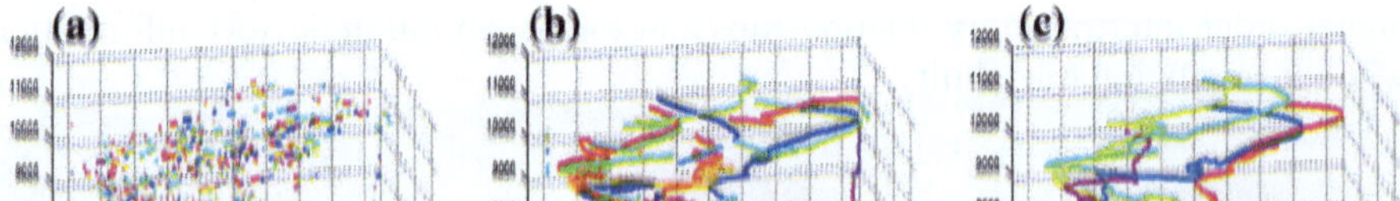

Fig. 6.3 Hierarchical data association. **a** Low-level tracklets Υ from noisy detections; **b** mid-level tracks Γ obtained via the Hungarian algorithm [10]; **c** N high-level player trajectories $\mathcal{T}$ via a cost flow network [30]

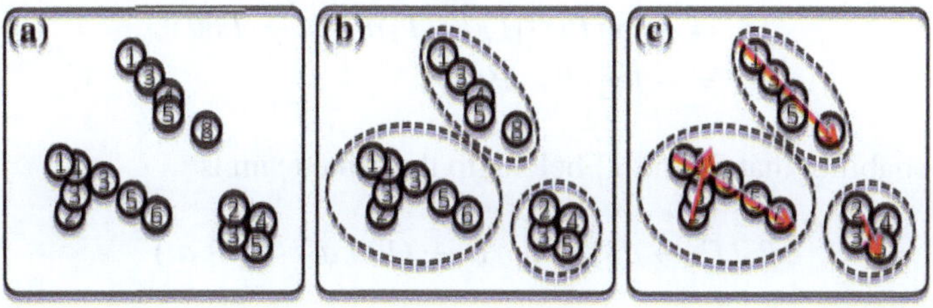

Fig. 6.4 Low-level Tracklet Extraction. Each detection is represented as a circle with a frame number. **a** Detection responses within a local spatial-temporal volume; **b** identified clusters; and **c** RANSAC-fitted constant velocity models (*red*)

to prefer shorter, more reliable tracks. Generally, mid-level tracks terminate when abrupt motions occur or when a player is not detected for more than 2 s.

6.3.2.3 High-Level Trajectories

MAP association is equivalent to the minimum cost flow in a network [30] where a vertex i is defined for each mid-level track Γ_i and edge weights reflect the likelihood and prior in (6.4). Unlike the Hungarian algorithm, it is possible to constrain solutions to have exactly N trajectories by pushing N units of flow between special source s and sink t vertices (see Fig. 6.5). The complete trajectory $\mathcal{T}_n$ of each player corresponds to the minimum cost path for one unit of flow from s to t. The cost c_{ij} per unit flow from i to j indicates the negative affinity, or negative log likelihood that Γ_j is the immediate successor of Γ_i, which we decompose into probabilities in continuity of appearance, time, and motion

Fig. 6.5 Cost flow network from mid-level tracks. Each *small circle* with a number inside indicates a detection and its time stamp. Colored edges on the *left* indicate mid-level track associations. The corresponding cost flow network is shown on the *right*. Each mid-level track Γ_i, as well as the global source s and sink t forms a vertex, and each directed edge in *black* from vertex a to b has a cost indicating the negative affinity of associating Γ_a to Γ_b

$$c_{ij} = -\log P(\mathcal{O}|\Gamma_i \rightarrow \Gamma_j)P(\Gamma_i \rightarrow \Gamma_j|\theta) \tag{6.5}$$
$$= -\log (P_a \cdot P_\tau \cdot P_m). \tag{6.6}$$

The probability that Γ_i and Γ_j belong to the same team is

$$P_a(\Gamma_i \rightarrow \Gamma_j) = a_i \cdot a_j + (1 - a_i) \cdot (1 - a_j) \tag{6.7}$$

where a_i and $1 - a_i$ are the confidence scores of the mid-level track belonging to team A and B, respectively.

Let t_{i0} and t_{i1} denote the start and end times of Γ_i, respectively. If Γ_j is the immediate successor of Γ_i, any nonzero time gap implies that missed detections must have occurred. Therefore, the probability based on temporal continuity is defined as

$$P_\tau(\Gamma_i \rightarrow \Gamma_j) = \exp(-\lambda(t_{j0} - t_{i1})). \tag{6.8}$$

Each mid-level trajectory Γ_i has "miss-from-the-start" and "miss-until-the-end" costs on edges (s, i) and (i, t), respectively. The weights are computed using (6.8) for temporal gaps (T_0, t_{i0}) and (t_{j1}, T_1), where T_0 and T_1 are the global start and end times of the sequence.

Before describing the form of $P_m(\Gamma_i \rightarrow \Gamma_j|\theta)$ in more detail, we first discuss how to extract a set of game context features θ from noisy detections $\mathcal{O}$.

6.4 Game Context Features

In team sports, players assess the current situation and react accordingly. As a result, a significant amount of contextual information is implicitly encoded in player locations. In practice, the set of detected player positions in each frame contains errors, including both missed detections and false detections. We introduce four game context features (two based on absolute position and two based on relative position) for describing the current game situation with respect to a pair of mid-level tracks that can be extracted from a varying number of noisy detected player locations $\mathcal{O}$.

6.4.1 Absolute Occupancy Map

We describe the distribution of players during a time interval using an occupancy map, which is a spatial quantization of the number of detected players, so that we get a description vector of constant length regardless of missed and false detections. We also apply a temporal averaging filter of 1s on the occupancy map to reduce the noise from detections. The underline assumption is that players may exhibit different motion patterns under different spatial distributions. For example, a concentrated distribution may indicate a higher likelihood of abrupt motion changes, and smooth

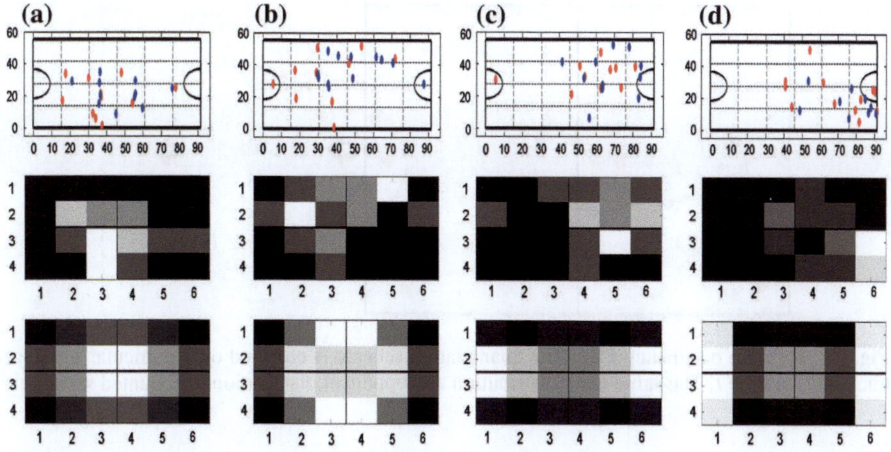

Fig. 6.6 Absolute occupancy map. Four clusters are automatically obtained via K-means: **a** center-concentrated, **b** center-diffuse, **c** goal, and **d** corner. The rows show: noisy detections (*top*), estimated occupancy map (*middle*), and the corresponding cluster center (*bottom*), which is symmetric horizontally and vertically

motions are more likely to happen during player transitions with a spread-out distribution.

We compute a time-averaged player count for each quantized area. We assume the same distribution could arise regardless of which team is attacking, implying a 180° symmetry in the data. Similarly, we assume a left/right symmetry for each team, resulting in a fourfold compression of the feature space.

Similar to visual words, we use K-means clustering to identify four common distributions (see Fig. 6.6) roughly characterized as: center-concentrated, center-diffuse, goal, and corner.

When evaluating the affinity for $\Gamma_i \rightarrow \Gamma_j$, we average the occupancy vector over the time window (t_{i1}, t_{j0}) and the nearest cluster ID is taken as the context feature of absolute occupancy $\theta_{ij}^{(A)} = k \in \{1, \ldots K\}$.

The spatial quantization scheme may be tuned for a specific sport, and does not necessarily have to be a grid.

6.4.2 Relative Occupancy Map

The relative distribution of players is often indicative of identity [19] or *role* [17]. For example, a forward on the right side typically remains in front and to the right of teammates regardless of whether the team is defending in the back-court or attacking in the front-court. Additionally, the motion of a player is often influenced by nearby players.

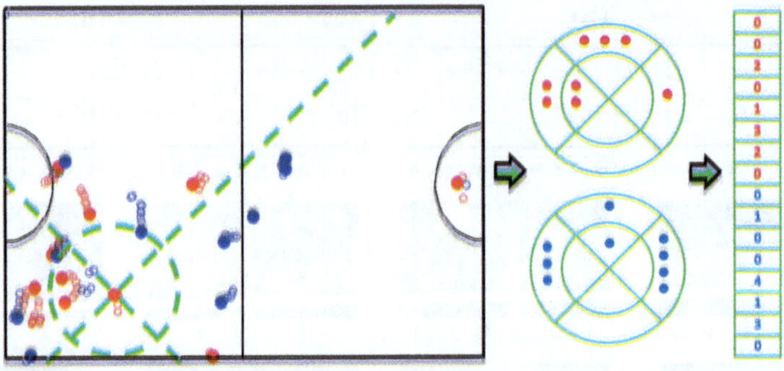

Fig. 6.7 Relative occupancy map. The quantization scheme is centered on a particular low-level tracklet Υ_l at time t. The same-team distribution and opponent distribution are counted separately

Therefore, we define a relative occupancy map specific to each low-level tracklet Υ_l which quantizes space similarly to the shape context representation: distance is divided into two levels, with a threshold of 4 m, and direction into four bins (see Fig. 6.7). The per-team occupancy count is then normalized to sum to one for both the inner circle and outer ring. Like absolute occupancy maps, we cluster the 16 bin relative occupancy counts (first 8 bins describing same-team distribution, last 8 bins describing opponent distribution) into a finite set of roles using K-means.

For each pair of possible successive $\Gamma_i \rightarrow \Gamma_j$ mid-level tracks, we extract the occupancy vector $\mathbf{v}_i$ and $\mathbf{v}_j$, with cluster ID k_i, k_j, from the end tracklet of Γ_i and the beginning tracklet of Γ_j. We also compute the Euclidian distance of $d_{ij} = |\mathbf{v}_i - \mathbf{v}_j|_2$. Intuitively, a smaller d_{ij} indicates higher likelihood that Γ_j is the continuation of Γ_i. The context feature of relative occupancy is the concatenation of $\theta_{ij}^{(R)} = (d_{ij}, k_i, k_j)$.

6.4.3 Focus Area

In team sports such as soccer or basketball, there is often a local region with relatively high player density that moves smoothly in time and may indicate the current or future location of the ball [13, 22]. The movement of the focus area in absolute coordinates also strongly correlates to high-level events such as turnovers. We assume the movement of individual players should correlate with the focus area over long time periods, thus this feature is useful for associations $\Gamma_i \rightarrow \Gamma_j$ with large temporal gaps (when the motion prediction is also less reliable). For example, mid-level trajectory Γ_i in Fig. 6.8 is more likely to be matched to Γ_{j1} with a constant velocity motion model. However, if the trajectory of the focus area is provided as in Fig. 6.8, it is reasonable to assume $\Gamma_i \rightarrow \Gamma_{j2}$ has a higher affinity than $\Gamma_i \rightarrow \Gamma_{j1}$.

We estimate the location and movement of the focus area by applying meanshift mode-seeking to track the local center of mass of the noisy player detections. Given a pair of mid-level tracks with hypothesized continuity $\Gamma_i \rightarrow \Gamma_j$, we interpolate

Fig. 6.8 Focus area. Kinematic constraints are less reliable across larger time windows. Because player motions are globally correlated, the affinity of two mid-level tracks over large windows should agree with the overall movement trend of the focus area

the trajectory within the temporal window (t_{i1}, t_{j0}) and calculate the variance of its relative distance to the trajectory of the focus area σ_{ij}. We also extract the average speed of the focus area v_f during the time window, which describes the momentum of the global motion. The focus area context feature is thus set as $\theta_{ij}^{(F)} = (\sigma_{ij}, v_f)$.

6.4.4 Chasing Detection

Individual players are often instructed to follow or *mark* a particular opposition player. Basketball, for example, commonly uses a one-on-one defense system where a defending player is assigned to follow a corresponding attacking player. We introduce chasing (close-interaction) links to detect when one player is marking another. If the trajectories Γ_i and Γ_j both appear to be following a nearby reference trajectory Γ_k, there is a strong possibility that Γ_j is the continuation of Γ_i (assuming the mid-level track of the reference player is continuous during the gap between Γ_i and Γ_j, see Fig. 6.9).

We identify chasing links by searching for pairs of low-level tracklets (Υ_i, Υ_k) that are less than 2 m apart and moving along similar directions (We use the angular threshold of 45° during the experiment). Let $\tau_{ij|k}$ be the temporal gap between Γ_i's last link with Γ_k and Γ_j's first link with Γ_k, and $\tau_{ij|k} = \infty$ when there are no links between either Γ_i or Γ_j and Γ_k. The chasing continuity feature $\theta_{ij}^{(C)}$ that measures whether trajectories Γ_i and Γ_j are marking the same player is given by

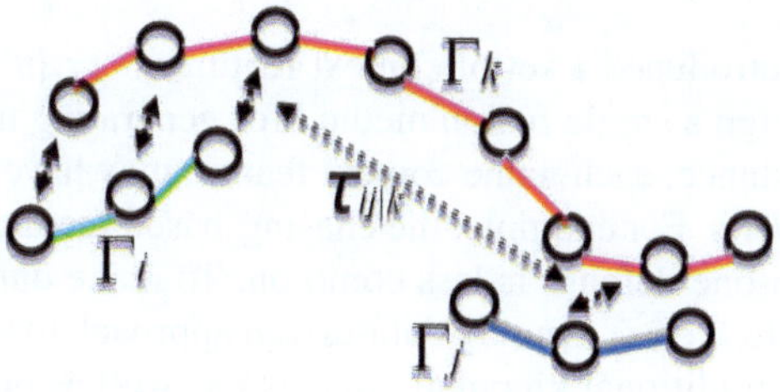

Fig. 6.9 Chasing. If Γ_i and Γ_j both correlate to a nearby track Γ_k, there is a higher likelihood that Γ_j is the continuation of Γ_i

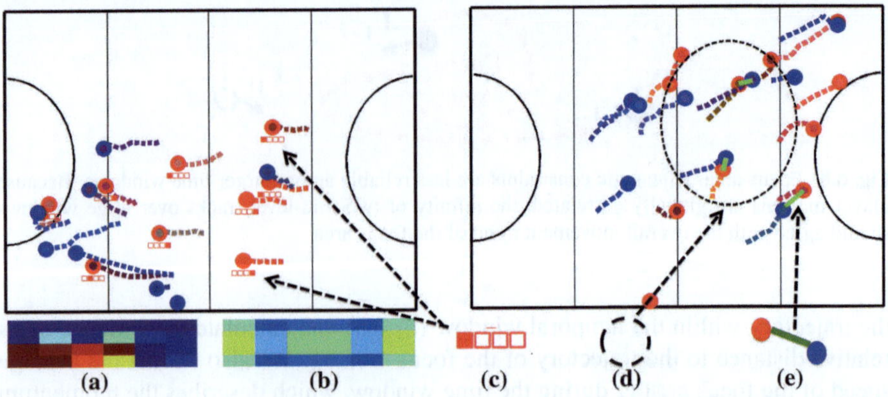

Fig. 6.10 Visualization of all game context features, where detections of different teams are plotted as *blue* and *red* dots. **a** The computed occupancy map based on noisy player detection; **b** the corresponding cluster center of the global occupancy map; **c** indicator of the role categories of each player based on its local relative occupancy map; **d** the focus area; and **e** chasing between players from different teams

$$\theta_{ij}^{(C)} = \min_{k=1,\ldots/i,j} \{\tau_{ij|k}\}. \tag{6.9}$$

Intuitively, the likelihood that (Γ_i, Γ_j) correspond to the same player increases as $\theta_{ij}^{(C)}$ decreases.

A visualization of all game context features is shown in Fig. 6.10. Features based on position appear on the left. The computed instantaneous occupancy map (a) and its corresponding cluster center (b) are shown underneath. Each mid-level track is assigned to one of the four role categories based on its local relative occupancy map as indicated in (c). Features based on motion appear on the right. The focus area (d) is shown as a dashed ellipse, and (e) detected correlated movements between opposition players is illustrated using green lines.

6.5 Context-Conditioned Motion Models

Although we have introduced a set of context features $\theta = \{\theta^{(A)}, \theta^{(R)}, \theta^{(F)}, \theta^{(C)}\}$, it is nontrivial to design a single fusion method for generating the final motion likelihood score. For instance, each game context feature may have varying importance between different sports. For example, the chasing-based feature is less important in sports where one-on-one defense is less common. To make our framework general across different sports, we use a purely data-driven approach to learn a motion model which uses both the traditional kinematic features as well as our game context features.

The kinematic features $\mathbf{K} = \{t_g, e_0, e_1, e_2, \Delta\mathbf{v}\}$ describe the motion smoothness between two successive mid-level tracks $\Gamma_i \rightarrow \Gamma_j$, and is based on the distance error with extrapolate constant position, constant velocity, and constant acceleration models, respectively. Additionally, the velocity change in velocity is also included (see Table 6.1).

We generate training data by extracting kinematic features $f_{ij}^{(K)}$ and game context features θ_{ij} for all pairs of mid-level tracks (Γ_i, Γ_j) that have a temporal gap $t_{g|i \rightarrow j} \in [0, 60)$ seconds. Using ground truth tracking data, we assign binary labels $y_{ij} \in \{1, 0\}$ indicating whether the association is correct or not (two trajectories belonging to the same ground truth player identity). However, the total number of incorrect associations are usually much more than the correct ones. To avoid severely unbalanced training data, we only select a subset of hard negative examples that has high motion smoothness.

A random forest containing 500 decision trees is then trained to learn the mapping $C(f_{ij}^{(k)}, \theta_{ij}) \rightarrow y_{ij}$. A random forest is robust against the overfitting that might occur when using limited training data via bootstrapping, especially when the data is not easily separable due to association ambiguity in the real world. More importantly, by recursively splitting the data with random subsets of features, the random forest model automatically optimizes local adaptivity, i.e., decisions for linking pairs of tracks having small or large temporal gaps may be split at different levels and handled with different feature sets. As confirmed in our experiments (see Sect. 6.6), the occupancy feature is more effective at handling short-term association (when feature t_g is small) and the chasing feature is more important in connecting trajectories with long temporal gaps (t_g is big).

During the testing stage, the average classification score across all trees provides a continuous affinity score to approximate $P(\Gamma_i \rightarrow \Gamma_j|\theta) = C(f_{ij}^{(K)}, \theta_{ij})$ in Eq. (6.5).

Table 6.1 Our context-conditioned motion models employ traditional kinematic features [10], such as the position extrapolation error when joining two tracks across a temporal gap

Feature ID	Symbol	Meaning
1	t_g	Temporal gap duration
2	e_0	Const-position extrapolation error
3	e_1	Const-velocity extrapolation error
4	e_2	Const-acceleration extrapolation error
5	$\Delta\mathbf{v}$	Change in velocity
6	σ_{ij}	Motion correlation with focus area
7	v_f	Velocity of focus area
8	d_{ij}	Consistency of local relative player distribution
9–12	k_i, k_j	Local occupancy cluster encoded into binary digit
13–14	$\theta_{ij}^{(A)}$	Global occupancy cluster encoded into binary digit
15	$\theta_{ij}^{(C)}$	Chasing gap

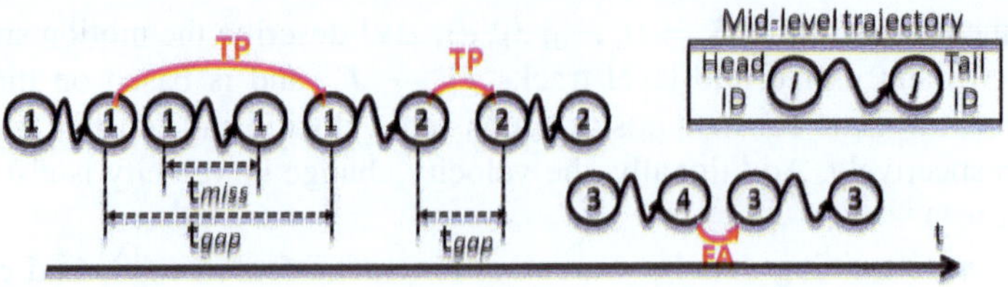

Fig. 6.11 Demonstration of evaluation metrics for high-level association (*red*)

6.6 Experiments

We validate our framework on two sports: field hockey with 20 players and basketball with 10 players. Player detection is transformed from multiple calibrated views using the method in [7] with frame rates of 30 (hockey) and 25 (basketball), respectively. We use simple RGB-based color histogram classifiers to estimate the confidence score $a_i \in [0, 1]$ of track i belonging to home team or the away team. We also discard tracks likely to correspond to the referees and goalies.

6.6.1 *Baseline Models and Evaluation Metrics*

To verify the contribution of the various *GCF*s, we construct five models for a quantitative comparison. All models apply hierarchical association and start with the same set of mid-level tracks $\{\Gamma\}$. The only difference between the models is the motion affinity used during the final association stage. Model 1 (K) only uses kinematic features ($f^{(K)}$) for training, which is equivalent to the combined algorithm of [10, 15, 30]. Models 2–4 use focus area features (F), chasing related features (C), and occupancy feature ($A + R$), respectively, in addition to motion-smoothness features. Model 5 uses all features ($f^{(K)}, \theta$).

We have also examined other features for describing aspects of game context, such as variance of track velocity or team separability. However we found these features to be less effective than the ones described in Sect. 6.4.

Three errors are commonly evaluated in the multitarget tracking literature: (1) the number of incorrect associations N_{err}, (2) the number of missed detections N_{miss}, and (3) the number of false detections N_{fa}. The Multiple Object Tracking Accuracy measure $MOTA = 1 - (N_{\text{err}} + N_{\text{miss}} + N_{\text{fa}})/N$ combines all three errors with equal weighting. However the equal weighting de-emphasizes N_{err} in a hierarchical association framework with a high frame rate. Therefore, we report the individual error sources and normalize for the situation of a known fixed number of objects: N^*_{err} is an average count of incorrect ID associations per minute per player; P_{miss} and P_{fa} are the proportion of missed and false mid-level trajectory segments of $\mathcal{T}_n$ as compared to the ground truth, ranging from 0 to 1.

In addition to overall tracking performance, we also evaluate in isolation the high-level association stage $\{\Gamma\} \rightarrow \mathcal{T}$, which is the key part of our framework. We report

Table 6.2 Quantitative evaluations on field hockey dataset

Features	N^*_{err}	P_{miss}	P_{fa}	Precision	Recall	$\bar{t}_{\mathrm{gap}}$ (s)
Kinematic	0.84	0.131	0.032	0.69	0.97	3.68
Kinematic + Focus	0.81	0.129	0.032	0.71	0.97	3.97
Kinematic + Chasing	0.82	0.128	0.032	0.70	0.97	3.56
Kinematic + Occupancy	0.80	0.128	0.033	0.71	**0.98**	3.62
All	**0.75**	**0.126**	**0.031**	**0.75**	0.97	3.95

association precision and recall rate, where precision $= N_{\mathrm{TP}}/(N_{\mathrm{TP}}+N_{\mathrm{FA}})$, and N_{TP}, N_{FA} are correct/incorrect number of associations of $\Gamma_l \rightarrow \Gamma_j$. We define recall $= 1 - T_{\mathrm{miss}}/T_{\mathrm{gap}}$, where T_{gap} is the accumulation of temporal gaps t_{gap} between high-level associations, and T_{miss} is the total length of mid-level tracks Γ_l being missed. The motivation is to exclude miss-associations in previous stages. An illustration of these metrics is given in Fig. 6.11. Finally, we also report the statistics of average length temporal gap $\bar{t}_{\mathrm{gap}}$ being correctly associated during the high-level association, which reflects the algorithm's ability to associate trajectories with long-term misses.

6.6.2 Field Hockey Dataset

We generated and labeled six field hockey sequences for a total length of 29 min, from three games played by different teams. The average player detection miss and false-alarm rates are 14.0 and 10.3 %, respectively, or the multitarget detection accuracy MODA $= 1 - (N_{\mathrm{miss}} + N_{\mathrm{fa}})/N = 0.75$. Our first experiment uses as much training data as possible: testing one sequence and using the remaining five for training.

The introduction of each individual *GCF* achieves better performance, and using all *GCF*s generally produces the best performance (see Table 6.2).

According to Table 6.2, all methods are good in terms of low false-alarm rate. Thus the major difference in their performances is reflected in the terms for incorrect association N^*_{err} and miss association P_{err}.

We can also introduce a weighting w_m on motion likelihood relative to the appearance likelihood into the objective function of Eq. (6.1), where w_m plays an essential role in the trade-off between miss-associations and false associations:

$$\log P(\mathscr{T}|\mathscr{O},\theta) = \log P(O|\mathscr{T}) + w_m \cdot \log P(\mathscr{T}|\theta) + c. \qquad (6.10)$$

Instead of the default setting of $w_m = 1$, a lower weight for the motion likelihood ($w_m < 1$) gives higher priority to optimizing the observation likelihood $P(O|\Gamma)$, which prefers to have fewer missing players. On the other hand, a higher weighting $w_m > 1$ encourages smoother motions and results in fewer false alarms but more missed detections. As we vary w_m from 0.2 to 3, the tradeoff curves are plotted in Fig. 6.12a.

Table 6.3 Quantitative evaluations on basketball dataset

Features	N^*_{err}	P_{miss}	P_{fa}	Precision	Recall	$\bar{t}_{gap}$ (s)
Kinematic	4.33	0.30	0.027	0.65	0.99	3.26
Kinematic + Focus	4.43	0.280	0.031	0.67	0.99	3.99
Kinematic + Chasing	**0.380**	**0.280**	0.024	0.71	0.99	5.09
Kinematic + Occupancy	4.32	0.280	0.025	0.68	0.99	3.60
All	3.81	0.281	**0.018**	**0.71**	**0.99**	3.81

We also conduct an experiment studying the cross-game-generalization of the *GCF*s. Instead of testing 1 sequence trained on the other 5, we perform all pairwise combinations (30 in total) of 1 sequence training with 1 other sequence testing. We then evaluate the resulting statistics for same-game learning and different-game learning, respectively, as summarized in Table 6.3.

It can be seen that the introduction of *GCFs* again improves the result both in the case of same-game and different-game learning, yet this time the amount of training data used is much smaller (4 min on average). On the other hand, same-game learning outperforms cross-game learning in terms of generalization, which matches our intuition that the game context features are more similar within the same game with the same players, e.g., the team distribution/tactics and the velocity/acceleration of players are more consistent.

6.6.3 Basketball Dataset

We also conduct the same evaluation on a basketball dataset of four sequences for a total length of more than 5 min. The dataset is more challenging due to a higher player density and less training data. Each sequence is tested while using the other three sequences for training. The average testing performance is reported in the trade-off curve of Fig. 6.12b and Table 6.4. As can be seen, the chasing feature is much more important for basketball sequences, indicating that one-on-one defensive situations occur more frequently in basketball than field hockey.

6.6.4 Classifier

In addition to random forests, we also examined the performance of linear SVMs for representing context-conditioned motion models. We utilize all the training data for a fivefold cross-validation scheme and evaluate the RoC curves (see Fig. 6.13). The experiments suggest the underlying motion models are not linear functions of the features because random forests outperform SVMs in all parameter configurations.

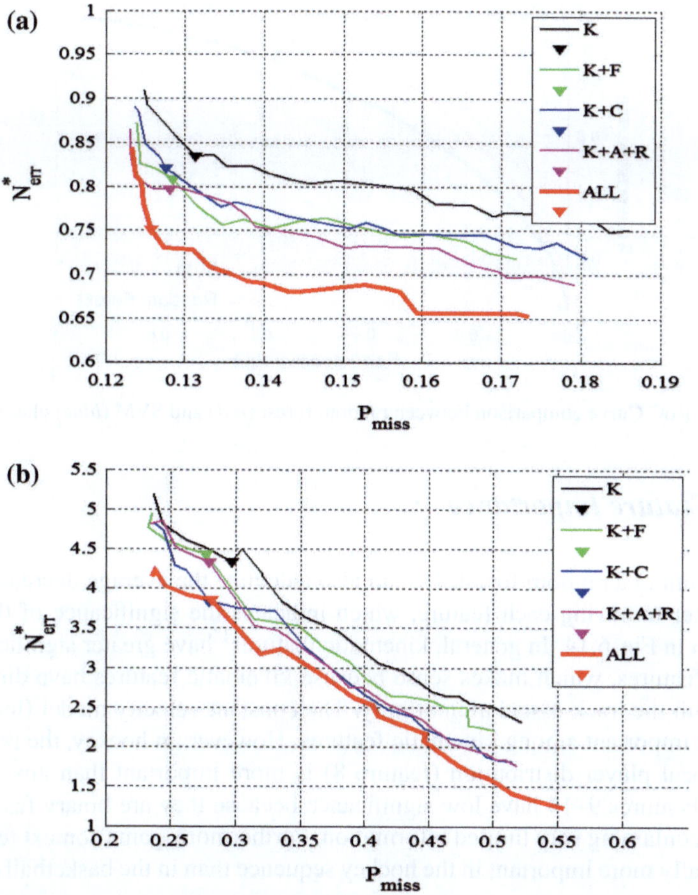

Fig. 6.12 Trade-off curve between P_{miss} and N^*_{err} for **a** field hockey sequences and **b** basketball sequences. N^*_{err} is an averaged association error per minute per person. The *triangle* marks indicate the default operating point ($w_m = 1$ in Eq. (6.10)). Our proposed method using all *GCF*s achieves more than 10 % of improvements on both cases

Table 6.4 Comparison of same/cross-game learning (hockey)

Features	Same game			Different game		
	N^*_{err}	P_{miss}	P_{fa}	N^*_{err}	P_{miss}	P_{fa}
Kinematic	0.810	0.141	0.034	1.240	0.130	0.036
Kinematic + Focus	0.840	**0.133**	0.034	1.230	0.125	0.034
Kinematic + Chasing	0.780	0.134	0.034	1.190	0.127	0.035
Kinematic + Occupancy	0.780	0.136	0.034	1.170	0.126	0.034
All	**0.770**	0.134	**0.033**	**1.140**	**0.124**	**0.034**

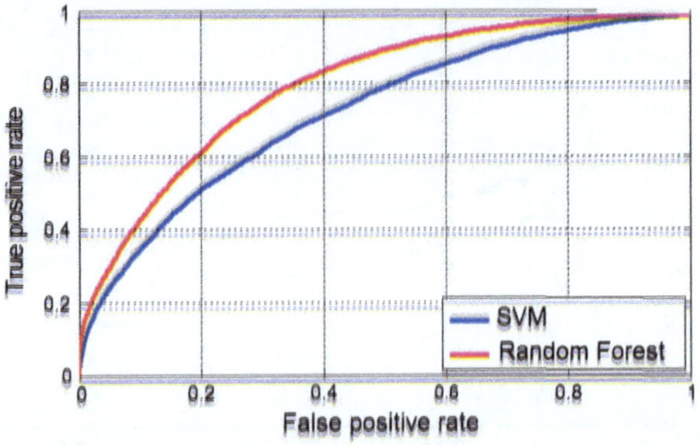

Fig. 6.13 RoC Curve comparison between random forest (*red*) and SVM (*blue*) classifier

6.6.5 Feature Importance

When training a random forest, we can also calculate the average decrease in Gini-index after removing each feature, which indicates the significance of the feature as shown in Fig. 6.14. In general, kinematic features[1] have greater significance than context features, which makes sense because kinematic features have direct correlation with the track association affinity. The constant velocity model (feature 3) is the most important among kinematic features. However, in hockey, the consistency of the local player distribution (feature 8) is more important than any kinematic feature. Features 9–14 have low significance because they are binary features with each bit containing very limited information. Furthermore, game context features are individually more important in the hockey sequence than in the basketball sequence.

6.7 Summary

In this work, we use hierarchical association to track multiple players in team sports over long periods of time. Although the motions of players are complex and highly correlated with teammates and opponents, the short-term movement of each player is often reactive to the current situation. Using this insight, we define a set of game context features and decompose the motion likelihood of all players into independent per-player models contingent on game state. Higher order interplayer dependencies are implicitly encoded into a random decision forest based on track and game context features. Because the conditioned model decomposes into pairwise terms, our formulation remains efficiently solvable using cost flow networks. We validate our approach on 30 min of international field hockey and 10 min of college basketball.

[1] Refer to Table 6.1 for the meaning of each feature number.

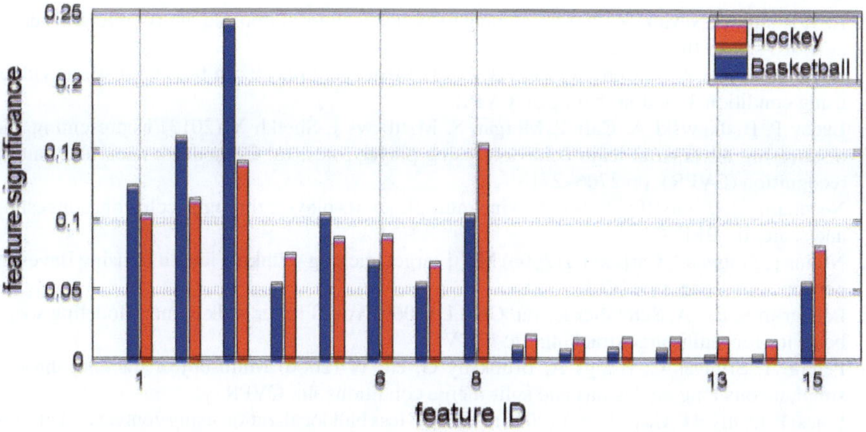

Fig. 6.14 Normalized feature significance in hockey (*red*) and basketball (*blue*) sequences

In both sports, motion models conditioned on game context features consistently improve tracking results by more than 10 %.

References

1. Ali S, Shah M (2008) Floor fields for tracking in high density crowd scenes. In: ECCV
2. Amit kumar KC, Vleeschouwer CD (2013) Discriminative label propagation for multi-object tracking with sporadic appearance features. In: ICCV
3. Andriyenko A, Schindler K (2011) Multi-target tracking by continuous energy minimization. In: CVPR
4. Andriyenko A, Schindler K, Roth S (2012) Discrete-continuous optimization for multi-target tracking. In: CVPR
5. Brendel W, Amer M, Todorovic S (2011) Multiobject tracking as maximum weight independent set. In: CVPR
6. Cai Y, de Freitas N, Little J (2006) Robust visual tracking for multiple targets. In: ECCV
7. Carr P, Sheikh Y, Matthews I (2012) Monocular object detection using 3d geometric primitives. In: ECCV
8. Collins R (2012) Multi-target data association with higher-order motion models. In: CVPR
9. Du W, Hayet J, Piater J, Verly J (2006) Collaborative multi-camera tracking of athletes in team sports, In: Workshop on computer vision based analysis in sport environments
10. Huang C, Wu B, Nevatia R (2008) Robust object tracking by hierachical association of detection responses. In: ECCV
11. Jiang H, Fels S, Little J (2007) A linear programming approach for multiple object tracking. In: CVPR
12. Khan Z, Balch TR, Dellaert F (2004) An MCMC-based particle filter for tracking multiple interacting targets. In: ECCV
13. Kim K, Grundmann M, Shamir A, Matthews I, Hodgins J, Essa I (2010) Motion fields to predict play evolution in dynamic sport scenes: In: CVPR
14. Kristan M, Pers J, Perse M, Kovacic S (2009) Closed-world tracking of multiple interacting targets for indoor-sports applications. CVIU 113(5):598–611

15. Li Y, Huang C, Nevatia R (2009) Learning to associate: hybrid-boosted multi-target tracker for crowded scene. In: CVPR
16. Lu W-L, Ting J-A, Murphy K, Little J (2011) Identifying players in broadcast sports videos using conditional random fields. In: CVPR
17. Lucey P, Bialkowski A, Carr P, Morgan S, Matthews I, Sheikh Y (2013) Representing and discovering adversarial team behaviors using player roles. In: Computer vision and pattern recognition (CVPR), pp 2706–2713
18. Needham CJ, Boyle RD (2001) Tracking multiple sports players through occlusion, congestion and scale. In: BMVC
19. Nillius P, Sullivan J, Carlsson S (2006) Multi-target tracking—linking identities using Bayesian network inference. In: CVPR
20. Pellegrini S, Ess A, Schindler K, van Gool L (2009) You'll never walk alone: Modeling social behavior for multi-target tracking. In: ICCV
21. Perera A, Srinivas C, Hoogs A, Brooksby G, Hu W (2006) Multi-object tracking through simultaneous long occlusions and split-merge conditions. In: CVPR
22. Poiesi F, Daniyal F, Cavallaro A (2010) Detector-less ball localization using context and motion flow analysis. In: ICIP
23. Rodriguez M, Ali S, Kanade T (2009) Tracking in unstructured crowded scenes. In: ICCV
24. Santiago C, Sousa A, Estriga M, Reis L, Lames M (2010) Survey on team tracking techniques applied to sports. In: AIS, pp 1–6
25. Shitrit H, Berclaz J, Fleuret F, Fua P (2011) Tracking multiple people under global appearance constraints. In: ICCV
26. Shitrit H, Berclaz J, Fleuret F, Fua P (2013) Multi-commodity network flow for tracking multiple people. In: PAMI
27. Xing J, Ai H, Liu L, Lao S (2011) Multiple player tracking in sports video: a dual-mode two-way Bayesian inference approach with progressive observation modeling. Trans Image Process 20(6):1652–1667
28. Yang B, Nevatia R (2012) Multi-target tracking by online learning of non-linear motion patterns and robust appearance models. In: CVPR
29. Yu T, Wu Y (2004) Collaborative tracking of multiple targets. In: CVPR
30. Zhang L, Li Y, Nevatia R (2008) Global data association for multi-object tracking using network flows. In: CVPR
31. Zhang T, Ghanem B, Ahuja N (2012) Robust multi-object tracking via cross-domain contextual information for sports video analysis. In: ICASSP
32. Zhao X, Gong D, Medioni G (2012) Tracking using motion patterns for very crowded scenes. In: ECCV

Chapter 7
Geometry Reconstruction of Players for Novel-View Synthesis of Sports Broadcasts

Tiberiu Popa, Marcel Germann, Remo Ziegler, Richard Keiser and Markus Gross

Abstract In this chapter, we present two methods for geometric reconstruction of players in standard sports broadcasts specifically designed to enable the broadcast director to generate novel views from locations where there is no physical camera (novel-view synthesis). This will significantly broaden the creative freedom of the director greatly enhancing the viewing experience. First, we propose a data-driven method based on multiview body pose estimation. This method can operate in uncontrolled environments with loosely calibrated and low resolution cameras and without restricting assumptions on the family of possible poses or motions. Second, we propose a scalable top-down patch-based method that reconstructs the geometry of the players adaptively based on the amount of detail available in the video streams. These methods are complementary to each other and together provides a more complete set of tools for novel-view synthesis for sport broadcasts.

7.1 Introduction

Novel-view video synthesis is an area of active research in computer vision whose goal is to produce views of a scene from a camera position where there is no physical camera present (i.e., virtual camera). It has a large variety of applications including

T. Popa (✉)
Concordia University, Montreal, Canada
e-mail: tiberiu.popa@concordia.ca

M. Germann · M. Gross
ETH Zurich, Zurich, Switzerland
e-mail: eth@masi.li

M. Gross
e-mail: grossm@inf.ethz.ch

R. Ziegler · R. Keiser
Vizrt Switzerland, Nyon, Switzerland
e-mail: rziegler@vizrt.com

R. Keiser
e-mail: rkeiser@vizrt.com

T.B. Moeslund et al. (eds.), *Computer Vision in Sports*,
Advances in Computer Vision and Pattern Recognition,
DOI 10.1007/978-3-319-09396-3_7

telepresence, games, movie production, interactive TV sports broadcasts, etc. This chapter focuses on novel-view video synthesis from conventional sports broadcasts footage [1, 2]. The goal is to extend the creative freedom of an editor or director by providing the possibility to place a virtual camera in the stadium without having to change or add anything in the already existing physical camera setup: no additional cameras or other sensor modalities and no additional constraints to the existing cameras' position or motion.

Typical novel-view synthesis pipelines [3], first, reconstructs the textured geometry of the scene by calibrating the existing video cameras and applying multiview stereo algorithms. Second, they render it from a new view point. As noted in [1, 4, 5] for sports broadcasts this is very challenging due to several factors. There are typically only few moving cameras available that cover the interesting part of the scene and can be calibrated. In some sports, they are positioned only on one side of the stadium. Although the cameras provide high resolution images, they are usually set to be wide angle for editorial reasons. Therefore, an individual player covers only a height between 50 and 200 pixels [1] (Fig. 7.1 Left). In sports broadcasts, the player motion is usually fast and thus often results in motion blur. Methods for per frame automatic calibration in such setups [6] suffer from errors and typically contain no radiometric calibration (Fig. 7.1 Right). All these factors have to be circumvented in order to create a convincing novel-view synthesis.

One key observation is that the field of play is for many sports planar and thus it is only the geometry of the players that has to be computed. Some of the most popular approaches in this field still use simple planar billboards [7] to represent the geometry of a player. Unfortunately, this approximation is not sufficient and invariably produces unwanted visual artifacts like ghosting.

In this chapter, we present two methods that can be used to robustly reconstruct the geometry of the player under challenging conditions with sufficient accuracy to be used for high-quality novel-view synthesis. The first method [5] is based on pose estimation of the players (Fig. 7.2). If the pose of each player is correctly reconstructed in 3D, the geometry of the players can be approximated using an articulated

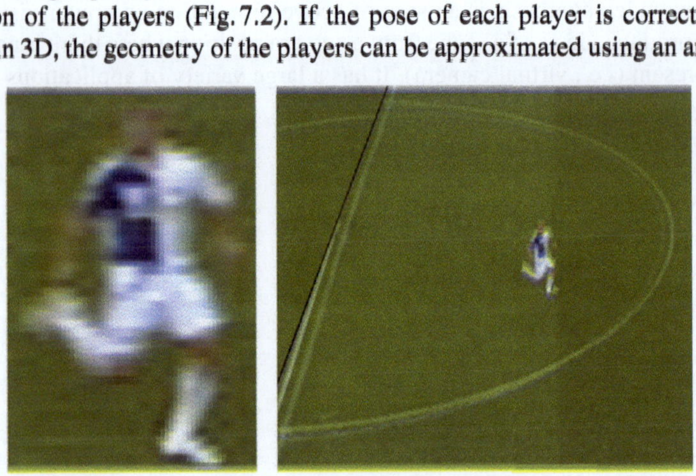

Fig. 7.1 *Left* Resolution of input images. *Right* Example with calibration errors visible on the ground as ghosting of lines

Fig. 7.2 Estimated poses in a soccer game. The image shows a projection of the 3D skeletons into a source camera

Fig. 7.3 Novel-view synthesis using our *top-down*, adaptive patch-based reconstruction technique: **a** and **b** Closeups of the two source camera images used. **c** Our reconstruction of the same view

template or articulated billboards [8] yielding good novel-view synthesis results. The second method [9] uses a robust, adaptive, top-down reconstruction technique that starts with a course initial geometry that is gradually refined based on color consistency (Fig. 7.3). These two methods are complementary: they use radically different approaches and thus they have different pros and cons. Therefore, depending on the particular context one might be more desirable than the other. A comparative analysis of these two methods will be provided at the end of this chapter.

7.2 Robust Data-Driven Pose Estimation of Players in Sport Broadcast Footage

Pose estimation or motion capture is a fundamental problem in computer vision [10, 11] with many applications. Many current commercially available motion capture systems [12] typically use optical markers placed all over the body to track the motion over time. These systems are very accurate, however, they are invasive and work under controlled environment. Therefore, they are unsuitable for our setup.

Markerless motion capture methods based on multiple video footage have received a lot of attention in the last decade [10, 11]. Most methods for multiple views 3D pose estimation use tracking algorithms to reconstruct the pose at time t from the pose at time $t - 1$ [13]. The tracking can be done either using optical flow [13] or stereo matching [14]. These methods can provide very accurate pose estimation, but they generally work in a controlled environment, require larger number of high-resolution cameras (usually at least four) and good spatial coverage of the scene (usually circular coverage) to resolve ambiguities due to occlusions. Other methods [15–17] construct a proxy geometry either using multiview silhouettes or multiview stereo. The skeleton is then fitted into this geometry. These methods provide very good results, but impose restrictions on the setup. They require a carefully built studio setup, many high-resolution cameras, and very good spatial coverage. Another class of algorithms is based on image analysis and segmentation [18, 19]. These algorithms use machine learning methods to discriminate between body parts. This analysis generally requires high-resolution footage, which is not available in our setup.

Due to the complexity of the problem, there still does not exist a universal solution for all the applications. The solutions strongly depend on the conditions and on the constraints imposed on the setup. In this chapter, we focus on pose estimation based on unconstrained broadcast footage. This implies several challenges to camera positions, object size, and temporal coherence. Although, the pose estimation can be computed based on a multicamera setup, there are only few cameras available, which additionally feature wide baselines. Moreover, the cameras are typically placed only on one side of the field providing limited coverage of the scene. The cameras provide high-resolution images, but are usually set to be wide angle for editorial reasons. Therefore, players typically cover only a height between 50 and 200 pixels. Furthermore, the motion of the players can be very complex and, especially in contact sports like football, there is a lot of occlusion.

We present a data-driven pose estimation algorithm that can operate in an uncontrolled, outdoors environment with loosely calibrated cameras, low resolution players, and in presence of occlusions. Our algorithm can use as little as only two cameras to estimate the pose. No restricting assumption is made on the family of possible poses or motions. By using temporal coherence for the initial pose estimation as well as pose refinement, the user interaction is limited to few clicks inverting arms and legs in failure cases. We use a database of poses and silhouette comparison to extract pose candidates in 2D and use camera calibration information to compute the corresponding 3D skeleton. We first perform a novel time consistent silhouette-based search in the database to extract the closest database candidate with temporal coherence. An additionally applied novel time consistency step is leading to the initial pose estimation. Because the exact real pose is generally not in the database, this will only result in a closest match, but not in an accurate pose. Therefore, we developed a novel space–time optimization technique that leverages the temporal information to automatically compute the accurate 3D pose.

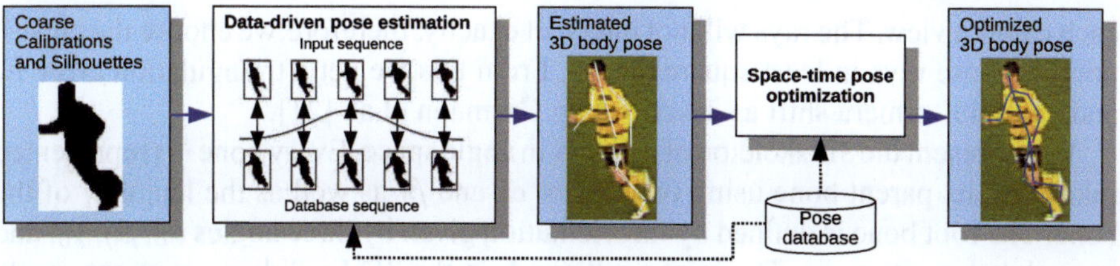

Fig. 7.4 Algorithm overview. *Left* the silhouettes obtained from each camera. *Middle* the estimated 3D pose obtained from queried to the motion capture database. *Right* the final 3D pose after the optimization procedure

7.2.1 Overview

Our algorithm consists of two steps as illustrated in Fig. 7.4. In the first step, the algorithm extracts 2D poses for each individual camera view using a spatial–temporal silhouette matching technique, yielding a triangulated 3D pose guess. This pose detection is inherently prone to ambiguities, namely left-right flips of symmetrical parts. Although the skeleton matches the silhouettes quite well, the arms or legs of the player can still be flipped. Due to occlusions and low resolution, these ambiguities are sometimes very difficult to spot even for the human eye. Therefore, we employ an optical flow-based technique to detect the cases where flips occur, and correct them to obtain a consistent sequence. It is important to note that optical flow is in such setups not reliable enough for tracking the entire motion of a player's body parts over an entire sequence, but it can be used for local comparisons as shown by Efros et al. [20].

However, in general, no pose from the database will match the actual pose exactly. As a consequence, in the second part of the algorithm, this initial 3D pose is refined by an optimization procedure, which is based on spatio-temporal constraints. The resulting optimized 3D skeleton matches the silhouettes from all views and features temporal consistency over consecutive frames.

The following sections present the algorithm in more detail. Section 7.2.2 describes how the initial pose is obtained. The optimization procedure to obtain the final, more accurate pose estimation is presented in Sect. 7.2.3. Finally, a selection of the results are presented in Sect. 7.2.4.

7.2.2 Initial Pose Estimation

The initial pose estimation is computed by first retrieving the 2D pose from each player and each camera view using a novel space–time data-driven silhouette-ased search. Once we find the 2D poses for every player in every camera, we can use the calibration information from the cameras to lift the 2D joints to 3D. We compute the 3D location of each joint by intersecting the rays corresponding to each 2D joint in each camera view. The rays will not intersect exactly, therefore,we choose the closest point to these rays in least-squares sense. From this,we get a triangulation error E_t and an initial camera shift as described by Germann et al. [21].

We represent the 3D skeleton of a pose S in angle space. Every bone i is represented relative to its parent bone using two angles α_i and β_i as well as the length l_i of the bone. The root bone is defined by its orientation given by three angles $\alpha_0, \beta_0, \gamma_0$, and by a global position p_0. The joint positions $\mathbf{j}_i$ in the 3D Euclidian space can easily be computed from this representation and vice versa.

7.2.2.1 Pose Database Construction

A large database that samples the entire range of human motion is important for our algorithm and is very difficult to create manually. Therefore, we use the CMU motion capture database [22]. A template mesh rigged with the same skeleton is deformed using linear blend skinning to match the pose of the database pose. From this,virtual snapshots are taken and the silhouette is extracted. This way we created a database of around 20,000 silhouettes.

Unfortunately, the CMU database has only a limited number of types of poses, mostly from running and walking sequences. Therefore, we manually added a set of 900 silhouettes from several soccer scenes. Figure 7.5 shows some database poses taken from real scenes. This is significantly fewer than the ones generated automatically, but enough to enlarge the span of example poses to obtain good results. It is important to note that the added example poses were not taken from the same sequences as we used to fit the poses. The database could continuously be enlarged by newly generated poses, resulting in a better initial pose estimation.

7.2.2.2 2D Pose Estimation

Similar to Germann et al. [21], we assume as an input a coarse binary silhouette mask for each player as well as coarse camera calibrations. We compare these silhouettes against the silhouettes from the database using the technique presented by Germann et al., that computes the quality of a match between the input silhouette and a database silhouette on a fix raster size (grid with height = 40 and width = 32) that is fitted to the segmentation.

Fig. 7.5 Example of database poses taken from real soccer footage

The silhouette extraction extends the algorithm presented by Germann et al. by leveraging temporal information. Instead of relying on a single frame matching, our approach considers a weighted sum of differences over a sequence. The resulting pixel error $E_q(s)$ of the binary input silhouette image I with index t based on the silhouette image I'_s with index s from the database is evaluated as follows:

$$E_q(s) = \sum_{i \in \{-\frac{n}{2},\dots,\frac{n}{2}\}} \theta_s(i) \frac{1}{|P|} \sum_{p \in P} |I_{t+i}(p) - I'_{s+i}(p)|. \tag{7.1}$$

n is the filter window size, and P is the set of all raster positions where the corresponding pixel is in both images not possibly occluded, i.e., part of another player's silhouette. The weights $\theta_s(i)$ describe a normalized Gaussian function with the center around s. For $I'_{s+i}(p)$ not included in the database, $\theta_s(i)$ is set to 0 before the normalization. Comparing sequences instead of single images, does not only add temporal coherence resulting in smooth motions, but also improves pose estimation. Even image parts occluded over few frames can be fitted more robustly. In general, this approach helps to prevent matching a silhouette that is similar but originated from a completely different pose.

Using this energy function, we search for each camera view for the best two pose hypotheses and select the best combination of those by choosing the lowest resulting triangulation error E_t.

7.2.2.3 Pose Consistency

The 2D pose detection step relies on silhouette matching, and therefore, is prone to ambiguities. Given a silhouette and an initial 2D pose for it taken from the database, we cannot decide if the labelings of left/right in arms and legs are correct. Figure 7.6 shows an example silhouette with two possible labelings for the legs. Figure 7.6 (left) and Fig. 7.6 (right) show two inconsistent labeling in the two cameras. Without additional information we cannot decide in such a situation which positions are correct, i.e., select the only one correct out of the four possibilities—especially when only two cameras are available. To correctly solve these ambiguities, we propose a two-step approach: first, the local consistency between each pair of consecutive 2D frames is resolved, resulting in an entire sequence of temporally consistent 2D poses. Second, the entire sequence is resolved globally.

Local Consistency. The goal of this step is to make sure that the 2D pose recovered from a camera at frames k and $k+1$ are consistent (i.e., there are no flips of arms or legs between consecutive frames). In other words, if a pixel at frame k belongs to the right leg, it should belong to the same leg in the frame $k+1$ as well. To assure this assumption, we assign to each pixel in both color images I_{C_k} and $I_{C_{k+1}}$ a corresponding bone, and we compute the optical flow [23] between the frames. The underlying idea is that a pixel in frame k and its corresponding pixel in frame $k+1$, computed using optical flow, should be assigned to the same bone. Therefore,

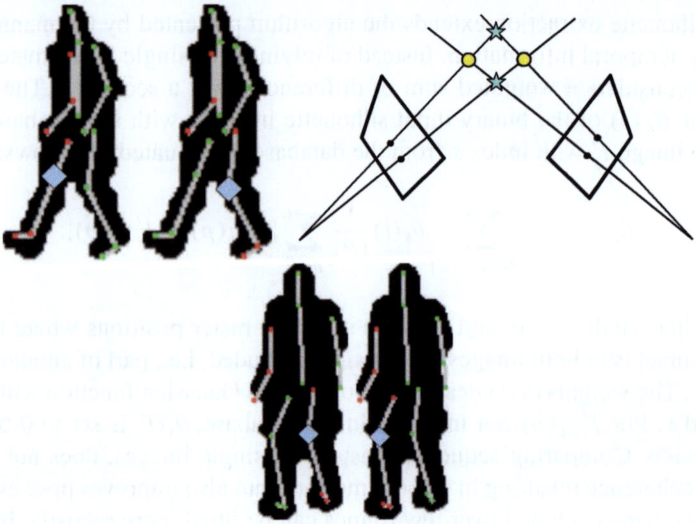

Fig. 7.6 Example for pose ambiguities. *Left* Possible labelings in first camera. *Middle* Schematic view from the *top* to illustrate the two possible positions of the knees. *Right* Possible labelings in the second camera

we compute this association for all combinations of possible labelings, compute the consistency of the pixels, and select the most consistent label configuration for the second frame. To make the approach more robust in respect to optical flow errors, we only consider pixels with good optical flow and where the corresponding pixel labels in both frames are of the same bone type, i.e., either both arms or both legs. This resolves most of the flips of arms or legs. For failure cases, the user can change the flipping for all subsequent frames of a sequence with one mouse click. This is the only user interaction in our system and for a view of a player takes only about 1 click per 10 frames.

Global Consistency. After the local consistency step, all consecutive frames should not have flips between them which means that the entire sequence is consistent. There is still the possibility that the entire sequence is flipped the wrong way. However, this is a simple problem as we only have a binary predicate to apply for the entire sequence. Therefore, the global consistency is checked for the possible global labelings of the arms and the possible global labelings of the legs. The final labeling is selected by choosing the labeling combination that minimizes the following error term:

$$E_g = \lambda_{\mathrm{DB}} E_{\mathrm{DB}} + \lambda_t E_t \qquad (7.2)$$

This is a weighted sum with constant parameters λ_{DB} and λ_t. E_{DB} ensures that the selected labeling/flipping results in plausible poses along the sequence. It penalties for the distance to the closest pose P in the database:

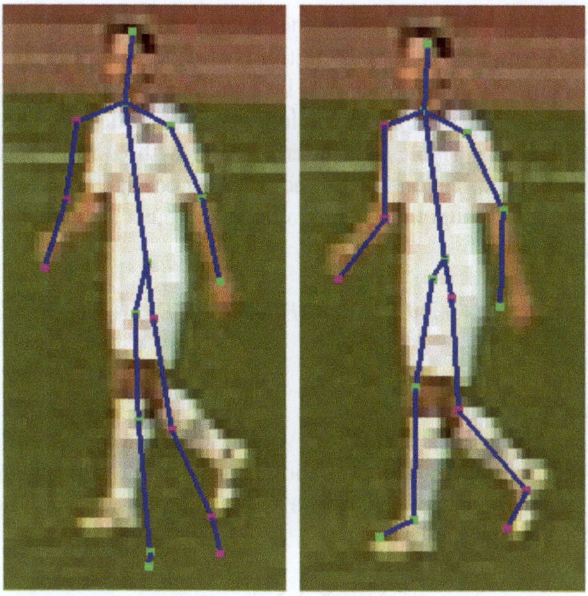

Fig. 7.7 Comparisons of the pose before (*left*) and after (*right*) the pose optimization

$$E_{\mathrm{DB}} = \min_{P} \frac{1}{2|J|} \sum_{i=0}^{|J|} (\alpha_i' - \alpha_i)^2 + (\beta_i' - \beta_i)^2 \tag{7.3}$$

where α and β are the joint angles of the triangulated joint positions J. α' and β' are the ones of the database pose P. Since the database contains only anthropometrically correct poses, this penalties for nonplausible poses.

7.2.3 Pose Optimization

The best 3D poses computed by the pose estimation are still limited to fit in each view to a pose of the database. The database is only a subset of all possible poses, and therefore, often does not contain the accurate solution. We developed a new optimization method to retrieve a more accurate pose as shown in Fig. 7.7. To guide our optimization method, we combine several spatial and temporal energy functions and minimize them using an optimization method.

7.2.3.1 Energy Function

The energy function is based on our representation of the skeleton S described in Sect. 7.2.2. All the parameters besides the bone length are variable per frame.

The lengths are also variable but stay the same over the entire sequence and are initialized as the average of the local lengths of all frames. This automatically introduces an anthropometric constraint, since bones should not shrink or grow over time. Another nice property of the chosen skeleton representation is that it significantly reduces the number of variables. In order to cope with calibration errors, we also optimize for the two-dimensional shift vector given per subject, camera, and frame.

We define our energy functional per frame and subject as the following weighted sum of error terms:

$$E(S) = \omega_s E_s + \omega_f E_f + \omega_{\text{DB}} E_{\text{DB}} + \omega_{\text{rot}} E_{\text{rot}} + \omega_p E_p + \omega_l E_l \tag{7.4}$$

Silhouette Matching Term E_s

The bones of the correct 3D skeleton should project onto the 2D silhouette in all cameras. The error term E_s penalizes the joint positions whose 2D projections are outside the silhouettes:

$$E_s = \frac{1}{|C||J_+|} \sum_{c \in C} \sum_{\mathbf{j} \in J_+} EDT_c(P_c(\mathbf{j})), \tag{7.5}$$

where C is the set of all cameras that cover a silhouette of this subject. J_+ is the union of the set J of all joints and the points that are exactly in the middle of a bone. The normalized Euclidean distance transform EDT returns for every 2D point in the camera image, the distance to the closest point inside the silhouette divided by the larger side of the silhouettes' bounding box. This normalization is important to make the error independent of the size of the subject in the camera image which may vary according to the zoom. $P_c(j)$ is the projection to transform the 3D joint $\mathbf{j}$ into camera space taking into account the camera shift.

Silhouette Filling Error Term E_f

Although the silhouette matching term E_s penalizes joints outside the silhouette, there is no restriction on them for where to be placed inside the silhouette. The filling error term E_f prevents them from just shrinking together somewhere inside the torso and especially makes sure that there are also joints in all the extremities:

$$E_f = \frac{1}{|C||R|} \sum_{c \in C} \min_{\mathbf{j} \in J} \sum_{r \in R} \text{dist}(P_c^{-1}(r), \mathbf{j}), \tag{7.6}$$

where R is the set of all grid points from Sect. 7.2.2.2 that are inside the silhouette. $P_c^{-1}(r)$ transforms such a grid point from camera space of camera c into a ray in world space while dist() describes the distance of a ray to a joint.

Distance to Database Pose E_{DB}

This was already defined in Sect. 7.2.2.3. It ensures that the final 3D pose is kinematically possible (e.g., the knee joint bends the right way) by taking into advantage the database of correct poses. It implicitly adds anthropometric constraints to our optimization.

Smoothness Error Terms E_{rot} and E_p

Human motion is generally smooth such that the skeletons of adjacent frames should be similar. This enables us to introduce temporal coherence to the pose optimization. Therefore, E_{rot} penalizes large changes of the internal angles of the skeleton of consecutive frames and E_p penalizes large motion:

$$E_{\mathrm{rot}} = \frac{1}{2|J|}\sum_{i=0}^{|J|}(\alpha_i' - \alpha_i)^2 + (\beta_i' - \beta_i)^2 \tag{7.7}$$

$$E_p = |\mathbf{p}_0 - \mathbf{p}_0'| \tag{7.8}$$

where α' and β' are the corresponding angles of the same subject in the previous frame and $\mathbf{p}_0'$ is the global position of the root joint in the previous frame. We also constraint the rotation of the root bone in a similar way, which we omitted here for simplicity.

Length Error Term E_l

The initialization of the bone lengths is already a good approximation, when handling a sequence of frames. Therefore, we try to keep the optimized pose close to these lengths:

$$E_l = \frac{1}{|J|}\sum_{i=0}^{|J|}(l_i - \hat{l}_i)^2 \tag{7.9}$$

where l_i is the final bone length and $\hat{l}_i$ is the initial bone length.

7.2.3.2 The Optimization Procedure

To minimize the energy term in Eq. 7.4, we employ a local optimization strategy where we iteratively optimize the variables one by one by performing line search along randomly picked directions [24]. For each variable, we select 10 random directions for optimization and we perform 20 global iterations. Due to the inherent non-

Table 7.1 The parameter values that we used for all our results, computed using our automatic parameter tuning system

Param.	ω_s	ω_f	ω_{db}	ω_{rot}	ω_p	ω_l	λ_{DB}	λ_t
	9	15	0.05	0.1	1	1	0.15	0.3

smooth nature of our objective functions, this method performed better in practice than Levenberg–Marquardt [25].

Figure 7.7 illustrates the effect of the optimization procedure. The leftmost example shows the influence of the silhouette filling error term: The arm of the player can be brought up or down to reduce the silhouette matching error term, but the silhouette filling error term is only reduced when moving the arm up. Figure 7.7 shows a clear improvement over the method by Germann et al. [21] which did not include a pose optimization at all and where each pose had to be corrected manually.

7.2.4 Results

We evaluated our system on four sequences of TV footage from real soccer games with two or three cameras, yielding roughly 1,500 poses to process.

For the optimization functions in Eqs. (7.4) and (7.2), we used the parameters shown in Table 7.1 for all our results.

Our pose estimation algorithm takes about 40 s per player per frame in a two-camera setup and about 60 s for a three-camera setup. We implemented a parallel version that runs a thread for every player. On an 8 core system, this gave a speedup of roughly a factor of 8.

Note that the initial pose estimation does not depend on the pose estimation of the previous frame. Thus, there is no drift and the process can recover from bad pose guesses.

Figure 7.8 shows a result of our pose estimation algorithm. Figure 7.9 shows how the pose estimation can be used to generate novel views.

7.3 Adaptive Geometry Reconstruction from Sport Broadcast Footage

The method presented in the previous chapter has two main shortcomings. First, it requires some manual intervention. When processing thousands of frames, even little manual intervention can be cumbersome. Second, it relies on a large pose database that it might not be easy to create. An alternative way to retrieve 3D geometric information is to exploit the 2D silhouettes in all the camera views and construct a visual hull of the scene, which can be used to render the scenes from an arbitrary viewpoint with the video camera images as textures [26–30]. Visual hull methods

Fig. 7.8 3D poses overlaid with the video footage

are suitable for novel-view synthesis of single objects. In crowded scenes, unless a large number of cameras are employed, extraneous so-called phantom geometry is generated [31]. Additionally, when using distant cameras, small calibration errors can cause entire arms or legs to be cut off. Guillemaut et al. [1, 4, 32] addresses many challenges for free viewpoint video in sports broadcasting by jointly optimizing scene segmentation and player reconstruction. Their approach is leading to a more accurate geometry than the visual hull, but still requires a fairly large number of cameras (6–12). Inamoto et al. [33] also use silhouettes and match dense correspondences on epipolar lines. These correspondences, will suffer from the same drawbacks as the visual hull when working with weak calibration. Also their method does only interpolate on the path between cameras whereas we allow arbitrary viewpoints in the area of the two cameras.

Rather than relying on silhouettes alone to reconstruct a proxy geometry, an alternative way is to use dense geometry reconstruction techniques [34–36]. The results are very convincing, but dense reconstruction is difficult to do in wide-baseline camera setups. An alternative approach suitable for setups where dense feature matching is difficult to accomplish, is patch-based reconstruction [37–40]. Patch-based reconstruction methods only require a sparse set of correspondences, but are limited to objects with a strong planarity assumption, and thus not suitable for reconstructing players.

Since our wide-base camera setup does not allow dense reconstruction, but it is possible to get reliable sparse matches [41], we propose a technique in the spirit of the patch-based reconstruction methods. However, instead of a bottom-up approach that tries to cluster pixels in planar patches, we propose a top-down approach that starts

Fig. 7.9 A rendering from a novel view where there is no existing video camera

by reconstructing the scene with a few large planar pieces and recursively subdivides the geometry and gradually adds geometric detail up to resolution limitations.

7.3.1 Overview

The backbone of our method is a top-down adaptive reconstruction technique that is able to retrieve a 2.5D triangulation of the players in each camera even in challenging setups consisting of only two wide-baseline cameras. The reconstruction starts with a simple triangulation (Fig. 7.10a). The triangles are placed according to a sparse 3D point cloud (Fig. 7.10b), which is generated using an extended version of the Daisy features [41]. If the triangles are too large and do not represent the shape of the object accurately (red triangles in Fig. 7.10c), they are subdivided. This process is repeated until the triangles are just small enough to approximate the shape of the object. This way the reconstruction method inherently adapts to the geometric complexity as well as to the resolution of the represented object. In an additional refinement

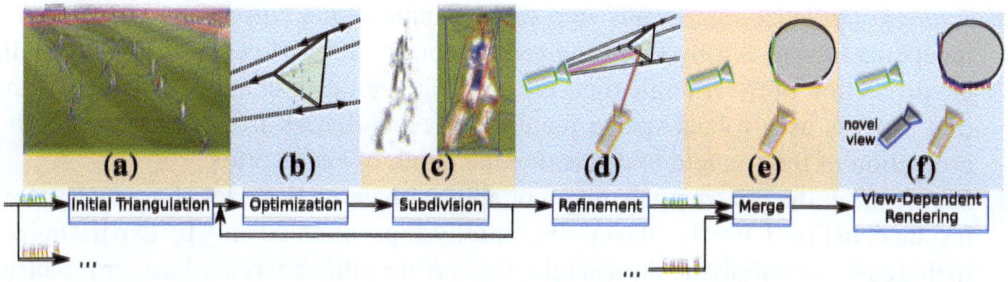

Fig. 7.10 Overview of the algorithm: **a–e** The adaptive reconstruction. **f** The view-dependent rendering

step, the vertex depths of those triangles that do not contain any features are set to optimal depth values of neighboring triangles including random perturbation tests. The adaptive level of detail and the reconstruction lead to a robust geometry. To cover also parts of the scene that are occluded in one camera, we repeat the reconstruction for each camera as a *base camera* and merge these 2.5D reconstructions into a final 3D geometry (Fig. 7.10e).

We render this geometry from an arbitrary viewpoint and blend the color information from the available cameras. However, inherent calibration errors will yield rendering artifacts such as ghosting. Therefore, we propose a method that morphs the geometry based on the viewing positions to compensate for calibration errors (Fig. 7.10f).

In Sect. 7.3.2, the adaptive reconstruction is elaborated in detail. The view-dependent geometry morph and rendering is described in Sect. 7.3.3. Our proposed method is evaluated and discussed in Sect. 7.3.4.

7.3.2 Adaptive Reconstruction

We chose to represent the geometry as a per camera triangle soup. The advantage of a triangle soup as opposed to a connected mesh is that it allows us to place these triangles independently solving implicitly for depth discontinuities. However, to avoid discontinuities on connected surface parts, we connect the triangles that are close together before the rendering stage. Our reconstruction algorithm proceeds as follows (Fig. 7.10):

1. *Initial Triangulation*: an initial set of triangles is created from the image of one of the cameras. The triangulation of this base camera is illustrated in Fig. 7.10a. The triangles are aligned with the view of the base camera such that the only degree of freedom is the depth of its vertices in camera coordinates. This allows for a low degree of freedom optimization that facilitates the process of positioning them in 3D, without sacrificing precision.

2. *Triangle Optimization*: in this step each triangle of the current set is positioned independently in 3D by optimizing the depth of its vertices only. As a result, the projection of the triangle onto the base camera never changes. The optimization process uses robust sparse feature correspondences from pixels inside the projection of the triangle to determine the depth of each vertex.
3. *Subdivision*: the 3D triangles may not approximate well the local geometry. For instance, in Fig. 7.10a the players are initially approximated only by two triangles. In this case, we subdivide the triangle if the error evaluated by a robust error metric of texture reprojection is too big. Figure 7.10c shows triangles to be subdivided in red. We repeat the optimization and subdivision step until the reprojection error is small for all triangles.
4. *Refinement*: due to occlusions and the low resolution of the image, it is not always possible to find image features in every triangle. If a triangle has no features, it inherits its vertex depths from the previous subdivision. However, these depths could be wrong and as a result we might have rendering artifacts such as missing parts of the players. To further refine the position of such triangles, we employ a heuristic to determine their 3D location based on depth guesses from the neighboring triangles combined with random perturbations.
5. *Merge:* We reconstruct a 2.5D geometry the same way for every input camera as base camera and build the union of these resulting in a final 3D reconstruction (Fig. 7.10e).

7.3.2.1 Inital Triangulation

The initial triangulation is done in 2D using a delaunay triangulation of the four corners of the image and the corners of the bounding boxes of each player (Fig. 7.10a). The bounding boxes of each player are computed automatically [42]. Note that we do not rely on an accurate bounding box detection. As one can see in Fig. 7.10a, players who are occluding each other are generally classified into one box. Also the goal keeper's box is shifted. This does not create any problems for the algorithm since it is only used as an initial triangulation. This procedure gives us a set of 2D triangles in a base camera, which we project to the ground plane to obtain an initial 3D triangle soup. The ground plane can be found automatically by the calibration method according to pitch lines such as described in [6].

7.3.2.2 Triangle Optimization

The main goal of this step is to optimize the 3D position of the triangles in the current set. The triangles are optimized independently while the only degree of freedom is the depth along the camera ray of their respective vertices as illustrated in Fig. 7.10b. Our optimization technique combines two criteria: one is based on a background color model and one based on robust feature matches.

Background Color Model.

Triangles are part of the background if more than 95 % of the pixels are classified as such by the background color model. An alternative way to accomplish this test is using a background subtraction technique as described in [43]. If the triangle is classified as background, its vertices are pushed to the ground.

The depth of nonbackground triangles relies on feature matching of pixels contained in the corresponding 2D triangles in the camera image. We first compute a robust set of matching pairs according to Sect. 7.3.2.2. Each 2D pair of matches represents a point in 3D that can be computed as the intersection of two rays. Due to calibration errors these rays usually do not intersect, and we use the point on the base camera's ray that is closest to the other ray, as explained in Sect. 7.3.3. The reconstructed set of 3D points belongs to the scene geometry of the base camera. By applying a RANSAC technique [44], we can accurately and robustly fit a plane to the set of 3D points. Once the best fitting plane is determined, we can solve for the depth values of every vertex, such that the optimized triangle lies in the plane.

Feature Matching

In order to position a triangle in 3D, we rely on image feature matching between the views. We selected Daisy features [41], which are designed for wide baselines. However, due to the low resolution of each player and the lack of features on the pitch, the feature detection contains a lot of wrongly matched pairs. Therefore, we added more constraints to the matching operator to get more reliable, and robust matches in three steps:

1. For every pixel in the base camera, we restrict the search space of possible matches in the second camera. This search space is defined by a band of $d = 20$ pixels around the epipolar line, whereof only pixels lying inside the bounding box are considered. This is illustrated as the yellow area in Fig. 7.11.
2. Only matches with a Daisy error value below 1.4 and below 0.8 times the average of the matches within this stripe are considered.
3. We verify that the match is symmetric. That is, if p_{c_0} is a pixel in the base camera and p_{c_1} is its corresponding Daisy match in the second camera, the Daisy match of pixel p_{c_1} has to lie within five pixels of p_{c_0}.

The resulting matches are a relatively sparse set of reliable matches that we use in the triangle optimization process (depending on the scene, it varies from 20 to 300 per player).

7.3.2.3 Adaptive Subdivision

If the scene geometry represented by a triangle significantly differs from a planar surface, a further subdivision of the triangle is required. The triangles are only refined if

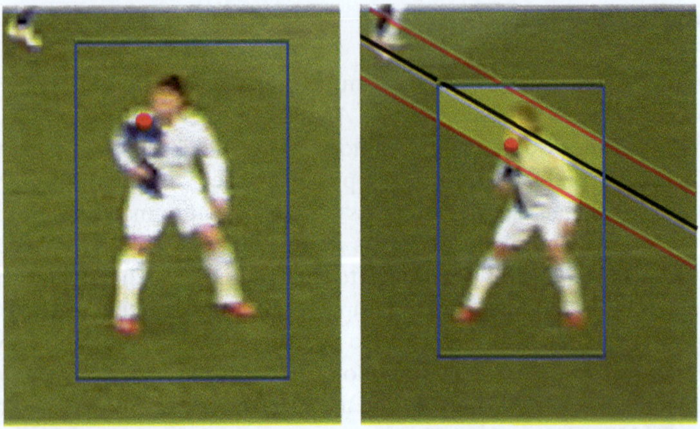

Fig. 7.11 Feature correspondence search for a pixel in the *left* image within a cropped epipolar stripe in the image of the other camera

the projective textures from the respective source cameras do not match. The resulting triangle soup only features small triangles where the underlying 3D geometry requires a refinement.

Error Metric

For every triangle, a color error value is computed to decide if the triangle has to be subdivided or not. To do so, the current geometry is used to reproject the textures from all cameras into the base camera. The error of a single triangle is then computed as the average of all pixel differences, which are not occluded in any of the cameras. To have comparable image sources, the appearances of the images are roughly adjusted by adding a compensating color shift as described in Sect. 7.3.3. An example of the initial per-pixel error viewed from the base camera is shown in Fig. 7.12 (right) where the entire geometry is approximated as the ground plane.

Fig. 7.12 Example for an initial color error when using the ground plane as the geometric proxy. The errors appear at pixels with wrong depth values

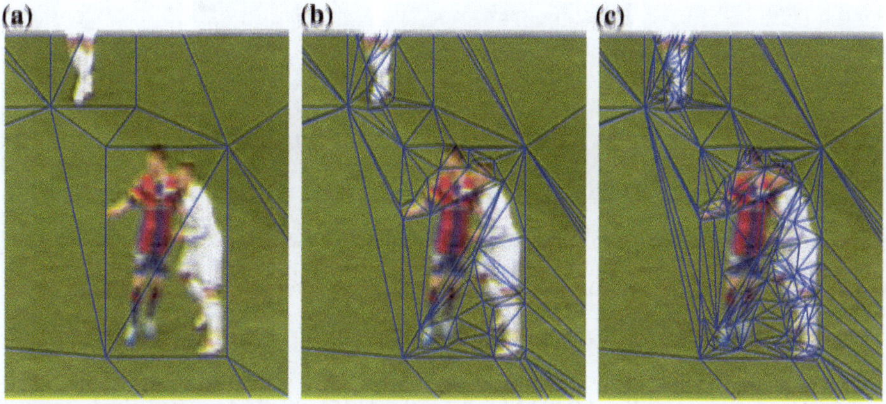

Fig. 7.13 **a** Initial triangulation. **b** First subdivision based on player's silhouettes. **c** Final subdivided geometry

Inaccurate calibration will inherently introduce a bias in this error metric as the projection of a 3D point into the cameras suffers from calibration errors. We address this problem by adding a geometric shift to each triangle vertex. This view-dependent geometry is described in detail in Sect. 7.3.3.

Subdivisions

The subdivision is a simple splitting of the triangle into two halves at the longest edge, including splitting of neighbors sharing the same edge. This directly inherits the position in 3D to the children. Therefore, even if no feature point is available for a child (e.g., at occlusions), it still inherits a most plausible 3D position and orientation. In the first iteration step, we use the background color model and a blob detection to get contour lines. These contour lines guide the first subdivision of the initial triangulation as shown in Fig. 7.13b. This speeds up the reconstruction and avoids high triangle counts, since it adds edges at potential depth discontinuities.

Figure 7.13c shows a final subdivision after 3 iteration steps of optimization and subdivision.

7.3.2.4 Refinement

Due to a lack of Daisy features, a small subset might not be positioned correctly in 3D and could also not be recovered by the inheritance of the subdivision. This may lead to rendering artifacts as shown in Fig. 7.14. To resolve these, we assume that neighboring triangles tend to have similar 3D depth values.

We try several positions using depth values from the neighboring triangles adding random perturbations. Finally, we select the one minimizing the color error.

Fig. 7.14 Two examples show the improvement of the result before and after applying the refinement step

Similar to the generalized PatchMatch method [45], this is done iteratively over all triangles 10 times with 10 random perturbations per vertex and iteration. Figure 7.14 shows the improvement of this step.

7.3.3 View-Dependent Geometry and Rendering

Our representation could be rendered as simple triangles in 3D with the color values from projective texturing of the source camera images, using some smart blending function [46]. Due to the inherent errors in the calibration process, the projection errors—even on a perfectly reconstructed geometry—result in rendering artifacts such as blurriness and ghosting. This problem is illustrated in Fig. 7.15. The blue dots are reliable feature matches from one camera to the other. If the calibration is correct then the corresponding rays (the red lines) would intersect. This is generally not the case. Wherever we position the 3D point, in at least one camera it will not project back to the 2D position where the feature point was detected. To solve this, we shift (morph) this point in 3D along the line of the shortest path between the two rays (the red arrow) when changing the viewing position. We call this shortest path a displacement. These displacements describe the geometric 3D morph function from every feature point in the base camera to the corresponding feature point in the other camera. To calculate the morph function of any view-dependent vertex (green dot), we interpolate all the displacements of neighboring features using a weighted average (the green arrow). The weighting function is a Gaussian, while only features lying in a radius of 1m of the vertex are considered being neighbors. This view-dependent rendering (Fig. 7.10f) is not a 2D morph but a morph of the 3D geometry and should not be confused with the merge of the 2.5D reconstructions (Fig. 7.10e). It resolves most of the rendering artifacts as demonstrated in Fig. 7.16.

More formally, let $\mathbf{v}_i(c)$ be the view-dependent position of vertex $\mathbf{v}_i$ in camera $c \in C$ as illustrated in Fig. 7.15. Let $\mathbf{v}_i(\hat{c})$ be the 3D position that we need to compute to render the vertex $\mathbf{v}_i$ from a novel-viewpoint $\hat{c}$. This view-dependent position can be interpolated between its corresponding positions of all cameras C.

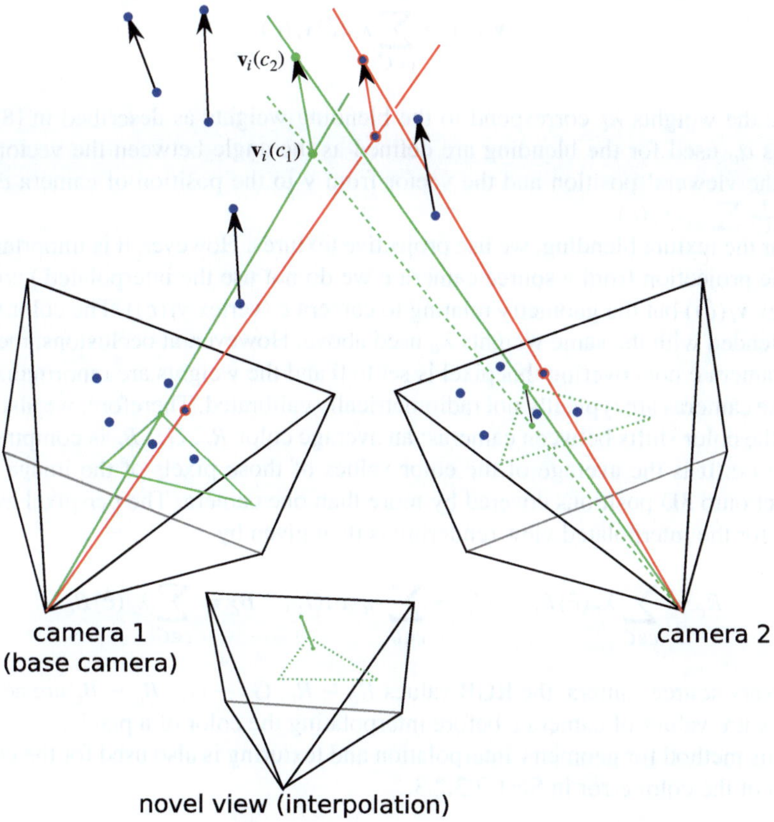

Fig. 7.15 Sketch of the view-dependent geometry. The *arrows* indicate the view-dependent geometric shift

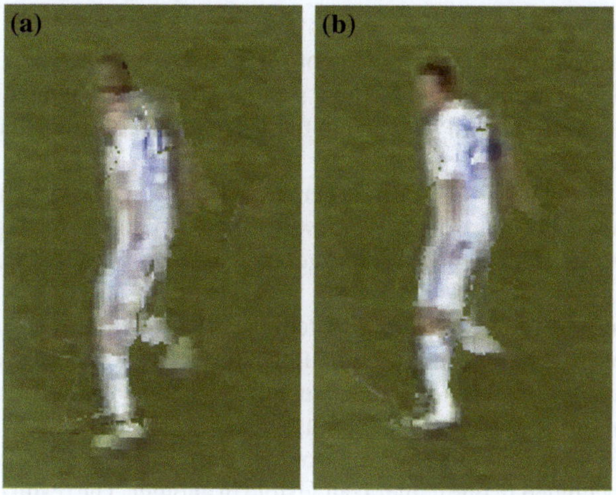

Fig. 7.16 **a** Rendering with one geometry. **b** Rendering with a view-dependent geometry

$$\mathbf{v}_i(\hat{c}) = \sum_{c \in C} \lambda_c(\hat{c}) \mathbf{v}_i(c) \tag{7.10}$$

where the weights λ_c correspond to the blending weights as described in [8]. The angles α_c used for the blending are defined as the angle between the vector from $\mathbf{v}$ to the viewers' position and the vector from $\mathbf{v}$ to the position of camera c, with $\mathbf{v} = \frac{1}{|C|} \sum_{c \in C} \mathbf{v}_i(c)$.

For the texture blending, we use projective textures. However, it is important that for the projection from a source camera c we do not use the interpolated geometry (vertex $\mathbf{v}_i(\hat{c})$) but the geometry relating to camera c (vertex $\mathbf{v}_i(c)$). The color values are blended with the same weights λ_c used above. However, at occlusions, the λ_c of any camera c not covering this pixel is set to 0 and the weights are renormalized.

The cameras are typically not radiometrically calibrated. Therefore, we also compute the color shifts between cameras: an average color R_c, G_c, B_c is computed per camera c. It is the average of the color values of those pixels of the image c that project onto 3D positions covered by more than one camera. The per-pixel average color for the interpolated view rendering is then given by

$$R_{\hat{c}} = \sum_{c \in C} \lambda_c(\hat{c}) R_c, \quad G_{\hat{c}} = \sum_{c \in C} \lambda_c(\hat{c}) G_c, \quad B_{\hat{c}} = \sum_{c \in C} \lambda_c(\hat{c}) B_c.$$

For every source camera, the RGB values $R_{\hat{c}} - R_c$, $G_{\hat{c}} - G_c$, $B_{\hat{c}} - B_c$ are added to the texture values of camera c before interpolating the color of a pixel.

This method for geometry interpolation and texturing is also used for the computation of the color error in Sect. 7.3.2.3.

7.3.4 Results

We demonstrate our method on footage of original TV broadcasts of several soccer scenes. All computations were done on a standard desktop computer (Core i7 CPU, 3.20 GHz). All results shown here and in the video are reconstructed using only two source cameras (Fig. 7.17).

Despite low resolutions and calibration errors (Fig. 7.1), our algorithm fully automatically reconstructs plausible novel views as shown in Fig. 7.18d. Figure 7.16 illustrates the effect of the view-dependent geometry that is able to reduce calibration error artifacts.

With our improved Daisy feature matching, the feature matches are reduced to a set of reliable correspondences. Sometimes this set contains only a few matches per player, but nevertheless our adaptive reconstruction method recovers a good approximation of the players' geometry as shown in Fig. 7.17.

Our method performs a reconstruction for each camera. This can be used to recover parts occluded in one camera but visible in another. The result of merging two reconstructions is shown in Fig. 7.18, where Fig. 7.18a shows a novel view using the

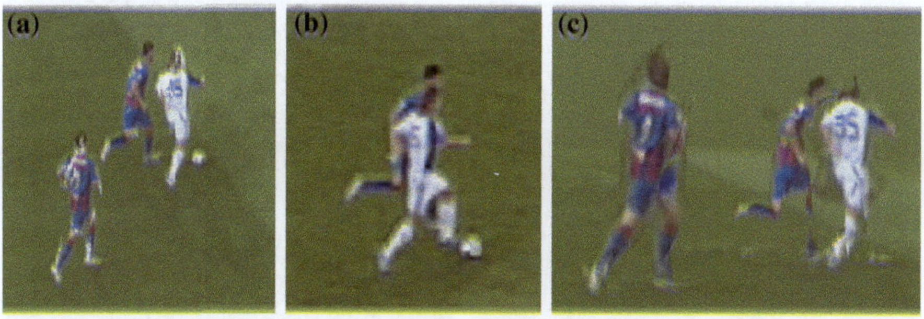

Fig. 7.17 Difficult occlusion. **a** View in camera 1 with feature points shown as *white dots*. **b** View in camera 2 where one player is almost entirely occluded. **c** Novel view

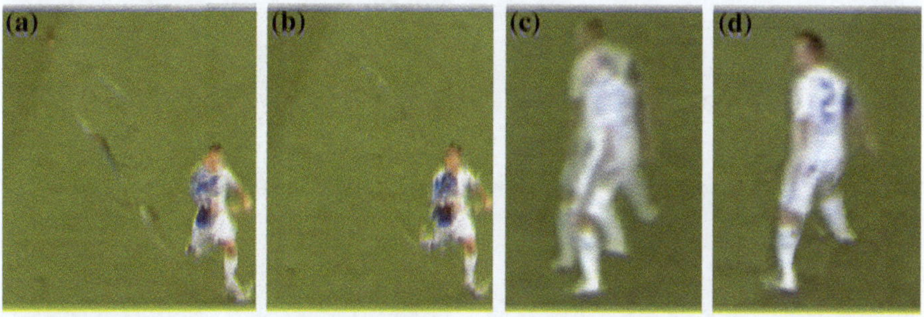

Fig. 7.18 **a** Reconstruction with triangulation in camera 1. The ghostings on the ground are parts not seen and thus not reconstructed in camera 1. **b** Merge of the reconstructions of camera 1 and camera 2. **c** A rendering using billboarding. **d** The same view using our method

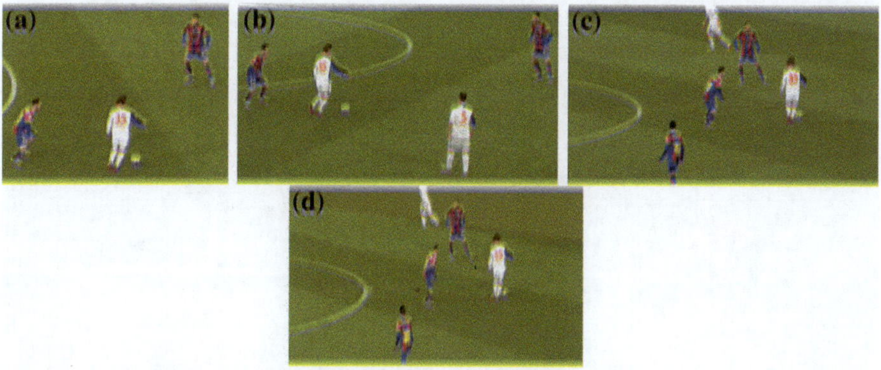

Fig. 7.19 Leave-one-out example: **a** and **b** Closeups of the two source camera images used. **c** High-resolution ground truth from a third (not used) camera that zoomed in. **d** Our reconstruction of the same view

Fig. 7.20 *Results* Each group shows on the *top* the two camera views, followed by a number of synthetic views

reconstruction of camera 1 only and Fig. 7.18b shows the same view with the unified reconstruction of the two cameras. With the reconstruction of only one camera, parts of players visible only in the other camera are not reconstructed and are thus projected onto the ground. With the merged reconstruction, we also get a valid depth for these parts allowing to reconstruct occlusions (Fig. 7.10e). Figure 7.17 demonstrates this with another example.

Figure 7.18c, d show a comparison to billboarding in a view halfway between the two source cameras. While billboarding shows ghosting (more than two legs) due to the planar representation, our method preserves the pose of the player in the novel view.

Figure 7.19 depicts a ground truth comparison to a third camera which was not used in the reconstruction. It demonstrates that the result of our reconstruction is correct and with similar quality as the input images. More results are shown in Fig. 7.20. The first two images are always the input images followed by the novel views. They show views not lying directly in between the cameras, e.g., top views or views from the height of the players' heads.

The rendering of novel views is done in real time, i.e., more than 60 frames per second for HD resolution. Our fully automatic algorithm for reconstruction takes on average 1 min per frame. The exact timing depends on the scene complexity, but none of our examples required more than 2 min to reconstruct. About 19 s of this time are Daisy feature vector computation and our feature matching. The rest of the time is spent about equally for positioning, and for the refinement. The time required per frame could be reduced by parallelization in several ways. First, the reconstruction for each camera is done completely independently (Fig. 7.10). Second, the refinement is done independently per triangle. Third, the feature matching could be parallelized.

7.4 Summary

In this chapter, we presented two player reconstruction methods designed for novel-view synthesis of sport broadcasts. The first one is based on accurate pose estimation from multiple cameras. To compute accurate 3D poses in such an uncontrolled environment, we rely on a rich database of poses and use the temporal coherence of human motion as a strong prior. Our algorithm works in two stages. First, it retrieves a good initial pose based on silhouette matching. Second, the initial estimation is improved using a novel optimization technique that combines spatial and temporal constraints to yield the final pose.

The second method is based on a multiview geometry reconstruction. We employ a novel, adaptive, top-down patch matching method where geometric detail is added gradually in the areas where it is needed based on a reliable sparse feature matching technique. It also robustly handles areas with no image features by inferring the position based on the neighboring triangles and back projection error.

The two methods presented use very different approaches with different pros and cons. The pose estimation method is inherently temporally consistent and can have additional useful applications in biomechanics. When an injury or trauma takes place, it is possible to study the footage leading up to the event and check for the moments when the body was outside the normal envelop. It is also possible to use this method to prevent injury, by using the footage of the skeletal movement to improve the design of the protective gear.

However, this method also has two disadvantages. First, it relies on a relatively large database of poses that can be difficult to construct. Moreover, some of these databases might be sport specific (i.e., a different database is required for soccer and hokey). Second, due to occlusions it may require occasional manual intervention to solve some ambiguities. When processing thousand of frames, even light manual interaction per frame may lead to a significant editing effort overall and a fully automatic method is desirable.

The second method, based on adaptive reconstruction, is more general, more robust and fully automatic, but it is not guaranteed to be temporally consistent. This second method is less sensitive to occlusions as it uses several heuristics that seem to work well in practice to fill in the geometry when it is only viewed from one camera. Therefore, it can generate convincing results even in two camera setups.

Novel views. As the main application of these methods is to enable virtual novel views, we provide some insight about the quality of the novel-view generation in both methods. The first method, based on pose reconstruction, is more flexible and can generate a wider range of virtual views not restricted to the path between two existing cameras. However, if the virtual pose is too far from an existing camera, some ghosting artifacts can still occur due to the billboard-based rendering. The second method, on the other hand, as it construct its geometry in a view-dependent way, it provides best results when the virtual viewpoint is along a path between two existing cameras. However, it is more robust to noise and to calibration errors making it more versatile.

Acknowledgments The image data is courtesy of Teleclub and LiberoVision.

References

1. Hilton A, Guillemaut J, Kilner J, Grau O, Thomas G (2011) 3D-TV production from conventional cameras for sports broadcast. IEEE Trans Broadcast 57(2):462–476
2. LiberoVision. www.liberovision.com
3. Kuster K, Bazin J-C, Martin T, Oztireli C, Popa T, Gross M (2014) Spatio-temporal geometry fusion for multiple hybrid cameras using moving least squares surfaces. In: Eurographics
4. Guillemaut J-Y, Kilner J, Hilton A (2009) Robust graph-cut scene segmentation and reconstruction for free-viewpoint video of complex dynamic scenes. In: ICCV
5. Germann M, Popa T, Ziegler R, Keiser R, Gross M (2011) Space-time body pose estimation in uncontrolled environments. In: 3DIMPVT
6. Thomas GA (2006) Real-time camera pose estimation for augmenting sports scenes. In: CVMP
7. Hayashi K, Saito H (2006) Synthesizing free-viewpoint images from multiple view videos in Soccer stadium. In: CGIV
8. Germann M, Hornung A, Keiser R, Ziegler R, Würmlin S, Gross M (2010) Articulated billboards for video-based rendering. In: Eurographics

9. Germann M, Popa T, Keiser R, Ziegler R, Gross M (2012) Novel-view synthesis of outdoor sport events using an adaptive view-dependent geometry. In: Computer graphics forum (Proceedings of the Eurographics)
10. Moeslund TB, Granum E (2001) A survey of computer vision-based human motion capture. In: CVIU
11. Moeslund TB, Hilton A, Krüger V (2006) A survey of advances in vision-based human motion capture and analysis. In: CVIU
12. Vicon (2010). http://www.vicon.com
13. Ballan L, Cortelazzo GM (2008) Marker-less motion capture of skinned models in a four camera set-up using optical flow and silhouettes. In: 3DPVT
14. Choi C, Baek S-M, Lee S (2008) Real-time 3d object pose estimation and tracking for natural landmark based visual servo. In: IROS
15. Theobalt C, de Aguiar E, Magnor MA, Theisel H, Seidel H-P (2004) Marker-free kinematic skeleton estimation from sequences of volume data. In: VRST
16. de Aguiar E, Stoll C, Theobalt C, Ahmed N, Seidel H-P, Thrun S (2008) Performance capture from sparse multi-view video. In: SIGGRAPH
17. Vlasic D, Baran I, Matusik W, Popović J (2008) Articulated mesh animation from multi-view silhouettes. In: SIGGRAPH
18. Mori G (2005) Guiding model search using segmentation. In: ICCV
19. Ferrari V, Marin-Jimenez M, Zisserman A (2008) Progressive search space reduction for human pose estimation. In: CVPR
20. Efros AA, Berg AC, Mori G, Malik J (2003) Recognizing action at a distance. In: ICCV
21. Germann M, Hornung A, Keiser R, Ziegler R, Würmlin S, Gross M (2010) Articulated billboards for video-based rendering. In: Eurographics
22. CGLM Database (2010). http://mocap.cs.cmu.edu
23. Bouguet J-Y (1999) Pyramidal implementation of the Lucas Kanade feature tracker: description of the algorithm. Technical report, Intel Corporation, Microprocessor Research Labs
24. Schreiner J, Asirvatham A, Praun E, Hoppe H (2004) Inter-surface mapping. In: SIGGRAPH
25. Mor J (1978) The Levenberg-Marquardt algorithm: implementation and theory. Lecture notes in mathematics, vol 630
26. Laurentini A (1994) The visual hull concept for Silhouette-based image understanding. PAMI 16(2):150–162
27. Matusik V, Buehler C, Raskar R, Gortler S, McMillan L (2000) Image-based visual hulls. In: SIGGRAPH
28. Li M, Magnor M, Seidel H-P (2004) A hybrid hardware-accelerated algorithm for high quality rendering of visual hulls. In: Graphics interface
29. Grau O, Thomas GA, Hilton A, Kilner J, Starck J (2007) A Robust free-viewpoint video system for sport scenes. In: 3DTV
30. Petit B, Lesage JD, Menier C, Allard J, Franco JS, Raffin B, Boyer E, Faure F (2010) Multicamera real-time 3D modeling for telepresence and remote collaboration. Int J Digit Multi Broadcast
31. Franco J-S, Boyer E (2009) Efficient polyhedral modelling from silhouettes. PAMI 31(3): 414–427
32. Guillemaut J-Y, Hilton A (2011) Joint multi-layer segmentation and reconstruction for free-viewpoint video applications. IJCV 93(1):73–100
33. Inamoto N, Saito S (2002) Intermediate view generation of soccer scene from multiple videos. In: ICPR
34. Matusik W, Pfister H (2004) 3D TV: a scalable system for real-time acquisition, transmission, and autostereoscopic display of dynamic scenes. In: SIGGRAPH
35. Bradley D, Popa T, Sheffer A, Heidrich W, Boubekeur T (2008) Markerless garment capture. In: SIGGRAPH
36. Ballan L, Brostow GJ, Puwein J, Pollefeys M (2010) Unstructured video-based rendering: interactive exploration of casually captured videos. In: SIGGRAPH

37. Fraundorfer F, Schindler K, Bischof H (2006) Piecewise planar scene reconstruction from sparse correspondences. Image Vis Comput 24(4):395–406
38. Stich T, Linz C, Albuquerque G, Magnor M (2008) View and time interpolation in image space. In: Pacific graphics
39. Sudipta SN, Steedly D, Szeliski R (2009) Piecewise planar stereo for image-based rendering. In: ICCV
40. Gallup D, Frahm J-M, Pollefeys M (2010) Piecewise planar and non-planar stereo for urban scene reconstruction. In: CVPR
41. Tola E, Lepetit V, Fua P (2010) Daisy: an efficient dense descriptor applied to wide baseline stereo. PAMI 32(5):815–830
42. Fleuret F, Berclaz J, Lengagne R, Fua P (2007) Multi-camera people tracking with a probabilistic occupancy map. PAMI 30(2):267–282
43. Zach C, Pock T, Bischof H (2007) A globally optimal algorithm for Robust TV-L1 range image integration. In: ICCV
44. Fischler MA, Bolles RC (1981) Random sample consensus: a paradigm for model fitting with applications to image analysis and automated cartography. Commun ACM 24:381–395
45. Barnes C, Shechtman E, Goldman DB, Finkelstein A (2010) The generalized PatchMatch correspondence algorithm. In: ECCV
46. Buehler C, Bosse M, McMillan L, Gortler S, Cohen M (2001) Unstructured Lumigraph rendering. In: SIGGRAPH

Chapter 8
Estimating Athlete Pose from Monocular TV Sports Footage

Mykyta Fastovets, Jean-Yves Guillemaut and Adrian Hilton

Abstract Human pose estimation from monocular video streams is a challenging problem. Much of the work on this problem has focused on developing inference algorithms and probabilistic prior models based on learned measurements. Such algorithms face challenges in generalisation beyond the learned dataset. We propose an interactive model-based generative approach for estimating the human pose from uncalibrated monocular video in unconstrained sports TV footage. Belief propagation over a spatio-temporal graph of candidate body part hypotheses is used to estimate a temporally consistent pose between user-defined keyframe constraints. Experimental results show that the proposed generative pose estimation framework is capable of estimating pose even in very challenging unconstrained scenarios.

8.1 Introduction

Pose estimation is an important problem and has received considerable interest in the computer vision community [11]. We consider the problem of estimating human pose in 2D from a single view video stream. There are many potential advantages to being able to analyse monocular video streams including lower equipment cost, lower complexity and higher portability of the camera set-up. Additionally, most of the content available to the user, despite recent advances in 3D film and stereoscopic displays, remains single view. Thus, for most practical purposes only a single video stream of the scene is available for analysis.

Monocular sports footage is challenging due to the complexity of the backgrounds and the highly articulated human body, engaged in fast-paced activities. Additional challenges posed by such data include motion blur, low foreground resolution,

M. Fastovets (✉) · J.-Y. Guillemaut · A. Hilton
University of Surrey, Guildford GU27XH, UK
e-mail: mykyta.fastovets@surrey.ac.uk

J.-Y. Guillemaut
e-mail: j.guillemaut@surrey.ac.uk

A. Hilton
e-mail: a.hilton@surrey.ac.uk

T.B. Moeslund et al. (eds.), *Computer Vision in Sports*,
Advances in Computer Vision and Pattern Recognition,
DOI 10.1007/978-3-319-09396-3_8

occlusions and self-occlusions and rapid configuration changes, camera movement and zoom. The goal of the proposed algorithm is not only to deal with such data, but to do so with sufficient reliability to be suitable for use in a broadcast/production environment and can be summarised as follows: *Given a monocular sequence of images with one or more athletes in each image, estimate the full-body 2D limb configuration and joint locations of the athletes in each image.*

The aim is to provide rapid, yet robust, user-assisted pose estimation and tracking. We opt for a generative model-based approach that requires no offline learning and is generic in the types of motion it is capable of handling but relies on a small amount of human interaction. As the target use scenario is within a production environment with the presence of human operators, complete automation is not critical. Although we focus our experiments on real athletic events footage, no assumptions are made about body size and appearance, type of motion and the scene.

The algorithm introduces an effective constraint on pose change over time for a full human skeletal model and is capable of estimating pose in unconstrained data requiring a relatively small number of keyframes. Figure 8.1 illustrates a sample result and compares to a standard off-the-shelf method, demonstrating full-body 2D pose estimation with the proposed approach.

Fig. 8.1 Comparison of the proposed method with interpolation in *green* and solution in *black* with a silhouette overlay (*left*) to an off-the-shelf implementation in [7] (*right*)

8.2 Previous Work

Human pose estimation algorithms in the literature can be separated into two distinct categories—*generative* and *discriminative*. Discriminative approaches are typically data driven and tend to rely on a mapping from image features (silhouettes, salient features, etc.) to pose information [1, 5]. The key idea behind discriminative approaches is that the number of typical human poses is far smaller than the number of kinematically possible ones. Discriminative methods learn a model that directly recovers pose estimates from observable image metrics. In other words, the state posterior is modelled directly by learning an image to pose mapping. Once this training process is complete, estimating pose is fast but heavily reliant on the training data.

Visual cues used in discriminative approaches often rely on salience or segmentation [13, 18] and attempt to exploit inherent symmetries in the human body [15]. The cues are used to produce part detections for most body parts. The recovery of human pose from these detections can then be formulated as either a combinatorial [13, 15, 16] or a parsing problem [18]. One of the difficulties associated with this class of approaches is their reliance on an accurate and robust part detector. Detectors often fail when background clutter is significant or when body parts have little visual distinction. Advantages of discriminative approaches include the ability to model occlusions as well as the freedom to formulate the pose recovery problem for use with efficient global search algorithms.

Generative approaches presuppose an explicitly known parametric body model (generally a kinematic tree) and estimate pose by inverse kinematics or numeric optimization of a model-image correspondence metric over the pose variables, using forward rendering to predict the images. Bottom-up Bayes' rule is used and the state posterior density is modelled using observation likelihood or a cost function. Decision-making can proceed even in the case of missing or incomplete data and assumptions as well as any prior information (such as pose constraints) are easily accommodated, but most importantly, there exists a bilateral dependence between the model and the data. Such algorithms generally incorporate a likelihood model capable of discriminating incorrect hypothetical poses from correct ones based on image evidence and an estimation algorithm able to generate possible pose hypotheses from the parametric body model [9, 10]. Model-based tracking is a derived technique which focuses on tracking the pose estimate from one time step to the next, starting from a known initialisation based on an approximate dynamical model. Most generative pose estimation frameworks suffer from the fact that the optimisation is prone to hitting local minima, requiring a good initialisation and often failing on complex motions [2].

Pictorial Structures (PS) is a probabilistic inference approach for a tree-structured graphical model where the overall cost function for a pose decompose across edges and nodes of the tree. PS recovers locations scales and orientations of rigid rectangular part templates that represent a body. PS is a well-developed detection method and can be used for tracking by detection [3, 4, 6]. A technique to extend existing training datasets is presented in [14]. These methods, however, require a large motion capture and image training dataset. Lan and Huttenlocher [10] use a spatio-temporal model though pictorial structures as states in a Hidden Markov Model (HMM). A recent development [3] introduces the idea that pictorial structures may be a generic multi-purpose solution to pose estimation, detection and tracking. The method is reliant on a strong discriminatively trained appearance model. Ferrari et al. [8] propose a temporal link between frames when estimating pose in videos, but the proposed algorithm only works for frontal upper body poses.

While there exist multiple pose estimation techniques capable of extracting human pose from monocular image streams, existing approaches do not provide a suitable solution to the problem of general pose estimation in sports footage due to the fast and extreme motion captured with moving and zooming cameras. Most algorithms focus on recovering pose from single images and/or do not make full use of the temporal constraint on limb motion [2, 3, 14, 17]. Available off-the-shelf single image methods such as [7] have trouble coping with the difficulty of the data, even when the human is detected. Figure 8.1 shows a side-by-side comparison of the output of the algorithm developed in [7] obtained using their online demo tool and the proposed method.

We propose a novel generative approach to pose estimation from sports video to avoid loss of generality and bypass the requirement for motion captured training data of specific athlete motions. The focus of the framework is on pose estimation with the assumption that a human is detected and an approximate foreground mask is available. Silhouette extraction is a well-studied problem and there is a wide variety of methods that deal with background subtraction, for example [20]. The diagram in Fig. 8.2 shows where our algorithm fits within a complete pose estimation framework.

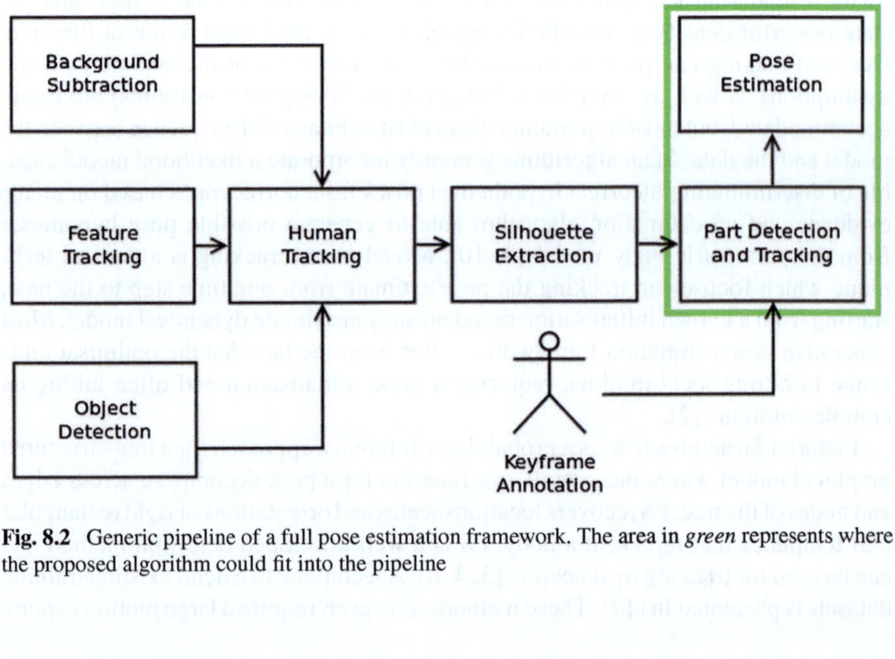

Fig. 8.2 Generic pipeline of a full pose estimation framework. The area in *green* represents where the proposed algorithm could fit into the pipeline

The contributions of this work are twofold. First, we propose a temporal smoothness term applied to the pictorial structures model and show that this term makes a significant impact on the outcome of the pose estimation problem. This temporal smoothness constraint should be useful in most existing pose estimation algorithms. Second, we propose a framework for estimating full-body pose in challenging circumstances by effectively moving the learning stage of the algorithm online. Generally, for a TV sequence of around 200 images, our algorithm will require 10–30 keyframes (depending on the difficulty of the motion) to produce high-quality results. The keyframes provide a motion prior and local part appearance models.

8.3 Methodology

The input into the algorithm is an image sequence along with a corresponding sequence of foreground masks and several user-created keyframes. The keyframes are used for building appearance models of body parts as well as to provide a body part location prior through motion interpolation. The process of pose estimation consists of two steps: body part detection and pose recovery.

We employ a human skeletal model consisting of $b = 13$ body parts (root (R), head (H), neck (N), right and left femur (RF, LF), tibia (RT, LT), metatarsal (RM, LM), humerus (RH, LH) and radius (RR, LR)) as depicted in Fig. 8.3.

Let $\mathbf{x}_t$ represent the state of the skeleton at time instant t. Let $\mathbf{p}_i$ represent the state (x, y, θ, s) of part i as per the standard PS model [6]. Then, $\mathbf{x}_t = \{\mathbf{p}_1, \mathbf{p}_2, \ldots, \mathbf{p}_b\}_t$.

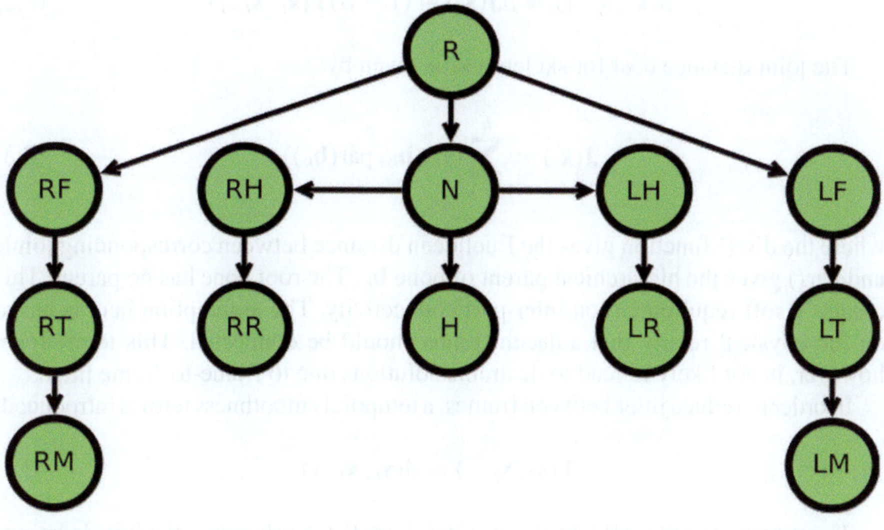

Fig. 8.3 Graph (tree) representation of the human kinematic skeletal model consisting of 13 body parts

Given a sequence of n frames, the problem of estimating human pose at each time instance can be written as:

$$\mathbf{X} = \mathbf{argmin_x} \alpha \sum_{t=1}^{n} \mathbf{D}(\mathbf{x}_t) + (1-\alpha) \sum_{t=1}^{n} \mathbf{S}(\mathbf{x}_t, \mathbf{x}_{t-1}) \tag{8.1}$$

where $\mathbf{X}$ represents the temporal sequence of poses $\{\mathbf{x}_1, \mathbf{x}_2 ... \mathbf{x}_t\}$, $\mathbf{D}(\mathbf{x}_t)$ represents the data term and $\mathbf{S}(\mathbf{x}_t, \mathbf{x}_{t-1},)$ the smoothness term at time instance t. The data term evaluates the cost of a state $\mathbf{x}_t$ with respect to image observations, while the smoothness term evaluates the temporal continuity of the sequence. Sections 8.3.1 and 8.3.2 explain in more detail how these terms are computed. In order to solve the problem, we first represent it as a factor graph and solve the resulting graph using an implementation of Generalised Belief Propagation [12]. Generalised Belief Propagation lends itself naturally to the problem of finding correct labels for body parts and although it provides an approximate solution, in practice the algorithm often converges to the global optima [19].

8.3.1 Smoothness Term

The smoothness term consists of two distinct components: an inter-limb distance cost $\mathbf{J}_{\mathbf{x}_t}$, representing joint connectivity, and a temporal distance term $\mathbf{T}_{\mathbf{x}_t}$, representing smoothness of motion across time:

$$\mathbf{S}(\mathbf{x}_t, \mathbf{x}_{t-1}) = \beta \mathbf{J}(\mathbf{x}_t) + (1-\beta)\mathbf{T}(\mathbf{x}_t, \mathbf{x}_{t-1}) \tag{8.2}$$

The joint distance cost for skeleton $\mathbf{x}_t$ is given by:

$$\mathbf{J}(\mathbf{x}_t) = \sum_{k=1}^{b} \text{dist}(\mathbf{b}_k, \text{par}(\mathbf{b}_k)) \tag{8.3}$$

where the dist() function gives the Euclidean distance between corresponding joints and par() gives the hierarchical parent of bone $\mathbf{b}_k$. The root bone has no parent. This creates a soft requirement on inter-part connectivity. The assumption here is based on the physical reality that adjacent limbs should be connected. This term alone, however, is not likely to lead to desirable solutions due to frame-to-frame jitter.

In order to reduce jitter between frames, a temporal smoothness term is introduced:

$$\mathbf{T}(\mathbf{x}_t, \mathbf{x}_{t-1}) = \text{d}(\mathbf{x}_t, \mathbf{x}_{t-1}) \tag{8.4}$$

The temporal term is effectively the Euclidean distance between the joint locations at t and $t-1$. Figure 8.4 illustrates the complete graph including the temporal term for three consecutive frames.

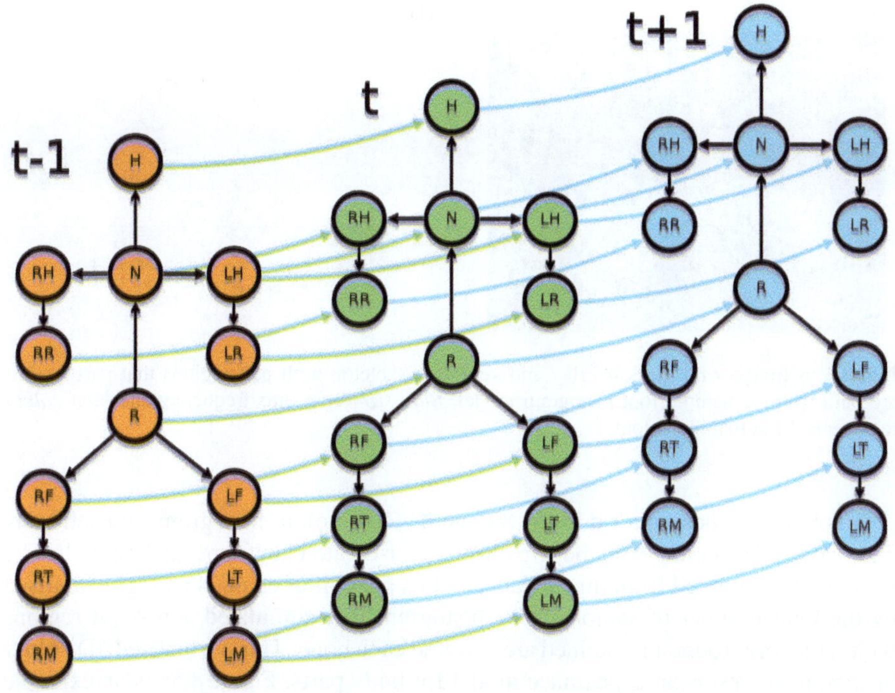

Fig. 8.4 Representation of temporal and inter-limb links for frames at time instances $t-1$, t and $t+1$. *Coloured* links represent the temporal constraint, while those in *black* represent the joint connectivity constraint

8.3.2 Data Term

The data term is defined simply as the sum of support scores $\mathbf{S}(k_{\mathbf{x}_t})$ assigned to each generated part candidate for configuration $\mathbf{x}_t$:

$$\mathbf{D}(\mathbf{x}_t) = \sum_{k=1}^{b} \mathbf{S}(k_{\mathbf{x}_t}) \tag{8.5}$$

To generate part candidates for part k a search region centred around the mid-point between the two joints of the interpolation for that part is created. At each pixel within the search region and the foreground mask, a rectangular template $\mathbf{R} = \{p_0, p_1, \ldots, p_q\}$ containing q pixels is centred with varying orientations and scales. Each instance of the template receives a support score $\mathbf{S}$ based on the strength of the support region as detailed in Eq. 8.6.

$$\mathbf{S}(k) = \frac{\sum_{i=0}^{n} \mathbf{d}(p_i)_k}{q} \tag{8.6}$$

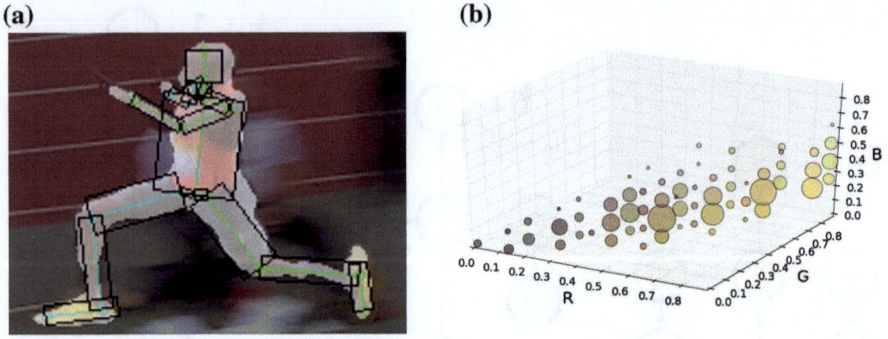

Fig. 8.5 **a** Image with mask overlay and keyframe skeleton with part regions that part models are built from. **b** Sample foot histogram model. *Blob size* represents frequency and *blob colour* represents the actual bin colour

To obtain the descriptor **d** in Eq. 8.6, an 8^3 RGB colour histogram for each body part using information from the two closest user-created keyframes is first built. The histogram is sampled from image data at 8 bits per colour channel and is normalised by the total number of samples. The histogram is accumulated across all regions within the foreground in a defined area around each bone. This normalised 3D colour histogram serves as an appearance model for body parts. Figure 8.5a is an example of regions from which the histogram model is built, while Fig. 8.5b shows a sample histogram of a foot model.

The histogram models provide k colour distribution functions, one for each body part. A k-dimensional vector is built at every pixel of the foreground region with each element giving the likelihood of the pixel belonging to a given part based on colour using the colour distribution functions previously obtained. This vector is then normalised by the maximum of its elements, creating k-dimensional descriptor **d** assigned to the pixel p(x, y) where each element of the descriptor is the probability of the pixel belonging to the corresponding body part. The rationale here is that each pixel in the foreground mask should, in principle, belong to one of the body parts. The normalisation allows for an effective ranking of probabilities of the pixel belonging to each distinct body part. This does, however, increase reliance on high-quality foreground masks as the algorithm will try to associate any background pixels that are within the foreground mask with human body parts. In practice, we find that obtaining sufficiently good masks is possible through readily available off-the-shelf methods.

Additionally, a 3D motion interpolation is computed using the two closest keyframes. The interpolation limits the search region and provides initial orientation and scale estimates for body part candidate generation. Interpolation is used to limit the search space and make the problem tractable on commodity hardware. The interpolation is computed using the manually annotated keyframes based on locations of joints in 3D space. Joint angles are represented in quaternions and linear interpolation is used to estimate the body state at each time instance.

8.4 Results and Evaluation

The framework is evaluated on three sports TV sequences with different camera angles, zoom and motion from two different sports—triple jump and hurdles. Due to the fast motion of the athlete's body, many frames suffer from motion blur effects. Additionally, we evaluate our algorithm on three of the HumanEva sequences: Box, Jog and Walk. Table 8.1 summarises the data used to evaluate the framework. The size of the athlete (height in pixels) differs in every sequence, ranging from 42 to over 800.

We use the interpolation between keyframes as the motion prior and assume that it gives a reasonable initial estimate. In order to help reduce the search space, we do not vary scale and vary limb orientation by 90° in each direction in increments of 10°. We also limit the search region for body parts to twice the interpolated limb length. This strikes a good balance between accuracy and computability allowing us to obtain results for 10 images (8 frames plus two keyframes) at speeds of around 15 (depending on foreground region size) seconds per frame on an Intel i5 processor with 4gb of RAM (Figs. 8.8, 8.9, 8.10, 8.11, and 8.12).

The error of a body part to ground truth is defined as the square of Euclidean distance to ground truth body part joints and is given by:

$$\mathbf{E_k} = \frac{\mathrm{d}(j_0, g_0)^2 + \mathrm{d}(j_1, g_1)^2}{2} \tag{8.7}$$

where j_0 and j_1 are estimated joint positions for the body part k and g_0 and g_1 are the ground truth positions. The graphs in Figs. 8.13, 8.14, and 8.15 show a comparison of RMS error at each time instance between 3D interpolation and our method for each of the three sequences. The ground truth is obtained by manual annotation of the sequences. The manual annotation of the sequence includes labelling of limbs as occluded to the point where even a human operator cannot reliably determine the location of the limb. Limbs labelled in this way are removed from error analysis as their true location is unknown.

The three HumanEva sequences were evaluated using the same error measure against the ground truth provided in the dataset. As the limb labelling scheme

Table 8.1 Summary of sequences used for framework evaluation

Name	Sport	Resolution	Frames	Keyframes	Average athlete height (pix)	Tuning frames
HurdlesSD	Hurdles	720 × 576	76	17	60	12
TriplejumpHD	Triple jump	1920 × 1080	198	42	800	10
TriplejumpSD	Triple jump	720 × 288	89	12	150	18
HumanEva Box	Triple jump	720 × 540	374	22	400	20
HumanEva Jog	Triple jump	720 × 540	391	17	400	30
HumanEva Walk	Triple jump	720 × 540	431	14	400	30

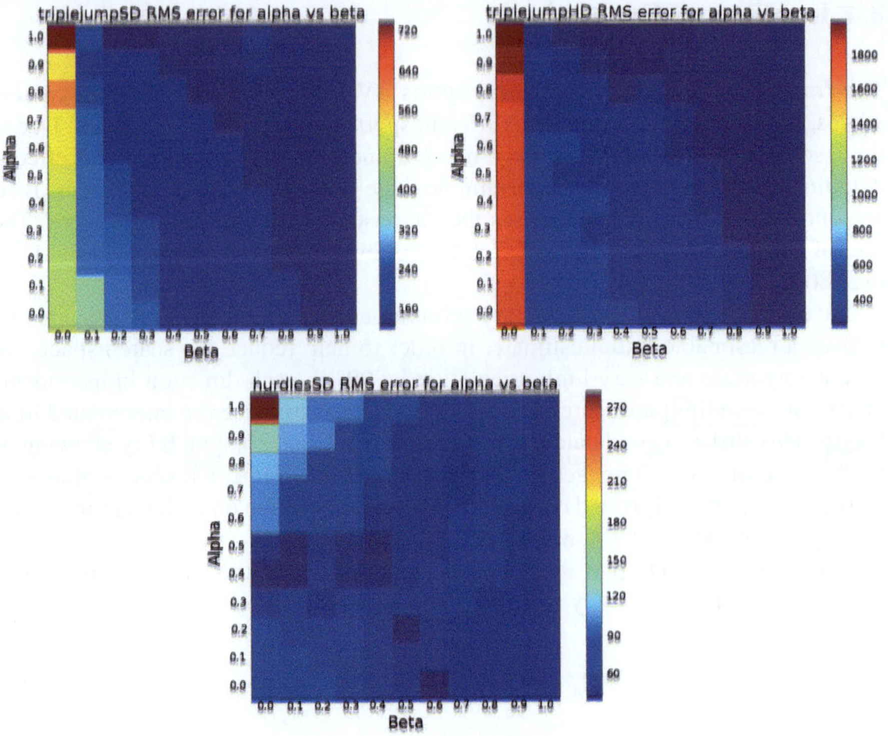

Fig. 8.6 Parameter tuning for the three TV sequences. Heat represents RMS error in *square* pixels

and the body model differ somewhat from our own the error measures are higher. Additionally, the human-labelled keyframes no longer correspond to ground truth and instead introduce some inherent error. We plot these errors, including keyframe errors in Figs. 8.16, 8.17, and 8.18 for the Box, Jog and Walk sequences, respectively. Our method is able to provide high quality results with far fewer keyframes required on these three sequences.

The parameters used for obtaining the results were experimentally derived using a short section of each of the tested sequences (see Table 8.1. Results of parameter tuning are presented in Figs. 8.6 and 8.7 for the TV and HumanEva sequences, respectively. As expected, the parameter tuning heat maps for the triplejump sequences appear similar with overlapping local minima. This is most likely due to the inherent similarity in the activity. Meanwhile, the heat map for hurdlesSD is significantly different. These results indicate not only that the temporal component has a quantifiable impact, but that parameter selection can be shared across sequences that are similar, e.g. same sport and somewhat similar camera angle. Though there is no one parameter set that is universally good.

Analysis of these sequences indicates that qualitatively our method is better than pure interpolation. The significance of improvement can depend on how good

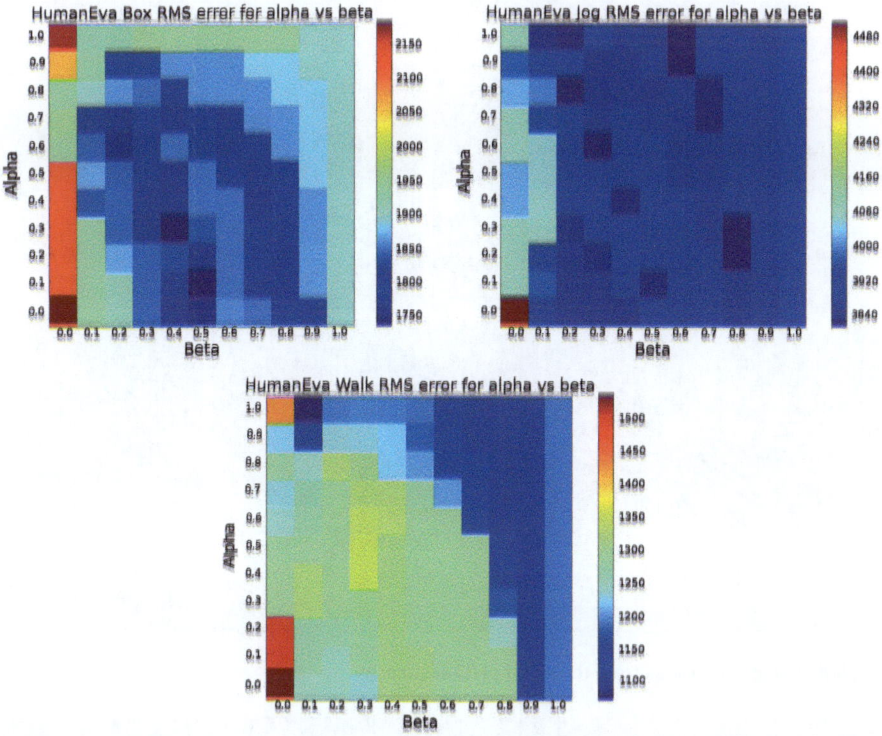

Fig. 8.7 Parameter tuning for the three HumanEva sequence. Heat represents RMS error in *square* pixels

interpolation is for a particular sequence. Since the interpolation we compare against is done on a 3D skeleton, it is fairly good at coping with normal human motion and is guaranteed connectivity and temporal consistence as long as it is across one gait cycle. Currently, we make use of interpolation as a motion prior and a constraint on the search space with the assumption that the interpolation provides a reasonable initial estimate of pose. Thus, even a seemingly small improvement in distance often has significant visual impact with regard to accuracy of body part locations. Furthermore, the problem of the interpolation straying significantly from the ground truth, preventing detection and potentially dragging the optimisation in the wrong direction is left for future work but has a definite impact on the results.

The error differences between interpolation and our method vary for the different sequences and sections of sequences. For example the graph for the triplejumpHD sequence 13 has a much more significant error gap than both triplejumpSD and hurdlesSD. Similarly, our method outperforms interpolation significantly on the HumanEva Box sequence for similar reasons. Large gaps can occur when the interpolation has strayed 90° of rotation away from ground truth (at the limit of our used range) but has stayed close enough to contain the image body parts within the search region.

Fig. 8.8 Sample solutions from the trijumpHD sequence

Fig. 8.9 Sample solutions from the trijumpSD sequence

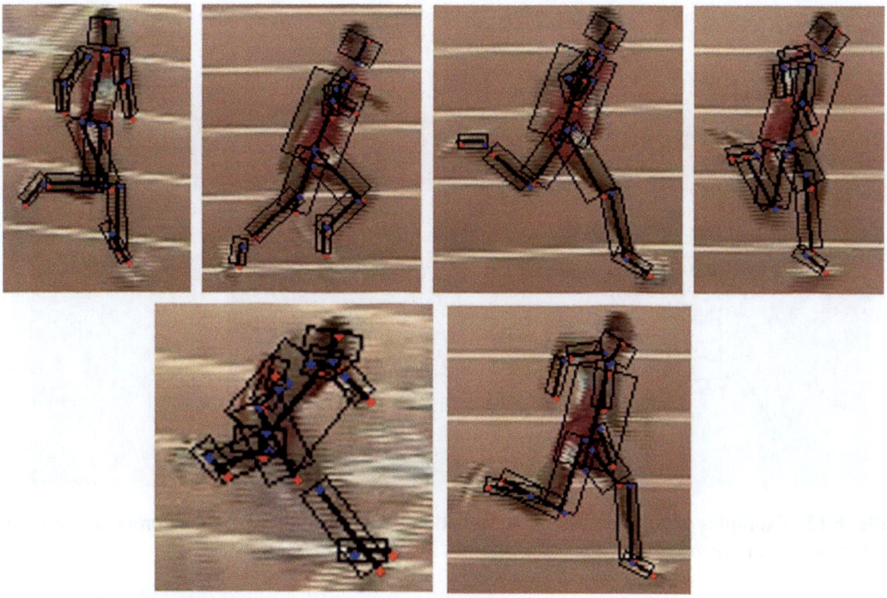

Fig. 8.10 Sample solutions from the hurdlesSD sequence

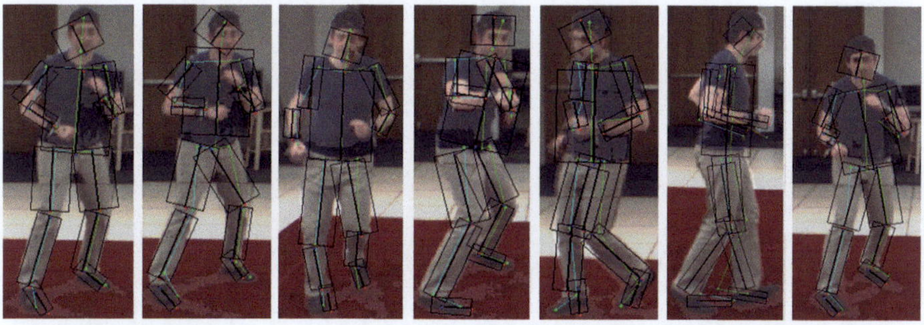

Fig. 8.11 Sample solutions from the Box, Jog and Walk HumanEva sequences

The HumanEva sequences require far fewer (generally one every 30–40 frames) keyframes due to the significantly slower motion and high framerate for the capture cameras. Additionally, the body part model used in the dataset does not include metatarsals. Feet are therefore excluded from the evaluation. The analysis of the HumanEva sequences also include a comparison of the method with the temporal component turned off, that is $\beta = 0$. Results indicate that the temporal smoothness term has a definite quantifiable impact on the result. The improvements are most noticeable at frames furthers away from keyframes, where detections relying on interpolation begin to fail. On these frames, improvements in accuracy over the non-temporal solve can in some cases reach 25–30 pixels.

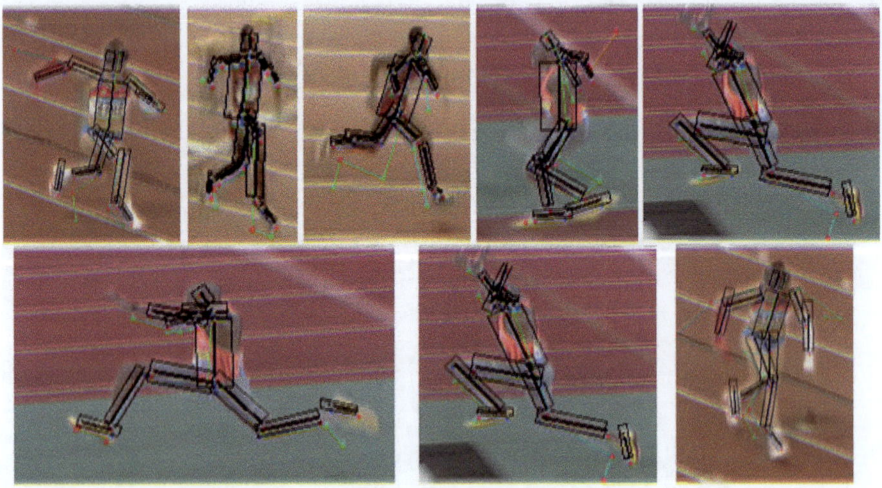

Fig. 8.12 Examples of solution where interpolation is significantly worse than proposed solution. Interpolation in *green*

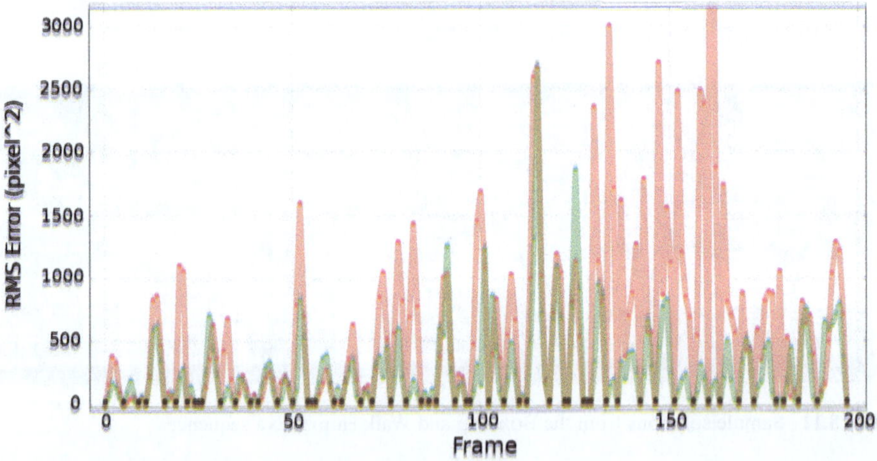

Fig. 8.13 Error to ground truth of our algorithm (*green*) and motion interpolation (*red*) for the triplejumpHD sequence. *Black* marks indicate keyframes

Figures 8.8, 8.9, and 8.10 show sample results from each sequence. The improvement over interpolation here is in many cases significant, despite the fact that keyframes are much sparser. A number of keyframes have high error when compared to the HumanEva ground truth as the human body models used differ. Our model is fully connected and joints are labelled visually, while motion capture data is derived from sensors attached to more anatomically correct joint locations. Figure 8.12 contains samples from the HumanEva sequences.

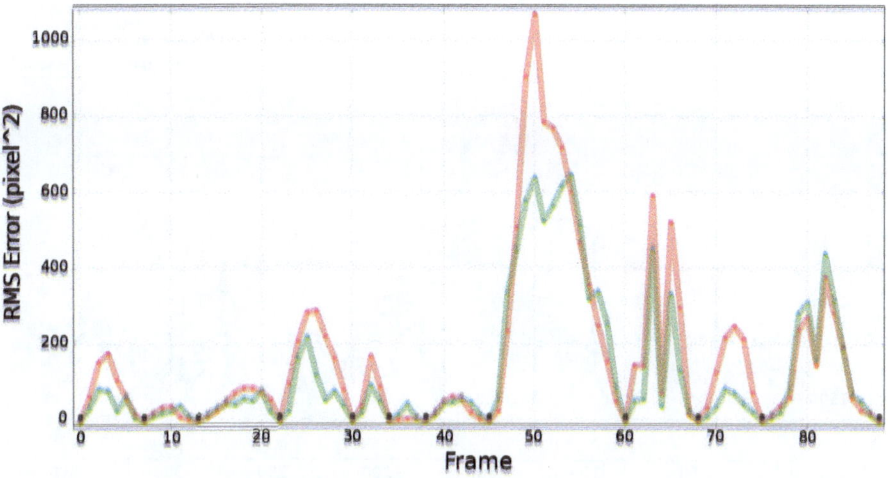

Fig. 8.14 Error to ground truth of our algorithm (*green*) and motion interpolation (*red*) for the triplejumpSD sequence. *Black* marks indicate keyframes

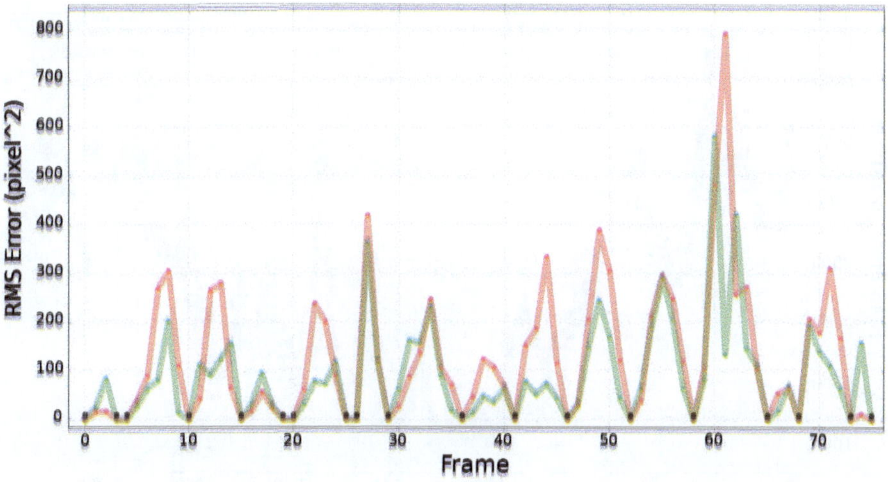

Fig. 8.15 Error to ground truth of our algorithm (*green*) and motion interpolation (*red*) for the hurdlesSD sequence. *Black* marks indicate keyframes

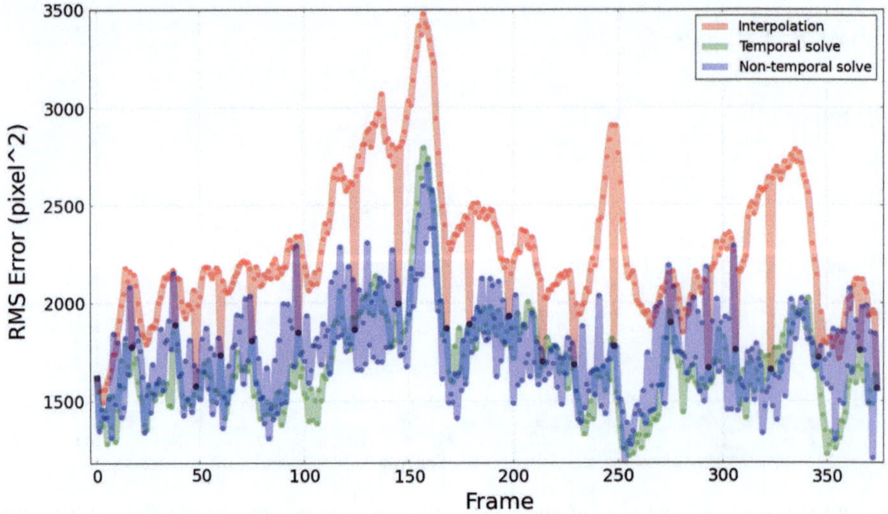

Fig. 8.16 Error to ground truth for the HumanEva Box sequence. *Black* marks indicate keyframes

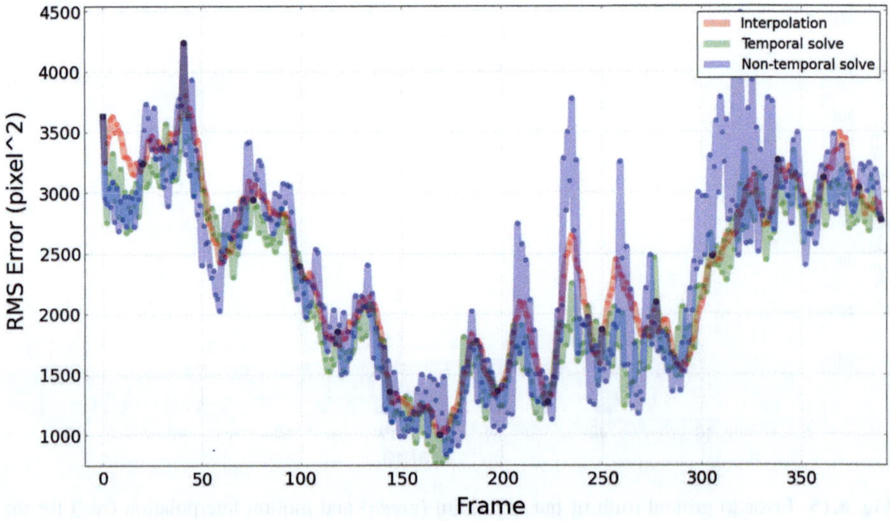

Fig. 8.17 Error to ground truth for the HumanEva Jog sequence. *Black* marks indicate keyframes

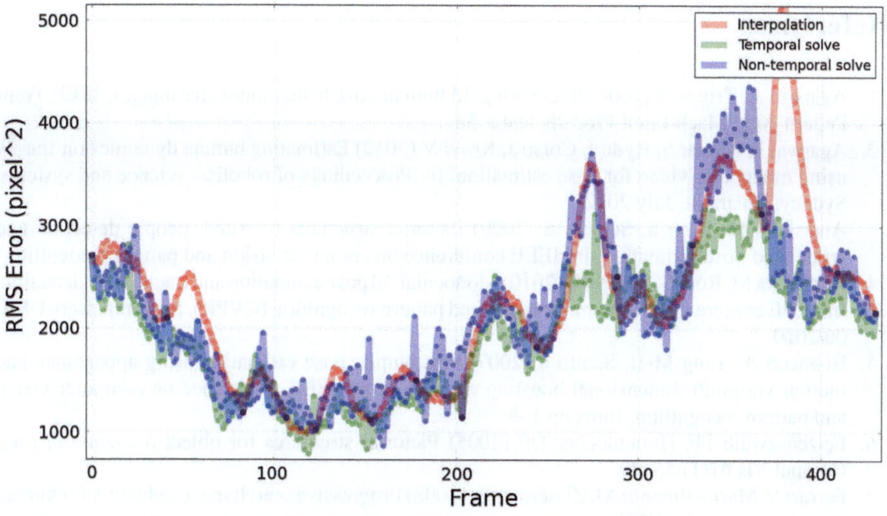

Fig. 8.18 Error to ground truth for the HumanEva Walk sequence. *Black* marks indicate keyframes

8.5 Conclusion and Future Work

We have presented a method for recovering human pose in challenging sports scenarios using only a single view but requiring some human interaction. The proposed framework is generic in terms of types of motion and pose the athlete could take. The algorithm has been tested on three challenging sports sequences of different sports as well as three sequences from the HumanEva dataset. Quantitative and qualitative analyses have shown that our method provides a significant improvement to using interpolation and is capable of recovering pose even in the most challenging of conditions. Sequences that are less difficult require significantly fewer keyframes for a successful solve.

Future work will focus on improving the appearance model as a stepping stone to weakening the reliance of the algorithm on keyframe interpolation and reducing the solution search space by generating higher quality body part candidates. This should also be useful in reducing the overall number of keyframes required for a high-quality solution.

Since our algorithm is capable of recovering joint locations another avenue for exploration is recovery of pose in 3D, which would allow for additional kinematic constraints to be added to the optimisation as well as derivation of useful metrics about the athlete.

References

1. Agarwal A, Triggs B (2006) Recovering 3d human pose from monocular images. IEEE Trans Pattern Anal Mach Intell Proc 28(1):44–58
2. Agarwal P, Kumar S, Ryde J, Corso J, Krovi V (2012) Estimating human dynamics on-the-fly using monocular video for pose estimation. In: Proceedings of robotics: science and systems, Sydney, Australia, July 2012
3. Andriluka M, Roth S, Schiele B (2009) Pictorial structures revisited: people detection and articulated pose estimation. In: IEEE conference on computer vision and pattern recognition
4. Andriluka M, Roth S, Schiele B (2010) Monocular 3d pose estimation and tracking by detection. In: IEEE conference on computer vision and pattern recognition (CVPR), San Francisco, USA, 06/2010
5. Bissacco A, Yang M-H, Soatto S (2007) Fast human pose estimation using appearance and motion via multi-dimensional boosting regression. In: IEEE conference on computer vision and pattern recognition, June, pp 1–8
6. Felzenszwalb PF, Huttenlocher DP (2005) Pictorial structures for object recognition. Int J Comput Vis 61(1):55–79
7. Ferrari V, Marin-Jimenez M, Zisserman A (2008) Progressive search space reduction for human pose estimation. In: IEEE conference on computer vision and pattern recognition, pp 1–8
8. Ferrari V, Marn-jimnez M, Zisserman A (2009) 2d human pose estimation in TV shows. In: In dagstuhl post-proceedings
9. Jiang H (2009) Human pose estimation using consistent max-covering. In: International conference on computer vision
10. Lan X, Huttenlocher D (2004) A unified spatio-temporal articulated model for tracking. In: Proceedings of the IEEE conference on computer vision and pattern recognition, June-2 July, vol 1, pp I-722–I-729
11. Moeslund TB, Hilton A, Krüger V, Sigal L (eds) (2011) Visual analysis of humans—looking at people. Springer, New York
12. Mooij JM (2010) libDAI: a free and open source C++ library for discrete approximate inference in graphical models. J Mach Learn Res 11:2169–2173
13. Mori G, Ren X, Efros AA, Malik J (2004) Recovering human body configurations: combining segmentation and recognition. In: Proceedings of the IEEE conference on computer vision and pattern recognition, pp 326–333
14. Pishchulin L, Jain A, Andriluka M, Thormaehlen T, Schiele B (2012) Articulated people detection and pose estimation: reshaping the future. In: 2012 IEEE conference on computer vision and pattern recognition (CVPR), Providence, United States, June 2012. IEEE, pp 1–8
15. Ren X, Berg AC, Malik J (2005) Recovering human body configurations using pairwise constraints between parts, vol 1, pp 824–831
16. Roberts TJ, McKenna SJ, Ricketts IW (2007) Human pose estimation using partial configurations and probabilistic regions. Int J Comput Vis Proc 73(3):285–306
17. Sapp B, Weiss D, Taskar B (2011) Parsing human motion with stretchable models. In: CVPR
18. Srinivasan P, Shi J (2007) Bottom-up recognition and parsing of the human body. In: Proceedings of the IEEE computer vision and pattern recognition, June 2007, pp 1–8
19. Yedidia JS, Freeman WT, Weiss Y (2000) Generalized belief propagation. In: IN NIPS 13. MIT Press, Cambridge, pp 689–695
20. Zhao T, Nevatia R (2003) Bayesian human segmentation in crowded situations. In: Proceedings of the IEEE conference on computer vision and pattern recognition, vol 2, June 2003, pp II-459-66

Part III
What are they Playing?

Chapter 9
Action Recognition in Realistic Sports Videos

Khurram Soomro and Amir R. Zamir

Abstract The ability to analyze the actions which occur in a video is essential for automatic understanding of sports. Action *localization* and *recognition* in videos are two main research topics in this context. In this chapter, we provide a detailed study of the prominent methods devised for these two tasks which yield superior results for sports videos. We adopt UCF Sports, which is a dataset of realistic sports videos collected from broadcast television channels, as our evaluation benchmark. First, we present an overview of UCF Sports along with comprehensive statistics of the techniques tested on this dataset as well as the evolution of their performance over time. To provide further details about the existing action *recognition* methods in this area, we decompose the action recognition framework into three main steps of feature extraction, dictionary learning to represent a video, and classification; we overview several successful techniques for each of these steps. We also overview the problem of *spatio-temporal localization* of actions and argue that, in general, it manifests a more challenging problem compared to action recognition. We study several recent methods for action localization which have shown promising results on sports videos. Finally, we discuss a number of forward-thinking insights drawn from overviewing the action recognition and localization methods. In particular, we argue that performing the recognition on *temporally untrimmed* videos and attempting to describe an action, instead of conducting a forced-choice classification, are essential for analyzing the human actions in a realistic environment.

K. Soomro (✉)
Center for Research in Computer Vision, University of Central Florida,
Orlando, FL 32826, USA
e-mail: ksoomro@cs.ucf.edu

A.R. Zamir
Gates Computer Science, #130, Stanford University, 353 Serra Mall, Stanford, CA 94305, USA
e-mail: zamir@cs.stanford.edu

T.B. Moeslund et al. (eds.), *Computer Vision in Sports*,
Advances in Computer Vision and Pattern Recognition,
DOI 10.1007/978-3-319-09396-3_9

9.1 Introduction

Developing automatic methods for analyzing actions in videos are of particular importance for machine understanding of sports. Action recognition, which is the problem of assigning a video to a set of predefined action classes, and action localization, defined as identification of the spatio-temporal location where an action takes place, are two of the fundamental and heavily studied topics in this context.

The majority of existing frameworks for action recognition consist of three main steps: feature extraction, dictionary learning to form a representation for a video based on the extracted features, and finally classification of the video using the representation. In the first step, a set of features, such as STIP [32, 33] or dense trajectories [77, 78], are extracted from a given video. These features are supposed to encode the information which is useful for recognition of the action in a numerical form such as a vector. Then, the extracted features are used for forming a representation of a video, which captures the actions that occur therein. Such representation may be as simple as a histogram of most frequent motions [32, 33, 75, 77, 78] or a semantically meaningful model such as action poses [76]. In the last step, a general model for each action of interest is learnt using the computed representation of a set of labeled training videos. Given the learnt models, a query video is then assigned to the most similar action class by the classifier.

Action localization, unlike action recognition, deals with the problem of identifying the exact location in space-time where an action occurs. It manifests a wider range of challenges, e.g., dealing with background clutter or the spatial complexity of the scene, and has been the topic of fewer research papers as compared to action recognition. The recent successful action localization techniques, which will be discussed in Sect. 9.4, typically attempt to segment the action utilizing cues based on the appearance, motion, or a combination of both [40, 69].

UCF Sports [57] is one of the earliest action recognition datasets that contains realistic actions in unconstrained environment. In this chapter, we provide a detailed study of the UCF Sports dataset along with comprehensive statistics of the methods evaluated on it. We also discuss the technical details of the prominent approaches for action localization and recognition which yield superior results for sports videos.

In Sect. 9.5, we discuss the insights acquired from summarizing the existing action recognition and localization methods, especially the ones evaluated on UCF Sports. In particular, we will argue that many of the existing action localization and recognition systems are devised for *temporally trimmed* videos. This is a significantly unrealistic assumption, and it is essential to develop techniques which are capable of performing the recognition or localization on temporally untrimmed videos. In addition, we discuss that describing an action using a universal lexicon of lower level actions, also known as action attributes [17, 37], is a worthwhile alternative to increasing the number of classes in action datasets and performing a forced-choice classification task. Lastly, we will discuss that the majority of existing action localization algorithms mostly perform an exhaustive search in, spatial, temporal, or spatio-temporal domain, in order to find a match for their action representation. This approach is

Fig. 9.1 UCF Sports Dataset: sample frames of 10 action classes along with their bounding box annotations of the humans shown in *yellow*

inefficient, as also observed in several recent object detection methods [9, 15, 72], and can be improved by employing a more efficient search strategy similar to selective search [25, 72] or object proposals [15].

9.2 UCF Sports Dataset

UCF Sports consists of various sports actions collected from broadcast television channels including ESPN and BBC. The dataset includes 10 actions: diving, golf swing, kicking, lifting, riding horse, running, skateboarding, swinging-bench, swinging-side, and walking. Figure 9.1 shows a sample frame of all ten actions. The dataset along with human bounding box and human gaze annotations is available to the public.[1]

The dataset includes a total of 150 sequences with the resolution of 720 × 480. Table 9.1 summarizes the characteristics of the dataset. Figure 9.2 shows the distribution of the number of clips per action as the number of clips in each class is not the same. Figure 9.3 illustrates the total duration of clips (blue) and the average clip length (green) for every action class. It is evident that certain actions are short in nature, such as kicking, as compared to walking or running, which are relatively longer and have more periodicity. However, it is apparent from the chart that the average duration of action clips shows great similarities across different classes. Therefore, merely considering the duration of one clip would not be enough for identifying the action.

Table 9.1 Summary of the characteristics of UCF Sports

Actions	10	Total duration	958 s
Clips	150	Frame rate	10 fps
Mean clip length	6.39 s	Resolution	720 × 480
Min clip length	2.20 s	Max num. of clips per class	22
Max clip length	14.40 s	Min num. of clips per class	6

[1] Download UCF Sports dataset: http://crcv.ucf.edu/data/UCF_Sports_Action.php.

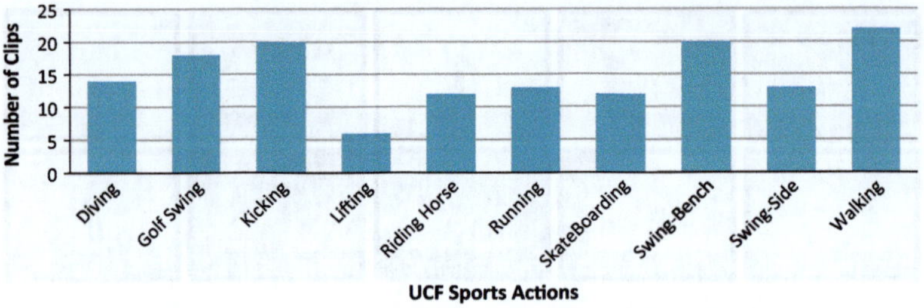

Fig. 9.2 Number of clips per action class

UCF Sports has been cited by more than 400 times since its introduction in 2008 and has been adopted by many state-of-the-art algorithms as an evaluation benchmark. Figure 9.4 shows number of citations per year and the cumulative count showing its rise every year.

Since its introduction, the dataset has been used for numerous applications such as: action recognition, action localization, and saliency detection. Saliency detection methods specify the region in the videos which attracts the human attention the most. The following sections explain how the methodologies applied on UCF Sports have evolved over time and describe the standard experimental setups. In the rest of this chapter, we focus on action recognition and localization as the two main tasks for analyzing the actions in videos.

9.2.1 Action Recognition

Action recognition is one of the heavily studied topics in computer vision. More than 80 % of the research publications which have utilized UCF Sports reported action recognition results on this dataset. Figure 9.5 shows how the accuracy of action recognition on UCF Sports has evolved every year since 2008. This figure reports yearly mean accuracy for two experimental setups: (1) Leave-One-Out and (2) Five-

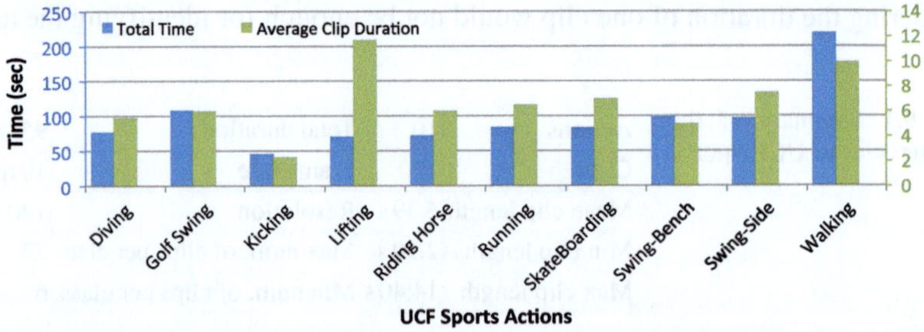

Fig. 9.3 The total time of video clips for each action class is shown in *blue*. Average length of clips for each action is shown in *green*

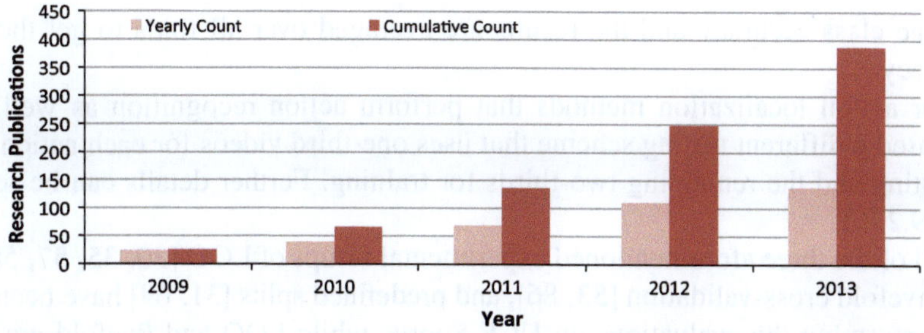

Fig. 9.4 Research publications in which UCF Sports was utilized. The chart shows yearly and cumulative counts until 2013

Fold cross-validation. The mean accuracy has gradually improved every year and the state-of-the-art method (96.6 % accuracy [23]) is able to recognize the minority of the actions correctly.

The early successful methods on UCF Sports were mostly based on sparse space-time interest points [32, 33] and cuboid descriptors. However, the more recent dense sampling [18, 50] and trajectory-based [77, 78] techniques have been able to outperform them and significantly improve the overall accuracy. Several of such methods for feature extraction [16, 32, 33], action representation [26, 76], dictionary learning [53], and classification [51, 57] will be discussed in more detail in Sect. 9.3.

9.2.1.1 Experimental Setup

The original way [57] to test on UCF Sports was to use a Leave-One-Out (LOO) cross-validation scheme. This scenario takes out one sample video for testing and trains using all of the remaining videos of an action class. This is performed for every sample video in a cyclic manner, and the overall accuracy is obtained by averaging the accuracy of all iterations.

An alternative experimental setup was proposed in [86] that uses a five-fold cross-validation scheme. Each fold consisted of one-fifth videos for testing and the remaining for training. For each fold the recognition accuracy is calculated using

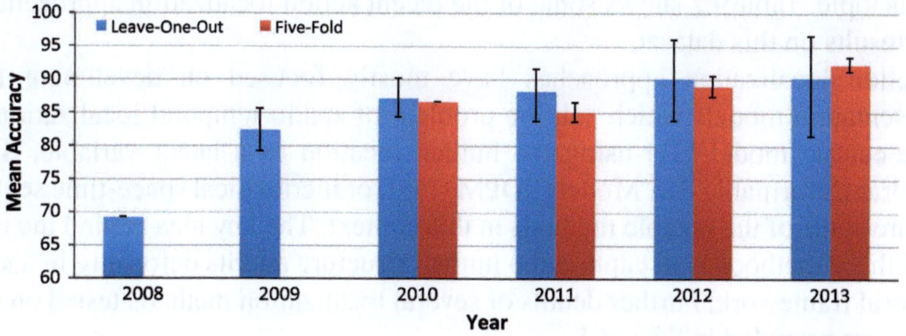

Fig. 9.5 Yearly mean accuracy of action recognition for two experimental setups: (1) Leave-One-Out (2) Five-Fold cross-validation. The brackets show the maximum and minimum accuracy for every year

average class accuracy and the results are averaged over all folds to get the final accuracy.

For action localization methods that perform action recognition as well, [31] proposed a different testing scheme that uses one-third videos for each action class as testing and the remaining two-thirds for training. Further details can be seen in Sect. 9.2.2.1.

All of the three aforementioned experimental setups of LOO [30, 35, 57, 58, 81, 87], fivefold cross-validation [53, 86], and predefined splits [31, 69] have been used for performing the evaluations on UCF Sports, while LOO and fivefold are more common. However, fivefold cross-validation and using splits are computationally less expensive as they require less training-testing iterations.

9.2.2 Action Localization

Action localization is an important problem with a wide range of applications such as human activity analysis, behavior recognition, video retrieval, and many others. Action localization is generally a more difficult task compared to action recognition. That is because a successful action localization requires the action class to be correctly recognized, and also its spatio-temporal location to be identified. Therefore, action recognition is a subproblem solved within action localization. In action recognition, at times it is feasible to recognize an action using only the background features, and without utilizing the temporal or motion information. Therefore, even though one could recognize such actions, detecting the exact spatio-temporal location of the action would require additional steps such as modeling the temporal movement of body parts. This becomes even more complex when practical challenges, e.g., occlusion or background clutter, are considered as well.

Action localization has been the subject of fewer research efforts compared to action recognition. This is observable in the statistics as less than 15 % of the research papers evaluated on UCF Sports have discussed action localization results. UCF Sports was one of the first datasets for which bounding box annotations of the actions were made available, and therefore it is an excellent dataset for studying the advances on this topic. Table 9.2 shows some of the recent action localization approaches and their results on this dataset.

Action localization approaches have mostly focused on developing action representation models which suit the problem of spatio-temporal localization. The figure-centric model [31] using the human location as a latent variable, Spatio-temporal Deformable Part Model (SDPM) [69], or hierarchical space-time segments [40] are some of the notable methods in this context. The key idea behind the majority of these methods is to capture the human structure and its deformity in a spatio-temporal framework. Further details of several localization methods tested on sports videos are provided in Sect. 9.4.

Table 9.2 Action localization results on UCF sports

Method	Year	Experimental setup	Evaluation metric	Accuracy (%)
Shapovalova et al. [61]	2013	Splits	ROC & AUC	32.3
Lan et al. [31]	2011	Splits	ROC & AUC	38
Tian et al. [69]	2013	Splits	ROC & AUC	42
Tran and Yuan [71]	2012	Splits	Average precision	55.34[a]
Ma et al. [40]	2013	Splits	Intersection-over-union	42.1
Gall et al. [21]	2011	Five-fold cross-validation	Average precision	54
Yao et al. [86]	2010	Five-fold cross-validation	Average precision	54
Cheng et al. [10]	2013	Five-fold cross-validation	Average precision	61.6
Thi et al. [68]	2012	Five-fold cross-validation	Binarized overlap	89
Raptis et al. [56]	2012	Leave-one-out cross-validation	Localization score	62.6

[a] Only three actions were used for localization: Horse Riding, Running and Diving

9.2.2.1 Experimental Setup

Similar to Sect. 9.2.1, the original experimental setup for action localization is to use Leave-One-Out (LOO) scheme. However, this setup has been criticized by Lan et al. [31] for two main reasons. The first reason is that no parameters (e.g., the SVM regularizer weightings, C) have been given and experiments show that the accuracy can change drastically by varying parameters. The second reason, which is more critical, is that many videos have similar backgrounds, and therefore a strong scene correlation exists between videos. Thus, while testing under LOO setting, the classifier may use the background features to classify the video which results in an artificially high accuracy. An empirical evidence for this issue has been provided in [31]. To alleviate this problem, an alternate experimental setup [31] is proposed. The new setup[2] splits the dataset into two uneven parts: two-third of videos for training and one-third for testing. To calculate the accuracy, an *intersection-over-union* criterion is used to plot ROC curves with a certain overlap threshold. The *intersection-over-union* computes the overlap between the predicted bounding box and the ground truth, and divides it by the union of both the bounding boxes, for every frame. This value is then averaged over all frames in a video. A 20 % overlap threshold is used for this experiment. Area Under Curve (AUC) against the overlap threshold, which shows how the performance varies if the threshold is changed, is used to compute the final performance. To calculate the overlap, the ground truth bounding box per frame is provided for the dataset. Figure 9.1 shows sample frames from UCF Sports dataset for each action class along with their annotated bounding boxes of humans.

The reported results in Table 9.2 show a variety of experimental setups and evaluation metrics. Due to the aforementioned issues, adopting the predefined splits of

[2] UCF Sports experimental setup for Action Localization: http://www.sfu.ca/~tla58/other/train_test_split.

[31] as the setup is recommended. As the evaluation metric, both Precision/Recall and ROC curves are appropriate. However, Precision/Recall has been a more popular choice for the other datasets, and therefore it is recommended for UCF Sports as well for the sake of consistency.

9.3 Action Recognition in Realistic Sports Videos

In this section, we provide an overview of some of the action recognition techniques which have shown superior results for sports videos. The overall recognition framework is broken down into three major steps of feature extraction, dictionary learning (for forming the representation of videos), and finally classification. The prominent methods for each step are elaborated in the rest of this section.

9.3.1 Feature Extraction

Classifying actions from videos requires extracting a set of data points, commonly termed features, that are expected to carry the information which is useful for distinguishing between various actions. Existing features can be classified into two main categories: (1) Low-level (Local) and (2) High-level (Holistic) features. Low-level features are the most commonly used features and are extracted by either detecting interest points or densely sampling them in a video. High-level features capture further structured information related to the action being performed. This high-level structure aims at gathering features such as shape [26], pose [76] or contextual information [81]. The general goal of feature extraction is to gather features that are generic enough and robust to backround variation. These features should be invariant to changes in scale, rotation, affine transformations, illumination, and viewpoint. However, capturing the required information while preserving the robustness to the aforementioned issues is a challenging problem. In the following sections, we will explore several low-level and high-level features that have performed well on UCF Sports.

9.3.1.1 Low-Level Features

Generally, low-level feature extraction is done by detecting sparse keypoints such as corners [24, 62], edges [8, 48], contours [49, 52], or blobs [42]. The corner detectors usually work by finding the locations that have large gradients in all directions; to find edges, an intensity derivative is applied in a specific direction. Contours find local silhouettes, and blobs aim at detecting regions within an image that have distinctive color properties compared to the neighboring areas. Once the keypoints are detected, a descriptor is formed around the point, which captures the local information. This descriptor can be scale-invariant such as Scale-Invariant Feature Transform

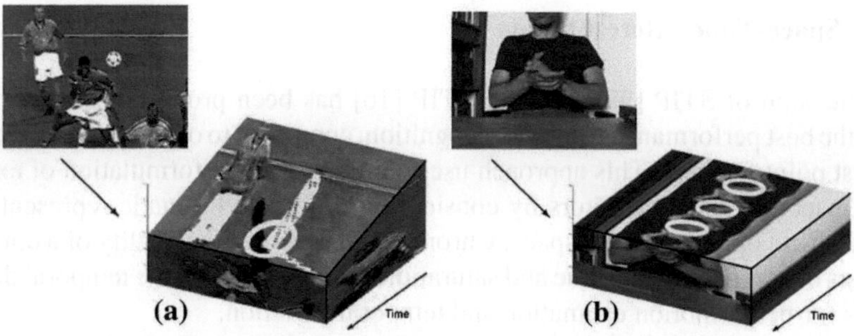

Fig. 9.6 Space-Time Interest Points (STIP) [32]: Features detected in **a** Football sequence when player is heading a ball. **b** Hand clapping sequence. The temporal slice of space-time volume shows that the detected events correspond to neighborhoods with high spatio-temporal variation

(SIFT) [38], texture-based [54], shape-context [5], gradient location and orientation histogram (GLOH) [46], steerable filters using Gaussian derivatives [20], moment invariants [73], and many more. Other useful information that local features can extract could be color, motion, trajectories, shape descriptors, and depth cues.

The aforementioned features were initially devised for images and capture the static information from the image. To extend this to videos and make use of temporal information, Space-Time Interest Points (STIP) [32, 33] were developed which are based on an extension of Harris corner detector. STIP can be described as the extention of spatial interest points into the spatio-temporal domain, where local structures which have significant local variations of image intensity values in space and nonconstant motion in time are detected. These local spatio-temporal features often correspond to interesting events in video data (see Fig. 9.6). Inspired by STIP, many variants have been proposed over time such as 3D-SIFT [60], HOG3D [29], extended SURF [80], and Local Trinary Patterns [87].

Although sparse keypoints have shown good classification performance, dense sampling has given further improvements in the image classification task [18, 50]. Dense sampling is different from sparse interest points in the sense that points are uniformly selected from the image, instead of using a criteria for selecting keypoints. That way, more information is gathered which can be learned by a classifier to give better performances in action recognition.

A more intuitive way of finding spatio-temporal characteristics is to track interest points throughout the video sequence. Some recent methods [43, 45, 65, 66] have shown improvement in action recognition performance using motion information of trajectories. These methods obtain feature trajectories by either using KLT tracker [39] in their approach [43, 45] or matching SIFT descriptors [38] between consecutive frames [66].

In the following sections, we describe two main low-level features that have given superior action recognition results on the UCF Sports dataset.

Color Space-Time Interest Points

An extension of STIP [32] to Color-STIP [16] has been proposed recently which gives the best performance in action recognition, compared to other sparse space-time interest point features. This approach uses a multichannel reformulation of existing STIP detectors and descriptors by considering different chromatic representations derived from opponent color space. Chromaticity specifies the quality of a color and consists of two parameters: hue and saturation. Adding Color to the temporal domain allows for better motion estimation and temporal variation.

The approach transforms *RGB* space to *Opponent* color space and comes up with a new photometric representation: I(ntensity), C(hromatic), N(ormalized chromatic) and H(ue). A combination of intensity and chromatic channels is used to give a three-channel representation: *IC*, *IN*, and *IH*. Multi-Channel Harris-STIP and Gabor-STIP detectors are formulated for each photometric channel and are represented using a Multi-Channel STIP descriptor. The Multi-Channel STIP descriptor is calculated by incorporating chromaticity in the HOG3D [29] descriptor. The final descriptor is a combination of two variants: (1) Channel Integration and (2) Channel Concatenation.

Many existing STIP-based approaches [32, 33] operate on image intensity, making them sensitive to highlights and shadows. They ignore the discriminative information by discarding chromaticity from the representation. By utilizing chromaticity in their enhanced appearance model, Color-STIP has shown to outperform other STIP-based methods.

Trajectories

Dense sampling of feature points and feature trajectories [39] have shown a notable improvement in image classification [18, 50] and activity recognition [45]. Inspired by these approaches, a recent method [77] computes dense trajectories by sampling dense points from each frame and tracking them based on displacement information from a dense optical flow field. By employing global smoothness constraints, dense trajectories are made to be more robust to irregular abrupt motion as well as shot boundaries.

Feature points are densely sampled on a grid, with uniform spacing, and tracked at multiple spatial scales to obtain dense trajectories (see Fig. 9.7). Each point is tracked between consecutive frames using median filtering in a dense optical flow field. These points from subsequent frames are then linked together to form a trajectory. To avoid the problem of drifting in trajectories, the length is limited to a fixed number of frames. Drifting usually occurs when a trajectory moves away from the initial position during the tracking process.

In order to encode various trajectory information, a novel descriptor is proposed which combines trajectory shape, appearance, and motion information. The shape of trajectory embeds local motion patterns and is described by a sequence of normalized displacement vectors. The motion and appearance information is captured by computing the descriptor within a space-time volume aligned with the trajectory.

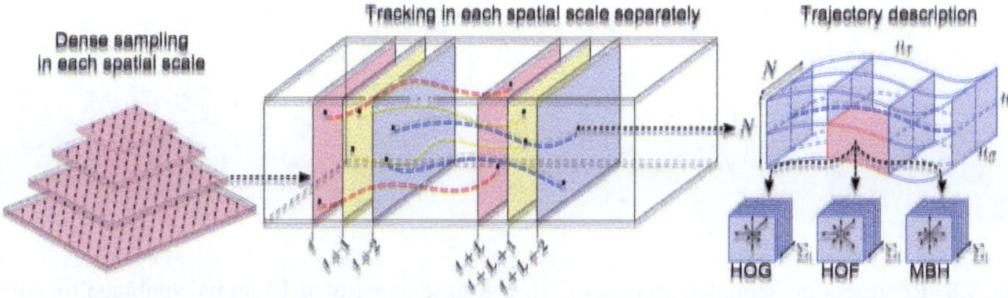

Fig. 9.7 Extracting Dense Trajectories [78]. *Left* Densely sampled feature points on each spatial scale. *Middle* Tracking feature points separately on each spatial scale using median filtering for L frames in a dense optical flow field. *Right* A $N \times N$ pixels neighborhood divided into $n_\sigma \times n_\sigma \times n_\tau$ grid is used to compute (*HOG*, *HOF*, *MBH*) descriptors along the trajectory

The volume is subdivided into a spatio-temporal grid to obtain local information. Histogram of Oriented Gradients (HOG) [11] encoding static appearance information, Histogram of Oriented Flow (HOF) [34] getting local motion information and Motion Boundary Histogram (MBH) [12] capturing relative motion information, are used as various descriptors for the trajectory volume.

Dense trajectories have shown to give better performance than Space-Time Interest Points (STIP) [33], as they capture appearance and dynamic motion information along the trajectory as compared to STIP, which uses cuboids instead. Experiments have shown dense trajectories to be further robust to camera motion and more informative for action classification.

9.3.1.2 High-Level Features

High-level features in action recognition represent an action by detecting high-level concepts [58] and often build upon local features [67]. The main idea is to preserve structural information of actions. These high-level features can be a spatio-temporal volume (STV) generated by 2D contours [88], 3D shapes induced by silhouettes [22], motion descriptor based on smoothed and aggregated optical flow [14], kinematic features [4] and so on.

The following sections introduce two of the recent high-level features that model the action remarkably well under varying background conditions and yield superior results on UCF Sports.

Spatio-Temporal Structures of Human Poses

An action can be considered as a mere articulation of parts. Hence, representing an action as poses is intuitively meaningful and has the capability of incorporating the variety of nonrigidness that a human body posesses when performing an action. In this context, [76] presents a pose-based action representation which models the spatio-temporal structures of human poses [85].

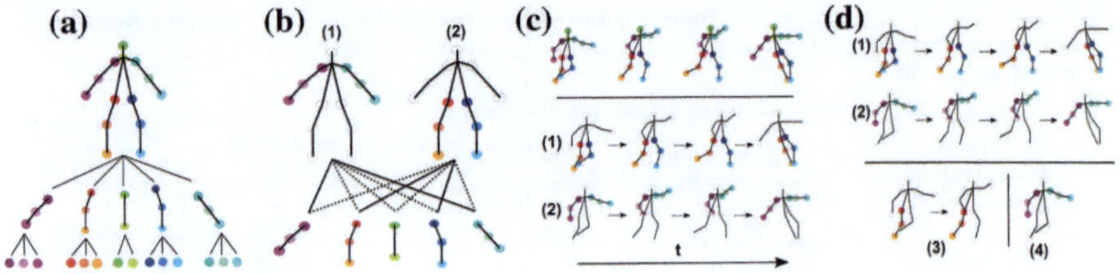

Fig. 9.8 Representing actions with poses [76]. **a** A pose consists of 14 joints combined together to form five body parts; **b** two spatial-part-sets showing co-occurring combinations of body parts for a particular action; **c** temporal-part-sets showing co-occurring sequences of body parts; **d** action representation consisting of spatial-part-sets *(4)* and temporal-part-sets *(1–3)*

Given a video, K-best pose estimations are obtained for each frame, and the best pose is inferred using segmentation cues and temporal constraints. To obtain the action representation, estimated joints are grouped into five body parts: Head, Left arm, Right arm, Left leg, and Right leg (see Fig. 9.8). Efficient Contrast mining algorithm is used to gather distinctive co-occurring spatial configuration of body parts, called spatial-part-sets, and co-occurring pose sequences of body parts in temporal domain, called temporal-part-sets. Similarly, for test videos, part-sets are detected using estimated poses and represented using a histogram of part-sets. This histogram is then classified using a Support Vector Machine (SVM). Representing actions in terms of poses and part-sets gives a better visual interpretation and is compact as compared to high-dimensional, low-level representations. It is also robust to variations in body part movements since it can model the temporal movements effectively.

Shape Models

A joint shape-motion descriptor is proposed in [26], which combines shape features from an appearance model and motion features from optical flow field to capture distinct properties of an action. The approach represents an action as a sequence of prototypes for flexible action matching in video sequences. In training, action interest regions are localized and shape-motion descriptors are extracted. Using hierarchical K-means clustering, an action prototype tree is learned in a joint shape and motion space. The training sequences are represented as a labeled prototype sequence. In testing, humans are detected and tracked using appearance information, while frame-to-prototype correspondence is established by maximizing joint probability of the actor location and action prototype by searching the learned prototype tree. Finally, the action is recognized using dynamic prototype sequence matching.

The shape descriptor for an action interest region is represented as a feature vector by dividing the region of interest into a square grid. Shape observations are gathered using background subtraction or from appearance likelihood maps. For the appearance likelihood map, an appearance model is built and is used to assign a probability to each pixel in the specified region. An accumulation of such probabilites

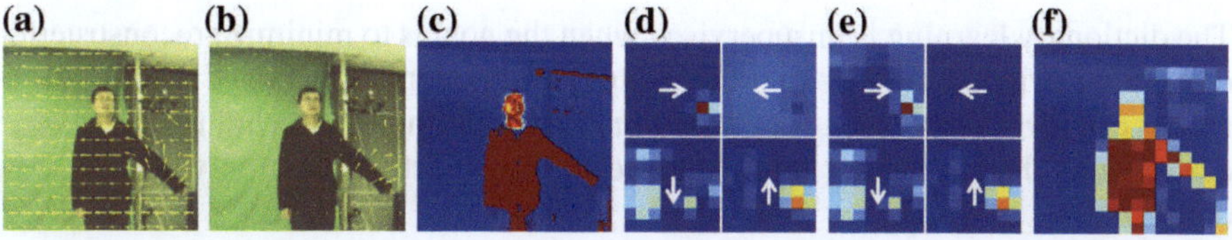

Fig. 9.9 Computing shape-motion descriptor [26]: **a** Raw optical flow field. **b** Motion-compensated optical flow field. **c** Appearance likelihood map. **d** Motion descriptor from the raw optical flow field. **e** Motion descriptor from the motion-compensated optical flow field. **f** Shape descriptor

for each grid square is used as a shape feature vector. The feature vector is L_2 normalized to get the final shape descriptor, as seen in Fig. 9.9f.

The motion descriptor for an action interest region is represented as a feature vector of Quantized, Blurred, Motion-compensated Flow ($QBMF$). The motion flow feature is calculated similar to [14], where optical flow is computed and divided into horizontal and vertial components and then background motion is removed by subtracting the medians of flow fields to get median-compensated flow fields. Motion-compensated flow fields (see Fig. 9.9b) are half-wave rectified into four nonnegative channels and each one of them is blurred using a Gaussian Kernel to get motion observations. The four channels are L_2 normalized and concatenated to get the raw motion descriptor. Finally, the raw motion descriptor is L_2 normalized to get the final motion descriptor. Figure 9.9d, e, shows the four channels of the motion descriptor, where grid intensity indicates motion strength and the arrow indicates the dominant motion orientation at that grid.

The results demonstrate good action recognition performance under moving camera and dynamic background. The reason is that the approach models the correlation between shape and motion using action prototypes in a joint feature space, which allows the method to tolerate such complex conditions.

9.3.2 Dictionary Learning

Dictionary learning is an important step in forming the representation of actions. It is most commonly employed in a Bag-of-Words (BoW) framework by using either low-level features such as STIP [32, 33] or high-level features such as human poses [76]. Typically, an unsupervised learning technique such as K-means is applied to cluster local features, and then the features from each video sequence are mapped to these cluster centers to get a histogram representation.

Sparse coding is also very popular and has been successfully applied to many computer vision problems such as image classification [84], visual saliency [83], and image restoration [55]. Sparse coding attempts to approximate an input sample using a linear combination of a few items from an overcomplete dictionary. Dictionary learning methods can be categorized into unsupervised and supervised learning.

The dictionary learning is unsupervised when the goal is to minimize reconstruction error of the original samples in order to build a dictionary. Supervised learning techniques can form a category specific dictionary that promotes discrimination between classes; this discriminatory term is added to the objective function which is to be optimized.

In the following sections, we will explore new techniques for dictionary learning that have produced notable results on UCF Sports dataset.

9.3.2.1 Multi-Task Sparse Learning

Multi-Task Sparse Learning (MTSL) [89] aims to construct a given test sample with multiple features and very few bases. In this framework, each feature modality is considered as a single task in MTSL to learn a sparse representation. These tasks are generated from multiple features extracted from the same visual input (video), hence they are interrelated. A Beta Process (BP) prior is used to learn a compact dictionary and infer sparse structure shared across all tasks.

Each video is represented using two types of features: (1) a histogram and (2) co-occurrence features. Histogram representation has achieved state-of-the-art performance and is frequently used in a bag-of-words framework. However, it ignores the geometric distribution of local features. Co-occurrence feature makes use of spatio-temporal proximity distribution of local features in a video to utilize geometric context.

A task is generated from each modality of features coming from the same video sequences. Each individual task is defined as learning a sparse representation of the video in one feature space. Multi-task learning improves the performance of each individual task by sharing information between related tasks. A target sample $y_j, j = 1, \dots, J$ with J tasks, obtained from a video is represented in terms of a dictionary D_j, a sparse coefficient θ_j and a residual error ε_j. A sparse coefficient vector is the product of a binary vector z_j, defining which dictionary terms are used to represent a sample, and a weight vector ω_j. A Beta Process is used to formulate the dictionary as well as the binary vector. A graphical model based representation of MTSL is shown in Fig. 9.10. The bottom layer consists of individual models with task-related parameters. In the middle layer, tasks are connected via common prior of the tasks and the top layer is the hyperprior invoked on the parameters of the prior. In the model, the variables are infered given the training samples. Gibbs sampling is used to update them iteratively. All variables except the dictionary D are initialized randomly. However, the dictionary is initialized using K-SVD [53]. K-SVD learns an overcomplete dictionary for sparse representation. Once initialized, MTSL obtains a compact and discriminative dictionary by Gibbs sampling. To classify a test video, the sparse representation is obtained by MTSL model using the learned dictionary. It is then classified using the reconstruction error accumulated over all the tasks.

This method classifies UCF Sports actions using a Leave-One-Out setup and achieves an accuracy of 92.67 %. MTSL approach combined multiple features efficiently to improve the recognition performance. Its robust sparse coding technique

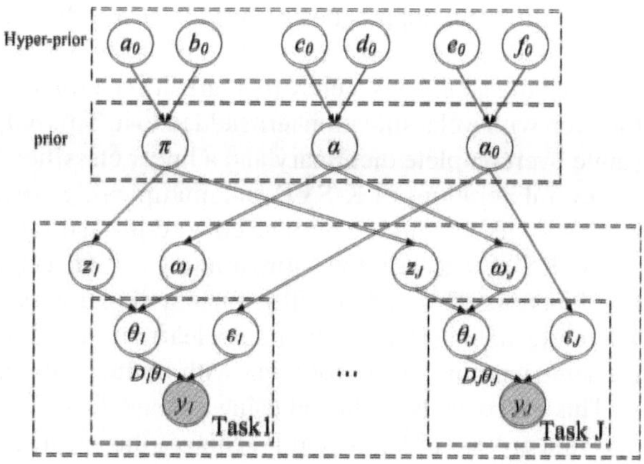

Fig. 9.10 Hierarchical Bayesian model representation of Multi-Task Sparse Learning (MTSL) approach [89]. Details of the parameters can be found in the paper

mines correlations between different tasks to obtain a shared sparsity pattern which is ignored if each task is learned individually. By using the Beta Process, the reconstruction coefficient vector is sparse, and it is distinct from the widely used l_1 regularized sparseness, which has many small coefficient values, but not exactly zero.

9.3.2.2 Label Consistent K-SVD

To learn a discriminative dictionary for sparse coding, a label consistent K-SVD (LC-KSVD) algorithm is proposed in [28]. During the dictionary learning process, the approach uses class label information of training data and associates label information with each dictionary item to enforce discriminability in sparse codes.

The above method presents a supervised learning algorithm to learn a reconstructive and discriminative dictionary for sparse coding. The objective function has a reconstruction error term and has two formulations for sparsity constraints: (1) L_0 norm and (2) L_1 norm. It also introduces a new label consistency constraint called "discriminative sparse code error." This term encourages the features from the same class to have similar sparse codes and those that belong to different classes have different sparse codes. Each item in the dictionary is chosen in a way that it represents a subset of training features that are ideally from a single class, so that each dictionary item can be associated to a particular label. This makes the correspondence between dictionary items and the class labels. The last term in the objective function is the classification error term. This term is a linear predictive classifier, and enables joint dictionary and classifier construction. The objective function is efficient and achieves a good classification performance; it also allows feature sharing among classes. By including the classification term, the objective function enforces a label consistency constraint on the sparse code with respect to the dictionary. It also makes the learned dictionary adaptive to underlying stucture of the training data. Learning the dictionary and classifier separately might make the dictionary suboptimal.

Two different approaches are presented for dictionary learning: (1) LC-KSVD1 (2) LC-KSVD2. The objective function for LC-KSVD1 uses the reconstruction error term and the label consistency regularization term. LC-KSVD2 has similar objective function with a classification term added to it. This helps the algorithm jointly learn a single overcomplete dictionary and a linear classifier. The parameters are initialized by several iterations of K-SVD and multiple ridge regression model. The dictionary is constructed by minimizing the error terms and satisfying the sparsity constraints.

LC-KSVD accesses the entire training set at every iteration to optimize the objective function. This can be difficult in a situation with limited memory resources. Therefore, an incremental dictionary learning algorithm is presented that can employ the same learning framework, but with limited memory resources.

This approach is evaluated using a Leave-One-Out experimental setup as well as five-fold cross-validation and it achieves the accuracies of 95.7 and 91.2 %, respectively. The results show that the method performs better than other sparse coding techniques that learn the dictionary and then use a one-against-all classifier to obtain classification results. Instead of iteratively solving subproblems to get a global solution, the proposed method is able to simultaneously learn the dictionary, discriminative sparse coding parameters, and the classifier parameters.

9.3.3 Action Classification

After passing through the stages of feature extraction and dictionary learning, the next step is to form a video representation. Features studied in Sect. 9.3.1 are generally used in the popular bag-of-words (BoW) [16, 77, 78] framework, where local features are extracted from video sequences and mapped to a prelearned dictionary. The dictionary is a collection of code words obtained by clustering features, generally by K-means. After assigning each feature to a specific code word in a dictionary, the video is represented using a histogram. This type of representation is simple and efficient. Histogram representations are relatively robust to occlusion and viewpoint changes.

Once a video representation is obtained, the final step is to classify the actions. The technique for classification can either be generative, e.g., HMM [1, 19, 82], or discriminative, e.g., CRF [44, 63]. It can also be as simple as a Nearest Neighbor classifier or more complex methods such as mapping to a Grassmann manifold [23, 51]. Over the years, a variety of techniques have been proposed for performing action classification on UCF Sports. Some of these methods are: template-based [57, 58], hough-based [10, 21, 86], manifold learning [23], randomized trees [51], multiple kernel learning [81], pattern mining [79], and several others. The following sections present some of the notable techniques that show superior classification results on UCF Sports.

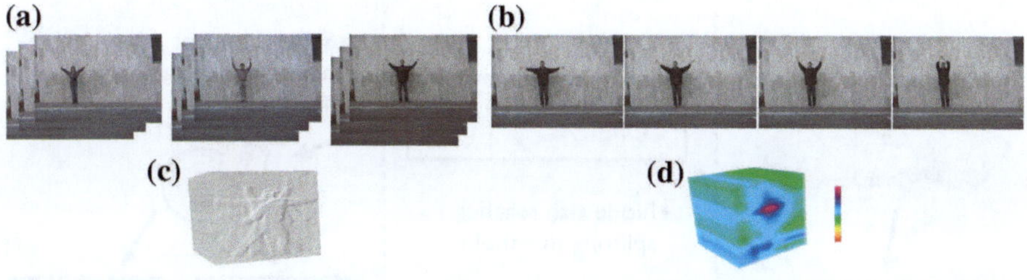

Fig. 9.11 Action MACH [57]: **a** Jumping Jack action from Weizmann action dataset. **b** 3D action MACH filter for Jumping Jack action. **c** Wave2 action from Weizmann action dataset. **d** Normalized correlation response for the Wave2 action using action MACH filter

9.3.3.1 Template-Based Method

Template-based matching emerged as an early solution for classifying actions. *Action Maximum Average Correlation Height (MACH)* filter proposed in [57] applies template-based matching to 3D spatio-temporal volume (video) having vector-valued data at each pixel location. The filter is generic and embeds intraclass variability into a single template. This capability enables the method to effectively discriminate a wide range of actions on UCF Sports dataset.

A *MACH* filter uses the training instances of a class to learn a single template by optimizing four performance metrics: Average Correlation Height (ACH), Average Correlation Energy (ACE), Average Similarity Measure (ASM), and Output Noise Variance (ONV). This gives a two-dimensional template which, when correlated with a testing image using a FFT transform in frequency domain, results in a response giving the most likely location of the object. The approach used in *Action MACH* extends this filter to be applied to spatio-temporal volumes and be able to fully utilize the temporal information.

During training, derivatives of spatio-temporal volumes, obtained from training video sequences, are represented in frequency domain by performing a 3D FFT transform. This 3D matrix is reshaped into a long column vector and is synthesized by minimizing average correlation energy, average similarity measure, output noise variance, and maximizing the average correlation height. After obtaining the 1D vector, an inverse 3D Fourier transform gives the *Action MACH* filter. However, this filter is only good for scalar values at each pixel location. To use vector-valued data, Clifford Fourier transform is applied, which is a generalization of the traditional scalar-valued Fourier transform.

Motion estimation in the video sequences is performed using Spatio-Temporal Regularity Flow (SPREF) [2]. SPREF computes the directions along which the sum of the gradients of a video sequence is minimized. Hence, a 3D vector field is generated having three values at each location that represent the direction along which the intensities of pixels change the least. This vector-valued data is then used to get the final *Action MACH* filter by applying Clifford Fourier transform (see Fig. 9.11a, b).

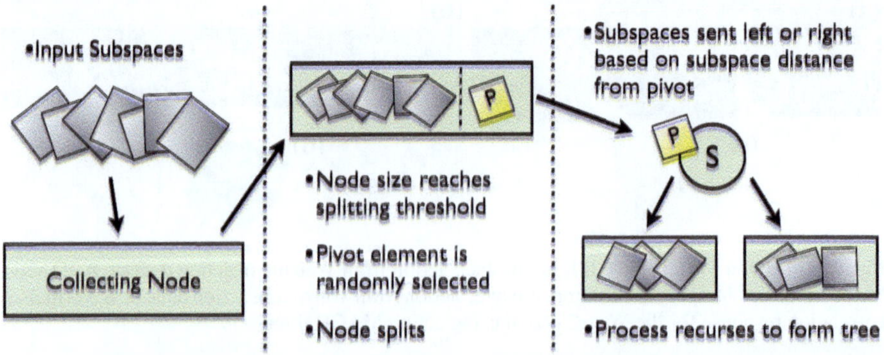

Fig. 9.12 Subspace tree construction [51]. *Left* Subspaces are added to a node. *Middle* If the node size exceeds a threshold it is split. *Right* The subspaces are split and assigned to *right* and *left* child node

To recognize an action in a test video sequence, the *Action MACH* filter is applied everywhere in the spatio-temporal volume (see Fig. 9.11c, d). The peak value in the response of the filter is compared to a threshold value and if it is greater, the video is classified to be of that particular action class. This approach was the first one to be applied on UCF Sports dataset and gave encouraging results.

9.3.3.2 Subspace Forest

A novel structure called Subspace Forest is introduced in [51], which proposes a randomized forest based approximate nearest neighbor (ANN) method for subspaces. This stucture is applied to action recognition, where actions are represented as subspaces on a Grassmann manifold. A Subspace tree is constructed during training, and, at testing stage, an ANN-based approach is used to classify each video sequence.

An action from a video is represented as a sequence of thumbnail-sized images called *tracklets*. Each *tracklet* is a three-dimensional cube with height, width, and frame as its axes. All tracklets are designed to be of an equal size. Every *tracklet* is mapped as one point on the Grassmann manifold. The Grassmann manifold $Gr(r,n)$ can be described as a set of r-dimensional linear subspaces of the n-dimensional vector space V. Points on the Grassmann manifold are subspaces and can be identified using orthogonal matrices. To map a *tracklet* on Grassmann manifold, the method first unfolds the *tracklet* along one of its axes and then applies QR factorization to get its orthogonal matrix. In this way, each *tracklet* is mapped onto the Grassmann manifold and represented by three subspaces coming from three tensor unfoldings. The distance between two tracklets is computed using the chordal distance by applying the component-wise sine function to the principal angles between subspaces.

A Subspace Tree (SSTree) is defined as a tree structure to sort points on Grassmann manifold. In this approach *tracklets*, obtained from video sequences, are sorted using their orthogonal basis. The SSTree is constructed by adding samples to an initially empty node, until the number of samples within a node become large enough to consider splitting (see Fig. 9.12). One of the elements of the node is selected as the pivot and chordal distance is computed between each element and the pivot. Based on the distance measure, i.e., greater or less than a threshold, the elements are added to the right and left child nodes, respectively. This recursive process forms the tree and all the samples are trickled down to the leaf nodes. The algorithm uses two different variations for splitting a node: (1) Median spliting (2) Entropy splitting. In median splitting, the pivot is selected randomly and the splitting threshold is selected by computing the median chordal distance between the pivot and all the remaining elements of the node. In entropy splitting, the pivot is also chosen randomly and the splitting threshold is selected using entropy over normalized histogram of distances computed between pivot and remaining elements. If the entropy falls below a threshold, then the distances are split into two clusters and the midpoint between cluster centers is used as a splitting threshold.

A variation of SSTree is also presented in an approach called Random Axes SSTree (RA-SSTree). In this tree structure, every new child node randomly selects an unfolding axes.

A Subspace Forest is defined as a collection of SSTrees. The forest size is chosen as a multiple of three for SSTree, so that all three unfolding axes of the *tracklet* have an equal number of SSTrees. In case of RA-SSTree, any number can be chosen.

To recognize the action class of a given video, first its *tracklet* is computed and then unfolded along X, Y, and T dimension to get three orthogonal matrices. All the orthogonal matrices are presented to the corresponding subspace trees in the forest to find out the approximate nearest neighbors (ANN). The final classification is done by the label of the K-Nearest-Neighbors (KNN) from each leaf node using a majority voting scheme.

Using subspace forest on Grassmann manifold, the method is able to achieve superior results as compared to *Action MACH*. The method has the ability to scale to larger real-world problems. It is also very simple to implement and has less parameters as compared to bag-of-features framework.

9.4 Action Localization in Sports Videos

The task of localization involves identifying the spatio-temporal volume in which the action is taking place. The simplest way to do this is to learn an action recognition classifier and use a sliding window approach. This method slides in the spatio-temporal volume of the video to select the subvolume with the maximum classifier score. By finding the volume with the highest score, a bounding box is placed at each frame to find the overlap with the ground truth. The label of the volume as well as the average percentage overlap (between ground truth and predicted bounding box) over all frames is used as a measure to judge whether the action was correctly localized.

Action *recognition approaches* that use a high-level representation, such as space-time shape models [22], silhouettes [74], human poses [76] or motion history images [7], have the potential ability to localize an action. However, this is not typically feasible in case of global action representations, e.g., bag-of-words histogram, which lose the spatial information.

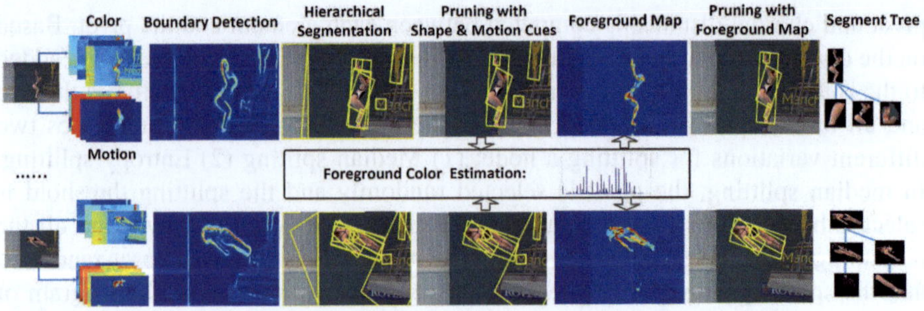

Fig. 9.13 Process to extract hierarchical space-time segments [40]. Each video is used to compute a boundary map using color and motion cues. The map is used to extract hierarchical segments. Irrelevant segments are pruned, firstly using shape and motion cues, then using foreground map to obtain a segment tree

Some of the recent methods achieving best localization performances are elaborated in the following sections.

9.4.1 Hierarchical Space-Time Segments

Representing an action by Hierarchical Space-Time Segments [40] has shown that preserving the static and nonstatic space-time segments along with their hierarchical relationships yields good action localization results. This approach uses a two-level hierarchiy: first level consists of root space-time segments and second level has parts of the root. Without utilizing bounding box annotations to train any body or body part detector, the algorithm uses an unsupervised approach to extract hierarchical space-time segments. Each step of the algorithm is elaborated below.

First, using color and motion information, a frame segmentation method is designed that preserves segments of the body and its parts, while suppressing the background. A boundary map is computed using color and motion channels to be utilized in forming an Ultrametric Contour Map (UCM). UCM gives a hierarchical segmentation of a video frame. The segment tree is traversed to prune irrelevant parts using motion and shape cues. For further pruning, a foreground map is built based on structure and global color cue over the whole video sequence, yielding a set of candidate segment trees, (see Fig. 9.13). In the remaining segment trees, each segment is tracked forward and backward in the video to get space-time segments. These space-time segments are used to train a Bag-of-Words framework with linear SVM. In testing, space-time segments are identified with a positive contribution to the video classification (see Fig. 9.14).

Thus, by using static and nonstatic parts, the method is able to achieve good classification and localization performance. The static information helps in extracting body parts that are not necessarily in motion, hence resulting in better localization. Sample results can be seen in Fig. 9.15. The method reports an accuracy of 42.1 % measured as average Intersection-Over-Union (IOU) over a subset of frames.

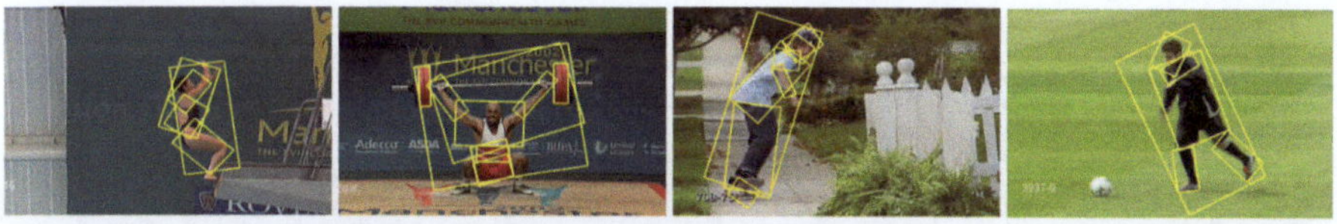

Fig. 9.14 Extracted segments from video frames [40]. Segments are outlined by *yellow* boxes. Boxes within a box show child–parent relationship

9.4.2 Spatio-Temporal Deformable Part Models

A natural extension of Deformable Part Models from 2D to a 3D for action localization is given by Spatio-Temporal Deformable Part Models (SDPM) [69]. In this method, a separate action model is learned for each class by selecting the most discriminative 3D subvolumes as parts and establishing spatio-temporal relations between them. The deformity in spatio-temporal volume that this approach yields empowers capturing the intraclass variabilities and becoming robust to background clutter.

The model consists of a root filter and many part models. Every part is defined by its part filter, anchor position, and coefficients of deformation cost. In the training stage, positive instances are selected from a single box of one cycle of an action. Negative instances are selected from positive volumes of other action classes, as well as by randomly drawing volumes from the background at multiple scales. HOG3D [29] features are extracted and a SVM is trained accordingly. Similarly, for training part models, HOG3D features are extracted at twice the resolution enabling them to capture more detail. Once SVM is applied, subvolumes having higher weights (i.e., more discriminative) are selected as parts, while others are ignored. After the initial model is obtained, latent SVM is used to update the model, while treating position of *i*th part as a latent variable (see Fig. 9.16)

In the testing stage, a spatio-temporal feature pyramid is built using HOG3D features at different spatial scales for the query video. A template-based sliding window approach is applied in 3D volume and the placement with the highest score is chosen to be the location of the action. This placement is defined by the location of the root and part filters (see Fig. 9.17).

Fig. 9.15 Action localization results [40]. *Green* area denotes the ground truth annotation, whereas the *red* area shows the localization result

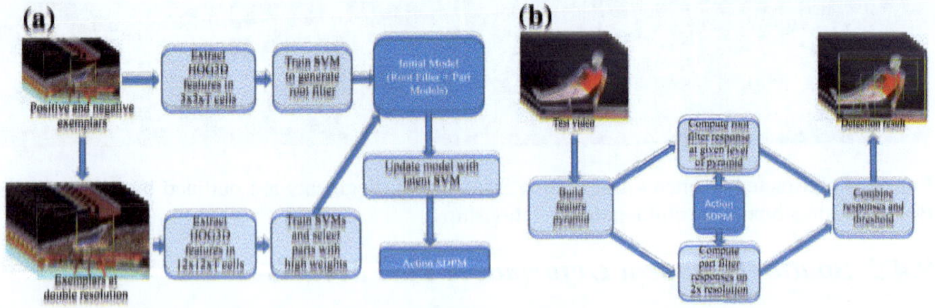

Fig. 9.16 Spatio-Temporal Deformable Part Models (STPM) [69]. **a** Training process shows the extraction of HOG3D features and learning the model using latent SVM. **b** Testing process with the final result showing the root (*yellow*) and its parts (*green*)

This approach has shown to be effective as the parts exclude most of the background giving better localization and focus on distinctive locations within an action. This method is different from other approaches as it explicitly models the intraclass variability using part deformations, and by using global and part templates, it is able to find the best location for an action in the scale, space, and time. The method achieves state-of-the-art results on UCF Sports dataset, as shown in Fig. 9.18.

9.5 Discussion

The earlier action recognition benchmarks [6, 59] were recorded in a controlled setting having static cameras with static and uncluttered backgrounds. The actions were performed by a few selected actors and appeared without any occlusions. This was improved by changing the source of videos to television broadcast and movies in datasets such as UCF Sports [34, 41, 47, 57, 70]. Action videos from these types of

Fig. 9.17 SDPM [69] localization. **a** Root and part filter locations in a training frame for *Swing-Bench* action. **b** Localization result in a test video. Root (*yellow*) and part (*red*, *magenta*, and *green*) locations are shown for both train and test examples. Each column shows the middle frame of a three temporal stage model

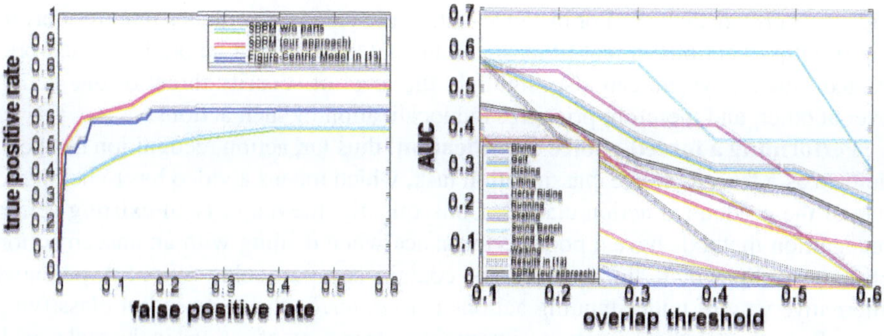

Fig. 9.18 SDPM [69] results. *Left* ROC at 0.2 overlap threshold; compared with figure-centric model [34]. *Right* Area Under Curve (AUC) for overlap threshold ranging from 0.1 to 0.6

sources presented a diversity of appearances, occlusion, and varying backgrounds. Although these videos were recorded in an unconstrained environment, they were produced by professional crew in favorable conditions, e.g., using selected viewpoints. Later, the focus shifted toward collecting videos from online repositories, e.g., YouTube. Videos collected from such sources were named to be videos "in the wild" [36, 64]. Since the videos are uploaded by a diverse group of users, they present a wide variety of challenges in a totally unconstrained environment. These datasets have been utilized for both localizing and recognizing actions. In the rest of this section, we discuss some of the common and crucial shortcomings in many of the existing action recognition and localization methods which are expected to be addressed in the future techniques.

Evaluating on temporally trimmed videos: even though the benchmarks have evolved to be more challenging by being recorded in an unconstrained setting and having a large number of action classes, the majority of the existing action datasets suffer from a crucial shortcoming: the collected videos are carefully trimmed to only contain the action of interest. Hence, the focus of the current action recognition methods has been toward classifying actions in temporally trimmed videos which is an unrealistic assumption. In addition, in many of the existing datasets, the action is performed by only a single person, as compared to a group of people. This makes these datasets even further simplistic and unrealistic compared to analyzing human actions in a natural setting. In videos having a single actor, the main task is to identify and recognize the motion of the actor, while separating it from background clutter. However, realistic scenarios would have several actions being performed simultaneously by different actors with massive inter- and intraclass variability. Therefore, the next generation of action recognition and localization methods are expected to address these two major shortcomings and be able to perform their task on temporally untrimmed videos [27] with potentially multiple actors performing various actions.

The task of recognizing multiple actions simultaneously will introduce new challenges to be explored such as: co-occurrence of actions, action-to-action occlusion, and interclass dependencies. Potential applications which would require localization of multiple actions include: video surveillance, automatic understanding of sports videos, or crowd analysis. For instance, automatic video surveillance requires detecting (multiple) actions in real time, so an unwanted event can be predicted and prevented. Such a system can also highlight the level of security threat of one action over another, and therefore prioritize the localization of such actions.

Performing a forced-choice classification: thus far, action recognition has been defined as a forced-choice classification task, which means a video has to belong to one of the predefined action classes. Consequently, the majority of existing action recognition methods have a poor performance when dealing with an unseen action class or a clip which simply does not contain any particular action. A potential alternative way of understanding actions is to *describe* them instead of classifying them. Even though there exists an extremely wide variety of actions in the real world, many of them share vast similarities in an atomic level. For example, the action of Pole Vault can be broken down into running, jumping, landing, and then standing up. Therefore, it is often feasible to describe an action using a universal lexicon of lower level actions, sometimes called action attributes [17, 37]. Hence, it is a worthwhile effort for the future action recognition techniques to understand the basic elements of human actions and devise a simple and comprehensive *description* for an action rather than a forced-choice classification.

Employing Exhaustive search as the search strategy: recently, several action localization methods that employ mid-to-high level representations [31, 69] which can effectively model the spatio-temporal structure of an action have been proposed. However, many of these approaches perform an exhaustive search using a sliding window, in temporal, spatial, or spatio-temporal domain, to find the desired location of the action. This approach is particularly inefficient as all possible spatio-temporal locations over different scales and aspect ratios have to be evaluated. Recently, efficient search strategies, such as selective search or object proposal [3, 9, 13, 15, 72], were shown to be more efficient than sliding window for object detection. Potentially, action localization methods can also adopt a similar approach [25] and utilize similar search strategies in order to increase the efficiency of their search in the spatio-temporal domain.

9.6 Conclusion

In this chapter, we overviewed the prominent action localization and recognition methods for sports videos. We adopted UCF Sports as the benchmark for evaluating the discussed techniques, as it includes a wide range of unconstrained videos categorized into 10 different sports collected from broadcast television channels. We provided an overview of the characteristics of UCF Sports as well as detailed statistics of the techniques evaluated on this dataset along with the evolution of their performance over time. To provide further technical details, we decomposed action recognition into three major steps of feature extraction, forming the video representation using dictionary learning, and classification. For each step, we studied the approaches which yield superior results on sports videos and discussed the reasons behind their success. Similarly, we presented the challenges faced in action localization, elaborated the reasons behind its intricacy, and overviewed several recent methods for this task, which have achieved promising results on sports videos. Lastly, we presented a number of insights acquired from summarizing the discussed action recognition and localization methods. We argued that conducting the recognition on temporally untrimmed videos and attempting to describe an action, instead of performing a forced-choice classification, are crucial for analyzing the human actions in a pragmatic environment.

References

1. Ahmad M, Lee SW (2008) Human action recognition using shape and CLG-motion flow from multi-view image sequences. Pattern Recognit 41(7):2237–2252
2. Alatas O, Yan P, Shah M (2007) Spatio-temporal regularity flow (SPREF): its estimation and applications. IEEE Trans Circuits Syst Video Technol 17(5):584–589
3. Alexe B, Heess N, Teh Y, Ferrari V (2012) Searching for objects driven by context. In: Neural information processing systems (NIPS)
4. Ali S, Shah M (2010) Human action recognition in videos using kinematic features and multiple instance learning. IEEE Trans Pattern Anal Mach Intell (TPAMI) 32(2):288–303
5. Belongie S, Malik J, Puzicha J (2002) Shape matching and object recognition using shape contexts. IEEE Trans Pattern Anal Mach Intell (TPAMI) 24(4):509–522
6. Blank M, Gorelick L, Shechtman E, Irani M, Basri R (2005) Actions as space-time shapes. In: Computer vision and pattern recognition (CVPR)
7. Bobick AF, Davis JW (2001) The recognition of human movement using temporal templates. IEEE Trans Pattern Anal Mach Intell (TPAMI) 23(3):257–267
8. Canny J (1986) A computational approach to edge detection. IEEE Trans Pattern Anal Mach Intell (TPAMI) 6:679–698
9. Carreira J, Sminchisescu C (2010) Constrained parametric min-cuts for automatic object segmentation. In: Computer vision and pattern recognition (CVPR)
10. Cheng SC, Cheng KY, Chen YPP (2013) GHT-based associative memory learning and its application to human action detection and classification. Pattern Recognit 46(11):3117–3128
11. Dalal N, Triggs B (2005) Histograms of oriented gradients for human detection. In: Computer vision and pattern recognition (CVPR)
12. Dalal N, Triggs B, Schmid C (2006) Human detection using oriented histograms of flow and appearance. In: European conference on computer vision (ECCV)
13. Dollar P (2010) A seismic shift in object detection. http://pdollar.wordpress.com/2013/12/10/a-seismic-shift-in-object-detection
14. Efros A, Berg A, Mori G, Malik J (2003) Recognizing action at a distance. In: International conference on computer vision (ICCV)
15. Endres I, Hoiem D (2014) Category-independent object proposals with diverse ranking. IEEE Trans Pattern Anal Mach Intell (TPAMI) 36:222–234
16. Everts I, van Gemert J, Gevers T (2013) Evaluation of color stips for human action recognition. In: Computer vision and pattern recognition (CVPR)
17. Farhadi A, Endres I, Hoiem D, Forsyth D (2009) Describing objects by their attributes. In: computer vision and pattern recognition (CVPR)
18. Fei-Fei L, Perona P (2005) A Bayesian hierarchical model for learning natural scene categories. In: Comput vision and pattern recognition (CVPR), vol 25, pp 24–531
19. Feng X, Perona P (2002) Human action recognition by sequence of movelet codewords. In: International symposium on 3D data processing, visualization, and transmission. IEEE, pp 717–721

20. Freeman WT, Adelson EH (1991) The design and use of steerable filters. IEEE Trans Pattern Anal Mach Intell (TPAMI) 13(9):891–906
21. Gall J, Yao A, Razavi N, Van Gool L, Lempitsky V (2011) Hough forests for object detection, tracking, and action recognition. IEEE Trans Pattern Anal Mach Intell (TPAMI) 33(11):2188–2202
22. Gorelick L, Blank M, Shechtman E, Irani M, Basri R (2007) Actions as space-time shapes. IEEE Trans Pattern Anal Mach Intell (TPAMI) 29(12):2247–2253
23. Harandi MT, Sanderson C, Shirazi S, Lovell BC (2013) Kernel analysis on Grassmann manifolds for action recognition. Pattern Recognit Lett 34(15):1906–1915
24. Harris C, Stephens M (1988) A combined corner and edge detector. In: Alvey vision conference, vol 15. Manchester, p 50
25. Jain M, van Gemert JC, Bouthemy P, Jégou H, Snoek C (2014) Action localization by tubelets from motion. In: Computer vision and pattern recognition (CVPR)
26. Jiang Z, Lin Z, Davis LS (2012) Recognizing human actions by learning and matching shape-motion prototype trees. IEEE Trans Pattern Anal Mach Intell (TPAMI) 34(3):533–547
27. Jiang YG, Liu J, Zamir AR, Laptev I, Piccardi M, Shah M, Sukthankar R (2014) Thumos challenge: action recognition with a large number of classes
28. Jiang Z, Lin Z, Davis L (2013) Label consistent K-SVD—learning a discriminative dictionary for recognition
29. Kläser A, Marszalek M, Schmid C (2008) A spatio-temporal descriptor based on 3d-gradients. In: British machine vision conference (BMVC)
30. Kovashka A, Grauman K (2010) Learning a hierarchy of discriminative space-time neighborhood features for human action recognition. In: Computer vision and pattern recognition (CVPR)
31. Lan T, Wang Y, Mori G (2011) Discriminative figure-centric models for joint action localization and recognition. In: International conference on computer vision (ICCV)
32. Laptev I (2005) On space-time interest points. Int J Comput Vis 64(2–3):107–123
33. Laptev I, Lindeberg T (2003) Space-time interest points. In: International conference on computer vision (ICCV)
34. Laptev I, Marszalek M, Schmid C, Rozenfeld B (2008) Learning realistic human actions from movies. In: Computer vision and pattern recognition (CVPR)
35. Le Q, Zou W, Yeung S, Ng A (2011) Learning hierarchical invariant spatiotemporal features for action recognition with independent subspace analysis. In: Computer vision and pattern recognition (CVPR)
36. Liu J, Luo J, Shah M (2009) Recognizing realistic actions from videos "in the wild". In: Computer vision and pattern recognition (CVPR)
37. Liu J, Kuipers B, Savarese S (2011) Recognizing human actions by attributes. In: Computer vision and pattern recognition (CVPR)
38. Lowe DG (2004) Distinctive image features from scale-invariant keypoints. Int J Comput Vis 60(2):91–110
39. Lucas B.D, Kanade T (1981) An iterative image registration technique with an application to stereo vision. In: International joint conference on artificial intelligence (IJCAI)
40. Ma S, Zhang J, Cinbis N, Sclaroff S (2013) Action recognition and localization by hierarchical space-time segments. In: International conference on computer vision (ICCV)
41. Marszalek M, Laptev I, Schmid C (2009) Actions in context. In: Computer vision and pattern recognition (CVPR)
42. Matas J, Chum O, Urban M, Pajdla T (2002) Robust wide baseline stereo from maximally stable extremal regions. In: British machine vision conference (BMVC)
43. Matikainen P, Hebert M, Sukthankar R (2009) Action recognition through the motion analysis of tracked features. In: ICCV workshops on video-oriented object and event classification
44. Mendoza M.Á, De La Blanca NP (2008) Applying space state models in human action recognition: a comparative study. In: International Workshop on Articulated Motion and Deformable Objects. Springer, pp 53–62

45. Messing R, Pal C, Kautz H (2009) Activity recognition using the velocity histories of tracked keypoints. In: International conference on computer vision (ICCV)
46. Mikolajczyk K, Schmid C (2005) A performance evaluation of local descriptors. IEEE Trans Pattern Anal Mach Intell (TPAMI) 27(10):1615–1630
47. Mikolajczyk K, Uemura H (2008) Action recognition with motion-appearance vocabulary forest. In: Computer vision and pattern recognition (CVPR)
48. Mikolajczyk K, Zisserman A, Schmid C (2003) Shape recognition with edge-based features. In: British machine vision conference (BMVC)
49. Nelson RC, Selinger A (1998) Large-scale tests of a keyed, appearance-based 3-d object recognition system. Vis Res 38(15):2469–2488
50. Nowak E, Jurie F, Triggs B (2006) Sampling strategies for bag-of-features image classification. In: European conference on computer vision (ECCV), pp 490–503
51. O'Hara S, Draper B (2012) Scalable action recognition with a subspace forest. In: Computer vision and pattern recognition (CVPR)
52. Pope AR, Lowe DG (2000) Probabilistic models of appearance for 3-d object recognition. Int J Comput Vis 40(2):149–167
53. Qiu Q, Jiang Z, Chellappa R (2011) Sparse dictionary-based representation and recognition of action attributes. In: International conference on computer vision (ICCV)
54. Randen T, Husoy JH (1999) Filtering for texture classification: a comparative study. IEEE Trans Pattern Anal Mach Intell (TPAMI) 21(4):291–310
55. Ranzato M, Poultney C, Chopra S, LeCun Y (2006) Efficient learning of sparse representations with an energy-based model. In: Neural information processing systems (NIPS)
56. Raptis M, Kokkinos I, Soatto S (2012) Discovering discriminative action parts from mid-level video representations. In: Computer vision and pattern recognition (CVPR)
57. Rodriguez M, Ahmed J, Shah M (2008) Action Mach: a spatio-temporal maximum average correlation height filter for action recognition. In: Computer vision and pattern recognition (CVPR)
58. Sadanand S, Corso JJ (2012) Action bank: a high-level representation of activity in video. In: Computer vision and pattern recognition (CVPR)
59. Schuldt C, Laptev I, Caputo B (2004) Recognizing human actions: a local SVM approach. In: International conference on pattern recognition (ICPR)
60. Scovanner P, Ali S, Shah M (2007) A 3-dimensional sift descriptor and its application to action recognition. In: ACM international conference on multimedia
61. Shapovalova N, Raptis M, Sigal L, Mori G (2013) Action is in the eye of the beholder: eye-gaze driven model for spatio-temporal action localization. In: Neural information processing systems (NIPS)
62. Shi J, Tomasi C (1994) Good features to track. In: Computer vision and pattern recognition (CVPR)
63. Sminchisescu C, Kanaujia A, Metaxas D (2006) Conditional models for contextual human motion recognition. Comput Vis Image Underst 104(2):210–220
64. Soomro K, Zamir AR, Shah M (2012) Ucf101: A dataset of 101 human action classes from videos in the wild. arXiv preprint arXiv:1212.0402 (2012).
65. Sun J, Mu Y, Yan S, Cheong L (2010) Activity recognition using dense long-duration trajectories. In: International conference on multimedia and expo
66. Sun J, Wu X, Yan S, Cheong L, Chua T, Li J (2009) Hierarchical spatio-temporal context modeling for action recognition. In: Computer vision and pattern recognition (CVPR)
67. Tamrakar A, Ali S, Yu Q, Liu J, Javed O, Divakaran, A, Cheng H, Sawhney H (2012) Evaluation of low-level features and their combinations for complex event detection in open source videos. In: Computer vision and pattern recognition
68. Thi TH, Cheng L, Zhang J, Wang L, Satoh S (2012) Integrating local action elements for action analysis. Comput Vis Image Underst 116(3):378–395
69. Tian Y, Sukthankar R, Shah M (2013) Spatiotemporal deformable part models for action detection. In: Computer vision and pattern recognition (CVPR)

70. Tran D, Sorokin A (2008) Human activity recognition with metric learning. In: European conference on computer vision (ECCV)
71. Tran D, Yuan J (2012) Max-margin structured output regression for spatio-temporal action localization. In: Neural information processing systems (NIPS)
72. Uijlings J, van de Sande K, Gevers T, Smeulders A (2013) Selective search for object recognition. Int J Comput Vis 104(2):154–171
73. van Gool L, Moons T, Ungureanu D (1996) Affine/photometric invariants for planar intensity patterns. In: European conference on computer vision (ECCV)
74. Wang Y, Huang K, Tan T (2007) Human activity recognition based on r transform. In: Computer vision and pattern recognition (CVPR)
75. Wang H, Ullah MM, Kläser A, Laptev I, Schmid C (2009) Evaluation of local spatio-temporal features for action recognition. In: British machine vision conference (BMVC)
76. Wang C, Wang Y, Yuille A (2013) An approach to pose-based action recognition. In: Computer vision and pattern recognition (CVPR)
77. Wang H, Kläser A, Schmid C, Liu C (2011) Action recognition by dense trajectories. In: Computer vision and pattern recognition (CVPR)
78. Wang H, Kläser A, Schmid C, Liu CL (2013) Dense trajectories and motion boundary descriptors for action recognition. Int J Comput Vis 103(1):60–79
79. Wang L, Wang Y, Gao W (2011) Mining layered grammar rules for action recognition. Int J Comput Vis 93(2):162–182
80. Willems G, Tuytelaars T, van Gool L (2008) An efficient dense and scale-invariant spatio-temporal interest point detector. In: European conference on computer vision (ECCV)
81. Wu X, Xu D, Duan L, Luo J (2011) Action recognition using context and appearance distribution features. In: Computer vision and pattern recognition (CVPR)
82. Yamato J, Ohya J, Ishii K (1992) Recognizing human action in time-sequential images using hidden Markov model. In: Computer vision and pattern recognition (CVPR)
83. Yang J, Yang M (2012) Top-down visual saliency via joint CRF and dictionary learning. In: Computer vision and pattern recognition (CVPR)
84. Yang J, Yu K, Gong Y, Huang T (2009) Computer vision and pattern recognition (CVPR)
85. Yang Y, Ramanan D (2011) Articulated pose estimation with flexible mixtures-of-parts. In: Computer vision and pattern recognition (CVPR)
86. Yao A, Gall J, van Gool L (2010) A Hough transform-based voting framework for action recognition. In: Computer vision and pattern recognition (CVPR)
87. Yeffet L, Wolf L (2009) Local trinary patterns for human action recognition. In: International conference on computer vision (ICCV)
88. Yilmaz A, Shah M (2005) A novel action representation. In: Computer vision and pattern recognition (CVPR)
89. Yuan C, Hu W, Tian G, Yang S, Wang H (2013) Multi-task sparse learning with beta process prior for action recognition. In: Computer vision and pattern recognition (CVPR)

Chapter 10
Classification of Sports Types Using Thermal Imagery

Rikke Gade and Thomas B. Moeslund

Abstract In this chapter we propose a method for automatic classification of five different sports types. The approach is based only on occupancy heatmaps produced from position data and is robust to detection noise. To overcome privacy issues when capturing video in public sports arenas we use thermal imaging only. This image modality also facilitates easier detection of humans; the detection algorithm is based on automatic thresholding of the image. After a few occlusion handling procedures, the positions of people on the court are calculated using homography. Heatmaps are produced by summarising Gaussian distributions representing people over 10-minute periods. Before classification the heatmaps are projected to a low-dimensional discriminative space using the principle of Fisherfaces. We test our approach on 2 weeks of video and get promising results with a correct classification of 89.64 %. In addition, we get correct classification on a publicly available handball dataset.

10.1 Introduction

In most societies, sports is highly supported by both governments and private foundations, as physical activity is considered a good way to obtain better health among the general population. The amount of money invested in sports facilities alone every year is huge, not only for new constructions, but also for maintenance of existing facilities. In order to know how the money is best spent, it is important to thoroughly analyse the use of these facilities. Such analyses should include information about how many people are present at any time, where they are and what they are doing. The first two issues are the subject of two recent papers by Gade et al. [6, 7].

R. Gade (✉) · T.B. Moeslund
Visual Analysis of People Lab, Aalborg University, Aalborg, Denmark
e-mail: rg@create.aau.dk

T.B. Moeslund
e-mail: tbm@create.aau.dk

T.B. Moeslund et al. (eds.), *Computer Vision in Sports*,
Advances in Computer Vision and Pattern Recognition,
DOI 10.1007/978-3-319-09396-3_10

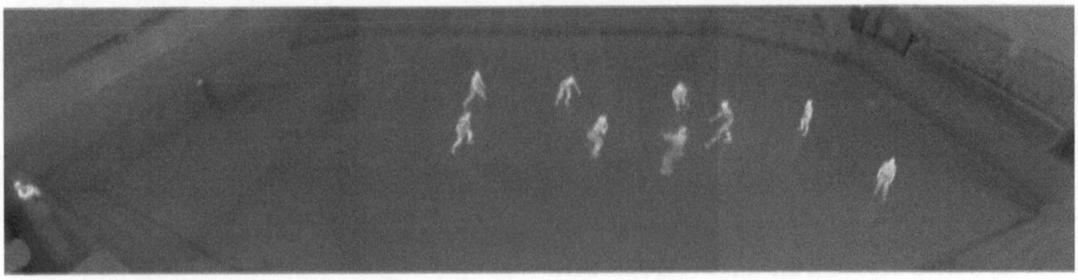

Fig. 10.1 Example of an input image

In this chapter we present a new method for automatic classification of sports types. We focus on the activities observed in public indoor sports arenas. In these arenas many types of activities take place, from physical education in schools, to elite training of a particular sport. For administrators as well as financial supporters of the arenas it is important to gain knowledge of how the arenas are used, and use that information for future planning and decisions on the layout of new arenas. In a future perspective it could also be of great value for the coaches and managers of a sports team to be able to automatically analyse when and where the certain activities are performed by the team.

Our goal for this work is to recognise five common sports types observed in an indoor arena; badminton, basketball, indoor soccer, handball, and volleyball. To overcome privacy issues we apply thermal imaging, which produces images where pixel values represent the observed temperature. Thereby, it is possible to detect people without identification. Figure 10.1 is an example of a thermal image from a sports arena.

Our hypothesis is that it is possible to classify five different sports types using a global approach based on position data only.

10.2 Related Work

Computer aided sports analysis has become a popular tool, particularly in team sports, since some of the first systems were developed in the 1980s [18]. Today the computer vision community works on a large variety of automatic solutions to replace manual tracking systems. Many works have already focused on automatic tracking of sports players [1]. These systems are typically used for game statistics and evaluation of individual performances. For game analysis purposes, automatic detection of play types or special team activities in a game is also an area of interest. With applications mainly in football, offensive play strategies are tried classified based on player trajectories [13, 14, 19]. However, in situations with a high degree of interaction between people, like most types of sport, tracking is still an unsolved problem. Many classification systems therefore rely on manually annotated trajectories, in order to avoid noisy data. The work of Bialkowski et al. [3] on recognising team activities in field hockey games is related to this work in the way that they use only position data.

Their approach is robust to noisy data and they test two different representations; team occupancy maps using different quantisation, and team centroids.

No previous work on recognising sports types has been based on thermal imaging. All existing works use visual cameras and a few include audio as well. For features, some works use edges that represent court lines and players. The sports categories can then be classified by edge directions, intensity or ratio [11, 24]. Also based on the visual appearance of the court is a method that uses the dominating colours of the image as features [16]. The dominant colour can also be combined with motion features [8, 20, 21] or combined with dominant grey level, cut rate and motion rate [17]. From the visual image SURF features [15] and autocorrelograms [22] can be extracted and used for classification. A combination of colour, edges, shape and texture has also been proposed by using six of the MPEG-7 descriptors [23]. One method is based only on location data and classifies sports categories by short trajectories [12].

After feature extraction the classification methods are based on well-known methods such as k-means and Expectation Maximization for clustering, and decision trees, SVM, Hidden Markov models, Neural Network and Naive Bayesian for classification.

As described here, most existing works are based on colour imaging, and many of them rely on the dominant colour of the fields as well as detection of court lines. These methods presume that each sports type is performed on a court designed mainly for one specific sport. In our work we aim to distinguish different sports types performed in the same arena, meaning that any information about the environment is not useful. Furthermore, due to privacy issues, we have chosen to use thermal imaging, which provides heat information only. Figure 10.1 shows an example of the thermal image, which is combined from three cameras in order to cover the entire court.

This work is based on occupancy heatmaps, which are summations of the registered positions of people over a given time span. It is believed that a heatmap for one sports type is unique among a limited number of sports types. This approach is also robust to noisy data, due to the summations over time. Figure 10.2 shows examples of signature heatmaps, which are typical heatmaps for each sports type. Two heatmaps of miscellaneous activities are also shown. Each heatmap covers a 10-minute period.

The approach of this work is to detect individual people and use a homography to calculate their position at the court. A summation of the positions over time results in the occupancy heatmaps. These heatmaps are classified after reducing the number of dimensions with PCA and Fisher's Linear Discriminant.

10.3 Image Acquisition

In order to detect individual people without occlusions, the ideal situation would be to capture images of the scene directly from above. However, installing a camera in the ceiling above the court is generally cumbersome and expensive and therefore

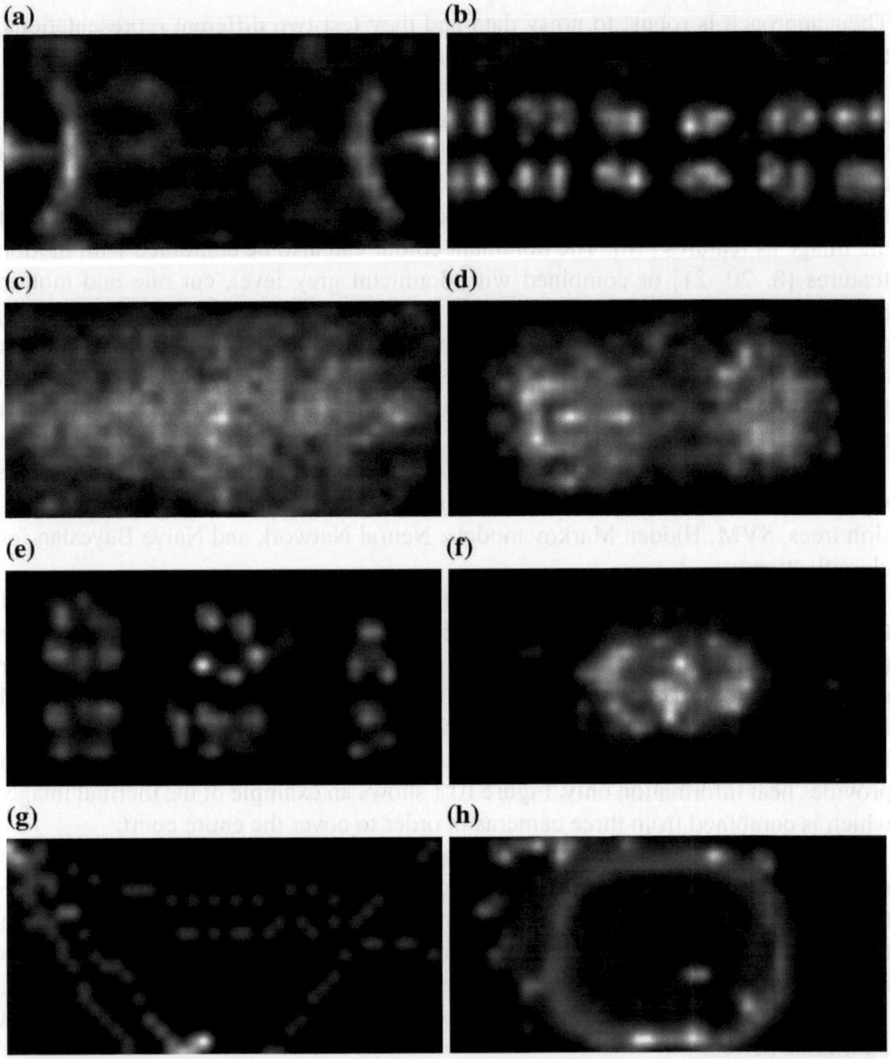

Fig. 10.2 Signature heatmaps of **a** handball, **b** badminton, **c** soccer, **d** basketball, **e** volleyball (three courts), **f** volleyball (one court), **g** miscellaneous, **h** miscellaneous

not realistic for temporary installations. Therefore, it must be installed on one of the walls or rafters around the court. A standard arena used in our experiments has a court size of 40×20 m, corresponding to a handball field, indoor soccer field, etc. As the lenses of commercial thermal cameras today have a maximum field-of-view of around 60°, more than one camera must be used to cover the entire court. The camera set-up used in this work consists of three thermal cameras placed at the same location in order to limit the work load of the set-up. The cameras are adjusted to have adjacent fields-of-view. This is illustrated in Fig. 10.3a. Figure 10.3b shows a picture of the camera box mounted in an arena.

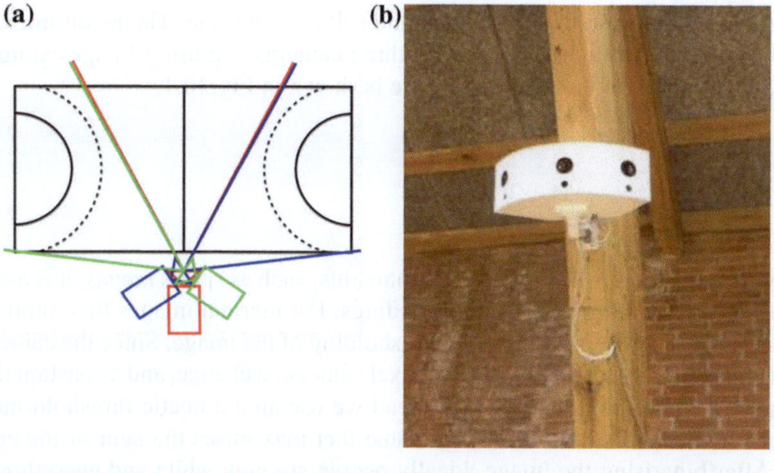

Fig. 10.3 **a** Illustration of the camera setup. **b** Image of the camera box mounted in an arena

Each camera is of the type Axis Q1922, which uses an uncooled microbolometer for detection. The resolution is 640 × 480 pixels per camera and the horizontal field-of-view is 57° per camera. This type of thermal camera is a passive sensor which captures long-wavelength infrared radiation (8–15 μm), radiated by all warm objects. The resulting image depicts the temperature of the scene [5].

To make the software system invariant to the cameras' set-up, the images are stitched together before processing. This requires the cameras to be perfectly aligned and undistorted in order to secure smooth "crossings" between two cameras. For calibration of the thermal cameras a special calibration board is made, consisting of 5 × 4 small incandescent light bulbs. A thermal image of the calibration board is shown in Fig. 10.4. With this board it is possible to adapt the traditional methods for estimating the intrinsic parameters of the cameras. The cameras are manually

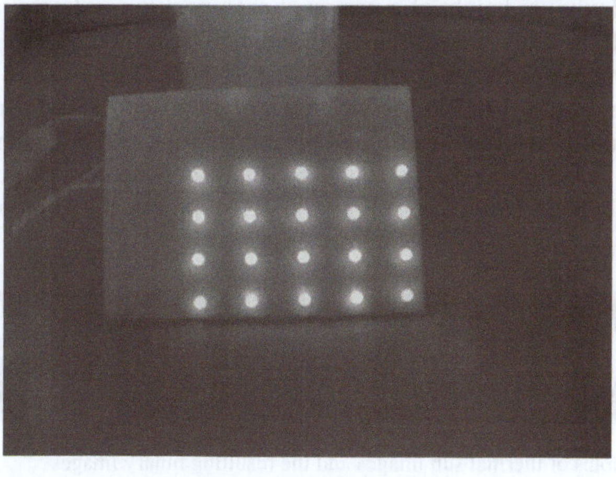

Fig. 10.4 Calibration using a board with incandescent light bulbs

aligned horizontally so that their pitch and roll are the same. The result mimics the well-known panorama effect, but with three cameras capturing images simultaneously. An example of the resulting image is shown in Fig. 10.1.

10.4 Detection

For temperature controlled indoor environments, such as sports arenas, it is assumed that people are warmer than the surroundings. For thermal images this implies that people can be segmented using only thresholding of the image. Since the camera has automatic gain adjustment, the level of pixel values can change, and a constant threshold value is therefore not suitable. Instead we use an automatic threshold method. This method calculates the threshold value that maximises the sum of the entropy [10]. After binarising the image, ideally people are now white and everything else in the image is black. There are, however, challenges to this assumption. Cold/wet clothes can result in parts of people being segmented as background, meaning that one person is represented by a number of unconnected blobs. Likewise, partial occlusions will challenge the detection of individual people, as more than one person is represented in one blob. Figure 10.5 shows some examples of the challenges after binarisation of the thermal images.

The next two sections present methods for reducing these problems.

10.4.1 Occlusion Handling

Two cases of occlusions are handled; people standing behind each other seen from the camera and people standing close to each other horizontally, e.g., in a group. In the first case, the detected blobs will appear taller than an object corresponding to one person. Maximum height of a person at each position is determined during the initialisation. If the blob exceeds the maximum height, it should be split horizontally. Since one or more people are partly occluded in these cases, it is not trivial to find the right place to split the blob. However, we often observe some narrowing or gap in the blob contour near the head of the person in front, which is generally the best point to split from. This point is found by analysing the convex hull and finding the convexity defects of the blob. Of all the defect points, the point with the largest

Fig. 10.5 Examples of thermal sub images and the resulting binary images

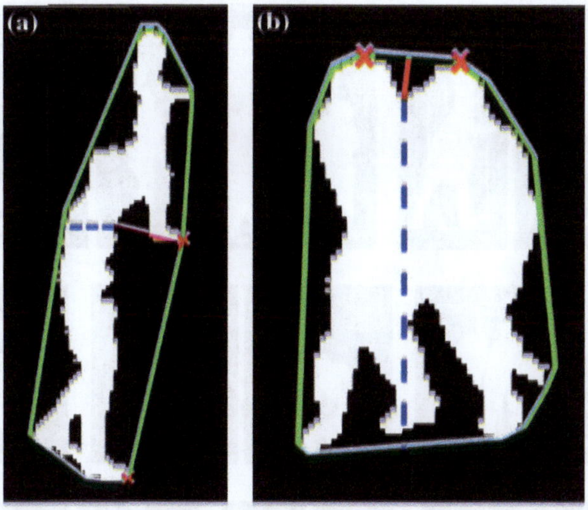

Fig. 10.6 Example of how to find the split location of tall (**a**) or wide blobs (**b**)

depth and a given maximum absolute gradient should be selected, meaning that only defects coming from the side will be considered, discarding e.g. a point between the legs. An example is shown in Fig. 10.6a, where the convex hull is drawn in green and the largest convexity defect is shown in red. From the defect point the blob is split horizontally, shown with the blue dashed line.

In the second case, wide blobs containing two or more persons standing next to each other must be identified. The height/width ratio and the perimeter are here considered as done in [6]. If the criteria are satisfied, the algorithm should try to split the blob. For this type of occlusion, it is often possible to see the head of each person, and split the blob based on the head positions. Since the head is narrower than the body, people can be separated by splitting vertically from the minimum points of the upper edge of a blob. These points can be found by analysing the convex hull and finding the convexity defects of the blob as shown in Fig. 10.6b. The convex hull is drawn with green, and the convexity defect of interest is drawn with red. The convexity defect start and end points, shown with red crosses, must both be above the defect point in the image, therefore other defects are discarded. The split line is shown with the blue dashed line.

More examples of blobs to be split are shown in Fig. 10.7a, b.

10.4.2 Joining of Blobs

Another challenge to the detection of individual people is separation of one person into several blobs. This happens when part of the body has a lower temperature, e.g. caused by loose, wet clothes or insulating layers of clothes. In order to detect the correct position of a person, the bottom part of the body must be identified. We adapt

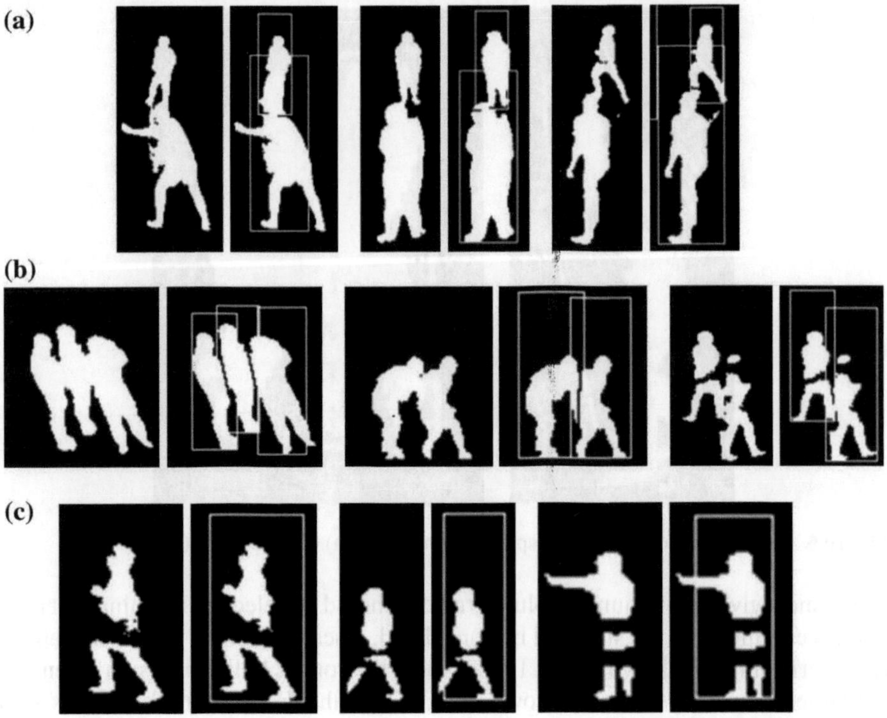

Fig. 10.7 Illustration of how blobs can be split (**a**), or joined (**b**), to single persons (**c**)

here the method presented in [7]. Each detected blob is considered a person candidate, and the probability of being a true person is tested. From the bottom position of the blob, a bounding box of the expected height of an average person and the width being one third of the height is generated. The probability for the candidate being true depends on the ratio of white pixels (r) in the rectangle. By tests it is found that most true detections have a ratio between 30 and 50 %, while less than 1 % of the true detections lie below 20 % or above 70 %. We choose to discard all detections below 20 % and assign a value between 0.8 and 1 to all other detections:

$$w_p(i) = \begin{cases} 0, & \text{if } r < 20\,\% \\ 0.8, & \text{if } r > 60\,\% \\ 0.9, & \text{if } r < 30\,\% \parallel 50 < r < 60\,\% \\ 1, & \text{otherwise} \end{cases} \quad (10.1)$$

This approach will reduce the detections of small body parts, as well as many non-human objects. However, a lot of false candidates will still exist. Many of them contain part of a person and overlap in the image with a true candidate. Due to the possibility of several candidates belonging to the same person, the overlapping rectangles must be considered. By tests from different locations and different camera placements, it is found that if two rectangles overlap by more than 60 %, they probably originate from the same person, or from reflections of that person. As only one position should be accepted per person, only one of the overlapping rectangles should be chosen. Due to low resolution images compared to the scene depth, cluttered scenes, and no restrictions on the posture of a person, the feet of a person cannot be recognised from the blobs. Furthermore, due to the possibility of reflections below a person in the image, it cannot be assumed that the feet are the lowest point of the overlapping candidates. Instead, the best candidate will be selected on the highest ratio of white pixels, as the probability of false candidates is lower here. The probabilities assigned to the approved candidates will be used later, when registering the positions of people.

Figure 10.7c shows three examples of blobs being joined to one detected person.

10.4.3 Region of Interest

As spectators, coaches and other persons around the court are of no interest in this work, the image must be cropped to the border of the court before processing. Since each sports type has its own court dimensions, a single choice of border is not feasible. Handball and soccer are played on a 40×20 m court, which is also the maximum court size in the observed arena. The volleyball court is 18×9 m, plus a free zone around the court, which is minimum 3 m wide, and the standard basketball court is 28×15 m. Badminton is played on up to six adjacent courts of 13.4×6.1 m. The court dimensions and layout in relation to each other are illustrated in Fig. 10.8. On the arena floor all court lines are drawn on top of each other, but here we have split it into two drawings for better visibility. Note that volleyball can be played on either three courts without free zones or on one court including the free zone.

During basketball and volleyball matches coaches and substitutes sit within the dimensions of the handball court, and would be unwanted detections if we cropped only to the largest court dimensions. Considering the illustrated court dimensions it is therefore decided to operate with two different court sizes, 40×20 m and 28×15 m. In test cases it is of course not known which sport is performed and thereby not known which court size to choose. Instead both options will be tried out for all data. The classification process is further described in Sect. 10.5.

10.4.4 Occupancy Heat Maps

The position of each person is registered in image coordinates as the bottom centre of the bounding box. The position then needs to be converted to world coordinates using a homography. Since the input image is combined from three cameras, each observing the left, middle or right part of the court, at least one homography for each camera is needed to calculate the transformation. This assumes that the cameras are

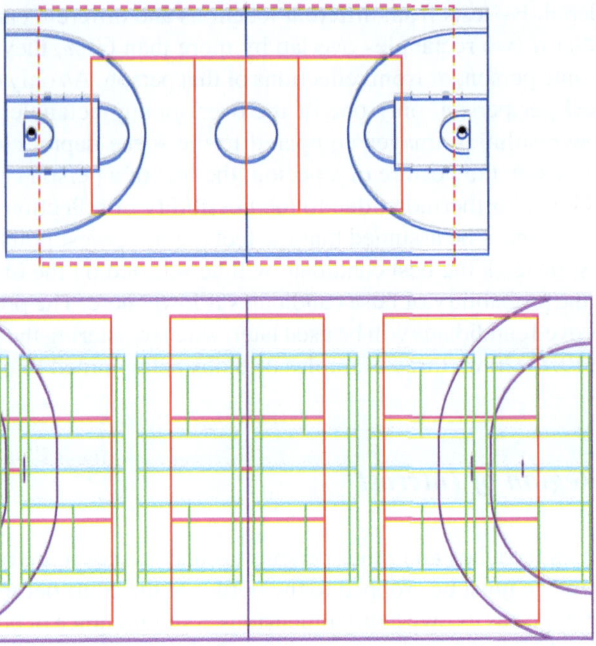

Fig. 10.8 The outlines of the different courts illustrated. *Red* volleyball, *blue* basketball, *purple* handball (and soccer), *green* badminton. Drawn in two figures to increase the visibility

perfectly rectified. For better precision, we instead divide the court into 5 × 5 m sq for each of which we calculate a homography. The corresponding points in image and world coordinates for each 5 m in both x- and y-directions are found during an initialisation. This initialisation must be performed one time for each set-up. In addition to finding the mapping between image and world coordinates, we also find the correlation between peoples' real height and their height in the images, corresponding to their distance to the camera. Furthermore, as the cameras are fixed relative to each other in one box and then tilted downwards when mounted in arenas, the result is that people in the image are more tilted the further they get from the image centre along the image x-axis. This means that a person's pixel height cannot always be measured vertically in the image. Therefore, the calibration must include the angle of a person standing upright at predefined positions on the court.

Figure 10.9 illustrates the result of an initialisation procedure. For each position in the 5 × 5 m grids a person stands upright, while the image coordinates of the feet and head are registered, resulting in a white line in the image, which gives the angle and height of a person. The world coordinate of the feet are also registered as well as the person's real height in metres.

The four corner points of each square are used to calculate the homographies, making it possible to map all image coordinates to world coordinates. Using interpolation from the corner points, an angle and maximum height are calculated for each pixel.

Fig. 10.9 Illustration of the initialisation process, each *white* line represents a standard person at that position

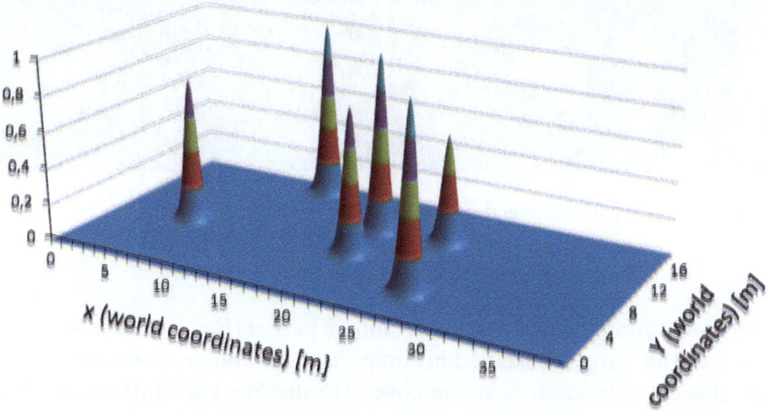

Fig. 10.10 Occupancy for one single frame. Each person is represented as a Gaussian distribution

When mapping the observations to a world-coordinate view of the court we need to represent the physical area of a person. A standard person is chosen to be represented by a three-dimensional Gaussian distribution with a standard height of 1, corresponding to 1 person, and a radius corresponding to 1 m for 95 % of the volume. To take into account the uncertainty of the detections, the height of Gaussian distributions is scaled by the probability factor w_p, described in Sect. 10.4.2.

Figure 10.10 shows an example of the occupancy calculated for a single frame. Six people are detected with different certainty factors.

The final occupancy heatmaps, as shown in Fig. 10.2, are constructed by adding up the Gaussians over time. The time span for each heatmap should be long enough to cover a representative section of the games and still short enough to avoid different activities to be mixed together. To decide on the time span, a study has been conducted between 5-, 10-, 20- and 30-minutes periods. An example of four heatmaps with the same end-time is shown in Fig. 10.11.

The comparison in Fig. 10.11 illustrates the situation where a handball team starts with exercises and warm-up, before playing a short handball match. The end-time for each heatmap is the same. The 30-minute period (Fig. 10.11d) is too long, the warm-up and game is mixed together such that no activity is recognisable. Between

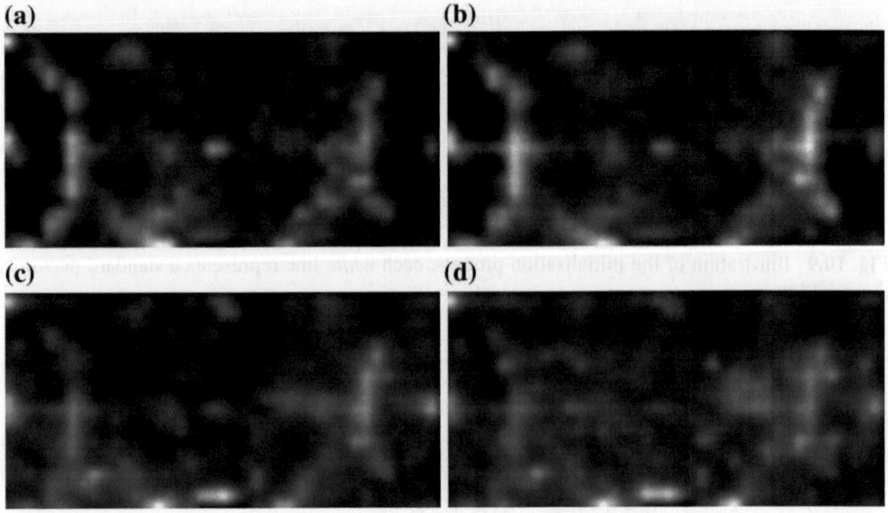

Fig. 10.11 Heatmaps with same end-time and different time span: **a** 5 min, **b** 10 min, **c** 20 min, **d** 30 min

the 5-, 10- and 20-minute periods the 10-minute period (Fig. 10.11b) shows the most clear pattern. The same is observed in comparisons for other sports activities, therefore it is chosen to let each heatmap cover 10 min. We will shift the starting time 5 min each time, so that the periods overlap and the resolution of classifications will be 5 min.

10.5 Classification

Each heatmap is an image with a resolution of 200 × 400 pixels, thus it can be considered a sample in an 80,000-dimensional space. Principal Component Analysis (PCA) is a well-known method for dimension reduction, but since it uses non-labeled data and seeks the dimensions with largest variance between all samples, there is a risk that the differences between classes are not conserved. Fischer's Linear Discriminant (FLD) seeks the directions that are efficient for discrimination between classes [4]. However, using FLD introduces the small sample size problem: In order to have a non-singular within-class scatter matrix (S_W) it is necessary to have more samples than dimensions. As we have an 80,000-dimensional space, it is not realistic to have a sample size of $n > 80{,}000$. In order to solve this problem we adapt the idea of Fisherfaces for face recognition [2]: First, project the sample vectors onto the PCA space of r dimensions, with $r \leq \text{rank}(S_W)$ and then compute the Fisherimage in this PCA space.

10.5.1 Dimensionality Reduction

Dimensionality reduction based on PCA is performed by pooling all training samples and calculating the directions with largest variance. The PCA will only have as many non-zero eigenvalues as the number of samples minus one, which will be significantly less than the original 80,000 dimensions. We choose to reduce the space to the 20 dimensions with largest eigenvalues. Although this is a reduction by 4,000 times in the number of dimensions 73 % of the total variance is still preserved. All heatmaps are projected to the new 20-dimensional space before further processing.

10.5.2 Fischer's Linear Discriminant

The optimal projection of the data is found using Fisher's Linear Discriminant, such that the ratio of the between-class scatter S_B and the within-class scatter S_W is maximised:

$$W_{\text{opt}} = \arg\max_{W} \frac{|W^T S_B W|}{|W^T S_W W|} \tag{10.2}$$

where W_{opt} is a matrix with orthonormal columns, consisting of the set of generalised eigenvectors of S_B and S_W corresponding to the m largest eigenvalues. There are at most $c - 1$ non-zero generalised eigenvalues, where c is the number of classes. The between-class scatter matrix S_B and the within-class scatter matrix S_W are defined as

$$S_B = \sum_{i=1}^{c} N_i(\mu_i - \mu)(\mu_i - \mu)^T \tag{10.3}$$

$$S_W = \sum_{i=1}^{c} \sum_{x_k \in X_I} N_i(\mu_i - \mu)(\mu_i - \mu)^T \tag{10.4}$$

where μ_i is the mean image of class X_i, and N_i is the number of samples in class X_i [2].

10.5.3 Final Classification

In the training phase, all data are projected to the new space found by FLD, and the mean coordinate for each class is calculated. When testing a new sample, the sample to classify is projected to the same space, and the nearest class is found using the Euclidean distance.

We use video from daily activities in a public sports arena, which includes a lot of undefined activities. Besides the five traditional sports types we therefore define a category of miscellaneous activities. This can include everything from specific exercises and warm-up, to cleaning the floor and an empty arena. This category is trained as a class in the same way as each sports type. Since miscellaneous contains very different heatmaps, it could be argued that this class will end up as a mean image of all other classes. However, by treating it as a class like the other sports types, the FLD will take care of projecting the data to a space that, as far as possible, discriminates the classes.

We use two different court dimensions for tests, as described in Sect. 10.4. The final classification for each time span should therefore choose between the classifications of these two heatmaps. If they agree on the same class, the final classification is simply that class. If one heatmap is classified as a sports type, while the other is classified as miscellaneous, the final classification will choose the regular sports type, as it is assumed that it is found the correct court size. If the heatmaps are classified as different sports types, the sample with shortest distance to the class mean will decide the classification.

10.6 Experiments

19 days of data has been captured in order to test the classification approach. Capturing from 7 am to 11 pm this is a total of 304 h of recordings, of which people are present in the arena in 163 and 141 h are empty. Video from the first week (7 days) is used for training data and the rest (12 days) is used for test. This approach is challenging, since the variety in the play can be large between different sessions. Many undefined activities are observed during a day, from warm-up and exercises, to more passive activities, such as transitions between teams, "team meetings", cleaning, etc. Only well-known sports types performed like in matches will be used for classification. Exercises related to a specific sport, such as practising shots at goal, will not be considered a specific sports type, but will be counted as miscellaneous activity. We do, however, allow variety in the play, such as different number of players and different number of courts in use for badminton and volleyball.

The sports types that are observed during both weeks and are used in this work are badminton, basketball, indoor soccer, handball and volleyball. As shown in Fig. 10.8, two different layouts of volleyball courts are observed, one with only one court in the middle of the arena (drawn on upper part of Fig. 10.8 and denoted volleyball-1) and the other version which fit three volleyball courts playing in the opposite direction (drawn with red on lower part of Fig. 10.8 and denoted volleyball-3). These are treated as two different classes, both referring to volleyball. This results in seven classes to classify, including miscellaneous.

For training and test of each sports type we use all heatmaps that are manually labelled to be a regular performed sport. In order to have a significant representation of the regular sports types in the total dataset we discard most of the empty hours and use

Table 10.1 Dataset used for training and test

Category	Training heatmaps	Test heatmaps
Badminton	35	19
Basketball	16	76
Soccer	20	36
Handball	18	15
Volleyball-1	33	20
Volleyball-3	15	8
Misc.	163	212
Total	300	386

only a few heatmaps from empty periods. Furthermore, the rest of the miscellaneous heatmaps are chosen as samples that represent the various kinds of random activities that take place in the arena. The number of heatmaps used for each class is listed in Table 10.1.

In order to test the system under real conditions, which will be continuous video sequences of several hours, we also perform a test on video captured on one day continuously from 7 am to 11 pm. This video contains recordings of volleyball, handball and soccer, as well as miscellaneous activities. The training data described in Table 10.1 is used again for this test. Lastly, we test our algorithm on a publicly available dataset from a handball game, while still using our own videos for training data. This will prove the portability of our method to other arenas and set-ups.

10.6.1 Results

10.6.1.1 12 Days Test

Table 10.2 shows the result for the first test with data from 12 days. The ground truth is compared with the classification.

This results in an overall true positive rate of 89.64 %. This result is very satisfying, considering that we classify seven classes based only on position data.

A low number of 14 heatmaps are wrongly classified as miscellaneous instead of the correct sports type. Four of them are from videos where only one of the three

Table 10.2 Classification result for data samples from one week

Truth	Badminton	Basketball	Soccer	Handball	Volleyball-1	Volleyball-3	Misc.
Badminton	**17**	0	0	0	0	0	2
Basketball	0	**69**	0	0	1	0	6
Soccer	0	0	**30**	0	4	0	2
Handball	0	0	0	**15**	0	0	0
Volleyball-1	0	0	0	0	**20**	0	0
Volleyball-3	0	0	0	0	0	**4**	4
Misc.	0	14	2	1	2	2	**191**

The number of heatmaps classified in each category

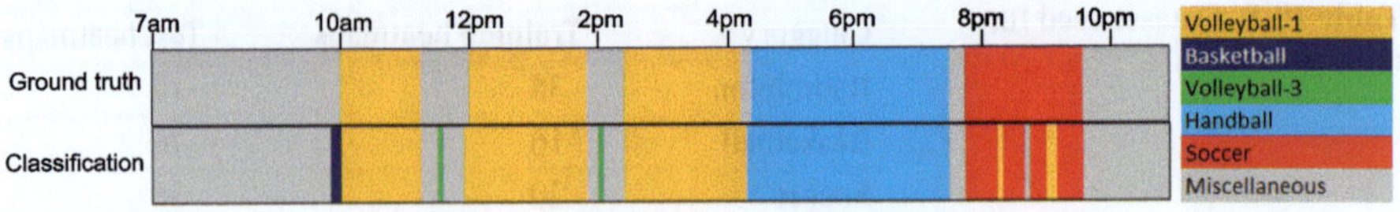

Fig. 10.12 Comparison of ground truth and classification of video from one full day

volleyball courts is used, and this situation is not represented in the training data. The error could therefore be reduced by capturing more training data. Of the basketball videos, a few heatmaps represent periods with unusually many players on the court, resulting in a different activity pattern and therefore they are classified as miscellaneous. Fourteen heatmaps manually labelled as miscellaneous are automatically classified as basketball. These heatmaps are borderline situations where exercises highly related to basketball are performed, and it could therefore be discussed whether these should be labelled basketball or miscellaneous. The same happens for a few miscellaneous heatmaps, classified as other sports types due to exercises highly related to the sport. Four heatmaps representing soccer are misclassified as volleyball played on the centre court. Inspecting these images, there are some similarities between the sports, depending on how they are performed.

10.6.1.2 Full Day Test

The result of classifying one full day from 7 am to 10 pm is illustrated in Fig. 10.12 with each colour representing a sports type and grey representing miscellaneous activities (including empty arena). The ground truth is shown in the upper row and automatic classification is shown in the bottom row.

The result is promising, showing that of the total of 191 heatmaps that are produced and classified for the full day, 94.24 % are correctly classified.

The green periods illustrate volleyball matches. Before these matches there is a warm-up period, where short periods of exercises are confused with basketball or volleyball played on the three courts. The last case is obvious, because some of their warm-up exercises include practising volleyball shots in the same direction as volleyball is normally played using the three courts. This test also shows like the previous test that soccer can be misclassified as volleyball in a few situations.

The results from this test show that our approach is satisfying even for the challenging situation of a full day's video, the true positive rate is indeed better than what was obtained in the first test.

10.6.1.3 CVBASE Dataset

The last test performed is classification of the sport from a publicly available dataset. In order to do that, we need a dataset with at least 10 min continuous recording of one of the five sports type considered in this paper. Furthermore, calibration data must be available, so that positions can be obtained in world coordinates. One suitable dataset

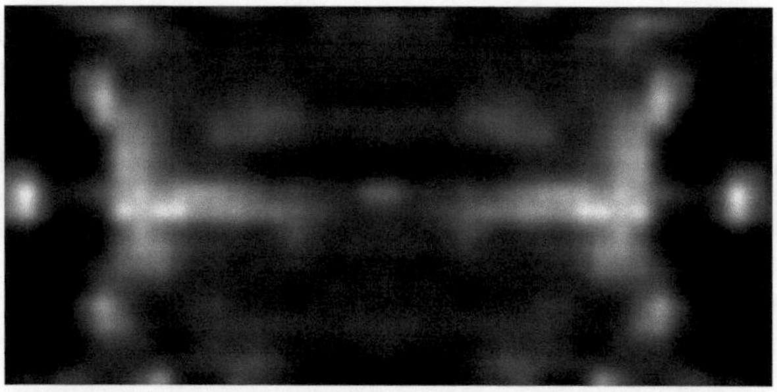

Fig. 10.13 Heatmap for the 10 min annotated positions of the CVBASE 06 handball dataset

is found, which is the handball dataset from CVBASE 06 [9]. This includes annotation of position data in world coordinates for seven players (one team) for 10 min of a handball match. Since we want to test the classification algorithm specifically, we use these annotations as input data instead of modifying our detection algorithm to work on RGB video. However, as we need position data from the players of both teams, we flip all positions along the x-axis (longest dimension of the court) and add these positions in order to represent the other team. The resulting heatmap for the 10-minute period is shown in Fig. 10.13.

Using the 1-week training data from our own recordings, this 10-minute period is correctly classified as handball. This proves the portability of our approach to other arenas and camera set-ups.

10.6.2 Comparison with Related Work

A comparison of our results with the reported results in related work is listed in Table 10.3. It should be noted that each work has its own dataset, making it hard to compare the results directly. All related works use normal visual cameras, where we

Table 10.3 Dataset used for training and test

Reference	Sports types	Video length	Result
Gibert et. al [8]	4	220 min	93 %
Mohan and Yegn. [11]	5	5 h 30 min	94.4 %
Lee and Hoff [12]	2	Approx. 1 h	94.2 %
Li et. al [15]	14	114 h	88.8 %
Mutchima and Sanguansat [16]	20	200 min	96.65 %
Sigari et. al [17]	7	(104 video clips)	78.8 %
Wang et. al [21]	4	(173 test clips)	88 %
Wang et. al [20]	3	16 h	100 %
Watcha. et. al [22]	7	233 min	91.1 %
Xu et. al [23]	4	1,200 frames	N/A
Yuan and Wan [24]	5	N/A	97.1 %
Our work	5	65 h	89.64 %

use thermal cameras. In addition to that, most work use video from different courts for each sports type, where we use video from one multi-purpose indoor arena.

Our result is comparable with the related work using an equal number of sports types. It is also seen that we test on a large amount of data compared to other works.

10.7 Conclusion

The work presented here shows that it is possible to classify five different sports types based only on the position data of people detected in thermal images. Heatmaps are produced by summarising the position data over 10-minute periods. These heatmaps are projected to a low-dimensional space using PCA and Fischer's Linear Discriminant. Our result is an overall recognition rate for five sports types of 89.64 %. This is a promising result, considering that our work is the first to use thermal imaging for sports classification. Furthermore, we use video from the same indoor arena, meaning that no information about the arena can be used in the classification. Our detection method is rather simple and the registered positions of people can be noisy, but since the classification method relies on summarised positions over time, the approach is robust to the noisy data.

For this work we have concentrated on sports played in match-like situations. Problems could rise if trying to classify a video of sport played in the opposite direction of usual, e.g. on half the court, or if trying to classify exercises related to one sports type. To overcome these limitations the future work will investigate the possibility of including local features. These could be clues from short trajectories, such as speed and path length and straightness to overcome these limitations. In relation to this, it could also be possible to extend the work to classify play types or other shorter activities within a sports game.

References

1. Barris S, Button C (2008) A review of vision-based motion analysis in sport. Sports Med 38(12):1025–1043
2. Belhumeur P, Hespanha J, Kriegman D (1997) Eigenfaces vs. Fisherfaces: recognition using class specific linear projection. PAMI 19(7):711–720. doi:10.1109/34.598228
3. Bialkowski A, Lucey P, Carr P, Denman S, Matthews I, Sridharan S (2013) Recognising team activities from noisy data. In: IEEE conference on computer vision and pattern recognition workshops. doi:10.1109/CVPRW.2013.143
4. Duda RO, Hart PE, Stork DG (2001) Pattern classification, 2nd edn. Wiley-Interscience, New York
5. Gade R, Moeslund TB (2013) Thermal cameras and applications: a survey. Mach Vis Appl. doi:10.1007/s00138-013-0570-5
6. Gade R, Jørgensen A, Moeslund TB (2012) Occupancy analysis of sports arenas using thermal imaging. In: Proceedings of the international conference on computer vision and applications
7. Gade R, Jørgensen A, Moeslund TB (2013) Long-term occupancy analysis using graph-based optimisation in thermal imagery. In: CVPR

8. Gibert X, Li H, Doermann D (2003) Sports video classification using HMMS. In: International conference on multimedia and expo (ICME). doi:10.1109/ICME.2003.1221624
9. Janez Pers MB, Vuckovic G (2006) CVBASE 06 dataset. http://vision.fe.uni-lj.si/cvbase06/dataset.html
10. Kapur J, Sahoo P, Wong A (1985) A new method for gray-level picture thresholding using the entropy of the histogram. Comput Vis Graph Image Process 29(3):273–285. doi:10.1016/0734-189X(85)90125-2. http://www.sciencedirect.com/science/article/pii/0734189X85901252
11. Krishna Mohan C, Yegnanarayana B (2010) Classification of sport videos using edge-based features and autoassociative neural network models. Signal, Image Video Process 4:61–73
12. Lee JY, Hoff W (2007) Activity identification utilizing data mining techniques. In: IEEE workshop on motion and video computing (WMVC). doi:10.1109/WMVC.2007.4
13. Li R, Chellappa R (2010) Recognizing offensive strategies from football videos. In: IEEE international conference on image processing
14. Li R, Chellappa R, Zhou S (2009) Learning multi-modal densities on discriminative temporal interaction manifold for group activity recognition. In: IEEE conference on computer vision and pattern recognition
15. Li L, Zhang N, Duan LY, Huang Q, Du J, Guan L (2009) Automatic sports genre categorization and view-type classification over large-scale dataset. In: 17th ACM international conference on multimedia (MM). doi:10.1145/1631272.1631380
16. Mutchima P, Sanguansat P (2012) TF-RNF: a novel term weighting scheme for sports video classification. In: IEEE international conference on signal processing, communication and computing (ICSPCC). doi:10.1109/ICSPCC.2012.6335651
17. Sigari M, Sureshjani S, Soltanian-Zadeh H (2011) Sport video classification using an ensemble classifier. In: 7th Iranian machine vision and image processing (MVIP). doi:10.1109/IranianMVIP.2011.6121538
18. Steiner H, Butzke M (1988) CASA computer aided sports analysis. In: Krause B, Schreiner A (eds) Hector. Springer, Berlin, pp 182–185
19. Varadarajan J, Atmosukarto I, Ahuja S, Ghanem B, Ahujad N (2013) A topic model approach to representing and classifying football plays. In: British machine vision conference
20. Wang J, Xu C, Chng E (2006) Automatic sports video genre classification using Pseudo-2D-HMM. In: 18th international conference on pattern recognition (ICPR). doi:10.1109/ICPR.2006.308
21. Wang DH, Tian Q, Gao S, Sung WK (2004) News sports video shot classification with sports play field and motion features. In: International conference on image processing (ICIP). doi:10.1109/ICIP.2004.1421545
22. Watcharapinchai N, Aramvith S, Siddhichai S, Marukatat S (2007) A discriminant approach to sports video classification. In: International symposium on communications and information technologies (ISCIT). doi:10.1109/ISCIT.2007.4392081
23. Xu M, Park M, Luo S, Jin J (2008) Comparison analysis on supervised learning based solutions for sports video categorization. In: IEEE 10th workshop on multimedia signal processing. doi:10.1109/MMSP.2008.4665134
24. Yuan Y, Wan C (2004) The application of edge feature in automatic sports genre classification. In: IEEE conference on cybernetics and intelligent systems. doi:10.1109/ICCIS.2004.1460749

Chapter 11
Event-Based Sports Videos Classification Using HMM Framework

Shyju Wilson, C. Krishna Mohan and K. Srirama Murthy

Abstract Sports video classification is an important application of video content analysis. Event detection or recognition in sports video is an important task in semantic understanding of video content. In this paper, we propose a framework based on hidden Markov models (HMM) to represent a video as a sequence of core events that occur in a particular sport. The objective is to observe a subset of (hidden) state sequences to see whether they can be interpreted as the core events of that sport. We propose a method for sports video classification based on the events in each sport category. The proposed method for detection of events is based on a subset of state sequences, unlike the traditional way of computing the likelihood as a sum or maximum overall possible state sequences. The neighboring frames are considered for the computation of event probability at any instant of time. We demonstrate the application of this framework to five sport genre types, namely basketball, cricket, football, tennis, and volleyball.

11.1 Introduction

Classification of digital video into various genres, or categories is an important task, which enables efficient cataloging and retrieval with large video collections. Efficient search and retrieval of video content have become more difficult due to the ever increasing amount of video data. The recent statistics of popular video sharing website YouTube shows that over 6 billion hours of videos are watched each month on YouTube (50 % more than last year) and 100 h of videos are uploaded onto YouTube every minute. This huge growth leads to the importance of efficient organization and retrieval of video data. Semantic analysis is a natural way for video management and

S. Wilson (✉) · C.K. Mohan · K.S. Murthy
Indian Institute of Technology Hyderabad, Hyderabad 502205, India
e-mail: cs10p006@iith.ac.in

C.K. Mohan
e-mail: ckm@iith.ac.in

K.S. Murthy
e-mail: ksrm@iith.ac.in

T.B. Moeslund et al. (eds.), *Computer Vision in Sports*,
Advances in Computer Vision and Pattern Recognition,
DOI 10.1007/978-3-319-09396-3_11

accessing. However, it remains a challenging issue. There are various approaches to content-based classification of video data. A video clip can be classified at various levels in the semantic hierarchy. At the highest level of hierarchy, video collections can be categorized into broad program genres such as cartoon, sports, commercials, news, and music. At the next level of hierarchy, domain videos such as sports can be classified into different subcategories. At a finer level, a video sequence itself can be segmented, and each segment can then be classified according to its semantic content. In [1], sports video segments are first segmented into shots, and each shot is then classified into playing field, player, graphic, audience, and studio shot categories. Semantic classification of basketball segments into goal, foul, and crowd categories [7] by using edge-based features is another work carried out at this level. In this study, we focus on classification of sports videos into different subcategories.

We address the problem of classification of sports videos into different categories. Each sports video category can be identified using actions in that particular sport. For instance, the act of a bowler delivering the ball to a batsman is unique to the game of cricket. Similarly, a player serving the ball into the opponent's court is specific to the game of lawn tennis. These actions help a human viewer to readily identify a given sport. What is important here is the sequence of changes that are integral to an action and which qualify the action. For instance, when a bowler delivers the ball, his bowling run up, bowling action, and speed of the delivery are not so much important as the act of delivering the ball. It is the act of delivering the ball that is significant, and is common across different bowlers. Such acts occur within a limited time duration. They help in uniquely characterizing a sport and can be useful for classification, provided they can be detected automatically from the video data. In this context, an event can be defined as any significant change during the course of the game. An activity may be regarded as a sequence of certain semantic events. Automatic detection of events from raw data is a challenging task, since the variations in the raw data make it difficult to interpret a change as an event. At the level of feature too, these changes cannot be observed by comparing low-level features across adjacent frames due to variability and noise. Moreover, the changes may span over a sequence of image frames. In this context, an event can be viewed as a feature at a higher level, while an activity (sequence of events) can be viewed as a signature of a given class. This necessitates the need to model the information present in a sequence of frames.

The problem of automatic detection of events in sports videos has been addressed in literature by modeling events that are defined a priori for a given sport (or a set of sports) [17, 25]. The main goal in such approaches is to classify the video of a given sport into different semantic events. In such approaches [17, 25], video sequences are presegmented into clips where each clip contains only one event. Another class of approaches performs automatic segmentation of the given video into shots. However, the detected events themselves are not used to distinguish between different categories of sports. In this paper, the objective is to automatically detect events from the video sequences in a generic manner without a priori knowledge of the events and without predefining the events. Moreover, the hypothesized events are used to distinguish between classes, since the nature of events is likely to differ among the classes. We propose a probabilistic approach to detect the events, using the framework of hidden Markov model (HMM). Since the variations in the events are reflected only indirectly through the feature vectors derived from the data, HMM is a better choice to capture the hidden sequence from the observed sequence of feature vectors.

Hidden Markov models have been used in the literature for identifying activities from observation sequences [5]. Given an HMM denoted by λ and an observation sequence $\mathbf{O}$, the probability $P(\mathbf{O}/\lambda)$ that this observation sequence is generated by the model, is calculated as either the *sum* or *maximum* overall possible state sequences to detect the activity [12]. The optimal state sequence is not driven by the events that occur during the activity, but by the likelihood of the observed data. No attempt has been made to examine the sequence of states to characterize any (hidden) activity in the sequence of events that may be present in the observed data. This study attempts to derive/interpret the sequence of events that may be present in a subset of (hidden) state sequences, and not from the raw data itself because the raw data may vary too much to interpret any change as an event [2]. In the case of sports video data, activities are characterized by certain events of interest that are embedded in the motion information, and occur within a limited time duration. These event probabilities obtained using the HMM framework are used to characterize the activity in a particular game.

Methods that model temporal information in video sequences focus on the detection of events in video sequences. These are predefined events that require manual effort to identify frame sequences containing those events. Moreover, the detected events are used mostly for indexing and retrieval, and not for classification. In this context, we note that the events being specific to sports categories can be used as features to classify a given video into one of those categories. We propose a novel method to identify and match events in video sequences using a framework based on hidden Markov models. Here, the events are not predefined, but hypothesized based on the sequence latent in a given video. Once the events are identified, they are further used for classification of a given video into one of the sports categories.

The remainder of this paper is organized as follows: Sect. 11.2 contains related works. In Sect. 11.3, we describe a method for detection of events in the framework of hidden Markov models. Section 11.3.1 describes the representation of motion-based features for detection of events. Once the events are hypothesized, a measure of similarity is required for comparison of events obtained from reference and test video data. In Sect. 11.4, a method is proposed for the comparison of events. Section 11.5 discusses experiments on video classification using five sports categories, and the performance of the system. Section 11.6 summarizes the study.

11.2 Related Work

In [25], an HMM-based framework is suggested to discover the hidden states or semantics behind video signals. The objective is to arrive at a sequence of semantics from a given sequence of observations by imposing temporal context constraints.

The framework is then applied to detect predefined events in sports categories such as basketball, soccer, and volleyball. An error weighted semicoupled hidden Markov model [9] is used with as state-based bimodal alignment strategy and bayesian classifier weighted scheme. For the optimal emotion recognition, audio video visual feature pair is classified into one of the emotional class by combining decisions from the classifier of audio and visual features. Hierarchical hidden Markov model (HHMM) [22] is used to classify video segment based on the motion feature distribution. Video Summarization is done through object and event detection.

Features indicating significant events are selected from video sequences [17]. These features include a measure of motion activity and orientation of edges, which help in detection of crowd images, on-screen graphics, and prominent field lines in sports videos. The evidence obtained by different feature detectors are combined using a support vector machine, which then detects the occurrence of an event. Another approach [14] models the spatio-temporal behavior of an object in a video sequence for identifying a particular event. The game of snooker is considered and the movement of snooker ball is tracked using a color-based particle filter. A few events are predefined in terms of actions, where an action can be a white ball colliding with a colored ball, or a ball being potted. An HMM is used to model the temporal behavior of the white ball along with algorithms for collision detection.

A symbolic description of events is provided in [21], where events are described in terms of rules using fuzzy hypotheses. These hypotheses are based on the degree of belief of the presence of specific objects and their interrelations, extracted from the video sequence. The method involves the extraction of main mobile objects in video sequences, also called fuzzy predicates. The input is defined on the set of fuzzy predicates, while the output is a fuzzy set defined on the events to be recognized. The association between the fuzzy predicates and the set of events is represented using a neurofuzzy structure. The approach is tested on soccer video sequences for detecting some predetermined events. In [10], Pyramidal Motion Feature (PMF) are used for human action recognition. The boosted keyframe, which is having more discriminative information, is selected using AdaBoost learning algorithm. The correlogram is used to represent action sequence which will be classified by Support Vector Machine (SVM). In [24], a multilayer framework based on HMMs is proposed for detection of events in sports videos on the basis that sports videos can be considered as rule-based sequential signals. At the bottom layer, event HMMs output basic hypotheses using low-level features. The upper layers impose constraints on the predefined events in basketball.

The deterministic approach to event detection is compared with probabilistic approach, in [8]. While the former depends on clear description of an event and explicit representation of the event in terms of low-level features, the latter is based on states and state transition models whose parameters are learnt through labeled training sequences. It is shown through automatic analysis of football coaching video, that the probabilistic approach performs more accurately while detecting events, mainly due to its ability to capture temporal patterns and yet, absorb small spatio-temporal variations. Thus, a common feature of most of these approaches is the use of HMM in a traditional framework for detection of predefined events. While the detected events are used for indexing, retrieval, and generation of summary/highlights, they are rarely used for classification of video sequences.

Another approach, described in [4] constructs two hidden Markov models, from principal motion direction and principal color of each frame, respectively. The decisions are integrated to obtain the final score for classification. In [26], a multilayered data association algorithm with graph-theoretic formulation for tracking multiple objects that undergo switching dynamics in clutter is described. A framework for analysis and summarization of soccer video is described in [3]. The method allows real-time event detection by cinematic features, and further filtering of slow motion replay shots by object-based features for semantic labeling. An automatic interpretation and evolution tracking of a tennis match using standard broadcast video sequences as input data is described in [6]. The method uses hierarchical structure consisting of hidden Markov models. This will take low-level events as its input, and will produce an output where the final state will indicate if the point is to be awarded to one player or another.

The framework described in [18] covers a scalable architecture for video processing and stages of shot boundary detection, salient object detection and tracking, and knowledge-base construction for effective spatio-temporal object querying. An approach for automatic detection of a falling person in video [20] uses both audio and video tracks to decide a fall in video. Human motion in video is modeled using hidden Markov models and audio information is used to distinguish a falling person from a person simply sitting down or sitting on a floor. In [15], a tool called temporal credal filter with conflict-based model change (TCF-CMC) is described to smooth belief functions online in transferable belief model (TBM) framework. It is an unsupervised and online criterion used in both assessment of filtering and detection of new actions. TCF-CMC modeling is based on joint belief functions and includes parameter adaptation.

Semantic model vectors [11], from low-level features, are used to bridge the semantic gap between low-level visual features and events in video. Sequences of feature are represented as string and similarities are measured by appropriate string matching technique [27]. The Levenshtein distance has been used for comparing two video clips with three operations viz. insertion, deletion, substitution of feature vectors. After shot boundary detection and keyframe extraction, efficient near duplicate keyframe (NDK) detection [23] is adopted to identify similar events and clustered them to form potential events. Four properties (video set, start and end time, key terms, representative NDK) are extracted to represent the event. Kevin Tang et al. works with variable duration hidden Markov model to detect events in the video. The Counter is assigned to each state and expect single state to generate several temporal segments that can be interpreted as event [19]. In our approach, event probability is calculated from subsequence of states rather than counting for event detection.

11.3 Detection of Events Using HMM

An event can be defined as any significant change during the course of the game. These changes cannot be observed at the pixel level by comparing the adjacent frames, because the raw data may vary too much to interpret any change as an event. At the feature level also, it may not be possible to detect the events because of the variability in the data and the presence of noise. Hence, in this paper, we propose a probabilistic approach to detect the events, by considering a sequence of frames, using HMM framework. Since the variations in the events are reflected only indirectly through the feature vectors derived from the data, HMM is a better choice to capture the unknown hidden sequence from the observation sequence of feature vectors. The events thus derived are associated with an event label which describes the nature of the event and a probability value which denotes the likelihood with which the event can occur.

Hidden Markov models are powerful tools for characterizing the temporal behavior of time sequences, and have been used in various ways for content-based video processing. The HMM is a Markov model in which the state is a probabilistic function of observation symbol. In general, each state in the HMM is modeled as a Gaussian mixture model. Typically, the number of states N is far less than the number of observation symbols T. The continuous density HMM model can be described by the parameter set $\lambda = (A, B, \Pi)$ where

$\Pi = \{\pi_1, \pi_2, \ldots \pi_N\}$ denote the initial state probability,
$A = \{a_{ij}\}$ denote the state transition matrix, and
$B = \{b_j(k)\}$ denote the probability distributions of individual states.

Given a large number of examples of an activity, the parameter set $\lambda = (A, B, \Pi)$ is estimated using the Baum-Welch algorithm [13]. Once the parameter set λ is estimated, the probability of a test observation sequence $\mathbf{O} = (\mathbf{o}_1\mathbf{o}_2\mathbf{o}_3 \ldots \mathbf{o}_T)$ being generated by the model λ can be computed in two ways:

1. Sum overall the possible state sequences
   $P(\mathbf{O}/\lambda) = \sum_{\{q_1,\ldots,q_T\}} P(q_1, \ldots, q_T, \mathbf{o}_1, \ldots, \mathbf{o}_T/\lambda)$,
   where $q_1, q_2, \ldots, q_T$ are the individual states and $\{q_1, q_2, \ldots, q_T\}$ is the state sequence.
2. Maximum of all the possible state sequences
   $P(\mathbf{O}/\lambda) = \max_{\{q_1,\ldots,q_T\}} P(q_1, \ldots, q_T, \mathbf{o}_1, \ldots, \mathbf{o}_T/\lambda)$.

The key idea in the traditional HMM formulation is that the sum or the maximum overall possible state sequences is considered in evaluating the probabilities. But the optimal state sequence obtained using these methods is not driven by the events that occur during the activity rather by the likelihood of the observed data. In this kind of formulation, there is no attempt to examine the sequence of states to characterize any hidden activity in the form of sequence of events that may be present in the observed data. Traditional method does not give any information regarding events. Here, we exploit events in the activity to classify the videos. This is the novelty in our approach.

In this paper, we propose a method to examine a subset of sequences and explore the possibility of interpreting them as sequence of events. The hypothesis is that, though the state sequences themselves may look different across examples of the same activity, certain (hidden) state transitions may be preserved in a subset of state sequences, and we call such transitions as events.

11.3.1 Features for Detection of Events

Motion is an important cue for understanding video and widely used in semantic video content analysis. Since features based on motion carry important information about the temporal sequence corresponding to a given sports category, we use motion-based features for event detection. The approach adopted here for extraction of motion information from the video is based on the work by Roach et al. [16]. From the video sequence, we derive the binary maps as shown in Fig. 11.1. These binary maps are representative of moving and nonmoving areas of the video sequence, where moving areas are highlighted in white. The binary maps are extracted by pixel-wise differencing of consecutive frames. We divide each frame into four subimages of equal size in order to capture the location specific information. The motion feature is computed as follows:

$$M(t) = \frac{1}{w \times h} \sum_{x=1}^{w} \sum_{y=1}^{h} P_t(x, y), \quad 0 < t \leq N, \tag{11.1}$$

where

$$P_t(x, y) = \begin{cases} 1, & \text{if } |I_t(x, y) - I_{t-1}(x, y)| > \beta \\ 0, & \text{otherwise.} \end{cases} \tag{11.2}$$

In the above equation, N is the total number of frames in the video clip, $I_t(x, y)$ and $I_{t-1}(x, y)$ are the pixel values at location (x, y) in tth and $(t-1)$th frames, respectively. Here β is the threshold, and w and h are width and height of the subimage, respectively. A 4-dimensional feature vector is derived from each pair of consecutive frames. Thus, the sequence of 4-dimensional feature vectors derived from a video clip of a particular sports category forms one observation symbol sequence for that category.

11.3.2 Exploring Events in Sequence of States

Let a given sports video clip be represented by an observation symbol sequence $\mathbf{O} = (\mathbf{o}_1\mathbf{o}_2\mathbf{o}_3 \ldots \mathbf{o}_T)$. Suppose that the underlying activity responsible for the

Fig. 11.1 Examples of binary maps for different sports categories. Each row shows two consecutive frames and the corresponding binary map for five different sports, namely, **a** basketball. **b** Cricket. **c** Football. **d** Tennis. and **e** Volleyball

production of the observation symbol sequence can be described by a sequence of events occurring at different time instances. So, to represent this activity, we need to detect the number of events, the nature of events, and the time instants at which they occur. As these events are localized in time, it is reasonable to expect that an event at time t is affected by observations in its immediate neighborhood. Hence, we define a variable $\eta_t^p(i, j)$ as given by [2]

$$\eta_t^p(i, j) = P(q_{t-p} = i, q_{t-p+1} = i, \ldots, q_t = i, \\ q_{t+1} = j, q_{t+2} = j, \ldots, q_{t+p+1} = j/\mathbf{O}, \lambda), \tag{11.3}$$

where $2p + 2$ frames around t are considered. The superscript p refers to support of p frames used on either side of the time instant t in order to detect an event. The $\eta_t^p(i, j)$ can be written as

$$\begin{aligned}\eta_t^p(i, j) &= \Big(P(q_{t-p} = i, q_{t-p+1} = i, \ldots, q_t = i, q_{t+1} = j, \\ &\qquad q_{t+2} = j, \ldots q_{t+p+1} = j, \mathbf{O}/\lambda)\Big) \div P(\mathbf{O}/\lambda), \\ &= \Big(\alpha_{t-p}(i) a_{ii}^p b_i(o_{t-p+1}) \ldots b_i(o_t) a_{ij} b_j(o_{t+1}) \ldots \\ &\qquad b_j(o_{t+p}) a_{jj}^p \beta_{t+p}(j)\Big) \div P(\mathbf{O}/\lambda),\end{aligned} \tag{11.4}$$

where α and β are forward and backward variables [12], respectively. We define one more variable e_t^p, similar to the one that is used in Viterbi maximization, as

$$e_t^p(k, l) = \max_{i,j} \eta_t^p(i, j) \quad i \neq j, \tag{11.5}$$

where

$$(k, l) = \arg\max_{i,j} \eta_t^p(i, j) \quad i \neq j. \tag{11.6}$$

Here $e_t^p(k, l)$ represents the probability with which there can be a transition from stable state k to stable state l, with a support of p frames for stable states, at the time instant t. At every instant of time, we hypothesize an event, and evaluate the event probability $e_t^p(i, j)$. Large values of e_t^p indicate the presence of an event, and the corresponding (k, l) pair indicates the state transition responsible for the event. The nature of the event is specified by state pair (k, l), and the intensity of the event is specified by the value of e_t^p.

For every symbol $\mathbf{o}_t$ in the given observation symbol sequence $\mathbf{O} = \{\mathbf{o}_1, \mathbf{o}_2, \ldots, \mathbf{o}_T\}$, an event probability value e_t^p and a state transition (k, l) are associated. The value of p determines the support given to the stable states on either side of the transition. A small value of p results in too many spurious events, whereas a large value of p might result in missing an event of interest totally. Hence, the value of p is determined by using the domain knowledge and some preliminary experimental studies. The event probability sequence e_t^p and the corresponding state transitions (k, l) form the signature for the activity in a particular sports category.

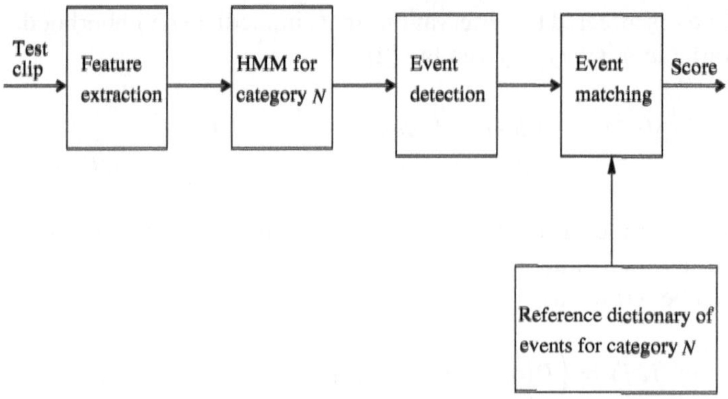

Fig. 11.2 Block diagram of the proposed video classification system using HMM framework

11.4 Matching of Events

We now describe a method for matching of events between a test video sequence and a reference video sequence. The block diagram of the proposed sports video classification system using HMM framework is shown in Fig. 11.2. Given L_1 observation symbols of a video category, a five state ergodic HMM model with one Gaussian per state is trained with motion features extracted from the video frames. The events (event probabilities and corresponding state transition) corresponding to the reference examples are obtained. These reference event sequences are used to create a dictionary of events for the given sports category. The distribution of the event probability values corresponding to a particular state transition (k, l) in the reference events is approximated by a Gaussian density $\mathscr{N}(\mu_{kl}, \sigma_{kl})$, where μ_{kl} and σ_{kl} denote mean and variance of the density function, respectively, given by

$$\mu_{kl} = \frac{1}{L_1} \sum_{t=1}^{L_1} e_t^p(k, l) \tag{11.7}$$

and

$$\sigma_{kl} = \sqrt{\frac{1}{L_1} \sum_{t=1}^{L_1} (e_t^p(k, l) - \mu_{kl})^2}. \tag{11.8}$$

So, every state transition is assigned a mean and a variance which represents the probabilities with which the event $e_t^p(k, l)$ occurs in that category. For a test video clip not presented during training, the events are obtained using a reference HMM. Let us denote by $\hat{e}_t^p(k, l)$, the event probability corresponding to the state transition (k, l) at time t, when a test sequence of observation symbols is presented to a reference model. Let L_2 denote the number of observation symbols in the test sequence. A similarity score s between the test video clip and the reference model is given by

$$s = \frac{1}{L_2}\sum_{t=1}^{L_2}\frac{1}{\sqrt{2\pi}\sigma_{kl}}\exp\left[-\frac{(\hat{e}_t^p(k,l)-\mu_{kl})^2}{2\sigma_{kl}^2}\right]. \tag{11.9}$$

There exists a possibility that two different categories may have similar distributions of event probabilities, i.e., two models may have the same score. In such a case, it is difficult to classify the videos without the sequence knowledge. But in practice, probability of occurring this kind of situation is very rare. In our approach, events are detected but not assigned label to the events.

11.5 Experiments and Performance Analysis

Experiments were carried out on about $5\frac{1}{2}$ h of video data (1,000 video clips, 200 clips per sports category, and each clip of 20 s duration) comprising of cricket, football, tennis, basketball, and volleyball categories. The video clips were captured at a rate of 25 fps, at 320 × 240 pixel resolution, and stored in AVI format. The data were collected from different TV channels in various sessions and ensure independence among videos in the same class. For each sports video category, 100 clips were used for training and the remaining 100 clips were used for testing.

11.5.1 Experimental Results

One HMM model is chosen for each category of sport for our study. The HMM model is trained using Baum-Welch algorithm for ten iterations. The choice of the number of states (N) of HMM is critical. It is difficult to arrive at the number of states from the physical process, since the process is not explicit. Hence, N needs to be determined experimentally by observing the classification performance. The classification performance was observed by varying N between 3 and 10. The values $N = 7$ and $N = 9$ were chosen based on the performance of classification. Also, the choice of the value of p is critical since it determines the support given to the stable states on either side of the transition. A small value of p results in too many spurious events, whereas a large value of p might miss an event of interest. Hence, the value of p is determined by using some preliminary experimental studies.

An ergodic HMM model is built for each class using 4-dimensional motion feature vectors. The performance of the event-based HMM classifier is given in Table 11.1 for the case with number of states $N = 7$ and number of mixtures $M = 1$. In Table 11.1, the entries in parenthesis denote the classification performance for $N = 7$ and $M = 2$. The classification performance for $N = 9$ and $M = 1, 2$ is given in Table 11.2. It is observed that the average performance for $N = 7$ is better for all sports except football. When $N = 9$, performance of football is increased very much. This can be attributed to the continuous motion in the football video compared to frequent

Table 11.1 Performance of correct video classification for $N = 7$ and $M = 1$ (in %)

	Basketball	Cricket	Football	Tennis	Volleyball	Avg. perf.
p=5	92 (62)	68 (56)	76 (58)	78 (80)	96 (96)	**82.0** (70.4)
p=7	90 (66)	58 (52)	80 (62)	78 (84)	98 (96)	80.8 (**72.0**)
p=10	82 (66)	56 (32)	88 (72)	78 (80)	98 (80)	80.4 (66.0)
p=13	72 (46)	56 (20)	90 (62)	80 (88)	98 (58)	79.2 (54.8)
p=15	60 (34)	48 (20)	92 (60)	74 (90)	98 (62)	74.4 (53.2)
p=17	48 (20)	42 (18)	92 (56)	74 (92)	98 (70)	70.8 (51.2)

The entries in parenthesis denote the performance for $N = 7$ and $M = 2$. The parameter p denotes the number of frames provided as support on either side of the time instant t. Entries in the last column denote the average performance of classification

Table 11.2 Performance of correct video classification for $N = 9$ and $M = 1$ (in %)

	Basketball	Cricket	Football	Tennis	Volleyball	Avg. perf.
p=5	94 (68)	56 (06)	96 (98)	60 (60)	82 (74)	**77.6 (61.2)**
p=7	84 (58)	48 (06)	98 (98)	60 (62)	78 (48)	73.6 (54.4)
p=10	76 (22)	36 (08)	98 (98)	60 (64)	82 (10)	70.4 (40.4)
p=13	58 (04)	34 (10)	98 (98)	60 (62)	88 (06)	67.6 (36.0)
p=15	44 (04)	38 (08)	98 (98)	60 (62)	86 (09)	65.2 (35.6)
p=17	44 (04)	24 (10)	96 (98)	60 (62)	84 (02)	61.6 (34.8)

The entries in parenthesis denote the performance for $N = 9$ and $M = 2$. The parameter p denotes the number of frames provided as support on either side of the time instant t. Entries in the last column denote the average performance of classification

changes in other categories. These continuous variations in the videos are better modeled using more number of states. This continuous variation also necessitates the choice of two mixtures per state ($M = 2$) for improved classification in the case of football category as shown in Table 11.2.

The confusion matrix for the best average classification performance ($N = 7$ or 9, $M = 1$, and $p = 5$) is given in Table 11.3. The relatively poorer performance for cricket and Tennis categories can be attributed to the inability of the models to detect the events. This is because basketball and volleyball videos have normally close-range view compared to other video categories, whereas the most parts of the videos of football, cricket, and tennis have taken from long-range view. But football is showing good performance because it is having continuous motion in the field and it can be captured well by increasing number of states. Both football and basketball have continuous motion because single camera is used to follow players or area of interest most of the times unlike the switching between multiple cameras in other cases. Another possibility of the relatively poorer performance of cricket and tennis is that the number of examples of a given event may be less in the training data, leading to poor representation of events.

Using the above method, we could detect significant changes in each sports category using motion information. The significant changes are considered as events

Table 11.3 The confusion matrix for the best classification performance (in %) ($M = 1$, and $p = 5$)

	Basketball	Cricket	Football	Tennis	Volleyball
Basketball ($N = 9$)	**94**	00	00	02	04
Cricket ($N = 7$)	02	**68**	16	12	04
Football ($N = 9$)	00	02	**96**	02	00
Tennis ($N = 7$)	00	06	16	**78**	00
Volleyball ($N = 7$)	00	04	00	00	**96**

which occurred repeatedly in the videos used for training. Some of the detected events are mentioned below. In the cricket, detected events are bowler releasing the ball, batsman hitting the ball, fielder picking up the ball, and fielder throwing the ball, etc. Two such cases events, of bowler releasing the ball and fielder picking the ball, are shown in Fig. 11.3. In the football, detected events are kicking the ball, change in the number of players in the field, etc. Goal is an important event in football, but it is unable to detect the goal as an event because occurring goal in football is very rare. In the basketball, detected events are catching ball, throwing ball, etc. In the volleyball, detected events are hitting ball, servicing ball, etc. In the tennis, detected events are servicing ball, hitting ball, etc.

11.5.2 Performance Analysis

We compare our proposed method with the traditional HMM. In traditional HMM method, the sum or the maximum of overall possible state sequences are considered in evaluating the probabilities, but it is not considering sequence of states to identify events in the activity. The proposed method is able exploit subsequence of states to identify events which helps to improve the classification performance. The Table 11.4 shows classification performance of sports videos (basketball, cricket, football, tennis, and volleyball) using traditional HMM with same features used in the proposed method. Most of the football videos are misclassified as cricket in the traditional method, but detection of sequence of events in our method plays important role to the classification of football videos. When the value of p increases, performance of football videos also increases. It means whenever more neighboring frames are considered for the detection of events, football can be classified well. This is attributed to the continuous motion in the football videos.

Basketball and volleyball videos are close-range videos compared to other categories and motion is also high in these categories. These common factors may be the reason for the misclassification of most of the volleyball videos as basketball in the traditional HMM. But in the proposed method, volleyball videos are classified correctly with high accuracy rate because events detected in volleyball help

Fig. 11.3 Sequence of image frames (from *top* to *bottom*) of two events of cricket category where the event of **a** bowler releasing the ball and **b** fielder picking up the ball are detected. The detected events are marked by a *circle*

to improve its classification. The overall performance of proposed method is better when compared to the traditional HMM.

Table 11.4 The confusion matrix for the classification performance using traditional HMM method (in %)

	Basketball	Cricket	Football	Tennis	Volleyball
Basketball ($N = 9$)	**95**	00	00	02	03
Cricket ($N = 7$)	03	**80**	02	01	04
Footbal ($N = 9$)	00	57	**43**	00	00
Tennis ($N = 7$)	00	21	04	**75**	00
Volleyball ($N = 7$)	48	07	00	00	**45**

N is number of states in each model of the category

11.6 Conclusion

We have presented a technique for classification of sports videos using events to represent class-specific information. The events were detected using a framework based on hidden Markov models. Each sports video category can be identified using actions in that particular sport. Activities are characterized by a sequence of semantic events that are embedded in the motion, and occur within a limited time duration. The event probabilities were used to characterize the activity. Value of p affects frequent or delayed changes of scene in the videos, it leads to the problem in the detection of events. Video classification is highly applicable in Content-Based Video Indexing and Retrieval. Our method works well with videos which is having well-defined events. Finally, the video classification was performed based on the similarity score obtained by matching the events. Whenever two categories have same distribution of events, it may not be possible to classify the videos without sequence knowledge. It is still challenging task to obtain sequence knowledge to improve the classification performance. This is our future work.

References

1. Assfalg J, Bertini M, Colombo C, Bimbo AD (2002) Semantic annotation of sports videos. IEEE Multimed 9(2):52–60
2. Cuntoor NP, Yegnanarayana B, Chellappa R (2005) Interpretation of state sequences in HMM for activity representation. In: Proceedings of international conference on acoustics, speech and signal processing, Philadelphia, USA
3. Ekin A, Tekalp AM, Mehrotra R (2003) Automatic soccer video analysis and summarization. IEEE Trans Image Process 12(7):796–807
4. Gibert X, Li H, Doermann D (2003) Sports video classification using HMMs. In: International conference on multimedia and expo, vol 2. Baltimore
5. Ivanov YA, Bobick AF (2000) Recognition of visual activities and interactions by stochastic parsing. IEEE Trans Pattern Anal Mach Intell 22(8):852–872
6. Kolonias I, Christmas W, Kittler J (2004) Tracking the evolution of a tennis match using hidden Markov models. Lecture Notes in Computer Science, vol 3138, pp 1078–1086
7. Lee MH, Nepal S, Srinivasan U (2003) Edge-based semantic classification of sports video sequences. In: International conference on multimedia and expo, vol 1. Baltimore, pp I-157-60

8. Li B, Sezan I (2003) Semantic sports video analysis: approaches and new applications. In: Proceedings of IEEE international conference on image processing, vol 1. Barcelona
9. Lin JC, Wu CH, Wei WL (2012) Errorweighted semi-coupled hidden Markov model for audio-visual emotion recognition. IEEE Trans Multimed 14(1):142–156
10. Liu L, Shao L, Rockett P (2013) Boosted key-frame selection and correlated pyramidal motion-feature representation for human action recognition. Pattern Recognit 46(7):1810–1818 doi:10.1016/j.patcog.2012.10.004. http://www.sciencedirect.com/science/article/pii/S0031320312004372
11. Merler M, Huang B, Xie L, Hua G, Natsev A (2012) Semantic model vectors for complex video event recognition. IEEE Trans Multimed 14(1):88–101
12. Rabiner LR (1989) A tutorial on hidden Markov models and selected applications in speech recognition. IEEE 77(2):257–286
13. Rabiner L, Juang B (1986) An introduction to hidden Markov models. IEEE Acoust Speech Signal Process Mag 3(1):4–16
14. Rae N, Dahyot R, Kokaram A (2004) Semantic event detection in sports through motion understanding. In: Proceedings international conference on acoustics, speech and signal processing. Dublin
15. Ramasso E, Rombaut M, Pellerin D (2007) State filtering and change detection using TBM conflict application to human action recognition in athletics videos. IEEE Trans Circuits Syst Video Technol 17(7):944–949
16. Roach M, Mason JS, Pawlewski M (2001) Motion-based classification of cartoons. In: Proceedings of international symposium on intelligent multimedia. Hong Kong, pp 146–149
17. Sadlier DA, OConnor NE (2005) Event detection in field sports video using audiovisual features and a support vector machine. IEEE Trans Circuits Syst Video Technol 15(10):1225–1233
18. Sevilmis T, Bastan M, Gudukbay U, Ulusoy O (2008) Automatic detection of salient objects and spatial relations in videos for a video database system. Image Vis Comput 26(10):1384–1396
19. Tang K, Fei-Fei L, Koller D (2012) Learning latent temporal structure for complex event detection. In: IEEE conference on computer vision and pattern recognition (CVPR). doi:10.1109/CVPR.2012.6247808, pp 1250–1257
20. Toreyin BU, Dedeoglu Y, Cetin AE (2006) HMM based falling person detection using both audio and video. In: Signal processing and communications applications. Antalya, pp 1–4
21. Tzouvaras V, Penakis GT, Stamou G, Kollias S (2003) Adaptive rule-based recognition of events in video sequences. In: Proceedings of IEEE international conference on image processing, vol 2. Barcelona
22. Wang F, Ngo CW (2012) Summarizing rushes videos by motion, object, and event understanding. IEEE Trans Multimed 14(1):76–87
23. Wu X, Lu YJ, Peng Q, Ngo CW (2011) Mining event structures from web videos. IEEE Multimed 18(1):38–51
24. Xu G, Ma YF, Zhang HJ, Yang S (2003) A HMM based semantic analysis framework for sports game event detection. In: Proceedings of IEEE international conference on image processing, vol 1. Barcelona
25. Xu G, Ma YF, Zhang HJ, Yang SQ (2005) An HMM-based framework for video semantic analysis. IEEE Trans Circuits Syst Video Technol 15(11):1422–1433
26. Yan F, Christmas W, Kittler J (2008) Layered data association using graph-theoretic formulation with applications to tennis ball tracking in monocular sequences. IEEE Trans Pattern Anal Mach Intell 30(10):1814–1830
27. Yeh MC, Cheng KT (2011) Fast visual retrieval using accelerated sequence matching. IEEE Trans Multimed 13(2):320–329

Part IV
What's Going on?

Chapter 12
Representing Team Behaviours from Noisy Data Using Player Role

Alina Bialkowski, Patrick Lucey, Peter Carr, Sridha Sridharan and Iain Matthews

Abstract Due to their unobtrusive nature, vision-based approaches to tracking sports players have been preferred over wearable sensors as they do not require the players to be instrumented for each match. Unfortunately however, due to the heavy occlusion between players, variation in resolution and pose, in addition to fluctuating illumination conditions, tracking players continuously is still an unsolved vision problem. For tasks like clustering and retrieval, having noisy data (i.e. missing and false player detections) is problematic as it generates discontinuities in the input data stream. One method of circumventing this issue is to use an occupancy map, where the field is discretised into a series of zones and a count of player detections in each zone is obtained. A series of frames can then be concatenated to represent a set-play or example of team behaviour. A problem with this approach though is that the compressibility is low (i.e. the variability in the feature space is incredibly high). In this paper, we propose the use of a bilinear spatiotemporal basis model using a *role representation* to clean-up the noisy detections which operates in a low-dimensional space. To evaluate our approach, we used a fully instrumented field-hockey pitch with 8 fixed high-definition (HD) cameras and evaluated our approach on approximately 200,000 frames of data from a state-of-the-art real-time player detector and compare it to manually labeled data.

A. Bialkowski (✉) · S. Sridharan
Queensland University of Technology, Brisbane, QLD, Australia
e-mail: a.bialkowski@connect.qut.edu.au

S. Sridharan
e-mail: s.sridharan@qut.edu.au

A. Bialkowski · P. Lucey · P. Carr · I. Matthews
Disney Research, Pittsburgh, PA, USA

P. Lucey
e-mail: patrick.lucey@disneyresearch.com

P. Carr
e-mail: peter.carr@disneyresearch.com

I. Matthews
e-mail: iainm@disneyresearch.com

T.B. Moeslund et al. (eds.), *Computer Vision in Sports*,
Advances in Computer Vision and Pattern Recognition,
DOI 10.1007/978-3-319-09396-3_12

12.1 Introduction

As the sophistication of analysis increases in professional sport, more organisations are looking at using player tracking data to obtain an advantage over their competitors. For sports like field-hockey, the dynamic and continuous nature makes analysis extremely challenging as game-events are not segmented into discrete plays, the speed of play is very quick (e.g. the ball can move at 125 km/h), and the size of the field is very large, with each player free to occupy any area at any time. A common approach to this problem is to use each player's x, y position in every frame to recognise team events [19, 20, 23]. However, as reliably tracking players in this environment over relatively long periods of time (i.e. >1 min) remains an unsolved computer vision problem, often large amounts of tracking data contains "holes" or "gaps" making analysis very difficult.

For tasks such as automatic event annotation (e.g. goals, corners, free-kicks), representations that describe the global pattern of team behaviours such as team-centroids or occupancy can be utilised on noisy detections. While these *macroscopic* representations can pick up on the global patterns, specific information such as individual player behaviours may be ignored which could be important for more specific events or retrieval tasks. As such, a *microscopic* representation (i.e. continuous tracks of each player) is preferred but this requires human intervention for long tracks. An example of this is shown in Fig. 12.1.

As player motion and position (i.e. proximity to teammates and opponents) is heavily linked to game-context and where the action on the field is taking place, these contextual features can be used to fill in the gaps of missed tracks caused by missed or false detections. In team sports, an important contextual feature is characterised by a *formation*: a coarse spatial structure which the players maintain over the course of the match. Additionally, player movements are governed by physical limits, such as acceleration, which makes trajectories smooth over time. These two observations suggest significant correlation (and therefore redundancy) in the spatiotemporal signal of player movement data. A core contribution of this work is to recover a low-dimensional approximation for a time series of player locations. The compact representation is critical for understanding team behaviour. First, it enables the recovery of a true underlying signal from a set of noisy detections. Second, it allows for efficient clustering and retrieval of game events.

A key insight of this work is that even perfect tracking data is not sufficient for understanding team behaviour, and an appropriate representation is necessary. A formation implicitly defines a set of *roles* or individual responsibilities which are then distributed amongst the players by the captain or coach. In dynamic games like field hockey, it may be opportunistic for players to swap roles (either temporarily or permanently). As a result, when analysing the strategy of a particular game situation, players are typically identified by the role they are currently playing and not necessarily by an individualistic attribute like name. In this paper, we present a *role representation* which provides a more compact representation compared to player identity, and allows us to use subspace methods such as the bilinear spatiotemporal basis model [3] to "denoise" noisy detections (which is common from a vision system).

Fig. 12.1 (*Top*) Detecting and tracking players over long-periods of time is challenging and often results in missed detections (*highlighted in red*) and false detections. (*Bottom*) In this paper, we evaluate two representations which are robust to false and missed detections: (1) an occupancy map (*left*), which is formed by quantising the field into discrete areas, and (2) a bilinear spatiotemporal model, which can be used to estimate continuous player tracks (*right*) from detection data and compactly represent spatiotemporal patterns

To enable this research we used player detection data captured via 8 fixed high-definition (HD) cameras, across seven complete field-hockey matches (over 8 h of match data for each camera). We utilise a state-of-the-art real-time player detector [9] to give player positions at every frame, affiliate detection results into teams using a colour histogram model, and then compare two approaches for representing the team behaviours: an occupancy map representation and a bilinear spatiotemporal basis model, which models the movement of players by role.

12.2 Related Work

Due to the host of military, surveillance and sport applications, research into recognising group behaviour has recently increased dramatically. Outside of the sports realm, most of this work has focussed on dynamic groups, where individual agents can leave and join groups over the period of observation. An initial approach was to recognise the activities of individual agents and then combine these to infer group activities [5]. Sukthankar and Sycara [33, 34] recognised group activities as a whole but pruned the size of possible activities by using temporal ordering constraints and agent resource dependencies. Sadilek and Kautz [30] used GPS locations of multiple agents in a "capture the flag" game to recognise low-level activities such as approaching and being at the same location. All of these works assume that the position and movements of all agents are known, and that all behaviours can be mapped to an activity within the library. Recently, Zhang et al. [37] used a "bag of words" and Support Vector Machine (SVM) approach to recognise group activities on the Mock Prison dataset [10].

Sports related research mostly centres on low-level activity detection with the majority conducted on American Football. In the seminal work by Intille and Bobick [18], they recognised a single football play *pCurl51*, using a Bayesian network to model the interactions between the players trajectories. Li et al. [24], modelled and classified five offensive football plays (dropback, combo dropback, middle run, left run, right run). Siddiquie et al. [31], performed automated experiments to classify seven offensive football plays using a shape (HoG) and motion (HoF) based spatio-temporal features. Instead of recognising football plays, Li and Chellapa [23] used a spatio-temporal driving force model to segment the two groups/teams using their trajectories. Researchers at Oregon State University have also done substantial research in the football space [15, 16, 32] with the goal of automatically detecting offensive plays from a raw video source and transferring this knowledge to a simulator. For soccer, Kim et al. [20] used the global motion of all players in a soccer match to predict where the play will evolve in the short-term. Beetz et al. [6] developed the *automated sport game models* (ASPOGAMO) system which can automatically track player and ball positions via a vision system. Using soccer as an example, the system was used to create a heat-map of player positions (i.e. which area of the field did a player mostly spend time in) and also has the capability of clustering passes into low-level classes (i.e. long, short etc.), although no thorough analysis was conducted due to a lack of data. In basketball, Perse et al. [28] used trajectories of player movement to recognise three type of team offensive patterns. Morariu and Davis [27] integrated interval-based temporal reasoning with probabilistic logical inference to recognise events in one-on-one basketball. Hervieu and Bouthemy [14] also used player trajectories to recognise low-level team activities using a hierarchical parallel semi-Markov model.

It is worth noting that an enormous amount of research interest has used broadcast sports footage for video summarisation in addition to action, activity and highlight detection [6, 12, 13, 17, 22, 25, 26, 36], but given that these approaches are not automatic (i.e. the broadcast footage is generated by humans) and that the telecasted view captures only a portion of the field, analysing groups has been impossible because some individuals are normally out of frame. Although similar in spirit to the research mentioned above, our work differs as: (1) we rely only on player detections rather than tracking, and (2) we compare across many matches.

12.3 Detection Data

12.3.1 Field-Hockey Test-Bed

In this work, we investigate the behaviours of several international field-hockey teams from player tracking data. To enable this research, we recorded video footage from a recent field-hockey tournament using eight stationary HD cameras which provide complete coverage of the 91.4 × 55.0 m playing surface, as displayed in Fig. 12.2.

12.3.2 Player Detection and Team Affiliation

For each camera, player image patches are extracted using a real-time person detector [9], which detects players by interpreting background subtraction results in terms of 3D geometry, where players are coarsely modelled as cylinders of height 1.8 m. This equates to 40–100 pixels height in the image depending on the distance

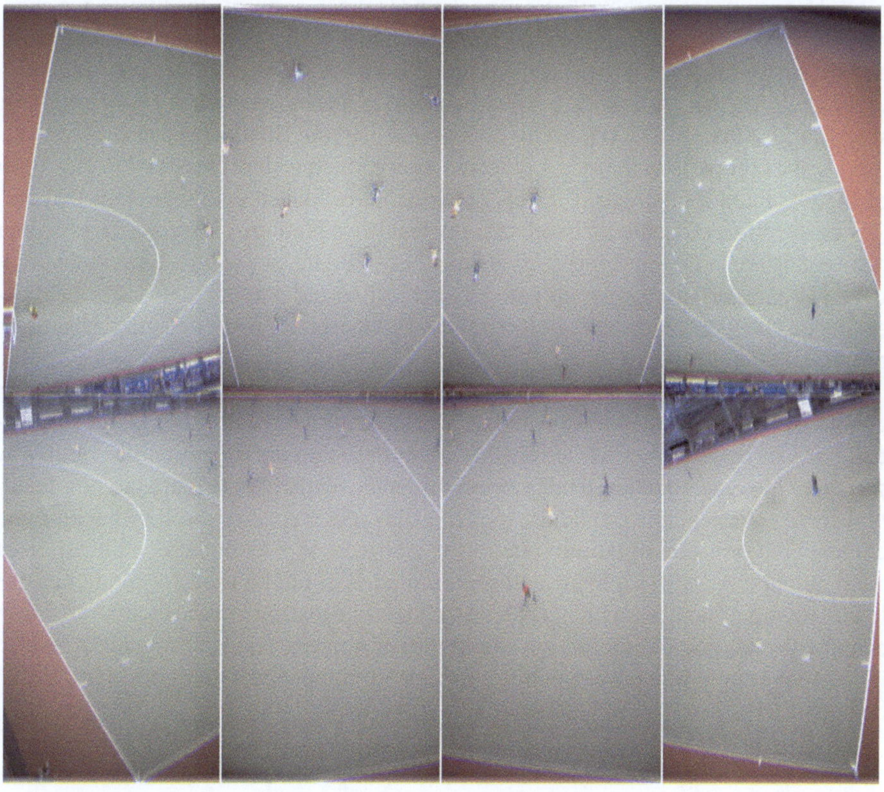

Fig. 12.2 View of the field-hockey pitch from the 8 fixed HD cameras

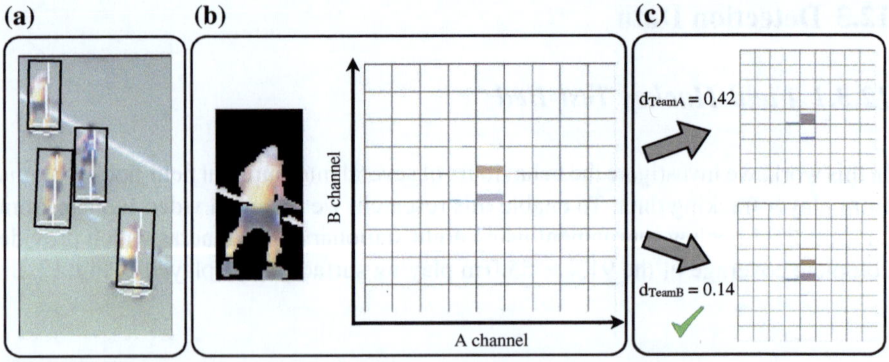

Fig. 12.3 **a** We detect players using a real-time person detector, and **b** represent the colours of each image patch using histograms of the foreground pixels in LAB colour space. **c** An image patch is then assigned to the closer of the two team histogram models (or "other" if the distance to each model exceeds a threshold)

from the camera, so for scale invariance, we normalise the image patches to a fixed size of 90 × 45 pixels. The image patches are then classified into teams using colour histograms of the foreground pixels, as illustrated in Fig. 12.3. The LAB colour space is used for representing the colours of each image patch, ignoring the luminance channel as it is affected by illumination changes. Nine bins are used for each dimension, and the histograms are normalised to sum to one.

Models for the two teams are learnt using *k*-means clustering from a training set of approximately 4,000 training histograms, and the Bhattacharyya coefficient is used as the comparison metric. A detected image patch is then classified to the closer of the two team models, or if it falls outside a threshold, it is classified as "others" (i.e. noise, referees, goalies). In our dataset, teams wear contrasting colours, so colour histograms are sufficient for distinguishing between the two teams. Detections from the eight cameras are then aggregated by projecting the player positions to field coordinates using each camera's homography, and merging player detections based on proximity (Fig. 12.4).

The performance of the detector and team classification compared to ground truth annotated frames using precision and recall metrics is shown in Table 12.1. From this table, it can be seen that while recall is high, the team classification has quite low precision in some matches. The poor performance is mainly attributed to non-team-players (referees, goalies, and false-positive player detections caused by background clutter) being misclassified into one of the teams, as they contain a combination of team colours. A more sophisticated representation could be used for modelling the teams as well as non-team image patches, and online learning of the colour models to adapt with changes in illumination would further improve results. From these results, it is evident that our team behaviour representation must be able to deal with a high degree of noise.

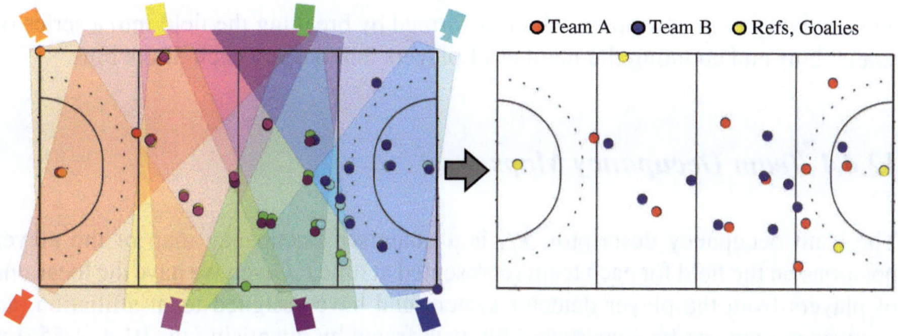

Fig. 12.4 (*Left*) We detect players in each camera using a real-time person detector and project these into real world co-ordinates. (*Right*) We then classify the detections into one of the two teams (or others) and aggregate the detections from each camera to extract the state of the game at each time instant

Table 12.1 Precision and recall values of the player detector and team affiliation classifier, after aggregating all cameras

Match code	No. of Frames	Precision			Recall		
		Detector (%)	Team A (%)	Team B (%)	Detector (%)	Team A (%)	Team B (%)
10-USA-RSA-1	14,352	81.1	67.2	77.7	89.0	98.3	98.4
24-JPN-USA-1	20,904	89.5	91.7	90.0	87.5	95.2	97.4
24-JPN-USA-2	7,447	85.8	72.4	79.7	90.0	97.6	97.0

12.4 Modelling Team Behaviours from Detections

An intuitive representation of team behaviours in sports would be to track all players (maintaining their identity) and the ball. For field-hockey, this would result in a 42 dimensional signal per frame (i.e. 21 objects with x and y coordinates—10 field players excluding the goalie × 2 teams, and the ball). However, since we cannot reliably and accurately track the player and ball over long durations, an alternative is to represent the match via player detections.

Player detection data can be modelled as a series of observations $\mathcal{O}$, where each observation consists of an (x, y) ground location, a timestamp t, and a team affiliation estimate $\tau \in \{\boldsymbol{\alpha}, \boldsymbol{\beta}\}$. At any given time instant t, the set of detected player locations $\mathcal{O}_t = \{x_A, y_A, x_B, y_B, \ldots\}$ is of arbitrary length because some players may not have been detected and/or background clutter may have been incorrectly classified as a player. Therefore, the number of player detections at any given frame is generally not equal to the actual number of players $2P$, where $P = 10$ players per team.

By representing the detections at each frame, we overcome the issue of tracking, but as a consequence we remove the player identity component of the signal and need another method to maintain feature correspondences. We propose to employ an *occupancy map* descriptor, which is formed by breaking the field into a series of spatial bins and counting the number of players that occupy each of the bins.

12.4.1 Team Occupancy Maps

The team occupancy descriptor, $\mathbf{x}_t^o$, is a quantised occupancy map of the player positions on the field for each team represented at time t. Given we have the locations of players from the player detector system and have assigned team affiliation, an occupancy map can be constructed for each frame by quantising the 91.4×55.0 m field into K bins, and counting how many player detections for that team fall within each location. The dimensionality of the formation descriptor is equal to twice the number of bins (i.e. $K \times 2$) so that both teams A and B are accounted for, resulting in $\mathbf{x}_t^o = [a_1, \ldots, a_K; b_1, \ldots, b_K]$, where a_k and b_k are the player counts in bin k for teams A and B respectively. Such an occupancy map can then be used to represent team activities by concatenating frames.

Depending on the level of complexity of the activity that we wish to recognise, we can use varying descriptor sizes (coarse/fine). We evaluate five different descriptor sizes: $K = 2(2 \times 1)$, $K = 8(4 \times 2)$, $K = 32(8 \times 4)$, $K = 135(15 \times 9)$ and $K = 540(30 \times 18)$, with examples illustrated in Fig. 12.5. The different quantisations represent how much tolerance there is in player's positions (e.g. in 15×9 quantisation, each player is assigned to an area of approximately $6\,\text{m}^2$).

12.4.2 Recognising Team Activities

To evaluate the different occupancy map representations, we conducted a series of isolated activity recognition experiments. We use the occupancy maps to recognise five activities, corresponding to important game states in field-hockey, shown in Fig. 12.6. As these activities coincide with a single event (e.g. the ball crossing the out line, or a goal being scored), they do not have distinct onset and offset times.

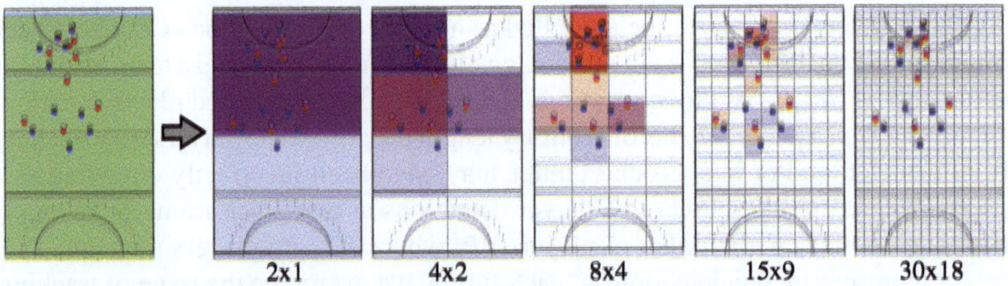

Fig. 12.5 Example team occupancy maps for different descriptor sizes

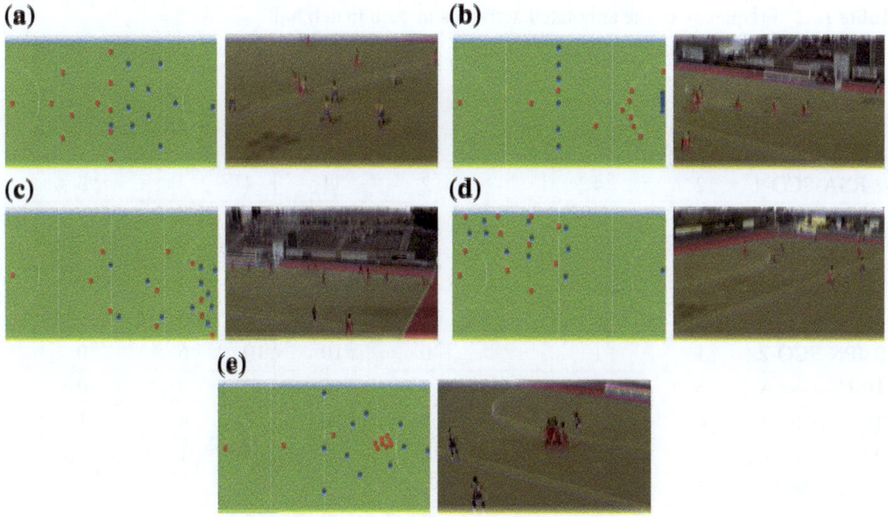

Fig. 12.6 Diagrams and examples of structured plays that occur in field-hockey. **a** Faceoff. **b** Penalty corner. **c** Long corner. **d** Defensive corner. **e** Goal

To account for this, we used the event as the start of the activity and went forward 10 s as the offset time, which gave us a series of 10 s play clips.

Since an activity can occur for either team, we compare the template descriptors in both orientations ($\mathbf{x}^{\theta} = [\mathbf{a}, \mathbf{b}]^T$, and $\mathbf{x}^{o} = [\mathbf{b}_{rot}, \mathbf{a}_{rot}]^T$, where $\mathbf{a}_{rot}$ represents a rotation of the field by 180° for team a's formation descriptor, so that the new descriptor is given by $\mathbf{a}_{rot}[k] = \mathbf{a}[K+1-k]$, for $k = 1, 2, \ldots, K$). We calculate the distance to the template in both orientations, and take the minimum as the distance measure.

Seven full matches (corresponding to over 8 hours of game play), were annotated with the 5 activities of interest: face-offs, penalty corners, goals, long corners and defensive corners as shown in Table 12.2. The annotated activities were split into testing and training sets using a leave-one-out cross-validation strategy, where one match half was used for testing and the remaining halves for training. We used a k-Nearest Neighbour classification approach, taking the mode activity label of the closest k examples in the training set, using L_2 as our distance measure. Confusion matrices using $k = 10$ are presented in Fig. 12.7.

Most activities are well recognised, however goals are often misclassified as the other activities because they are less structured, with a lot of variability possible. Defensive corners and long corners are sometimes confused with one another as the main difference is the team which maintains possession, which is not discernible from the occupancy descriptors. The best accuracy was achieved using an 8×4 descriptor with an accuracy of 78.2 %. Quantising at a finer level beyond this, resulted in a slightly reduced accuracy, which can be explained by players not aligning to the exact locations in the training activity templates, due to variability in activities (and our distance metric only compares corresponding field locations between occupancy

Table 12.2 Frequency of the annotated activities in each match half

	Face off	Penalty corner	Goal	Long corner		Defensive corner	
				(L)	(R)	(L)	(R)
1-JPN-USA-1	3	2	2	11	5	4	4
1-JPN-USA-2	2	6	1	4	10	7	3
2-RSA-SCO-1	2	4	2	11	4	3	3
2-RSA-SCO-2	3	9	2	3	12	4	3
5-USA-SCO-1	3	4	2	7	4	1	7
5-USA-SCO-2	3	8	2	3	3	2	2
9-JPN-SCO-1	2	4	2	8	7	5	2
9-JPN-SCO-2	1	1	0	10	10	6	0
10-USA-RSA-1	5	9	5	5	5	8	0
10-USA-RSA-2	6	4	5	6	7	4	1
23-ESP-SCO-1	3	4	2	7	6	1	1
23-ESP-SCO-2	3	7	2	9	5	2	1
24-JPN-USA-1	4	3	3	9	6	5	1
24-JPN-USA-2	2	2	1	5	9	7	6
Total	42	67	31	98	93	59	34

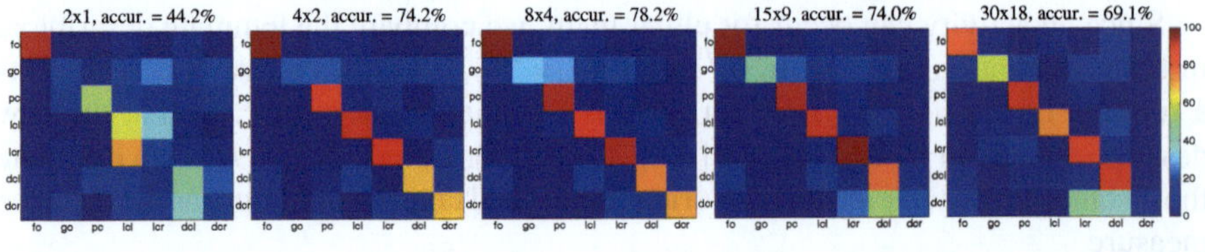

Fig. 12.7 Confusion matrices for isolated activity recognition using different occupancy map descriptor sizes

maps). A more coarse descriptor is able to represent the activity with tolerance for player position variations. This indicates that the annotated activities can be described by the distribution of the players on a relatively macroscopic scale rather than the exact positions approximated with the finer descriptors.

Despite their simplicity, it is evident that occupancy maps can be used to recognise important game states in the presence of noise and without any tracking information. However, if we wish to recognise the fine behaviours of teams (i.e. at the level of individual player behaviours), an occupancy map representation requires a very high dimensionality feature vector (e.g. a grid of 30×18 requires 540 feature dimensions per frame to represent player locations to a precision of $\sim 3\ m^2$). In addition, when modelling longer term behaviours, occupancy map descriptors are not very compressible in the temporal domain, because they do not directly model player movements (which are smooth) but occupancies in different zones of the field, which are discrete and do not vary smoothly or predictably in time, particularly with noisy detections.

In order to model individual behaviours in team sports compactly, we need a method to clean-up noisy detections and a representation which exploits the high degree of correlation between players. Player tracks could allow this, but we must overcome the issue of noisy detections (i.e. missed and false detections).

12.5 Representing Adversarial Movements

The task of tracking players across time is equivalent to generating a vector of ordered player locations $\mathbf{p}_t^\tau = [x_1, y_1, x_2, y_2, \ldots, x_P, y_P]^\mathsf{T}$ for each team τ from the noisy detections $\mathcal{O}_t$ at each time instant. The particular ordering of players is arbitrary, but must be consistent across time. Therefore, we refer to $\mathbf{p}_t^\tau$ as a *static labeling* of player locations. It is important to note that $\mathbf{p}_t^\tau$ is not simply a subset of $\mathcal{O}_t$. If a player was not detected, an algorithm must somehow infer the location of the unseen player.

We focus on generic team behaviours and assume any observed arrangement of players from team α could also have been observed for players from team β. As a result, there is a 180° symmetry in our data. For any given vector of player locations $\mathbf{p}_t^\tau$, there is an equivalent complement $\overleftrightarrow{\mathbf{p}}_t^\tau$ from rotating all (x, y) locations about the centre of the field and swapping the associated team affiliations.

12.5.1 Formations and Roles

In the majority of team sports, the coach or captain designates an overall structure or system of play for a team. In field hockey, the structure is described as a *formation* involving *roles* or individual responsibilities (see Fig. 12.8). For instance, the 5:3:2 formation defines a set of roles $\mathcal{R}$ = {left back (LB), right back (RB), left halfback

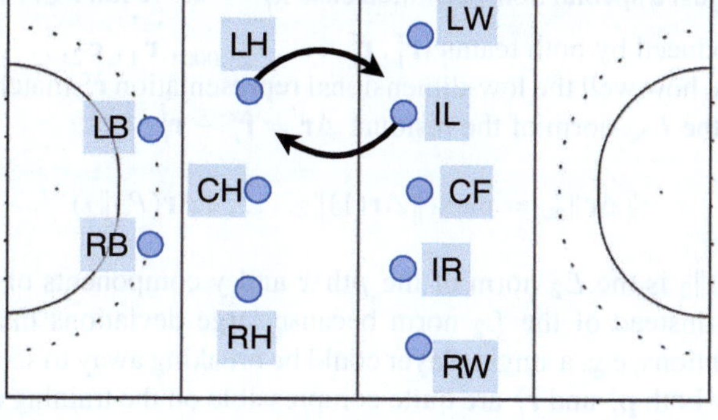

Fig. 12.8 The dynamic nature of the game requires players to switch roles and responsibilities on occasion, for example, the *left* halfback LH overlaps with the inside *left* IL to exploit a possible opportunity

Table 12.3 We manually labelled player location, identity and role at each frame for parts of four games from an international field-hockey tournament

Match code	No. of frames
10-USA-RSA-1	3,894
10-USA-RSA-2	8,839
24-JPN-USA-1	4,855
24-JPN-USA-2	7,418

(LH), center halfback (CH), right halfback (RH), inside left (IL), inside right (IR), left wing (LW), center forward (CF), right wing (RW)}. Each player is assigned exactly one role, and every role is assigned to only one player at any instant in time. Due to the dynamic nature of team sports, roles are generally not fixed and players will swap roles throughout a match, temporarily adopting the responsibilities of another player. Mathematically, assigning roles is equivalent to permuting the player ordering $\mathbf{p}_t^{\mathcal{T}}$. We define a $P \times P$ permutation matrix $\mathrm{x}_t^{\mathcal{T}}$ at time t which describes the players in terms of roles $\mathbf{r}_t^{\mathcal{T}}$

$$\mathbf{r}_t^{\mathcal{T}} = \mathrm{x}_t^{\mathcal{T}} \mathbf{p}_t^{\mathcal{T}} \tag{12.1}$$

By definition, each element $\mathrm{x}_t^{\mathcal{T}}(i, j)$ is a binary variable, and every column and row in $\mathrm{x}_t^{\mathcal{T}}$ must sum to one. If $\mathrm{x}_t^{\mathcal{T}}(i, j) = 1$ then player i is assigned role j. In contrast to $\mathbf{p}_t^{\mathcal{T}}$, we refer to $\mathbf{r}_t^{\mathcal{T}}$ as a *dynamic labeling* of player locations.

Because the spatial relationships of a formation are defined in terms of roles (and not individualistic attributes like name) and players swap roles during the game, we expect the spatiotemporal patterns in $\{\mathbf{r}_1^{\mathcal{T}}, \mathbf{r}_2^{\mathcal{T}}, \ldots, \mathbf{r}_T^{\mathcal{T}}\}$ to be more compact compared to $\{\mathbf{p}_1^{\mathcal{T}}, \mathbf{p}_2^{\mathcal{T}}, \ldots, \mathbf{p}_T^{\mathcal{T}}\}$. Additionally, we expect a team to maintain its formation while moving up and down the field. As a result, position data $\tilde{\mathbf{r}}_t^{\mathcal{T}}$ expressed relative to the mean (x, y) location of the team should be even more compressible. To test these conjectures, we manually tracked all players over 25,000 time-steps (which equates to $8 \times 25{,}000 = 200{,}000$ frames across 8 cameras), and asked a field hockey expert to assign roles to the player locations in each frame. A breakdown of the manually labelled data is given in Table 12.3.

For brevity, we explain the analysis in terms of roles $\mathbf{r}_t^{\mathcal{T}}$ since the original player ordering $\mathbf{p}_t^{\mathcal{T}}$ is just a special non-permuted case $\mathrm{x}_t^{\mathcal{T}} = \mathtt{I}$. We ran PCA on the temporal data series produced by both teams $\{\mathbf{r}_1^{\mathcal{T}}, \mathbf{r}_2^{\mathcal{T}}, \ldots, \mathbf{r}_{25{,}000}^{\mathcal{T}}, \overset{\leftrightarrows}{\mathbf{r}}{}_1^{\mathcal{T}}, \overset{\leftrightarrows}{\mathbf{r}}{}_2^{\mathcal{T}}, \ldots, \overset{\leftrightarrows}{\mathbf{r}}{}_{25{,}000}^{\mathcal{T}}\}$. This was to measure how well the low-dimensional representation $\hat{\mathbf{r}}_t^{\mathcal{T}}$ matches the original data $\mathbf{r}_t^{\mathcal{T}}$ using the L_∞ norm of the residual $\Delta\mathbf{r} = \hat{\mathbf{r}}_t^{\mathcal{T}} - \mathbf{r}_t^{\mathcal{T}}$

$$\|\Delta\mathbf{r}\|_\infty = \max(\|\Delta\mathbf{r}(1)\|_2, \ldots, \|\Delta\mathbf{r}(P)\|_2) \tag{12.2}$$

where $\|\Delta\mathbf{r}(p)\|_2$ is the L_2 norm of the pth x and y components of $\Delta\mathbf{r}$. We chose the L_∞ norm instead of the L_2 norm because large deviations may signify very different formations, e.g. a single player could be breaking away to score. Figure 12.9 illustrates how both $\mathbf{p}_t^{\mathcal{T}}$ and $\mathbf{r}_t^{\mathcal{T}}$ are quite compressible on the training data. However, when we test on unseen data (with role labels), the dynamic role-based ordering $\mathbf{r}_t^{\mathcal{T}}$

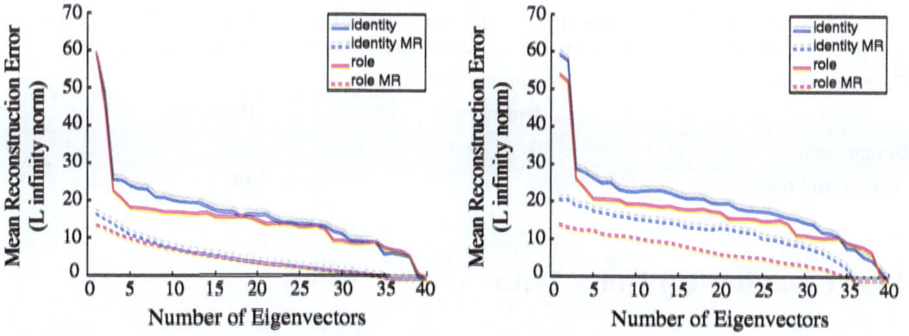

Fig. 12.9 Plot showing the reconstruction error as a function of the number of eigenvectors used to reconstruct the signal using the L_∞ norm for original and mean-removed features for both identity and role representations on training data (*left*) and unseen test data (*right*)

is much more compressible than the static ordering $\mathbf{p}_t^{\tau}$. Relative positions are more compressible than absolute positions in both orderings.

12.5.2 Incorporating Adversarial Behaviour

A player's movements are correlated not only to teammates but to opposition players as well. Therefore, we anticipate that player location data can be further compressed if the locations of players on teams A and B are concatenated into a single vector $\mathbf{r}_t^{AB} = [\mathbf{r}_t^A, \mathbf{r}_t^B]^\mathsf{T}$.

In Fig. 12.10, we show the mean formations for the identity and role representation. We can see that the role representation has a more uniform spread between the players, while the identity representation has a more crowded shape, which highlights the constant swapping of roles during a match. In terms of compressibility, Table 12.4 shows that using an adversarial representation gains better compressibility for both cases, and that using both a role and adversarial representation yields the most compressibility.

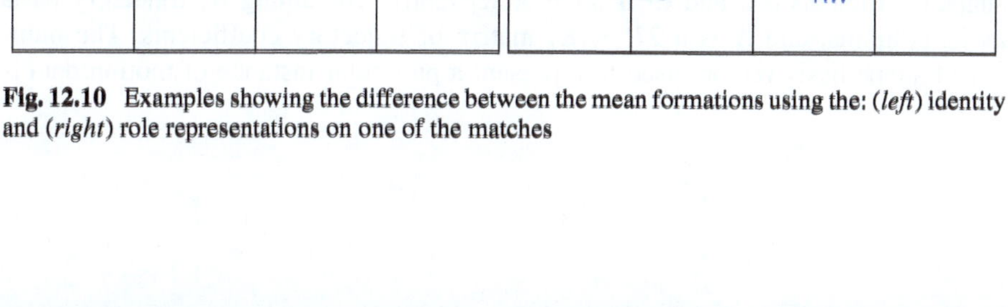

Fig. 12.10 Examples showing the difference between the mean formations using the: (*left*) identity and (*right*) role representations on one of the matches

Table 12.4 Showing the compressibility of different representations. Compressibility in this context refers to the percentage of features required to represent 95 % of the original signal

Representation	Compressibility	
	Identity (%)	Role (%)
Single team	30	25
Adversarial teams	20	**15**

12.6 Cleaning-Up Noisy Data

12.6.1 Spatiotemporal Bilinear Basis Model

The representation of time-varying spatial data is a well-studied problem in computer vision (see [8] for overview). Recently, Akhter et al. [3], presented a bilinear spatiotemporal basis model which captures and exploits the dependencies across both the spatial and temporal dimensions in an efficient and elegant manner, which can be applied to our problem domain. Given we have P players per team, we can form our role-based adversarial representation, $\mathbf{r}$, as a spatiotemporal structure $\mathbf{S}$, given $2P$ total players sampled at F time instances as

$$\mathbf{S}_{F\times 2P} = \begin{bmatrix} r_1^1 & \dots & r_{2P}^1 \\ \vdots & & \vdots \\ r_1^F & \dots & r_{2P}^F \end{bmatrix} \tag{12.3}$$

where r_j^i denotes the jth index within the role representation at the ith time instant. Thus, the time-varying structure matrix $\mathbf{S}$ contains $2FP$ parameters. This representation of the structure is an over parameterization because it does not take into account the high degree of regularity generally exhibited by motion data. One way to exploit the regularity in spatiotemporal data is to represent the 2D formation or shape at each time instance as a linear combination of a small number of shape basis vectors $\mathbf{b}_j$ weighted by coefficients ω_j^i as $\mathbf{s}^i = \sum_j \omega_j^i \mathbf{b}_j^T$ [7, 11]. An alternative representation of the time-varying structure is to model it in the trajectory subspace, as a linear combination of trajectory basis vectors, $\boldsymbol{\theta}_i$ as $\mathbf{s}_j = \sum_i a_i^j \boldsymbol{\theta}_i$, where a_i^j is the coefficient weighting each trajectory basis vector [1, 35]. As a result, the structure matrix can be represented as either

$$\mathbf{S} = \boldsymbol{\Omega}\mathbf{B}^T \quad \text{or} \quad \mathbf{S} = \boldsymbol{\Theta}\mathbf{A}^T \tag{12.4}$$

where $\mathbf{B}$ is a $P \times K_s$ matrix containing K_s shape basis vectors, each representing a 2D structure of length $2P$, and $\boldsymbol{\Omega}$, is an $F \times K_s$ matrix containing the corresponding shape coefficients ω_j^i; and $\boldsymbol{\Theta}$ is an $F \times K_t$ matrix containing K_t trajectory basis as its columns, and $\mathbf{A}$ is a $2P \times K_t$ matrix of trajectory coefficients. The number of shape basis vectors used to represent a particular instance of motion data is

$K_s \leq \min\{F, 2P\}$, and $K_t \leq \{F, 2P\}$ is the number of trajectory basis vectors spanning the trajectory subspace.

Both representations of **S** are over parameterisations because they do not capitalise on either the spatial or temporal regularity. As **S** can be expressed exactly as $\mathbf{S} = \boldsymbol{\Omega}\mathbf{B}^T$ and also $\mathbf{S} = \boldsymbol{\Theta}\mathbf{A}^T$, then there exists a factorization

$$\mathbf{S} = \boldsymbol{\Theta}\mathbf{C}\mathbf{B}^T \tag{12.5}$$

where $\mathbf{C} = \boldsymbol{\Theta}^T\boldsymbol{\Omega} = \mathbf{A}^T\mathbf{B}$ is a $K_t \times K_s$ matrix of spatiotemporal coefficients. This equation describes the bilinear spatiotemporal basis, which contains both shape and trajectory bases linked together by a common set of coefficients.

Due to the high degree of temporal smoothness in the motion of humans, a predefined analytical trajectory basis can be used without significant loss in representation. A particularly suitable choice of a conditioning trajectory basis is the Discrete Cosine Transform (DCT) basis, which has been found to be close to the optimal Principal Component Analysis (PCA) basis if the data is generated from a stationary first-order Markov process [29]. Given the high temporal regularity present in almost all human motion, it has been found that the DCT is an excellent basis for trajectories of faces [2, 3] and bodies [4]. Figure 12.11 shows that due to the highly structured nature of the game, and the fact that human motion over short periods of time is very simple, we can gain enormous dimensionality reduction especially in the temporal domain. From this, we can effectively represent 5 s plays with no more than $K_t = 3$ and $K_s = 33$ with a maximum error of less than 2 m. In terms of dimensionality reduction, this means we can represent temporal signals using $3 \times 33 = 99$ coefficients. For 5 s plays, this means a reduction of over 60 times. We found greater compressibility could be achieved on longer plays.

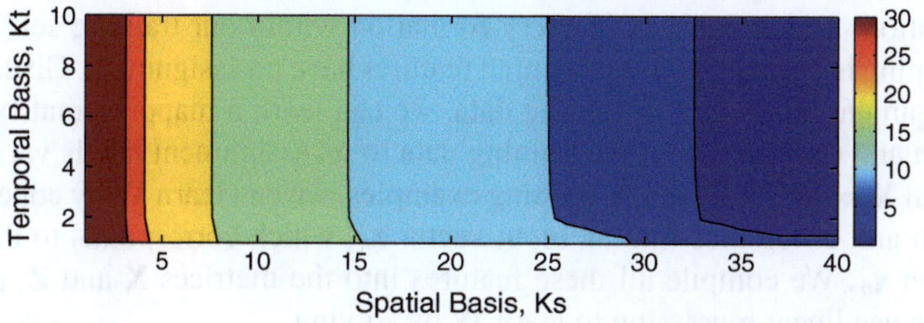

Fig. 12.11 Plot showing the mean reconstruction error of the test data as the number of temporal basis (K_t) and spatial basis (K_s) vary for 5 s plays (i.e. $K_{t\max} = 150$). We magnified the plot to show the first 10 temporal basis to highlight that only $K_t = 3$ is required to represent coarse player motion

12.6.2 The Assignment Problem

In the previous section, roles were specified by a human expert. We now address the problem of automatically assigning roles to an arbitrary ordering of player locations $\mathbf{p}_t^\tau$. Assuming a suitably similar vector $\hat{\mathbf{r}}^\tau$ of player locations in role order exists, we define the optimal assignment of roles as the permutation matrix $\mathbf{x}_t^{\tau\star}$ which minimises the square L_2 reconstruction error

$$\mathbf{x}_t^{\tau\star} = \arg\min_{\mathbf{x}_t^\tau} \|\hat{\mathbf{r}}^\tau - \mathbf{x}_t^\tau \mathbf{p}_t^\tau\|_2^2. \tag{12.6}$$

This is the linear assignment problem where an entry $\mathrm{C}(i, j)$ in the cost matrix is the Euclidean distance between role locations

$$\mathrm{C}(i, j) = \|\hat{\mathbf{r}}^\tau(i) - \mathbf{p}_t^\tau(j)\|_2. \tag{12.7}$$

The optimal permutation matrix can be found in polynomial time using the Hungarian (or Kuhn-Munkres) algorithm [21].

12.6.3 Assignment Initialization

To solve the assignment problem, we need a reference formation to compare to. Using the mean formation (see Fig. 12.10) is a reasonable initialization as the team should maintain that basic formation in most circumstances. However, in different areas of the field there are subtle changes in formation due to the what the opposition are doing as well as the game-state. To incorporate these semantics, we used a codebook of formations which consists of every formation within our training set. However, this mapping is difficult to do as the input features have no assignment. Given we have the assignment labels of the training data, we can learn a mapping matrix $\mathbf{W}$ from the mean and covariances of the training data to its assignment labels via the linear transform $\mathbf{X} = \mathbf{W}^T\mathbf{Z}$. Given N training examples, we can learn $\mathbf{W}$ by concatenating the mean and covariance into an input vector $\mathbf{z}_n$, which corresponds to the labeled formation $\mathbf{x}_n$. We compile all these features into the matrices $\mathbf{X}$ and $\mathbf{Z}$, and given these, we use linear regression to learn $\mathbf{W}$ by solving

$$\mathbf{W} = \mathbf{X}\mathbf{Z}^T(\mathbf{Z}\mathbf{Z}^T + \lambda\mathbf{I})^{-1} \tag{12.8}$$

where λ is the regularization term. Using this approach, we can estimate a labelled formation from the training set which best describes the current unlabeled one. In terms of assignment performance on the test set, this approach works very well compared to using the mean formation for both the identity and role labels as can be seen in Table 12.5. Figure 12.12 shows the confusion matrices for both Team A and Team B for both representations. It is worth noting that the role representation gave far

Table 12.5 Accuracy of the assignment using a mean formation as well as a codebook of possible formations

	Prototype	Hit rate	
		Team A	Team B
Identity	Mean formation	38.36	29.74
	Codebook	49.10	37.15
Role	Mean formation	49.47	50.30
	Codebook	**74.18**	**69.70**

better results than the identity representation, which is not surprising seeing that only spatial location is used. In terms of the role representation (bottom two plots), it can be seen that there is little confusion between the 3 defenders (LB, CH, RB) and the 3 forwards (LW, CF, RW). However, the midfield 4 (LH, RH, IL, IR) tend to interchange position a lot causing high confusion. Noticeably, there is a discrepancy between Team A and Team B which is understandable in this case as Team B interchanges positions more than twice the amount than Team A upon analysis of the ground-truth.

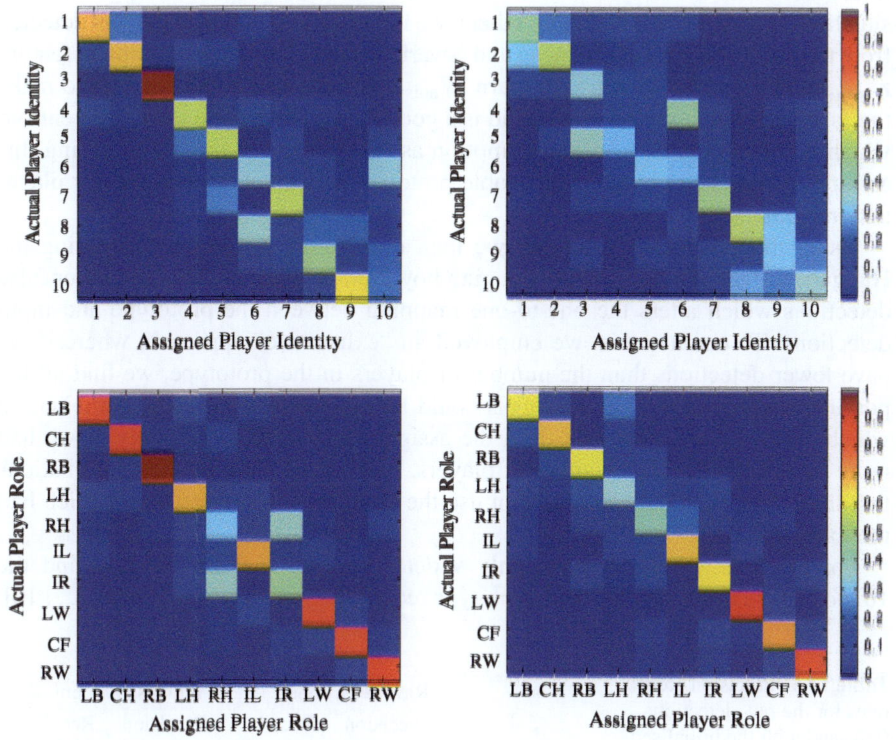

Fig. 12.12 Confusion matrix showing the hit-rates for correctly assigning identity (*top row*) and role (*bottom*) for Team1 (*left*) and Team 2 (*right*) on the test set

12.7 Interpreting Noisy Data

In practice, we will not obtain perfect data from a vision-system so our method has to be robust against both missed and false detections. Given the four annotated matches (presented in Table 12.3), the precision and recall rates for the detector and the team affiliation are given in the left side of Table 12.6. In this work, we consider a detection to be made if a player was within 2 m of a ground-truth label.

12.7.1 Assigning Noisy Detections

To determine whether or not we should make the assignment or discard the detection, some type of game context feature is required (e.g. the part of the field most of the players are located). To do this, we employed a similar strategy to the one we proposed in Sect. 12.6.3. However, instead of learning the mapping from the clean features $\mathbf{Z}$, we learn from the noisy features $\mathbf{Z}_{\text{noisy}}$. As the player detector has systematic errors (there are some "black-spots" on the field due to reduced camera coverage, or game situations where players bunch together), we include the number of players detected from the system as well as the mean and covariance in our noisy game context feature $\mathbf{z}_{\text{noisy}}$, which we can then use to learn $\mathbf{W}_{\text{noisy}}$. We are able to do this as we make the assumption that the clean centroid is a good approximation to the noisy centroid which was found to be a valid assumption as can be seen in Fig. 12.13. Using this assumption, we can obtain a reasonable prototypical formation to make our player assignments.

Using the estimated prototype, we then make the role assignments using the Hungarian algorithm. This is challenging however, as we may have missed or false detections which alters the one-to-one mapping between the prototype and input detections. To counter this, we employed an "exhaustive" approach, where if we have fewer detections than the number of players in the prototype, we find all the possible combinations that the labels could be assigned then use the combination which yielded the lowest cost from the assignments made. Conversely, if we had more detections than the number of players, we find all the possible combinations that the detections could be and then use the combination of detections which had the lowest cost.

For example, given we have only 9 detections for a team, we first find the 10 possible combinations that prototype could be (i.e. $[1, \ldots, 9]$, $[2, \ldots, 10]$,

Table 12.6 Precision-Recall rates for the raw detections (left) and with the initialised assignments (right)

	Raw detections		With assignment	
	Precision	Recall	Precision	Recall
Detections	77.49	89.86	**91.90**	80.46
Team A	72.54	86.14	**86.69**	74.17
Team B	79.84	89.66	**92.91**	82.85

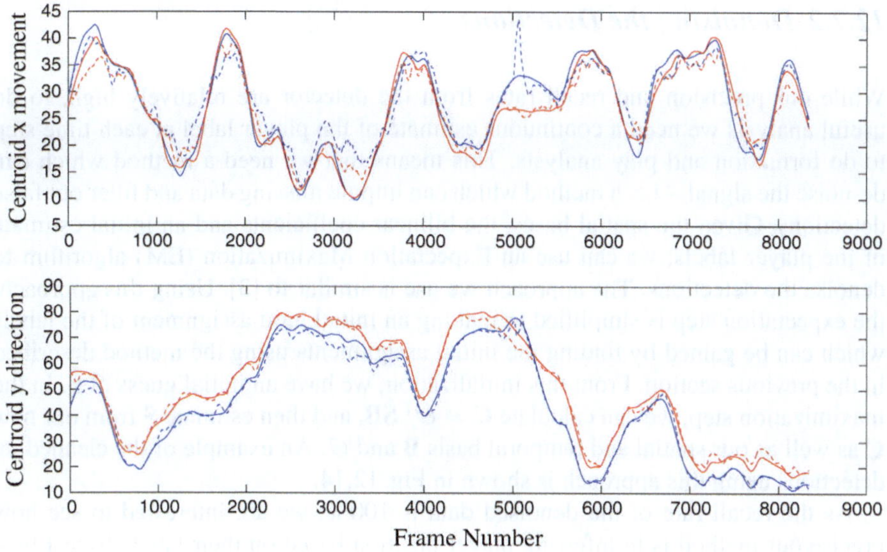

Fig. 12.13 As the centroids of both the clean (*solid*) and noisy (*dashed*) of both teams (*blue* = team1, *red* = team2) are roughly equivalent, we learn a mapping matrix using linear regression to find a formation from the training set which can best describe the noisy test formation

[1, 2, 4, ..., 10], [1, 2, 3, 5, ..., 10] etc.). For each one of these combinations, we then perform the Hungarian algorithm and calculate the cost of the made assignments. After we have exhaustively gone through all possible combinations, we make the assignment based on the combination with the lowest cost. Or given we have 11 detections for a team, we first find the 11 possible combinations that the detections could be, find the cost for each set and choose the one with the lowest cost. However, sometimes we get false positives which means that even though we may get 10 detections for a team we may only have 7 or 8 valid candidates. Employing this approach greatly improves the precision rate, while the recall rate decreases which is to be expected (see right side of Table 12.6). Even despite the drop in recall, we still assign role reasonably well (over 55 % compared to 66 % on the clean data) as can be seen in Table 12.7.

Table 12.7 Detection rates assigning roles to the noisy data. The column on the far right gives the effective hit-rate (i.e. missed detections omitted) of the correct assignments

	Correct	Incorrect	Missed	Hit rate
Team A	41.89	32.89	25.22	56.02
Team B	45.92	35.56	18.53	56.36

12.7.2 Denoising the Detections

While our precision and recall rates from the detector are relatively high, to do useful analysis we need a continuous estimate of the player label at each time step to do formation and play analysis. This means that we need a method which can de-noise the signal—i.e. a method which can impute missing data and filter out false detections. Given the spatial bases, the bilinear coefficients and an initial estimate of the player labels, we can use an Expectation Maximization (EM) algorithm to denoise the detections. The approach we use is similar to [3]. Using this approach, the expectation step is simplified to making an initial hard assignment of the labels which can be gained by finding the initial assignments using the method described in the previous section. From this initialization, we have an initial guess of $\hat{\mathbf{S}}$. In the maximization step, we can calculate $\mathbf{C} = \Theta^T \hat{\mathbf{S}}\mathbf{B}$, and then estimate $\mathbf{S}$ from our new $\mathbf{C}$ as well as our spatial and temporal basis $\mathbf{B}$ and Θ. An example of the cleaned up detections using this approach is shown in Fig. 12.14.

As the recall rate of the denoised data is 100 %, we are interested to see how precise our method is in inferring player position based on their label. To test this, we calculated the precision rate for the detections and the denoised detections against a distance threshold—that is, the minimum distance a player had to be to ground-truth to be recognised as a correct detection). The results are shown in Fig. 12.15. As can be seen from these figures, the detections from the player detector are very accurate and do not vary with respect to the error threshold (i.e. it either detects a player very precisely or not at all). Conversely, the denoised data is heavily smoothed due to the bilinear model, so we lose some of the finer detail to gain a continuous signal.

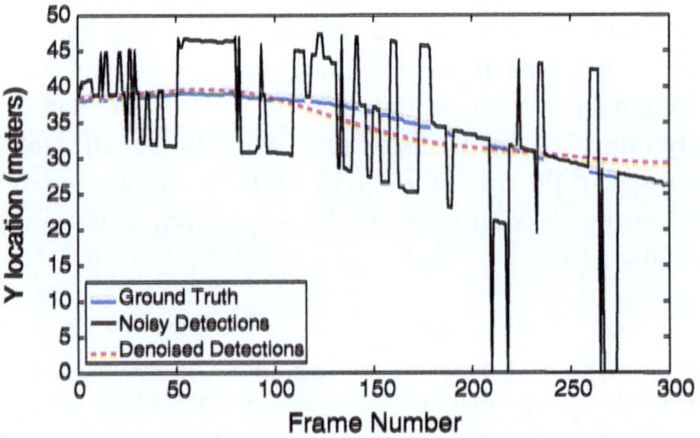

Fig. 12.14 Given our noisy detections (*black*), using our bilinear model we can estimate the trajectory of each player over time. We can see our estimate (*red*) is close to the ground-truth (*blue*)

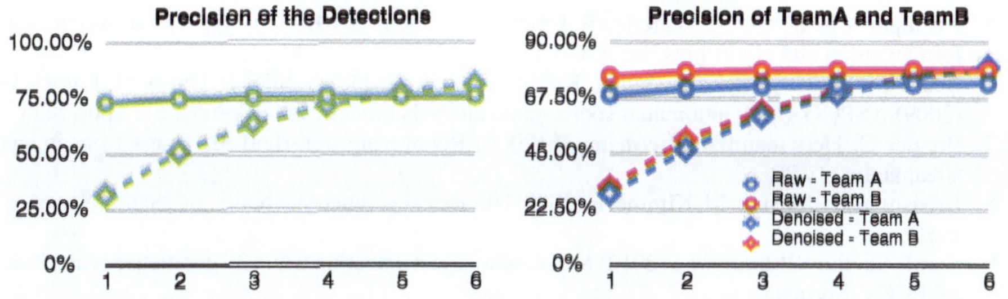

Fig. 12.15 Precision accuracy versus the distance threshold from ground truth (in metres) (*left*) the overall detections, (*right*) the detections based on team affiliation. The *solid lines* refer to the raw detections and the *dashed lines* refer to the denoised signal

12.8 Summary

Accurately tracking players over long durations of time is an unsolved computer vision problem, and prevents automated analysis of team sports using traditional representations based on player tracks. In this paper, we instead directly modelled team behaviours from raw player detections, and compared two representations which are robust to missed and false detections: (1) occupancy maps and (2) a bilinear-spatiotemporal basis model. We demonstrated that occupancy map features can accurately represent global group behaviours, and can be used to recognise group activities corresponding to important game states from raw player detections, without player tracking or ball information. However, one of the challenges of an occupancy map representation is that high dimensionality is required, and it is difficult to model team behaviours at the level of individual players. To overcome this, we proposed the use of a bilinear spatiotemporal basis model using a *role representation* to clean-up the noisy detections which operates in a low-dimensional space. This provides a very compact representation of group behaviours, and can facilitate tasks such as clustering and retrieval. We evaluated our approach on approximately 200,000 frames of field-hockey data from a state-of-the-art real-time player detector.

Acknowledgments The QUT portion of this research was supported by the Queensland Government's Department of Employment, Economic Development and Innovation.

References

1. Akhter I, Sheikh Y, Khan S, Kanade T (2008) Nonrigid structure from motion in trajectory space. In: NIPS
2. Akhter I, Sheikh Y, Khan S, Kanade T (2010) Trajectory space: a dual representation for nonrigid structure from motion. T. PAMI
3. Akhter I, Simon T, Khan S, Matthews I, Sheikh Y (2012) Bilinear spatiotemporal basis models. ACM Trans Graph
4. Arikan O (2006) Compression of motion capture databases. ACM Trans Graph 25(3)

5. Avrahami-Zilberbrand D, Banerjee B, Kraemer L, Lyle J (2010) Multi-agent plan recognition: formalization and algorithms. In: AAAI
6. Beetz M, von Hoyningen-Huene N, Kirchlechner B, Gedikli S, Siles F, Durus M, Lames M (2009) ASPOGAMO: automated sports game analysis models. Int J Comput Sci Sport 8(1)
7. Bregler C, Hertzmann A, Biermann H (2000) Recovering non-rigid 3D shape from image streams. In: CVPR
8. Bronstein A, Bronstein M, Kimmel R (2008) Numerical geometry of non-rigid shapes. Springer, Berlin
9. Carr P, Sheikh Y, Matthews I (2012) Monocular object detection using 3d geometric primitives. In: ECCV. Springer
10. Chang M, Krahnstoever N, Ge W (2011) Probabilistic group-level motion analysis and scenario recognition. In: ICCV
11. Cootes T, Taylor C, Cooper D, Graham J (1995) Active shape models—their training and applications. Comput Vis Image Underst 61(1):38–59
12. D'Orazio T, Leo M (2010) A review of vision-based systems for Soccer video analysis. Pattern Recognit 43(8)
13. Gupta A, Srinivasan P, Shi J, Davis L (2009) Understanding videos, constructing plots: learning a visually grounded storyline model from annotated videos. In: CVPR
14. Hervieu A, Bouthemy P (2010) Understanding sports video using players trajectories. In: Zhang J, Shao L, Zhang L, Jones G (eds) Intelligent video event analysis and understanding. Springer, Berlin
15. Hess R, Fern A (2009) Discriminatively trained particle filters for complex multi-object tracking. In: CVPR
16. Hess R, Fern A, Mortensen E (2007) Mixture-of-parts pictorial structures for objects with variable part sets. In: ICCV
17. Huang C, Shih H, Chao C (2006) Semantic analysis of soccer video using dynamic bayesian networks. T. Multimed 8(4)
18. Intille S, Bobick A (1999) A framework for recognizing multi-agent action from visual evidence. In: AAAI
19. Intille S, Bobick A (2001) Recognizing planned, multi-person action. Comput Vis Image Underst 81:414–445
20. Kim K, Grundmann M, Shamir A, Matthews I, Hodgins J, Essa I (2010) Motion fields to predict play evolution in dynamic sports scenes. In: CVPR
21. Kuhn HW (1955) The Hungarian method for the assignment problem. In: Naval research logistics quarterly
22. Lazarescu M, Venkatesh S (2003) Using camera motion to identify different types of American football plays. In: ICME
23. Li R, Chellappa R (2010) Group motion segmentation using a spatio-temporal driving force model. In: CVPR
24. Li R, Chellappa R, Zhou S (2009) Learning multi-modal densities on discriminative temporal interaction manifold for group activity recognition. In: CVPR
25. Liu T, Ma W, Zhang H (2005) Effective feature extraction for play detection in American football video. In: MMM
26. Money A, Agius H (2008) Video summarisation: a conceptual framework and survey of the state of the art. J Vis Commun Image Represent 19(2):121–143
27. Morariu V, Davis L (2011) Multi-agent event recognition in structured scenarios. In: CVPR
28. Perse M, Kristan M, Kovacic S, Pers J (2008) A trajectory-based analysis of coordinated team activity in basketball game. Comput Vis Image Underst
29. Rao K, Yip P (1990) Discrete cosine transform: algorithms, advantages, applications. Academic, New York
30. Sadilek A, Kautz H (2008) Recognizing multi-agent activities from GPS data. In: AAAI
31. Siddiquie B, Yacoob Y, Davis L (2009) Recognizing plays in American football videos. Technical report University of Maryland

32. Stracuzzi D, Fern A, Ali K, Hess R, Pinto J, Li N, Konik T, Shapiro D (2011) An application of transfer to American football: from observation of raw video to control in a simulated environment. AI Mag 32(2)
33. Sukthankar G, Sycara K (2008) Hypothesis pruning and ranking for large plan recognition problems. In: AAAI
34. Sukthankar G, Sycara K (2012) Activity recognition for dynamic multi-agent teams. ACM Trans Intell Syst Technol
35. Torresani L, Bregler C (2002) Space-time tracking. In: CVPR
36. Xu C, Zhang Y, Zhu G, Rui Y, Lu H, Huang Q (2008) Using webcast text for semantic event detection in broadcast. T. Multimed 10(7)
37. Zhang Y, Ge W, Chang M, Liu X (2012) Group context learning for event recognition. In: WACV

Chapter 13
Recognizing Team Formation in American Football

Indriyati Atmosukarto, Bernard Ghanem, Mohamed Saadalla and Narendra Ahuja

Abstract Most existing software packages for sports video analysis require manual annotation of important events in the video. Despite being the most popular sport in the United States, most American football game analysis is still done manually. Line of scrimmage and offensive team formation recognition are two statistics that must be tagged by American Football coaches when watching and evaluating past play video clips, a process which takes many man hours per week. These two statistics are the building blocks for more high-level analysis such as play strategy inference and automatic statistic generation. In this chapter, we propose a novel framework where given an American football play clip, we automatically identify the video frame in which the offensive team lines in formation (*formation frame*), the line of scrimmage for that play, and the type of player formation the offensive team takes on. The proposed framework achieves 95 % accuracy in detecting the formation frame, 98 % accuracy in detecting the line of scrimmage, and up to 67 % accuracy in classifying the offensive team's formation. To validate our framework, we compiled a large dataset comprising more than 800 play-clips of standard and high definition resolution from real-world football games. This dataset will be made publicly available for future comparison.

I. Atmosukarto (✉)
Advanced Digital Sciences Center (ADSC), Singapore, Singapore
e-mail: indria@adsc.com.sg

B. Ghanem · M. Saadalla
King Abdullah University of Science and Technology (KAUST), Thuwal, Saudi Arabia
e-mail: bernard.ghanem@kaust.edu.sa

M. Saadalla
e-mail: mohamed.saadalla@kaust.edu.sa

N. Ahuja
University of Illinois Urbana-Champaign (UIUC), Champaign, USA
e-mail: n-ahuja@illinois.edu

T.B. Moeslund et al. (eds.), *Computer Vision in Sports*,
Advances in Computer Vision and Pattern Recognition,
DOI 10.1007/978-3-319-09396-3_13

13.1 Introduction

Sports coaches and analysts often analyze large collections of video to extract patterns and develop strategies in their respective sport. Before any extensive video analysis can be conducted, these sports experts must annotate the video data to provide context to the video clips. It is quite natural for humans to commit errors during annotation due to the high visual similarity, repetitive nature, and sheer volume of video data. If they have the budget, which few do, American Football teams employ highly experienced staff (video coaches) specifically for video annotation. Even dedicated video coaches are prone to error when manually annotating football clips and extracting important details from them. Automatic annotation of important events and statistics in American Football videos will save tremendous time and resources for the teams and the coaches, thus allowing coaches more time doing what they love best, being on the field training their teams.

Automated annotation of American football videos has many potential users, including coaches and players, but also sports analysts, content providers such as sports broadcasting companies, mobile service providers, and even end users. Coaches will use the automatic annotations to learn about the strengths and weakness of their own and other teams. To optimize video streaming over limited mobile bandwidth, cell phone companies want to detect significant events of a game for optimal streaming. Advertising companies want to automatically insert advertisements at the most significant points in a game. Broadcast companies want to enrich the game content with other materials to retain audiences and improve audiences' game watching experience. Sport analysts want to enrich their interpretation of the game and accumulate more detailed statistics that would not be possible with manual processing.

American football (hereafter referred to as 'football') is a very structured game where players move according to a number of set plays. A football play is defined as an offense's attempt to advance the ball forwards. There are two general football play types: offense/defense (o/d) and special teams. In this paper, we concentrate on two important details which must be recorded in every o/d play, namely the line of scrimmage and offensive formation type. The *line of scrimmage* is an imaginary line along the width of the field, upon which the ball is placed before the beginning of each play. A *formation* is defined as the spatial configuration of a team's players before a play starts. Before each play starts, the players go to a pre-determined place on the field on their side of the line of scrimmage. This is when a team is said to be in 'formation'. The play begins when a player lifts the ball off the ground ('snaps') and ends when the player with the ball either scores or is brought to the ground ('tackled'). Automatically detecting the line of scrimmage in a play clip is a challenging computer vision problem primarily due to high player occlusion and appearance similarity. Automatically detecting the offense formation in a play clip is difficult primarily due to significant occlusion, intra-class variation, inter-class similarity, and player appearance similarity.

Detecting the line of scrimmage and the offensive team formation are two fundamental building blocks without which any future action recognition and play understanding work is incomplete. The results of this solution can be used for more extensive analysis of football games such as offensive and defensive personnel detection, play detection, and ultimately playbook inference. A playbook is essentially a notebook that contains the collection of description and diagrams of all possible plays for a team.

In this chapter, we propose a novel framework to automatically identify the line of scrimmage and offensive team formation in football (refer to Fig. 13.1) [1]. The proposed framework uses the gradient information of the video frames projected onto the field using the method proposed in [13]. Projecting the frames not only removes camera motion but also allows player locations to be normalized on to the field of play irrespective of the view recorded by the camera. This solution is robust enough to identify features from any video as it is agnostic to colour information.

Our proposed framework consists of four components described as follows: (1) we automatically identify the frame in which the formation occurs, (2) we use the identified formation frame to automatically estimate the line of scrimmage, (3) we use the estimated line of scrimmage to differentiate players from the two teams and automatically identify which team is on offense, and (4) we use features extracted from the offensive side of the line of scrimmage to classify the offensive team's formation in the play clip.

The rest of the chapter is organized as follows. We discuss some existing work on sports video analysis in general and play analysis and formation detection in American football. In Sect. 13.3, we illustrate our proposed framework and describe each of the framework modules in detail. In Sect. 13.4, we validate our framework by extensively testing our methods on different American football play datasets. We conclude our chapter in Sect. 13.5 by summarizing our work and discussing ideas for future work.

Fig. 13.1 The goal of our work is to automatically recognize and label offensive team formation that occur at the beginning of an American football play

13.2 Related Work

Work on sports video analysis mainly focus on specific sports domain, thus allowing research and development to leverage upon the specific domain knowledge and structure of the particular sport being analyzed. There has been extensive work in the soccer domain focused on predicting important events in soccer games [11, 16, 23, 28, 30, 34–36, 39, 42, 47, 53, 56]. Zhu et al. [56] constructed a novel trajectory-based representation constructed based on multiple trajectories of players and the ball to recognize events such goal, side or center attacks, group or individual attacks. Zawbaa et al. [53] applied machine learning techniques such as neural network and SVM classifiers to detect important regions in the game such as goal posts and goal nets. Similarly, Saba and Altameem [42] applied similar artificial intelligence techniques to detect important events in soccer games.

Some work have focused on visualization of the games to enrich the experience of the audiences and fans of the sport [15, 21, 25, 40, 43]. Hilton et al. [21] presented a framework and prototype system for stereo 3DTV and free viewpoint production and visualization of soccer games. Hamid et al. [15] presented a framework for visualization of virtual offside line in soccer games. Ren et al. [40] used motion cues and temporal information of the ball trajectory from multiple fixed cameras to reconstruct its trajectories in 3D. Visualization of the ball trajectory in 3D will also enrich the experience of fans watching the game. Kim et al. [25] used motion fields to predict the play evolution in the game of soccer. Predicting regions of interest in dynamic scenes such as soccer has many applications, including automatic camera control, summary highlights and rich sports visualization and analysis.

Recently, some work have started to focus on automated soccer video analysis aimed as a teaching and training tools for coaches and players [3, 50]. Some of the work proposed to recognize soccer team strategies [14, 31, 32]. In other sports domains, work in tennis video analysis have focused on event detection and recognition (e.g. service or net playing) [17]. Another theme of research in sports video analysis have been on team activity analysis in group sports such as handball [10] or basketball [6, 26, 38, 55]. Lastly, many researchers working on sports video analysis have focused on automatic highlight detection and summarization [37, 41, 51, 52].

Work in American football video analysis have focused mostly on action and multi-agent activity recognition, specifically on recognizing and classifying the different types of football plays. Work in this domain can be categorized into tracking-based and non-tracking based methods. Swears and Hoogs [46] avoids the need to specifically track players in football plays. They present a framework to model multi-agent activities in the context of football plays. The goal of their work is to determine as early as possible the play type the offensive team is executing. The temporal interactions of the players (agents) are modeled using a Non-Stationary Kernel HMM (NSK-HMM). Their approach uses supervised learning to learn a playbook model based on exemplars from the different play types. Siddiquie et al. [44] used a different approach that does not make use of tracking, instead they utilized spatio-temporal features to represent shape and motion of the players. In addition, they propose a new Multiple Kernel Learning (MKL) formulation to combine different features and identify the discriminative features for play type classification. In the other tracking-based category, Varadarajan et al. [48] addressed a similar play type classification problem and modeled offense plays with the help of supervised topic models and player tracking [54]. Li and Chellappa [29] used probabilistic generative model to characterize players' motion, while Intille and Bobick[22] used Bayesian network model to model players' activities. Stracuzzi et al. [45] developed a complete framework that automatically learned plays from videos and then transferred the knowledge to be applied to new views for execution of plays in a simulated environment. Lazarescu and Venkatesh [27] and Fan [12] avoided the use of player or ball tracking and used camera motion information to classify different American football play types. Other type of work on event detection in football includes automatically detecting the start of an American football play in videos, an event called 'moment of snap' [33]. Their framework include a novel representation of motion changes based on quantization of motion in the video, which they denoted as Variable Threshold Images. Kim et al. [24] detected and predict regions of interest in dynamic scenes based on the global motion tendency and Gaussian process regression.

Little work has been done in automated offensive team formation recognition. Given a formation image, Hess et al. [19, 20] used a mixture-of-parts pictorial structure model (MoPPS) to localize and identify football players in order to recognize the formation in the image. Pictorial structures are graphical models representation that encodes the formation as a set of parts with deformable connections between the parts. The parts are described by their local appearances while the connections are described by their location. The best formation is essentially the pictorial structure assignment that minimizes the overall cost of the graphical model. Their work was tested on a limited dataset, the learning method for MoPPS model was computationally expensive and parameters of the model were hand-coded. In addition, their work assumes that the formation image is given. In most cases, video coaches work with play clips, and in essence a video coach has to go through the whole play clip to find the formation image. Selecting the formation image can be tedious and subjective as the differences between consecutive frames may not be noticeable to human eyes. Our work automatically finds the formation frame in the play clip, identifies the line of scrimmage, and labels the formation in the detected formation frame.

There has been some existing work on soccer team formations [2, 3, 49]. Visser et al. [49] used grid-based position of the players on the field as input vector to a neural network, while Ayanegui-Santiago [2] used a similar neural network model that took into consideration the relations between the players. However, work on soccer team formation tend to not be directly applicable to the American football domain as soccer tends to be more fluid and dynamic, changing over the course of the game, while American football games tend to be more structured and inherently repetitive.

13.3 Proposed Framework

Our proposed solution aims to identify the formation of the team playing offense in a game of football. Figure 13.2 shows the block diagram of our overall proposed framework. The input to our framework is a single football video play clip. The proposed approach consists of two major modules: *pre-processing* of the play video clip and *formation recognition* of the offensive team in the play clip. This chapter will mostly discuss the formation recognition module.

Given a registered play clip, the framework will first identify the frame in which the two teams are lined up in formation. Once this frame is detected, the field line that separates the two teams at formation time (otherwise known as the line of scrimmage) is determined in the formation frame. We utilize the spatial distribution of the two teams to identify the offensive team. Finally, we extract features from the offense region to train a linear SVM to classify the different offensive formations.

13.3.1 Pre-processing

Pre-processing of a given play clip includes registering the video to the reference field image and foreground/background identification. We use the robust registration method in [13] to map each frame of each play clip to the field image (refer to Fig. 13.2 (Pre-Processing module)). Since camera motion (zoom, pan and tilt) and viewpoint vary between plays and within the same play, registering frames unto the same coordinate system (the overhead field image) is crucial for formation recognition. The registration method matches entire images or image patches. The matching process computes an optimal homography between every pair of frames in the play

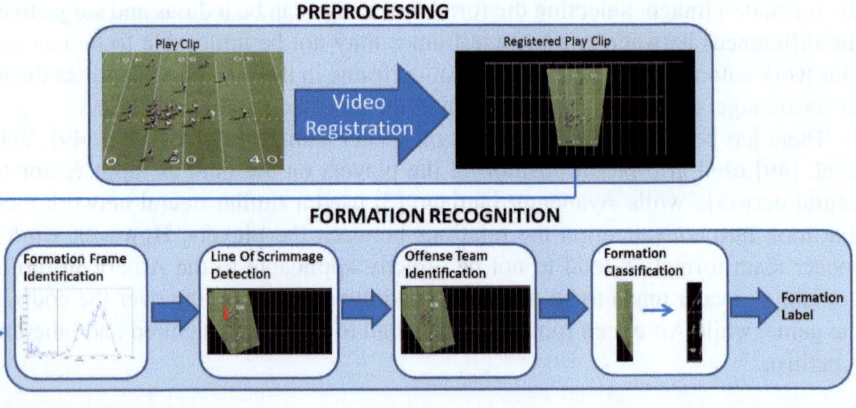

Fig. 13.2 Overall framework for automatic offensive team formation recognition in American football play

clip by assuming that outlier pixels are sufficiently sparse in each frame. For a given play clip, an overhead view of the playing field is not necessarily given, which precludes matching any frame of the clip to the reference. In this case, user interaction is required to register a single frame to the reference, whereby the user selects at least four corresponding pairs of points between the two images. Coupling this homography with the homographies computed between consecutive frames of the clip, we can register the entire play clip unto the reference field image. Note that user interaction is only required once for each different field.

After registering the clip to the field, we proceed to discriminate and extract the foreground (players) from the background (e.g. field patterns such as markers, lines, and logos). One way this can be done is through player detection and classification (as in [4]), where a classifier's confidence at each region of each frame designates the likelihood that a player exists at that region. However, this process requires training samples for players from different teams and from different camera viewpoints. Also, since the video frames are captured from far-field, the player resolution is usually low, so learning appearance-based classifiers leads to substantial false positives, especially at markers and mid-field logos. So, to avoid view dependent classification from far-field, we resort to background subtraction after all the frames of a play clip are registered to the same field image. This process can also be viewed as video stitching, where the panoramic generated by the stitch is the background with the rest constituting the foreground. Although many background subtraction methods exist in the literature (e.g. [8, 9]), the majority assume that the camera to be static and thus do not address the problem of camera motion. In our case, since frames are registered in the same coordinate system, conventional background subtraction methods can be applied; however, special care has to be taken because not *all* pixels are necessarily visible in all frames. Instead, we proceed to extend the robust registration work in [13] to allow for robust video stitching in the presence of incomplete data and sparse error. This sparse error corresponds to pixels that do not satisfy the homography mapping, specifically pixels belonging to players on the field. Sparsity here is a valid assumption, since the frames are imaged in the far-field and players generally constitute a small fraction of the pixels in a frame.

13.3.1.1 Robust Video Stitching

To mathematically formalize the stitching problem, we are given a set of F frames of a play clip registered to the field image. The projection of the kth frame into the reference frame is denoted as $\mathbf{i}_k \in \mathbb{R}^M$. As such, each of the mapped frames into the reference cover a subset of the whole panoramic view of the field. This panoramic image contains M pixels. We denote this panoramic image (sometimes known as the intrinsic image) in vector form as $\mathbf{v}$. The goal of our analysis is to reconstruct the panoramic $\mathbf{v}$ in the presence of sparse error and frame-to-frame global illumination change, modeled by $\mathbf{u} \in \mathbb{R}_+^F$. To solve for $\mathbf{v}$, we formulate the video stitching problem as a rank-1 matrix completion problem with sparse error. This problem is stated in Eq. (13.1), where $\mathbf{I} \in \mathbb{R}^{F\times M}$ is the concatenation of all the mapped frames (refer

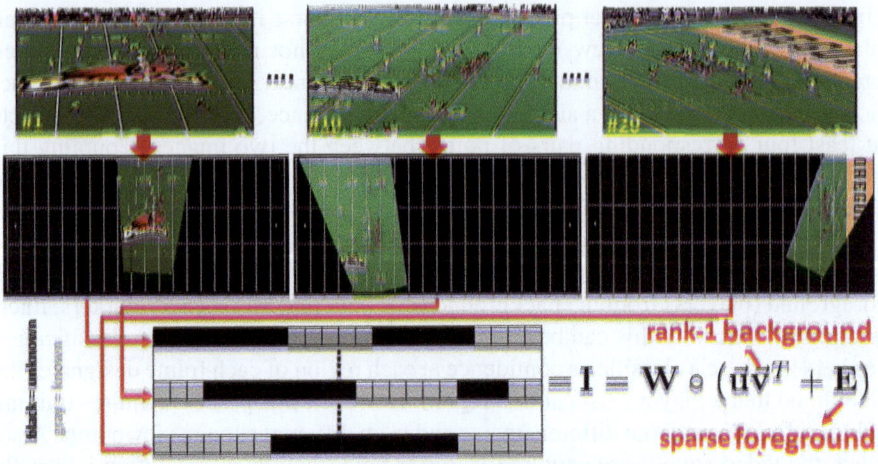

Fig. 13.3 Robust video stitching for foreground/background estimation. Each frame in the play clip is projected into the overhead field reference using the registration method in [13]. The projection of frame j (jth row of $\mathbf{I}$) constitutes a small part of the panoramic image $\mathbf{v}$ and contributes sparse error (jth row of $\mathbf{E}$). The visible pixels of the panoramic in each frame of the clip are defined in a binary matrix $\mathbf{W}$. The global illumination variation in the clip is addressed by the positive coefficients $\mathbf{u}$

to Fig. 13.3 for an illustration), $\mathbf{W} \in \mathbb{R}^{F \times M}$ is the concatenation of pixel weights (weighted observable supports) for all the mapped images in the reference image, and $\mathbf{E} \in \mathbb{R}^{F \times M}$ is the sparse error matrix. Here, we denote $\mathbf{W} \circ \mathbf{I}$ as the Hadamard product between the two sparse matrices $\mathbf{W}$ and $\mathbf{I}$. In the simplest case $\mathbf{W}$ is a sampling matrix, where each element is a binary value indicating whether or not the pixel is visible in that frame. More generally, $\mathbf{W}$ can be considered a weighting matrix for each frame or even for each pixel of each frame in the clip.

$$\min_{\mathbf{u},\mathbf{v},\mathbf{E}} \quad \|\mathbf{E}\|_{1,1} \qquad (13.1)$$
$$\text{subject to:} \quad \mathbf{W} \circ \mathbf{I} = \mathbf{W} \circ \left(\mathbf{u}\mathbf{v}^T + \mathbf{E}\right)$$

In fact, Eq. (13.1) can be viewed as the rank-1 version of robust PCA (RPCA [5]). Apart from being a valid assumption for video, where frame-to-frame lighting variations are not significant, the rank-1 model for $\mathbf{W} \circ \mathbf{I}$ precludes the computational infeasibility of RPCA on such large scale data, especially since RPCA involves expensive SVD operations. To put this in context, F is usually on the order of hundreds of frames, while M is in the order of 10^5–10^6 pixels. Equation (13.1) is non-convex due to the non-convex equality constraint. In this way, the formulated optimization problem is similar to GRASTA [18], except there is no tracking of an orthonormal subspace basis. Ideally, without illumination change due to camera settings, we have $\mathbf{u} = \mathbf{1}$. Therefore, to solve Eq. (13.1), we resort to an alternating descent approach, which alternates between fixing $\mathbf{u}$ and updating $\mathbf{E}$ and $\mathbf{v}$ via the inexact augmented Lagrangian method (IALM) and fixing $\mathbf{v}$ and $\mathbf{E}$ and updating $\mathbf{u}$ using a similar method. Although in general, this strategy does not guarantee the global solution (and a local solution at best); however, for most cases when the image sequences are captured by the same camera over time, the local solution that is obtained by initializing $\mathbf{u} = \mathbf{1}$ leads to a reasonable solution. For the case of spatially varying illumination change from image to image, there is a need to produce a higher rank approximation to the error-less $\mathbf{I}$, which can be approximated greedily by recursively solving Eq. (13.1) with $\mathbf{I}$ replaced by $\mathbf{I} - \mathbf{u}\mathbf{v}^T$. We do this to keep the computational complexity of the stitching process to a minimum. It is easily shown that each IALM iteration only involves simple and highly parallelizable matrix operations (e.g. matrix subtraction and addition) and *no* SVD operations are needed. As compared to RPCA, one interesting property of this solution is that it can be executed both in batch (all frames together) and incremental (e.g. one frame at a time) modes.

In Fig. 13.4, we show an example of applying robust video stitching to a football play clip, where the different frames are stitched together to generate the panorama and their respective sparse errors. Clearly, the error values are high at player locations and low in the background. As a result, the video stitching method is able to weigh each pixel in a frame as either background or foreground, thus essentially identifying only the moving objects or players in the play clip. This is especially useful for

Fig. 13.4 Robust video stitching for foreground/background estimation. The *top row* shows the stitched panoramic $\mathbf{v}$ (or background) computed by solving Eq. (13.1). A frame in the play clip and its corresponding error (or foreground) are shown in the *bottom row*. *Colder* colors designate smaller error values

removing large mid-field logos and field markers, which tend to be misclassified as moving players. It is worthwhile to note that the background is separated from the foreground even though the foreground is static for many frames, especially at the beginning of the play. As such, the output of the registration/stitching module is subsequently used in the formation recognition module to weigh pixels in the registered field, as described in the next sub-section.

13.3.2 Formation Frame Detection

The first task in the formation recognition module is to identify the frame in which the teams position themselves in a predefined formation before the start of play. Intuitively, the formation frame is the frame with the least player motion. At this frame, the frame-to-frame pixel displacement in the formation frame has the least motion magnitude among all other frames in the play. Given that the video frames are registered to a reference field image, the frame with the least motion magnitude is easily identified by calculating the frame-to-frame mean-squared error (MSE) for all pixels across the entire video sequence followed by a 5 tap median filter. We identify the formation frame as the last frame after which the MSE values are substantial and monotonically increasing. This is done to ensure that the motion of players in the frames is due to all players moving and *not* due to man-in-motion events (usually known as 'audible' in football) that may occur before the actual start of the play. Man-in-motion is defined as the event where a player on offense is moving backwards or parallel to the line of scrimmage right before the snap. In American football, only one offensive player can be in motion at any one time, the player cannot move toward the line of scrimmage at the snap, and may not be a linesmen (player who is on the line of scrimmage). To formalize, we build an SVM classifier on the MSE differences between frames of a play and learn its parameters using a small set of formation frames labelled by a sports expert. In Fig. 13.5 (top), we plot MSE values of all the frames in a given play clip. The index of the formation frame is marked by the red line. Figure 13.5 (bottom) shows the detected formation frame in the clip and its projection on the field respectively. In what follows, the detected formation frame is used to detect the line of scrimmage and recognize the play formation of the offensive team.

13.3.3 Line of Scrimmage Detection

Using our pre-processing robust video stitching technique (Sect. 13.3.1), we reduce the effect of background pixels including the logos on the field. As a result, player (foreground) density is highest at the line of scrimmage relative to any other area in the projected formation frame. We exploit this information to identify the line of scrimmage. Colour can be seen as a feature for identifying players on offense, since

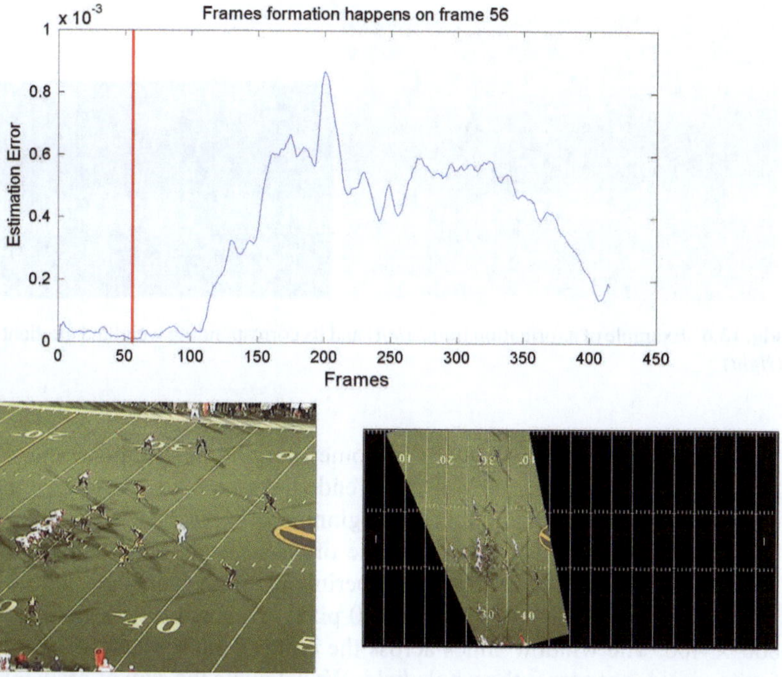

Fig. 13.5 Formation frame detection. MSE values of all frames in a sample play clip are plotted in the *top row*. The index of the formation frame is designated in *red*. The detected formation frame and its projection onto a reference field image are shown in the *bottom row*

the two teams wear opposing colored jerseys. A possible way to identify the team on offense would be to require the user to label at least one offensive player per play clip. However, most standard techniques for identifying players using colour models such as hue and saturation would fail to identify the players alone, owing to the fact that hue and saturation values also exist on the field leading to a number of false positives. Over and above that, opposing teams wear complementary colours such as a black jersey with white shorts and white jersey with black shorts making even semi-supervised methods ineffective in identifying players on offense. In this paper, we take a color agnostic approach and exploit the fact that the line of scrimmage is the region of the field in the formation frame that has the highest player density. In our case, this means that the line of scrimmage is the region where the image gradient density of the foreground is highest. Figure 13.6 shows the gradient intensity of the projected formation frame, weighted by the foreground (error) values obtained in the pre-processing step. Note that we only use the gradient information in the y-(vertical) direction as this would avoid including the gradient information from vertical lines such as that of yard lines. A sliding window approach is used to find the region with the highest density in the gradient image.

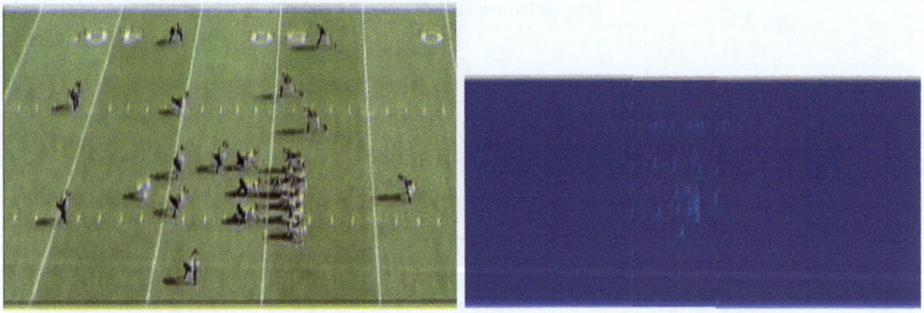

Fig. 13.6 Example of a formation frame (*left*) and its corresponding weighted gradient information (*right*)

After each play, the ball is placed somewhere in the middle of the width of the field closest to where the previous play ended. As such, to account for the variation in the offensive team position at the beginning of a play, we use a sliding window. The window's size was set to cover the offensive team and changes according to the size of the field image. For our experiments on the standard definition dataset, we set the window size to be 20 × 160 pixels respectively for field size image of 800 × 400. The window slides across the entire length of the projected formation frame region, not across the whole field. We calculate the sum of gradient intensities in each window in Eq. (13.2) and determine the line of scrimmage in Eq. (13.3). Figure 13.7 (left) shows an example of the sliding window, while Fig. 13.7 (right) shows the detected line of scrimmage marked in red.

$$Dens(y) = \sum_{i=1}^{M_W} \sum_{j=1}^{N_W} \left| \frac{\partial I_W}{\partial x} \right| \tag{13.2}$$

$$\text{line-of-scrimmage} = \arg\max_y Dens(y) \tag{13.3}$$

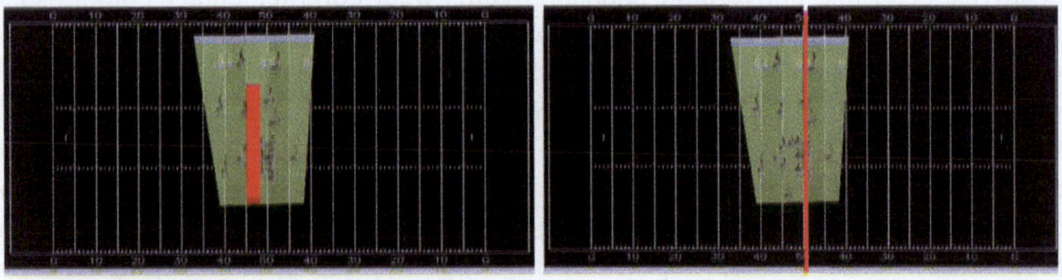

Fig. 13.7 A sliding window (shown in *red* on the *left*) is used to calculate the density of gradient intensity. The corresponding detected line of scrimmage is marked in *red* on the *right*

13.3.4 Offensive Team Identification

Football presents many technical hurdles for analysis. This is especially due to frequent and substantial player occlusion. However, football is highly repetitive and structured in nature. We exploit this repetition to distinguish offense from defense. The offensive team tends to be compactly positioned at the line of the scrimmage when in formation. There are at least five offensive players near the ball ('offensive line') in close proximity in front of the quarterback. The defense on the other hand, is usually more spread out, especially along the line of scrimmage. Therefore, the team on offense is determined as the side of the line of scrimmage (left or right) where the spatial distribution of players (foreground) on that side has minimum variance. The foreground distribution on either side of the line of scrimmage is estimated by a spatial pmf as shown in Eq. (13.4). Here, we model the probability that a player exists at pixel (x, y) as a function of the gradient intensity and foreground (error) value at (x, y).

$$p(x, y|d) = \frac{\partial I(x, y)/\partial x}{\sum_{(x,y)\in d} \partial I(x, y)/\partial x}; \quad [d \in \{\text{left, right}\}] \tag{13.4}$$

The side d with the minimum variance is determined to be offense.

$$o = \underset{d\in\{\text{left,right}\}}{\arg\min}\ \sigma\,(p(x, y|d)) \tag{13.5}$$

13.3.5 Formation Classification

At this stage, the formation frame, line of scrimmage, and the offensive team of a given play clip have been extracted. We proceed to learn a discriminative model to classify a play clip as one of five major formation types for offense. These formation types (classes) and the ground truth labeling of a play clip dataset are obtained from a football expert. We implemented and tested two classification schemes to compare and obtain the best classification performance. Results of the different classification schemes are presented in the next section.

In the first classification scheme, we distinguish between the five formation classes by learning a multi-class linear SVM classifier on a training subset of the play clip dataset. The feature used to learn the SVM is the spatial distribution of gradient intensity for the offensive side of the line of scrimmage. Since the location of an offensive team can vary on the field, we make the feature translation invariant by centering the spatial distribution at the field pixel (on the offensive side) with maximum gradient intensity. Note that we reflect the formation frame about the line of scrimmage to ensure that the offensive team is always on the left side of the line of scrimmage. The SVM classifier parameters are learned using a popular and publicly available SVM solver.

Due to the inherent hierarchical properties of the formation labels, in our second classification scheme we learn a structured SVM classifier. While SVM classifier supports binary, multi-class classification, and regression, structured SVM allows structured output labels such as trees. To learn the structured SVM model, we extract multi-scale Histogram Of Oriented Gradient(HOG) [7] applied on the error maps obtained the Robust Video Stitching method (Sect. 13.3.1). We begin by extracting the HOG of the whole error map and then subdivide the map into sub-maps and extract HOG descriptor for each of the submaps. The final feature vector is formed by concatenating the HOG across all scales and divisions. To reduce dimensionality complexities, we apply Principal Component Analysis (PCA) to the feature vector before learning our structural SVM model.

13.4 Experimental Results

In this section, we present experimental results that validate the effectiveness of our formation recognition framework. We tested our approach on three separate datasets. We provide both quantitative and qualitative results on these datasets.

13.4.1 Datasets

We evaluate the performance of our detection and classification framework by applying it to real-world football videos. There is no publicly available dataset that accurately represents video captured and used by American Football teams. Typically, a football coach would segment the video of a whole game into single play clips, identify their respective formation frames, and then classify the formation type. To evaluate our framework, we test it on three separate datasets, two of which we compiled ourselves and plan to make publicly accessible. To the best of our knowledge, our dataset is the largest dataset for American football plays.

The two datasets we compiled are denoted **SD (standard definition)** dataset and **HD (high definition)** dataset. They comprise 274 and 541 distinct offensive plays respectively. In both cases, the football game videos were collected from several college and show the sideline view of the game. The videos were recorded by the teams. The videos were manually segmented such that each clip shows a single play. In dataset **SD**, play clips are standard resolution 640 × 480. In dataset **HD**, they are high-definition 1,440 × 1,080 resolution. All play clips were registered to the football field reference image using the video registration and stitching method discussed in Sect. 13.3.1. The groundtruth data for the formation frame, line of scrimmage, and formation label were annotated by a sports domain expert with more than 6 years of experience in studying and analyzing football games. The third dataset, denoted **OSU** dataset, was obtained from the Oregon State University

Table 13.1 Hierarchy of the formation classes in the dataset

Top level label	Second level label	# instances
Ace	Ace.3WR	30
IForm	IForm.2WR	40
	IForm.3WR	19
Shotgun	Shotgun.2WR.1RB	21
	Shotgun.3WR.1RB	110
	Shotgun.3WR.2RB	85
	Shotgun.4WR.1RB	106
	Shotgun.5WR	26

Digital Scout Project [20]. This dataset consists of 51 formation frame images and their corresponding homography matrices for projection to the reference field image.

There exist more than a hundred known formation types (class labels in our case) in the sport of football. However, due to the limited amount of data available, we categorize the plays in each dataset into two different levels of categorization. Table 13.1 shows the hierarchy of the formation classes. At the coarse level of classification, the plays were classified into three different categories: *Ace*, *IForm*, or *ShotGun*. These top labels in the taxonomy were determined by the location of the quarterback (QB) and running backs (RB). *Ace* formation means there is one running back directly behind the quarterback, who is very close to the ball. *IForm* is similar to Ace, except there are two running backs directly behind the quarterback instead of one. In *Shotgun* formation, the quarterback is several yards away from the ball at the start of the play. At the second level, the classes were determined by the number of running backs (RB) and wide receivers (WR). The *Ace* formation consists of one subclass: Ace.3WR. The *IForm* class is subdivided into IForm.2WR and IForm.3WR, while the *ShotGun* formation consists of five subclasses: Shotgun.2WR, Shotgun.3WR.1RB, Shotgun.3WR.2RB, Shotgun.4WR.1RB, and Shotgun.5WR. The small inter-class variability in the datasets makes formation classification a challenging problem. Figure 13.8 shows examples of the different formations.

13.4.2 Quantitative Results

We tested and evaluated each of the modules in our framework separately.

13.4.2.1 Formation Frame Detection

To evaluate the performance of our formation frame detection method described in Sect. 13.3.2, a formation frame is marked as accurately labelled if the detected formation frame is within 1 s (30 frames) of the groundtruth formation frame index.

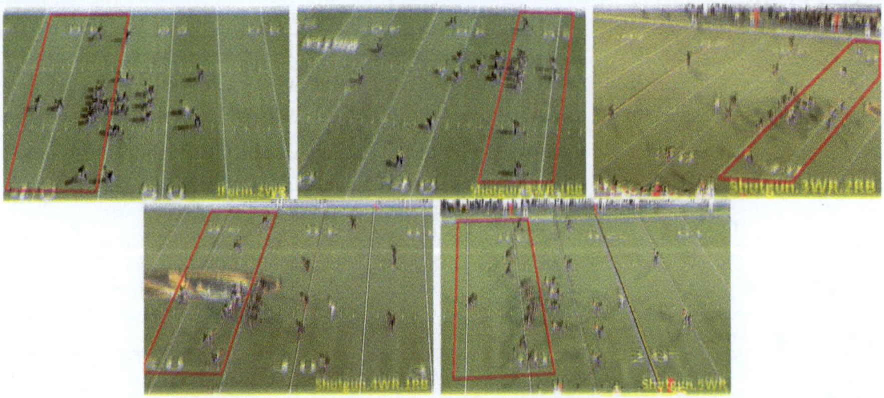

Fig. 13.8 Examples of 5 offensive team formation classes (*red bounding box*). It can be seen that the inter-class variation between the different formations is very small, making the classification problem a challenging task

This evaluation criterion was deemed acceptable by the sports expert. In this setup, the formation frame was accurately detected 94.53 % of the time on the **SD** dataset using 274 play clips. We could not test this module on the OSU dataset as the dataset consists only of frame images and not play video clips.

13.4.2.2 Line of Scrimmage Detection

After identifying the formation frame, we use the foreground (error) values for each pixel in the projected formation frame (computed in our pre-processing stage described in Sect. 13.3.1) as well as the gradient intensity to automatically detect the line of scrimmage, as described in Sect. 13.3.3. In fact, weighting the pixels of the formation frame with the foreground values significantly reduces false positive detection arising from regions of high gradient density such as field logos or markers.

To test our automatic line of scrimmage detection method, we use the groundtruth formation frame in the datasets. For the **SD** dataset, we achieve 97.5 % accuracy in detecting the line of scrimmage within 10 pixels of its actual location on the field. This translates to within a yard accuracy. The detection results improve significantly on the **HD** dataset, where we achieve a 97.9 % detection accuracy within 3 pixels on an **HD** reference field. This translates to a 6 in. accuracy on the physical field. As mentioned earlier, the **OSU** dataset only contains formation images and no play clips. Hence, we could not directly apply the robust registration/stitching method in Sect. 13.3.1 to obtain the per-pixel foreground values in the formation frame. Instead, we apply the video stitching method on the given formation frames in the dataset to generate an overhead panoramic stitching of the field. The resulting panoramic image of the **OSU** field is shown in Fig. 13.4 (top). This image is subtracted from each of the projected formation frames to produce the foreground error values (i.e. background subtraction). We obtained a detection accuracy of 90.2 % on the OSU dataset.

13.4.2.3 Formation Classification

To validate our formation classification method (described in Sects. 13.3.4 and 13.3.5), we test on the union of the three datasets. Special care has to be taken because of the imbalance in the combined dataset. We adopt the oversampling paradigm to alleviate this imbalance. The hierarchy of the classes and the number of instances in each class are reported in Table 13.1.

All classification model training and testing are performed using fivefold cross validation. In our first classification scheme, we trained a multi-class linear SVM classifier. We perform two levels of classification. For top level classification, we train the classifier to classify formations into one of three super classes: Ace, IForm, and ShotGun. The classification rate for the top level classification is 67.1 %. At the next level of classification, we train two classifiers, one each for labeling the IForm and ShotGun formations into their subclass labels respectively. The classification rate for labeling IForm formations into two subclasses, IForm.2WR and IForm.3WR, is 65.01 %, while the classification rate for classifying ShotGun formations into the 5 different subclasses is 36.43 %. Figure 13.9 shows the confusion matrix for classification of the ShotGun formations into the subclasses. The classification rate is lower compared to the classification of the IForm formation due to the fact that the differences between the subclasses are very subtle with the distinction being just the placement of one player in the formation. We also compared the performance of the hierarchical classifier to a simple multi-class classifier. When using a flat multi-class classifier, we obtained an overall classification accuracy of 31.1 %. The confusion matrix is shown in Fig. 13.10. Again the confusion mainly occurs within the ShotGun formation as the difference between the classes is very subtle.

Fig. 13.9 Confusion matrix for classification of ShotGun formations into five subclasses

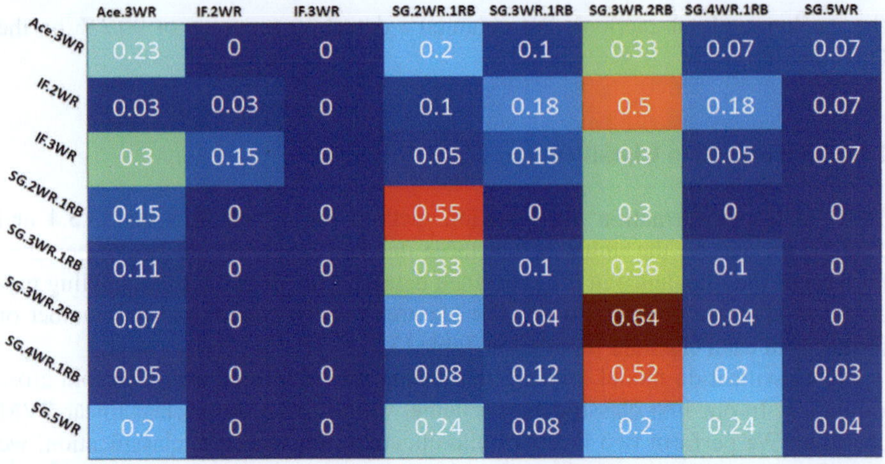

Fig. 13.10 Confusion matrix for simple multi-class classification using all 8 formation classes

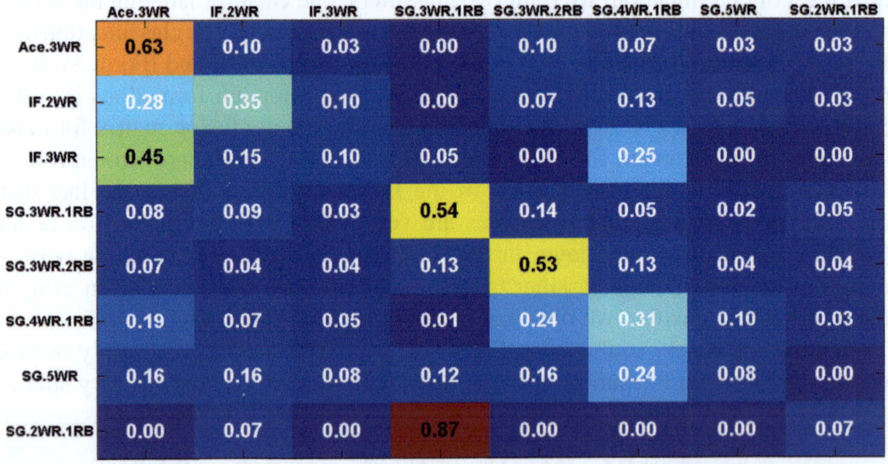

Fig. 13.11 Confusion matrix for the overall classification using all 8 formation classes and structured SVM. The results show an improvement over the linear SVM classification performance

Using our structured SVM classifier, we saw an improvement of at least 3 % in both levels of classification. When performing top level classification where we trained the structured SVM to classify the formations into one of the three upper classes, the structured SVM classifier achieved accuracy of 71 %. The overall classification accuracy for all 8 classes improved to 39 %. Figure 13.12 shows the confusion matrix for the top level classification using structured SVM, and Fig. 13.11 shows the confusion matrix for the overall classification scheme using all 8 formation classes with structured SVM. The classification performance may further improve as we add more training data to ensure a more balanced dataset.

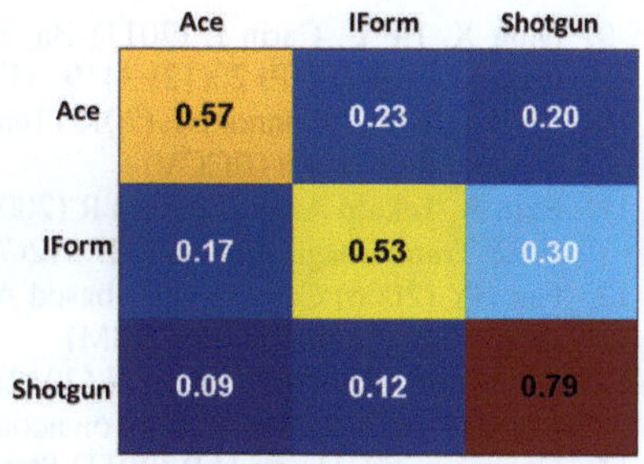

Fig. 13.12 Confusion matrix for the top-level classification using the 3 *top* formation classes and structured SVM. The results show an improvement over the linear SVM classification performance

13.5 Conclusion

In this chapter, we propose a framework for automatic recognition of offensive team formation in American football plays. We show promising results that our method is able to automatically label formations on three different datasets. The framework that we have developed serves as a building block that is part of our tool prototype for automatic analysis of American football games. Future work utilizing this formation classification framework include automatic personnel identification or identifying all players that are on the field, automatic play classification, and strategical playbook inference of a team.

Acknowledgments This study is supported by the research grant for the Human Sixth Sense Programme at the Advanced Digital Sciences Center from Singapore's Agency for Science, Technology and Research (A*STAR). We also would like to thank Shaunak Ahuja and Karthik Muthuswamy for their contributions.

References

1. Atmosukarto I, Ghanem B, Ahuja S, Muthuswamy K, Ahuja N (2013) Automatic recognition of offensive team formation in American football plays. In: Computer vision and pattern recognition workshops (CVPRW)
2. Ayanegui-Santiago H (2009) Recognizing team formations in multiagent systems: applications in Robotic Soccer. Lecture Notes in Computer Science. Springer, Berlin, pp 163–173
3. Beetz M, von Hoyningen-Huene N, Kirchlechner B, Gedikli S, Siles F, Durus M, Lames M (2009) ASPOGAMO: automated sports game analysis models. Int J Comput Sci Sport 8(1): 1–21
4. Berclaz J, Fleuret F, Turetken E, Fua P (2011) Multiple object tracking using k-shortest paths optimization. IEEE Trans Pattern Anal Mach Intell (TPAMI) 33(9):1806–1819
5. Candes E, Li X, Ma Y, Wright J (2011) Robust principal component analysis? J ACM 58(3): 1–11
6. Chen HT, Chou CL, Fu TS, Lee SY, Lin BSP (2012) Recognizing tactic patterns in broadcast basketball video using player trajectory. J Vis Commun Image Represent 23:932–947
7. Dalal N, Triggs B (2005) Histograms of oriented gradients for human detection. In: IEEE computer vision and pattern recognition
8. De la Torre F, Black M (2003) A framework for Robust subspace learning. Int J Comput Vis (IJCV) 54(1–3):117–142

9. Ding X, He L, Carin L (2011) Bayesian robust principal component analysis. IEEE Trans Image Process (TIP) 20(12):3419–3430. doi:10.1109/TIP.2011.2156801
10. Direkoglu C, O'Connor NE (2012) Team activity recognition in sports. In: European conference on computer vision (ECCV)
11. Ekin A, Tekalp AM, Mehrotra R (2003) Automatic soccer video analysis and summarization. IEEE Trans Image Process (TIP) 12(7):796–807
12. Fan GY (2006) Camera view-based American football video analysis. In: IEEE international symposium on multimedia (ISM)
13. Ghanem B, Zhang T, Ahuja N (2012) Robust video registration applied to field-sports video analysis. In: IEEE conference on acoustic, speech and signal processing (ICASSP)
14. Gonzalez AB, Uresti JAR (2011) Strategy patterns prediction model (SPPM). In: MICAI
15. Hamid R, Kumar R, Hodgins J, Essa I (2013) A visualization framework for team sports captured using multiple static cameras. Comput Vis Image Underst (CVIU)
16. Hamid R, Kumar RK, Grundmann M, Kim K, Essa I, Hodgins J (2010) Player localization using multiple static cameras for sports visualization. In: IEEE computer vision and pattern recognition (CVPR)
17. Han J, Farin D, de With PH (2008) Broadcast court-net sports video analysis using fast 3d camera modeling. IEEE Trans Circuits Syst Video Technol 18(11):1628–1638
18. He J, Balzano L, Szlam A (2012) Incremental gradient on the Grassmannian for online foreground and background separation in subsampled video. In: IEEE computer vision and pattern recognition (CVPR)
19. Hess R, Fern A (2007) Toward learning mixture-of-parts pictorial structures. In: ICML workshop on constrained optimization and structured output spaces
20. Hess R, Fern A, Mortensen E (2007) Mixture-of-parts pictorial structures for objects with variable part sets. In: IEEE international conference on computer vision (ICCV)
21. Hilton A, Guillemaut JY, Kilner J, Grau O, Thomas G (2011) 3D-TV production from conventional cameras for sports broadcast. IEEE Trans Broadcast: Spec Issue 3D-TV Horiz 57(2): 462–476
22. Intille S, Bobick A (2001) Recognizing planned, multiperson action. Comput Vis Image Underst (CVIU) 81:414–445
23. Kataoka H, Aoki Y (2011) Football players and ball trajectories projection from single camera's image. In: Frontiers of computer vision
24. Kim K, Lee D, Essa I (2012) Detecting regions of interest in dynamic scenes with camera motions. In: IEEE computer vision and pattern recognition (CVPR)
25. Kim K, Grundmann M, Shamir A, Matthews I, Hodgins J, Essa I (2010) Motion fields to predict play evolution in dynamic sport scenes. In: IEEE computer vision and pattern recognition (CVPR)
26. Lai JH, Chen CL, Wu PC, Kao CC, Hu M, Chien SY (2012) Tennis real play. IEEE Trans Multimed 14(6)
27. Lazarescu M, Venkatesh S (2003) Using camera motion to identify types of American football plays. In: IEEE international conference on multimedia and expo (ICME)
28. Leo M, Mazzeo PL, Nitti M, Spagnolo P (2013) Accurate ball detection in Soccer images using probabilistic analysis of salient regions. In: Machine vision and applications (MVA)
29. Li R, Chellappa R (2010) Recognizing offensive strategies from football videos. In: IEEE international conference on image processing (ICIP)
30. Liu Y, Liang D, Huang Q, Gao W (2006) Extracting 3d information from broadcast soccer video. In: Image and vision computing (IVC), pp 1146–1162
31. Lucey P, Bialkowski A, Carr P, Foote E, Matthews I (2012) Characterizing multi-agent team behavior from partial team tracings: evidence from English premier league. In: Association for the advancement of artificial intelligence
32. Lucey P, Oliver D, Carr P, Roth J, Matthews I (2013) Assessing team strategy using spatiotemporal data. In: ACM conference on knowledge discovery and data mining (KDD)
33. Mahasseni B, Chen S, Fern A, Todorovic S (2013) Detecting the moment of snap in real-world football videos. In: AAAI

34. Miura J, Shimawaki T, Sakiyama T, Shirai Y (2009) Ball route estimation under heavy occlusion in broadcast Soccer video. In: Computer vision and image understanding (CVIU), p 113
35. Motoi S, Misu T, Nakada Y, Yazaki T, Kobayashi G, Matsumoto T, Yagi N (2011) Bayesian event detection for sport games with hidden Markov model. In: Pattern analysis application
36. Naik V, Rathod G (2013) An algorithm for retrieval of significant events near goal post from soccer videos using fuzzy systems. Int J Emerg Technol Adv Eng 3(3)
37. Perin C, Vueillemot R, Fekete JD (2013) Soccerstories: a kick-off for visual soccer analysis. IEEE Trans Vis Comput Graph 19(12)
38. Perse M, Kristan M, Kovacic S, Vuckovic G, Pers J (2009) A trajectory-based analysis of coordinated team activity in a basketball game. Comput Vis Image Underst (CVIU) 113: 612–621
39. Poppe C, Bruyne S, Verstockt S, de Walle R (2010) Multi camera analysis of Soccer sequences. In: IEEE international conference on advanced video and signal based surveillance
40. Ren J, Orwell J, Jones GA, Xu M (2008) Real time modeling of 3d Soccer ball trajectories from multiple fixed cameras. IEEE Trans Circuits Syst Video Technol 18(3)
41. Rodriguez-Perez S, Montoliu R (2013) Bag-of-words and topic modeling-based sports video analysis. In: IbPRIA
42. Saba T, Altameem A (2013) Analysis of vision based systems to detect real time goal events in soccer videos. Appl Artif Intell: Int J 27(7)
43. Sankoh H, Sugano M, Naito S (2012) Dynamic camera calibration method for free-viewpoint experience in sport videos. In: ACM multimedia
44. Siddiquie B, Yacoob Y, Davis LS (2009) Recognizing plays in American football videos. Technical report, University of Maryland
45. Stracuzzi DJ, Fern A, Ali K, Hess R, Pinto J, Li N, Konik T, Shapiro D (2011) An application of transfer to American football: from observation of raw video to control in a simulated environment. AI Mag 32:107–125
46. Swears E, Hoogs A (2012) Learning and recognizing complex multi-agent activities with applications to American football plays. In: IEEE workshop on applications of computer vision (WACV)
47. Tabii Y, Thami ROH (2009) A framework for Soccer video processing and analysis based on enhancing algorithm for dominant color extraction. Int J Image Process 3(4)
48. Varadarajan J, Atmosukarto I, Ahuja S, Ghanem B, Ahuja N (2013) A topic model approach to represent and classify American football plays. In: British machine vision conference (BMVC)
49. Visser U, Drcker C, Hbner S, Schmidt E, Weland HG (2001) Recognizing formations in opponent teams. Lecture Notes in Computer Science. Springer, Berlin
50. von der Grun T, Franke N, Wolf D, Witt N, Eidloth A (2011) A real time tracking system for football match and training analysis. In: Microelectronic systems
51. Yu X, Farin D (2005) Current and emerging topics in sports video processing. In: IEEE international conference on multimedia and expo (ICME)
52. Zawbaa HM, El-Bendary N, Hassanien AE, Kim TH (2011) Machine-learning based video summarization system. In: MulGraB
53. Zawbaa HM, El-Bendary N, Hassanien AE, Kim TH (2012) Event detection based approach for soccer video summarization using machine learning. Int J Multimed Ubiquitous Eng 7(2)
54. Zhang T, Ghanem B, Ahuja N (2012) Robust multi-object tracking via cross-domain contextual information for sports video analysis. In: IEEE conference on acoustic, speech and signal processing (ICASSP)
55. Zhu G, Xu C, Huang Q, Gao W, Xing L (2006) Player action recognition in broadcast tennis video with applications to semantic analysis of sports game. In: ACM multimedia (MM)
56. Zhu G, Huang Q, Xu C, Rui Y, Jiang S, Gao W, Yao H (2007) Trajectory based event tactics analysis in broadcast sports video. In: ACM multimedia (MM)

Chapter 14
Real-Time Event Detection in Field Sport Videos

Rafal Kapela, Kevin McGuinness, Aleksandra Swietlicka and Noel E. O'Connor

Abstract This chapter describes a real-time system for event detection in sports broadcasts. The approach presented is applicable to a wide range of field sports. Using two independent event detection approaches that work simultaneously, the system is capable of accurately detecting scores, near misses, and other exciting parts of a game that do not result in a score. The results obtained across a diverse dataset of different field sports are promising, demonstrating over 90 % accuracy for a feature-based event detector and 100 % accuracy for a scoreboard-based detector detecting only scores.

14.1 Event Detection in Sports

Sport has always been one of the most popular of television broadcasts [1, 2]. Sports broadcast viewing figures are consistently high, particularly for events like the Olympics and national or regional finals of nationally popular games. Given such wide appeal and popularity, there has been significant interest in algorithms for automatic event detection in sports broadcasts [3]. This is motivated by potential applications such as automatic highlight generation for summarization for emerging second screen applications, indexing for search, and retrieval in large archives, mobile content delivery either offline or as an added value in-stadium user experience.

R. Kapela (✉) · A. Swietlicka
Faculty of Computing, ul. Piotrowo 3A, Poznan, Poland
e-mail: rafal.kapela@put.poznan.pl

A. Swietlicka
e-mail: aleksandra.swietlicka@put.poznan.pl

N.E. O'Connor · K. McGuinness
Insight Centre for Data Analytics, Dublin City University,
Glasnevin, Dublin 9, Ireland
e-mail: noel.oconnor@dcu.ie

K. McGuinness
e-mail: kevin.mcguinness@dcu.ie

T.B. Moeslund et al. (eds.), *Computer Vision in Sports*,
Advances in Computer Vision and Pattern Recognition,
DOI 10.1007/978-3-319-09396-3_14

Many of these applications either require or would benefit significantly from real-time event detection, however, this aspect has been largely overlooked to date in the relevant literature.

14.1.1 Sport Event Detection Approaches

A range of event detection algorithms have been presented in recent years, taking into account the broad diversity of different sports. It has been shown in [4] that about 97 % of interesting moments during a game are followed by a close-up shot presenting a player who scored or who caused some interesting action. In addition, features like end of a pitch, audio activity, or crowd shot detection have been shown to be very useful in event detection [4]. The system present in [4] was proven to work with different sports such as soccer, rugby, field hockey, hurling, and Gaelic football. A Support Vector Machine (SVM) was used as a event classifier. However, the algorithm was too computationally expensive for real-time implementation, mainly due to the use of the Hough transform.

A very similar approach was presented in [5]. To detect an event the authors declare so-called "plays" where mainly a color histogram is calculated and some heuristics are applied about the regions of histogram detection. An event is categorized using Hidden Markov Models (HMM) based on the sequence of camera shots. In this work events were detected in baseball, American football, and Japanese sumo wrestling. Another example of this kind of approach was presented in [6] where, based on simple visual features like pitch orientation and close-up detection, the authors achieved good accuracy. However, computation time is not evaluated in the paper and there is a large drop in accuracy when the SVM is trained on the samples that do not belong to the same game.

It is worth noting that the three approaches described above [4–6] are capable of extracting not only goals but also other exciting moments like penalties and near misses. In [7], very simple features like pixel/histogram change ratio between two consecutive frames, grass ratios, and background mean and variation in addition to time and frequency domain audio features were used to detect events in soccer games. The authors report high-accuracy using simple features, but again do not discuss computation time performance.

Although the acceptance of the MPEG-7 standard in the community has been rather low, there are approaches based on MPEG-7 descriptors. In [8] a goal detection system based only on MPEG-7 audio descriptors was proposed. Some implementations of the proposed feature extraction process are very fast and make the system applicable in real-time scenarios. However, the system is designed for soccer games alone, does not detect anything other than goals, and was tested on very few test samples (only 8 goal scenarios).

One event detection technique extensively investigated for broadcast videos is replay detection, since replays already contain interesting moments selected by a director. Some examples of these techniques for either slow or normal motion replay detections are presented in [9–11]. Although all of these feature very good precision and recall (from about 60 to 100 %), event detection based on replay extraction techniques are not really appropriate for real-time applications (i.e., they occur after the real event and a specific one may occur several times during a game so this approach requires building some sort of indexing system to store and match following scenes).

Finally, in [12, 13], very different approaches are taken. The former utilizes the information produced by people during a game and tweeted by the popular Twitter website to detect events in different games (soccer and rugby were tested). The latter approach uses web-casted text for the same purpose. These are, at first sight, universal approaches, however they can suffer from quite large false positive detection rates, need constant connection to the Internet and introduce some ambiguity in the form of delay between detected and real events making the detection of event boundaries more difficult.

14.1.2 Field Sports as a Specific Genre of Team Sports

In general, from a content analysis point of view, sport broadcasts can be classified into two main categories [3]: a single/dominant camera or multipoint/view camera capture broadcasts. In sports like tennis or badminton, there is typically one camera view that dominates the broadcast (e.g., the full court in tennis) and contains almost all the semantically meaningful elements required to analyze the game. Yet in sports like football, hurling, soccer, baseball, hockey, basketball, there is no such well-defined camera view that dominates the course of play. This is mainly due to the fact that the playing field is too large to present all the necessary details with a single camera broadcast.

Most existing event detection algorithms focus on a particular type of sport (e.g., tennis, soccer, cricket) and are not robust for other types of sports, thereby limiting their applicability. This reflects the fact that different sports present different characteristics either in the rules for that sport or the manner in which they are captured for broadcast. So far there have been very few attempts to make event detection more general so that the same system/algorithm could be used for more than just a single sport. Although this may seem to be complex and challenging it could be very convenient from the perspective of a sports broadcaster, avoiding the need for development and deployment of multiple different algorithms and systems. For this reason, in this chapter we focus on a generic subset of all sports that can be designated as "field sports", a term originally introduced in [4] to refer to any sport played on a grass pitch (soccer, rugby, field hockey, etc.) featuring two teams competing for territorial advantage. In this work, however, we extend this definition to include other sports that exhibit similar characteristics but that are not necessarily played on a grass pitch. Specifically, we extend the definition of field sports to include sports played in a playing arena that features some kind of scoring posts (e.g., goal post in soccer or basket in basketball), whereby the overall objective is territorial advancement with a view to obtaining a score. Since most field sports have similar characteristics, broadcasters use the same scene compilation techniques to present the action on the field to the viewer. Thus, once a robust and accurate algorithm is developed, it can be applied to different kinds of field sports without any modification.

14.2 The Architecture of the Event Detection System

The top-view architecture of the system is presented in Fig. 14.1. After video decoding the stream analysis is split into two independent threads. The first, termed the *scene thread*, works on extracted video frames and audio packets. The second, the *scoreboard thread* needs only video frames. The common data is stored in a shared buffer in order to simplify the processing flow. The two threads are described in more detail in the following sections. All their features are presented in the bottom-up approach—we start with a description of the low-level modules that gather the data extracted by feature detectors. All these data are then sent to the mid-level modules where, depending on the processing thread, it is either used to detect the text (scoreboard) region or predict what kind of scene is presented to the viewer. The top module gathers the events from both threads, summarizing the description of the system. The inputs (i.e., recognized score change or specific—event related sequence of shots) to this module are treated separately which means that there are two kinds of event markers at the system output. In general the primary design constraint was the latency introduced by the modules working at all levels throughout the system. This is reflected in the following sections, where time efficiency is the main parameter investigated in each module. The two threads are described in detail below.

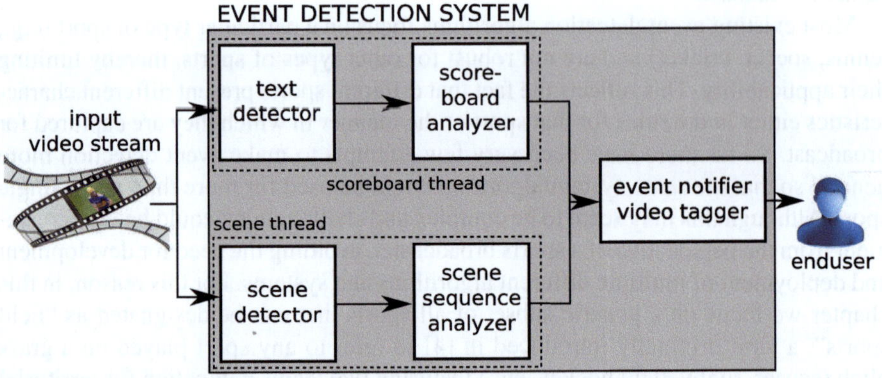

Fig. 14.1 The block schematic of the system—the two parallel threads are responsible for the analysis of the specific aspects of the video stream in order to determine if the particular part of the video is interesting from the user's point of view

14.3 Feature-Based Event Detection System

The scene analysis thread is responsible for detection of events that can subsequently be observed on the scoreboard (i.e., goals) but also situations like close-misses or any other actions that can be classified as interesting from the viewer's point of view. It belongs to the class of the algorithms that analyze the sequence of shots presented. Earlier works on event detection state that 97 % of the interesting moments are followed by close-up shots (i.e., shots that present a player) [4]. If we add to this the information about where the action has taken place (e.g., end of pitch/court—close to the goal-post/basket) before the close-up shot occurred, we can more precisely distinguish between usual and unusual events.

The scene analysis thread utilizes extracted video frames and audio packets in order to detect the events. Most of the information needed for this task is stored in visual data. For this reason we have chosen 14 different classes that represent most of the situations presented on the field/court during a match. In order to evaluate the generalization properties of the algorithm some of the classes were split into three subclasses: shot with simple background (a dominant color easily distinguishable), shot with complex background (no dominant color in the background) and a mixture of the two—Table 14.1.

However, we have also included simple audio analysis for better robustness of the algorithm. The reason for this was that we have observed how usually the interesting moment in the game is followed with increased audio activity intervals (e.g., round of applause or excitation of the commentator). From a real-time perspective audio track analysis does not introduce significant overhead in processing time since the decoder does audio extraction in parallel to the analysis of the video stream and moreover, we are only calculating a temporal energy of the audio signal which is a relatively simple operation.

Table 14.1 The abbreviations of descriptors used in the system

Abbreviation	Descriptor focus
CLHS	Close up shot head with simple background
CLHC	Close up shot head complex background
CLH	Close up shot head mixture background
CLWUS	Close up shot waist up simple background
CLWUC	Close up shot waist up complex background
CLWU	Close up shot waist up mixture background
SPS	Short distance shot presenting player(s) simple background
SPC	Short distance shot presenting player(s) complex background
SP	Short distance shot presenting player(s) mixture background
SS	Short distance shot presenting spectators
LC	Long distance shot presenting center of the field
LR	Long distance shot presenting right side of the field
LL	Long distance shot presenting left side of the field
LS	Long distance shot presenting spectators

14.3.1 Feature Detection

As mentioned in the introduction, to date there have been many features proposed to detect different scenes in a game. However, the majority of these approaches are either not suitable for real-time analysis of the game or, taking into account that we deal with not only one type of the sport, too simple to distinguish robustly between the type of the scenes. For these reasons we had to propose our own scene detection techniques [14] or simplify the existing ones to meet the real-time requirement.

In [14] we compared state-of-the-art image description techniques and proposed a dataset of images especially chosen for this task. The mentioned dataset meets two very important requirements in order to provide a tool for unique categorization of scene detection algorithms:

- it contains variety of field sports (specifically, soccer, rugby, Gaelic football, hurling, basketball, and cricket);
- provides a representative variety of images that can be assigned to particular classes (i.e., 14 types of scenes ranging from head close-up shots to shots with long perceptive distance to the players).

Our work in [14] shows that local feature detection algorithms like Scale Invariant Feature Transform (SIFT) [15] and Histogram of Oriented Gradients (HoG) [16] algorithms, that are characterized with the highest accuracy are too slow to be part of a system that has to work under real-time constraints. More recent local feature descriptors have been proposed, similar to SIFT and Speeded-Up Robust Features (SURF), which are much faster to compute as they produce a binary output (e.g., to produce the response, the algorithm only has to compare a fixed number of region intensities around the key-point). These include: Binary Robust Independent Elementary Features (BRIEF) [17], Fast Retina Keypoint (FREAK) [18], Binary Robust Invariant Scalable Keypoints (BRISK) [19] and An Efficient Dense Descriptor Applied to Wide Baseline Stereo (DAISY) [20]. Depending on the descriptor length and local region filtering they could be from several up to several tens of times faster than the SURF local descriptor [21, 22]. The fastest is BRIEF (up to sixty times faster than SURF) ensuring at the same time an acceptable recognition rate [22]. Note, that a scene description algorithm for sport videos does not need to provide scale and rotation invariance for two reasons:

- the broadcasted videos always present non-rotated scenes;
- we want to distinguish between long and close-up shots of the players and the field/court, thus the scale invariance has to be restrained to some, albeit relatively small, range.

As the BRIEF descriptor satisfies the above considerations and is computationally efficient, it was chosen for this application scenario.

14.3.2 Feature Aggregation

Once a set of binary local descriptors have been extracted for a frame, a method is needed to aggregate these into a single fixed-length descriptor that can be used for classification. The most widely known technique is the bag of visual words method, in which a histogram of local descriptors is created from a pre-trained codebook where each bin represents a cluster of similar local descriptors. This very simple and effective algorithm is also suitable for binary data and outperforms, in terms of computational complexity, other state-of-the-art techniques, for example, Fisher kernels [23] or VLAD [24].

Bag of visual word aggregation is usually implemented using k-means to generate the code book. However, clustering binary data with k-means algorithm is not straight forward as descriptors should be compared using Hamming distances rather than Euclidean, and substituting Euclidean distances may lead to unexpected results [25]. We therefore took a different approach for cluster generation. The algorithm is as follows:

1. Calculate local descriptors for all images from the training set.
2. For each of these, find N nearest neighbors based on Hamming distance (based on a number of experiments we noticed that N should be equal to 2–5 % of the number of descriptors, in our case $N = 150$). The sum of all the distances to a particular node is an estimate of a local density around it.
3. Sort the list by the local density estimate.
4. Choose a vector from this list, either from the top, bottom, or randomly, and store it as a cluster.
5. Remove the vector that produced the cluster and all its neighbors.
6. Repeat points 4–5 until all clusters are selected.

Intuitively there would be tendency to pick only clusters from the top, but experiments show that also selecting random vectors and vectors from the bottom has a positive effect on accuracy. Accuracy is improved because the candidates with less neighbors simply represent the regions of lower densities. Experimental results are presented in the Sect. 14.5.

We applied a moving window approach where the average of the SVM responses over a fixed time period is calculated when detecting the 14 classes defined in Sect. 14.3. Then these 14 values and the audio intensity descriptor are sent to the event recognition module.

14.3.3 Event Recognition

Figure 14.2 shows an example of the behavior of the description vectors (outputs from scene recognition SVMs). For a close-up shot one can observe that all the descriptors prefixed with CL (close-up) are dominant, whereas in a long-distance

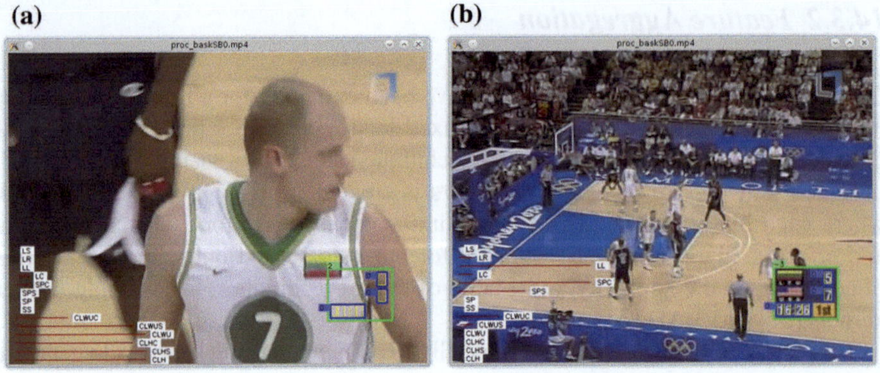

Fig. 14.2 Example of the behavior of visual descriptors (averaged responses from SVMs) **a** a close-up shot; **b** long-distance shot

shots the LL (long-left) descriptor is dominant with the additional feedback that some players/spectators detected could be at a short perceived distance to the camera. Note, that the difference between short and long type of shots is quite fuzzy (e.g., in basketball long type of shot presents players at a scale analogous to short distance shots in soccer, Gaelic football, or hurling). However, this does not negatively impact on effective event recognition.

Intuitively, an initial approach would be to train a deterministic classifier like an SVM to take all the responses of scene classifiers and detect if the shot presented belongs to an event class. Our experiments, however, show that we also need an additional input about previous SVMs responses and also responses from the event classifier.

14.3.3.1 State Machine

A state machine can be one of the simplest ways of singling out all of the important scenes from the given game. Tha main difficulty in this case is however the optimal choice of the number of states. After analysis of the correlation between the values of the descriptors and the ground-truth probes we have chosen four states:

A—an interesting event has been detected, e.g. there was a goal;
B—an interesting event just happened;
C—an idle state, when all the descriptors have values less than 0.5;
D—all other situations.

We assumed that the most interesting moments of the game take place at the end of the arena, so state A occurs when the descriptor of the end of the field or court is higher than 0.8, plus very often after an event, there is a close-up shot. This is reflected by keeping track of an upward trend of the set of close-up descriptors.

After analyzing the amount of transitions between the proposed states it is obvious that the biggest probability of transition is between the same states. This unfortunately leads to insufficient accuracy of around 46 %. This is caused by the fact that the state machine usually stays in the same state, and breaking the loop is almost impossible. This is unacceptable since we can of course reduce the number of states to two and propose a random classifier with an accuracy better than 46 %. As a conclusion of this analysis, these results forced us to look for other solutions and to consider dependency between descriptors at a higher level than just their values.

14.3.3.2 Decision Tree

Because of the real-time requirement on the system, using a decision tree for event detection was a natural choice to investigate. Also, going deeper into the analysis of values of each descriptor we decided to think about constructing a decision tree that would give the information about the significance of a single frame. We started with an analysis of the end-of-pitch/court descriptor since most of the events begin with this kind of scene and then they are followed with a close-up shot. Note, that from an event detection point of view we do not need to have the information about left or right side of a pitch/court. For this reason we shortened the number of elements in the description vector to nine values. The new one encompasses the following features: LLR equal to maximum of LL and LR; LC, LS, SP, SS, CLH, CLHS, CLHC, audio activity (AA).

Thus, for the end-of-pitch/court descriptor we can have two situations: the video sequence comprises or does not comprise an event. Table 14.2 shows both situations, where the first nine values refer to the audiovisual descriptors and the last one gives the information whether this frame belongs to an event or not. As can be seen, the first situation ensures that this scene is taking place at the end of the court but the value notifying about an event is false, which means that nothing interesting has happened. In the second case we have the opposite situation—a scene is not happening at the end of the arena but the frame belongs to an event. Accordingly, we can easily find two lines, where values of descriptors are exactly the same but can be distinguished by the event flag. This was a reason to create two separate decision trees. The first one assumes nine descriptors as values that classify each frame independently and the second one eighteen descriptors, including also the previous time instant.

Constructing the tree manually would result in a tree that has $11(N-1) \cdot 101$ nodes, where N stands for the length of the input vector. We would start with the first descriptor and consider all possible eleven values (i.e., the average of ten previous

Table 14.2 The disambiguation between scene descriptors

LLR	LC	LS	SP	SS	CLH	CLHS	CLHC	AA	EVENT
1.0	0.0	0.0	0.6	0.0	0.0	0.0	0.0	1.0	False
0.0	0.0	0.9	0.2	0.9	0.0	0.0	0.4	0.4	True

SVM 0/1 responses), each going to the next node representing the next descriptor which would also has eleven possible branches, etc. Then the last tree level would have 101 branches since this is the number of all possible values for audio descriptor. To avoid this and create an efficient decision tree we used the algorithm described in [26], based on the Gini diversity index, which measures the node impurity and is given with a formula:

$$g(n) = 1 - \sum_{l} \frac{n_l^2}{N^2} \tag{14.1}$$

where $n = (n_1, n_2, \ldots, n_k)$ is a vector of non-negative real numbers representing the number of examples of each class and

$$N = \sum_{l} n_l \tag{14.2}$$

represents the total number of examples at a given node. A node with just one class (a pure node) has the Gini index zero, otherwise the Gini index is positive. The algorithm is also available in MATLAB [26].

Depending on the amount of data and on the number of descriptors (9 or 19) the constructed tree has 2,000–2,500 nodes. In the case, with 9 descriptors we reached 94 % accuracy and with 18–99 % (see the Sect. 14.5 for details).

14.3.3.3 Artificial Neural Networks

An artificial neural network, thanks to its auto-associative memory capabilities, also seems to be an appropriate solution for the detection of interesting events since they can track regularities that occur in the sequences of values of descriptors, which are practically impossible to do with the naked eye. Optimizing this kind of classification method, since many local minima exist, is a non-convex problem but thanks to choosing a fixed but random starting point it gives good results and can be treated as a deterministic method.

We naturally considered at first a feedforward structure, where we simply used values of nine descriptors on the input and the network was trained to recognize if a given frame belongs to the event segment of a video. The structure of this neural network assumed 18 neurons and linear activation function in the hidden layer and a sigmoid activation function in the output layer. We used the Levenberg-Marquardt algorithm [27, 28] for training and the gradient of error function reached a minima after 10 iterations. Fast convergence indicates that the neural network was able to learn the classification task. We can assume this because fast convergence implies that the network was able to recognize quickly all the learning data not causing a divergence in the validation error at the same time. This is also a clue based on which we can say that the positive and negative training datasets are not overlapping each other. The accuracy reached around 65 % on average for all sports. More details on how we split the dataset to train and test subsets is given in Sect. 14.5. We therefore experimented with a more sophisticated recursive network structure.

The natural choice was the Elman neural network [29], which assumes the recursion from a chosen number of neurons in the hidden layer. In this case we decided to consider two structures of the neural network:

- based only on nine values of descriptors at a certain moment of time;
- based on nine values of descriptors at a certain moment of time, values of descriptors at a moment preceding the considered moment of time and the information about whether the previous moment/frame was considered to be an event or not.

In the hidden layer we used 20 neurons where ten had a feedback to the input layer. Linear and sigmoid activation functions were used in hidden and output layer respectively. The Levenberg-Marquardt algorithm was used also for training, which was able to train the whole network in only 30 iterations. After a number of simulations, the architecture with 19 inputs appeared to be the most effective. The accuracy of this network was above 90 % for all sports in our dataset.

14.4 Scoreboard-Based Event Detection

The detection of an event in sport video broadcasts may seem to be an easy task. Very often there is a scoreboard in one of the corners on the screen to notify the viewers that an event occurred. So naturally a first approach would be to analyze this region of the screen to detect any interesting moments in a game. However, this is not an easy task from a computer vision point of view, taking into account the variety of shapes, fonts, and behaviors of these regions. For sports with relatively simple scoring systems, like soccer, Gaelic football, hurling, and rugby, the scoreboards tend to share some characteristics. There is usually information about the teams, points that they have scored, and the remaining/elapsed time. However, even in this case there is significant diversity in the possible layouts. Figure 14.3 shows some examples of the scoreboards in our dataset.

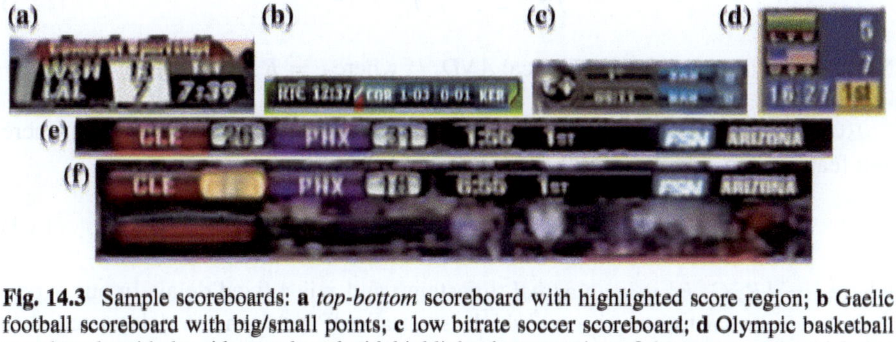

Fig. 14.3 Sample scoreboards: **a** *top-bottom* scoreboard with highlighted score region; **b** Gaelic football scoreboard with big/small points; **c** low bitrate soccer scoreboard; **d** Olympic basketball scoreboard; **e** side-by-side scoreboard with highlighted score regions; **f** the same scoreboard during a transition effect

These are just representatives of the vast range of scoreboards possible. Examples Fig. 14.3a shows the top-bottom layout of the scoreboard. Note, that the gap between the two scores and digits in the same score on the scoreboard Fig. 14.3a is very small, which significantly affects the digit segmentation/extraction process. Since the score region can be highlighted, the process that finds the digits needs to be invariant to different backgrounds and complex objects like country flags in the region where text is detected Fig. 14.3d. Scoreboard Fig. 14.3b represents a Gaelic football scoreboard where the score for both teams can be further split into big and small points. Another issue in text detection and recognition in the images is the quality of the image itself. Example Fig. 14.3c represents a scoreboard region extracted from the video of very low bitrate or resolution. Note, that even if the text region is correctly recognized the score itself is almost invisible, or at least very difficult to extract. These aspects that make the extraction of the score difficult are exacerbated by the fact that almost every broadcaster has implemented a different style of the scoreboard behavior that can be changed at short notice. There are two major features that can vary from broadcaster to broadcaster:

- the amount of time the scoreboard is visible on the screen (even when the score is recognized, due to the fact that in replays usually this information is invisible, it is not possible to simply assume that it will be there every time we need it);
- transition effects cause changes such as color change or some additional graphical effects Fig. 14.3e, f.

Clearly, the implementation of the scoreboard-based event detection system is not a straightforward task.

14.4.1 Scoreboard Detection

The scoreboard/text region detection process is run independently on each of the three channels of the RGB color space, and then merged into a single text region image representation in a logical *AND* manner presented with Eq. (14.3).

$$I^{\text{text}} = I^R \wedge I^G \wedge I^B \tag{14.3}$$

Note, that in order to perform logical *AND*, I^i where $i = R, G, B$ has to be a binary image.

Every channel is a logical *OR* combination of present and past video frames where text features are calculated with respect to the Eq. (14.4):

$$I^i = I^i_{t,t-\tau} \vee I^i_{t,t-2\tau} \vee I^i_{t-\tau,t-2\tau} \tag{14.4}$$

where $i = \{R, G, B\}$, t is an actual timestamp and τ is a fixed delay. In our experiments τ is equal to one second which is a tradeoff between the delay needed to detect a change by the algorithm and delay needed for the scoreboard to apply the text transition effect. As it can be seen, we take three different pairs resulting from all different combinations of an actual frame and two frames from the past delayed by the same amount of the time between each of them. For every pair we calculate following formula (note, that for clarity we drop the i index) (14.5):

$$I_{t0,t1} = I^{\text{col}}_{t0,t1} I^{\text{var}} I^{\text{edg}}_{t0,t1} \tag{14.5}$$

Equation (14.5) shows the three features extracted for text region detection:

$$\begin{aligned}
I^{\text{col}}_{t0,t1} &= \overline{|I^{\text{col}}_{t0} - I^{\text{col}}_{t1}|} \\
I^{\text{var}} &= \frac{1}{L} \sum_{p=1}^{L} \left(p_{x,y} - \bar{I}_{x,y}\right)^2 \\
\bar{I}_{x,y} &= \frac{1}{L} \sum_{p=1}^{L} p_{x,y} \\
I^{\text{edg}}_{t0,t1} &= \overline{|I^{\text{edg}}_{t0} - I^{\text{edg}}_{t1}|} \\
I^{\text{edg}}_{t} &= \max\left(I^{\text{vertical}}_{t}, I^{\text{horizontal}}_{t}, I^{\text{diagonal}}_{t}\right)
\end{aligned}$$

where $p_{x,y}$ is a pixel of x, y coordinates, L is the number of pixels in the local variance mask and I^{vertical}_{t}, $I^{\text{horizontal}}_{t}$, I^{diagonal}_{t} are vertical, horizontal, and diagonal gradients of a frame t. These kind of gradients are proven to work well in text detection process [30].

Taking all the above into account a text region is a region where:

1. The color distribution does not change (even if it is transparent to some extent) and the font color does not change.
2. Text is a region of a high edge density that also usually does not change between the two frames.
3. Local variance of a text region is big.

This is always true for all three RGB channels. Figure 14.4 shows a sample soccer video frame and a response from text region identification algorithm. It can be seen that the presented algorithm works for multiple regions that have different characteristics (i.e., different colors, partially transparent background, etc.).

The next step after finding the text candidate regions is to create consistent text regions on which the digit identification algorithm can run. This is done by a project and split algorithm that works in the following manner:

1. Project the text candidate images horizontally onto the y axis (projection axis number 1 in Fig. 14.5);
2. Based on the projection curve detect consistent regions of values above a threshold, equal to 5 in our experiments—a good tradeoff between noise removal and small text region extraction (regions 1 and 2 in Fig. 14.5);

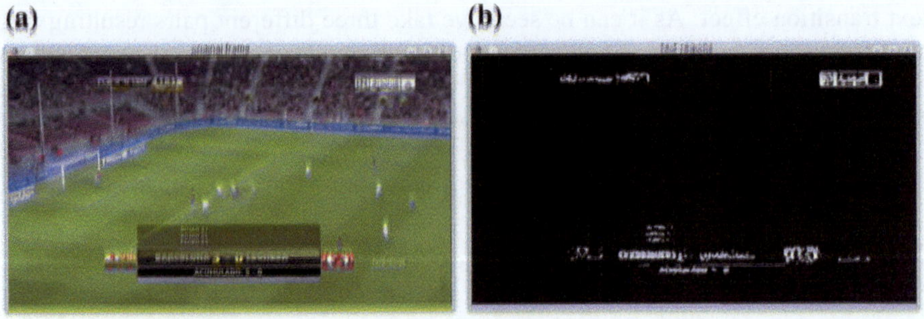

Fig. 14.4 Sample video frame from a basketball game (**a**) and its text region candidates (**b**)

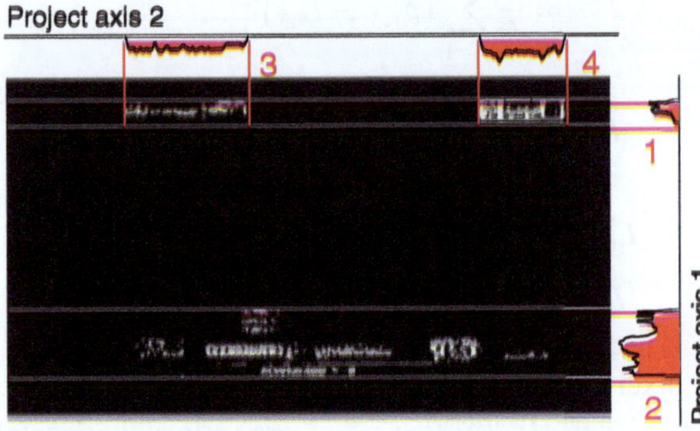

Fig. 14.5 Project and split algorithm

3. Store all the region candidates in memory;
4. Take region candidate from the queue;
5. Project region in the opposite direction (projection axis number 2 in Fig. 14.5);
6. Based on the projection curve detect consistent regions of values above threshold (regions 3 and 4 in Fig. 14.5);
7. If the detected region width/height is equal to the original width/height before projection store ready text region in the memory;
8. Go to step 4.

The above procedure can be implemented using recursion. The first few steps are shown in Fig. 14.5.

14.4.2 Event Detection

Figure 14.6 shows the processing flow in the scoreboard-based event detection task. The input to the algorithm are the extracted text regions described in the previous section. The following stages are described herein.

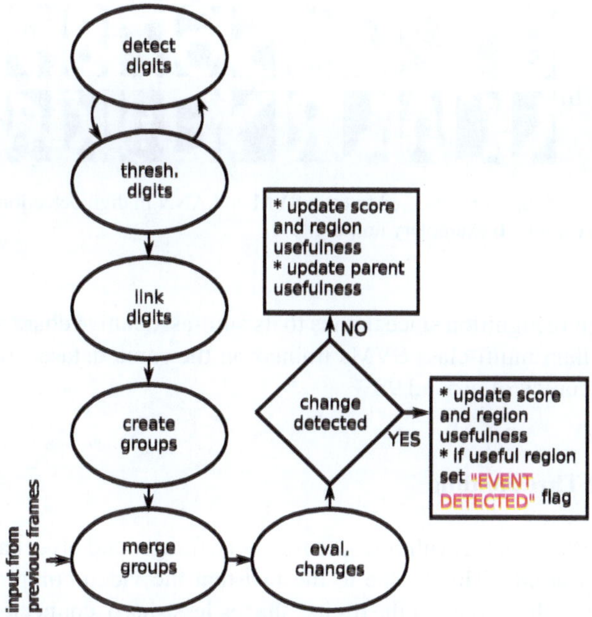

Fig. 14.6 The flow of scoreboard-based event detection

14.4.2.1 Digit Detection

Since the scoreboard region is typically designed for better visibility with high contrast we assume that either the text color is very dark or very bright. This approach allows us to deal with the challenge of different font colors (Fig. 14.3a). Based on this assumption, the detection phase is performed twice: the first time it seeks black digits on white background and second, white digits on black background. The digit identification algorithm finds foreground objects, extracts their features, and applies a cascade classifier to detect if the region contains a digit and, if so, what digit. The levels of the classifier validate the following features:

- region height;
- region width/height ratio;
- region no. foreground pixels to no. background pixels ratio;
- a Support Vector Machine (SVM) response.

An SVM is trained to recognize digit/non-digit image blocks based on concatenated horizontal and vertical projections of this block [31]. A feed-forward artificial neural network trained on the same input as in the SVM is then used to distinguish between digits. A dataset of figures containing differently shaped digits and non-digits was created to train both an SVM and ANN. Figure 14.7 shows some exemplary images from this dataset. It contains 5,000 images distributed equally between different digit and non-digit classes. We have chosen an ANN for

(a)

(b)

Fig. 14.7 Samples of digit images used to train SVM and ANN in digit detection and recognition tasks: **a** exemplary digits; **b** exemplary non-digits

multi-class digit recognition since thanks to its auto-associative characteristics it performed better than multi-class SVMs trained on the same dataset. Both classifiers obtained an accuracy of around 98 %.

14.4.2.2 Digit Thresholding

The digit identification algorithm works for every foreground object and is repeated for varying thresholds. This is due to the fact that the video compression process softens the edges, thus, making the digits' shapes less sharp, connected to other digits or the background. Introducing a loop where the input region is thresholded with increasing threshold value assures that in some range of this value the extracted digit will be recognized correctly. After a set of experiments we decided to implement ten thresholds with spacing equal to ten (0–100 for black digits, 150–250 for white). Based on experiments we performed, this is a more robust and efficient solution than thresholding with adaptive threshold value which is not very robust to quantization noise or performing image segmentation based on a Gaussian mixture model where the number of Gaussians is unknown. For every iteration of the loop the digit recognition result is remembered and a voting is performed afterwards so that the output of this algorithm is a digit with the highest number of votes.

14.4.2.3 Digit Linking and Digit Group Creation

The first of these two processes looks for digits that are in close proximity and links them together. The idea behind this process is to link the digits that comprise a single score or the time information in the scoreboard. Note, that the distance between two digits to be linked has to be adaptive and is a function of a region height and font characteristics. The second process takes all the links into consideration and performs digit grouping, i.e., a single group consists of the digits that were linked together. Note, that a particular digit in a digit group does not have links with all the members in the group (transitional links are allowed). Each group is assigned a specific number called the *usefulness* which stands for the number of digit changes within the group.

14.4.2.4 Digit Group Merging and Changes Evaluation

If at least one digit group was detected in the text region candidate the procedure assigns a scoreboard candidate flag to this region and tries to find any equivalent results (scoreboard candidates and digit groups) from the previously processed frames. The features taken into account are the dimensions, location, and number of digit groups in the scoreboard candidates. If the first two match then the scoreboard candidates are merged together. During the merge process the recognized digits and usefulness scores are updated. If there was a digit change this information is sent to the following step where changes evaluation takes place. During this process the usefulness of the scoreboard candidate and digit group where the change was detected are taken into account. First, since there was a change, digit group usefulness is decreased. If the usefulness of a digit group and its parent (scoreboard candidate) are sufficiently high an *event detected* flag is set. If not, the algorithm updates the usefulness of a scoreboard region.

Figure 14.8 shows an example scoreboard recognized by our approach. After the digits are detected (yellow bounding boxes) and grouped into digit groups (blue bounding boxes) a text region becomes a scoreboard region. This is visualized with a green bounding box. Scoreboard region and digit groups are given usefulness parameters visualized with numbers at the upper left corners. The pictured situation was captured after few seconds from the beginning of the video and it shows that the regions that change often (e.g., time region) are marked with negative usefulness whereas score digit groups and their parent (scoreboard region) have all high usefulness numbers.

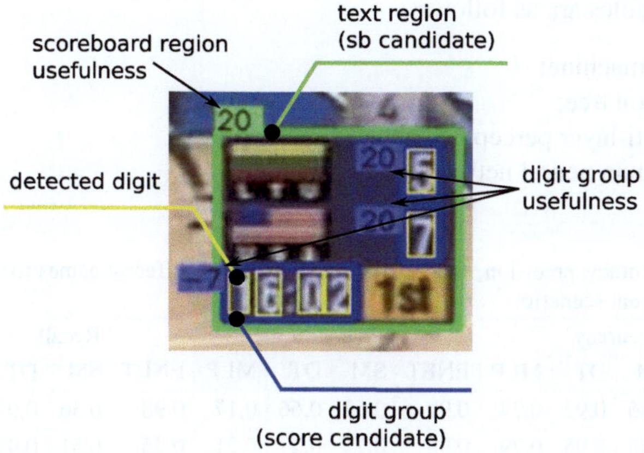

Fig. 14.8 Exemplary scoreboard region (*green* bounding box) with detected digits (*yellow* bounding boxes), digit groups (*blue* bounding boxes)

14.5 Event Detection Results

This section presents results obtained from testing our event detection algorithms on datasets proposed especially for this task. We discuss the accuracy and the time performance separately. Results obtained from both investigations allow us to conclude that the system is capable of extracting the interesting events in a real-time.

14.5.1 Accuracy

The dataset comprises 40 h of basketball, soccer, rugby, cricket, Gaelic football, and hurling videos. The duration of the videos in each sport group is balanced equally in order to avoid biasing the obtained results. Also accuracy, precision, and recall are calculated for each sport to show that exactness/quality and completeness/quantity of results are consistent. For every sport the ground-truth dataset is split into submodules in order to detect three types of events:

1. Goal event—an event that ends with a change of the game score;
2. Exciting event—an event that could be extremely exciting to the viewer, e.g., skillful dribble before the goal or a close-miss;
3. General event—type of an event that includes both previous events, plus additional, less exciting moments.

In Tables 14.3, 14.4 and 14.5 we present calculated values of accuracy, precision and recall for the three possible scenarios presented above. All the abbreviations used in the above tables are as follows:

SM—state machine;
DT—decision tree;
MLP—multi-layer perceptron neural network;
ENET—Elman neural network.

Table 14.3 Accuracy, precision, and recall calculated for six different games for the classification of the general event scenario

	Accuracy				Precision				Recall			
	SM	DT	MLP	ENET	SM	DT	MLP	ENET	SM	DT	MLP	ENET
Rugby	0.66	0.92	0.74	0.99	0.63	0.66	0.17	0.98	0.36	0.97	0.04	0.98
Soccer	0.58	0.95	0.79	0.98	0.7	0.77	0.21	0.95	0.51	0.97	0.04	0.96
Basketball	0.74	0.99	0.85	0.99	0.62	0.95	0.17	0.92	0.32	0.91	0.19	0.92
Cricket	0.42	0.95	0.9	0.99	0.7	0.67	0.1	0.93	0.26	0.73	0.04	0.97
Gaelic football	0.59	0.98	0.92	0.99	0.3	0.81	0.18	0.97	0.39	0.92	0.05	0.97
Hurling	0.44	0.95	0.8	0.99	0.79	0.77	0.36	0.99	0.73	0.98	0.08	0.99

Table 14.4 Accuracy, precision, and recall calculated for six different games for the classification of the goal scenario

	Accuracy				Precision				Recall			
	SM	DT	MLP	ENET	SM	DT	MLP	ENET	SM	DT	MLP	ENET
Rugby	0.55	0.96	0.94	0.99	0.22	0.61	0.01	0.88	0.4	0.73	0.00	0.99
Soccer	0.56	0.95	0.83	0.96	0.72	0.75	0.23	0.81	0.5	0.92	0.07	0.96
Basketball	0.53	0.99	0.67	0.99	0.62	0.95	0.02	0.82	0.47	0.98	0.22	0.93
Cricket	0.8	0.96	0.96	0.94	0.33	0.59	0.07	0.57	0.42	0.79	0.03	0.97
Gaelic football	0.78	0.98	0.85	0.98	0.57	0.77	0.09	0.71	0.6	0.73	0.1	0.97
Hurling	0.59	0.94	0.68	0.99	0.46	0.59	0.55	0.92	0.46	0.96	0.05	0.99

Table 14.5 Accuracy, precision, and recall calculated for six different games for the classification of the exciting event scenario

	Accuracy				Precision				Recall			
	SM	DT	MLP	ENET	SM	DT	MLP	ENET	SM	DT	MLP	ENET
Rugby	0.44	0.97	0.65	0.94	0.52	0.48	0.83	0.88	0.72	0.99	0.28	0.74
Soccer	0.73	0.97	0.82	0.95	0.48	0.75	0.27	0.82	0.51	0.99	0.53	0.8
Basketball	0.58	0.99	0.93	0.99	0.32	0.97	0.52	0.71	0.72	0.99	0.17	0.95
Cricket	0.41	0.95	0.27	0.96	0.41	0.34	0.73	0.78	0.36	0.99	0.19	0.72
Gaelic football	0.46	0.99	0.26	0.98	0.77	0.49	0.14	0.22	0.39	0.76	0.75	0.78
Hurling	0.74	0.99	0.57	0.99	0.6	0.52	0.48	0.7	0.4	0.93	0.24	0.78

The training was performed with use of probes collected only from one game (in this case—basketball) and simulated on six different games: rugby, football, basketball, cricket, Gaelic football, and hurling. In order to figure out the optimal split between training and testing subclasses of the given data we ran a number of experiments. Naturally, we tried a training dataset that is equally distributed among all classes and sports but this did not give the most effective results. Surprisingly the optimal division seems to be in the case when we take most of the samples from one game and train the classifier and test it on the remaining data points. This is due to the fact that a large training dataset from one sport only will cover most of the situations that the system could deal with and are simply impossible or at least very difficult to analyze by a human. Concluding, as the training data we used 70 % of probes collected from the basketball game, which is around 19,600 frames.

It can be seen from the results that the system's accuracy in the case of a decision tree classifier is usually above 95 % and never lower than 92 %. The results for the Elman neural network are between 96 and 94 %. This proves, that both classifiers are well trained and are capable of recognizing event sequences from videos or even sports that they have never seen before.

Regarding the efficiency of the scoreboard-based event detection (which can only detect scores), once the scoreboard is detected correctly, as was presented in Sect. 14.4.2 it is just a matter of tracking the changes inside this region. If the change

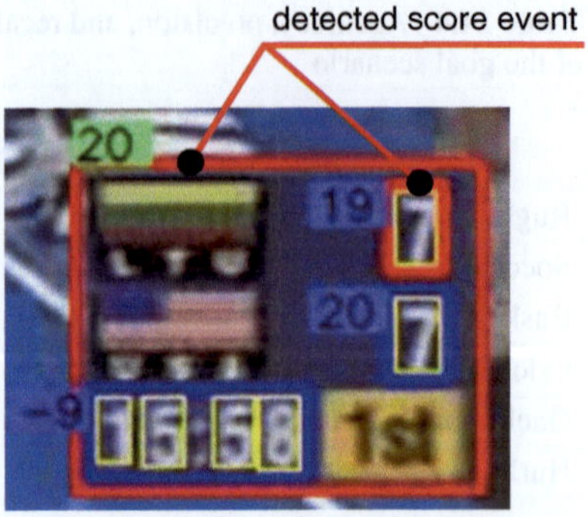

Fig. 14.9 Exemplary scoreboard region highlighting detected scoreboard-based event

appears in the digit region that does not change often and the digits present a number that is reasonably similar to the probable score of the game we say that there was a goal/event. Note, that the system is not constrained to count a score from zero since otherwise it would have to analyze every video from the beginning of the game. Figure 14.9 shows an exemplary visualization performed by the system when the change in the score is detected.

The only feature of the video that can affect this process is the perceptual quality of the scoreboard which is dependent on video bitrate and resolution. For example in our tests the system could easily recognize scoreboards in videos of resolution 640×480 whereas this was not the case for videos of resolution 768×76 due to a specific font used However, for videos where scoreboard regions can be clearly recognized by subjective viewing (about 80 % in our dataset) its effectiveness was always 100 %.

14.5.2 Time Performance

Given the classification methods presented in Sects. 14.3.3 and 14.4.2 it is important to highlight the time performance of the proposed detection techniques. Given the low accuracy of the state machine we do not take it into consideration.

As mentioned, the accuracy of the decision tree and Elman neural network are always higher than 92 % which makes them good candidates for the final event detector. Looking more closely at the two classification algorithms, the main differences that make them the best candidate for this task would be a train/predict time performance and the nature of the algorithm itself. The decision tree algorithm needs less than a second to create a tree (either in the case of nine or eighteen descriptors) while the Elman neural network needs more than a minute to perform the training. The prediction time is very similar for both cases: 0.0219 s for the decision tree and 0.0269 s for the neural network. Since training can be done offline it is not particularly crucial unless the system is required to change its behavior or gain some additional knowledge about events in interactive mode training time is very important. In addition, the great disadvantage of the neural network is that as a non-deterministic algorithm it will always give different results for every training, while it always starts with different values of weights. Thus, it is very unpredictable and each has to be validated separately. Moreover, the output of the neural network is a value between 0 and 1, and setting up the threshold for event detection can be a difficult task.

Figure 14.10 shows the breakdown of the time performance of the feature-based event detection algorithm. This is the time needed to prepare data for the final classifier (decision tree or Elman neural network). As can be seen, keypoint detection, feature extraction and matching (i.e., assigning all the descriptors to particular nodes) consume the most time, whereas creation of bag-of-words histogram and SVM prediction can almost be disregarded.

The time performance of the scoreboard-based event detection significantly depends on the behavior of the scoreboard region. In general it can be split, according to Fig. 14.6 into the following stages: preprocessing, digit detection, digit linking, digit grouping, group merging, evaluation/event detection. All stages except the last one are done only a few times at the beginning of each game unless the behavior of the scoreboard prevents the algorithm from detecting a stable scoreboard region (e.g., when scoreboard appears only for a few seconds after the score changes). The times for particular stages are as follows:

- preprocessing—30 ms;
- digit detection—135 ms;
- digit linking—6 μs;
- digit grouping—30 μs;
- group merging—250 μs;
- evaluation/event detection—55 μs.

So after the scoreboard is detected and digit groups are recognized the scoreboard-based event detection algorithm only needs 55 μs to detect an event. Finally, it should be noted, that the given times for scoreboard-based and feature-based event detection are not cumulative since both techniques work in parallel with no interdependency.

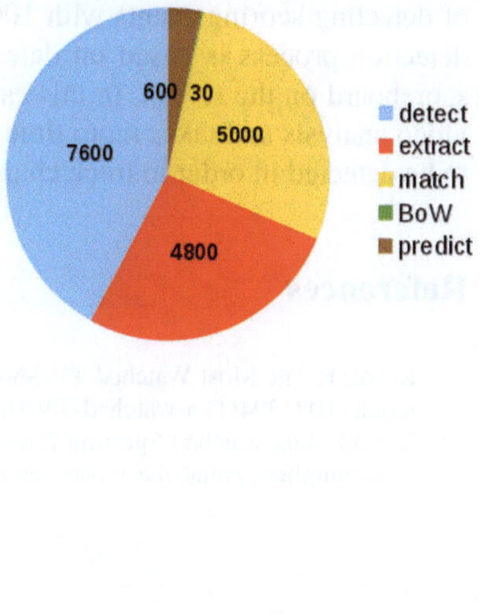

Fig. 14.10 Breakdown of processing time in the various stages of the feature-based event detection algorithm; all times are given in μs

14.6 Summary

This chapter describes a real-time field sports video event detection system that is capable of detecting goals/scores, close-misses, and also other exciting moments with high accuracy across multiple sports. Unlike previous work in sports scene classification, we pay particular attention to computational requirements, deriving an algorithm that is comparable with the state of the art in terms of accuracy, but which requires significantly less computational resources. For concreteness, our experimental evaluation focuses on field sports video as this covers multiple individual sports such as basketball, soccer, rugby, football, all genres of hockey, etc.; however, as our descriptor avoids using sports video specific mid-level features, like grass ratios, it is sufficiently general to be applicable in other contexts. The system is composed of two event detection modules that work in parallel performing complementary event detection tasks.

The first one is based on audio-visual low-level features and can be trained for different events such as goals, or very interesting moments such as a close miss. A feature of the approach is minimal ambiguity, as its response is considered in terms of event probability rather than a deterministic response. We also validated different event classification techniques and present results (accuracy, precision and recall) for each of them with respect to different sport videos processed by the system. The simplest approach is to use a state machine. However, the results showed that this solution does not give satisfactory results. To overcome this, we evaluated more sophisticated methods like deterministic decision trees or non-deterministic artificial neural networks. Both these solutions give good results, the difference is mainly in training time. It is important to notice that training either the decision tree or the Elman neural network based on the probes from one game only does not have negative influence on accuracy for any other game, which is always higher than 92 %. Using mixed values from different games could result in overfitting since it is very hard to judge if the game events encoded with low-level features are similar or not. For this reason we think it is better to use most of one game to train the event classifier since we can be sure it covers most of the possible cases on the field/court. The second, independent thread complements the first mentioned and is capable of detecting scoring events with 100 % accuracy with high resolution footage. The detection process is based on detection of changes in the score presented on the scoreboard on the screen. In this case, time performance is not constant during the video analysis and takes more time at the beginning where the scoreboard area has to be detected in order to track changes in the scores of the teams played.

References

1. Revoir P, The Most Watched TV Shows of All Time. http://www.dailymail.co.uk/tvshowbiz/article-1071394/The-watched-TV-shows-time-old-programmes.html
2. The 50 Most-watched Sporting Events of 2012. http://www.sportsmediawatch.com/2013/01/2012-numbers-game-the-most-watched-sporting-events-of-the-year/

3. Kokaram A, Rea N, Dahyot R, Tekalp AM, Bouthemy P, Gros P, Sezan I (2006) Browsing sports video. IEEE Signal Process Mag 23(2):47–58
4. Sadlier DA, O'Connor NE (2005) Event detection in field sports video using audio-visual features and a support vector machine. IEEE Trans Circuits Syst Video Technol 15:1225–1233
5. Li Baoxin S, Ibrahim M (2001) Event detection and summarization in sports video. In: Proceedings of the IEEE workshop on content-based access of image and video libraries (CBAIVL'01). IEEE Computer Society, Washington
6. Ye Q, Qingming H, Wen G, Shuqiang J (2005) Exciting event detection in broadcast Soccer video with mid-level description and incremental learning. In: Proceedings of the 13th annual ACM international conference on multimedia. Hilton, Singapore, pp 455–458. doi:10.1145/1101149.1101250
7. Chen SC, Shyu ML, Zhang C, Luo L, Chen M (2003) Detection of soccer goal shots using joint multimedia features and classification rules. In: Proceedings of the fourth international workshop on multimedia data mining (MDM/KDD2003), pp 36–44
8. Kim HG, Roeber S, Samour A, Sikora T (2005) Detection of goal events in Soccer videos. In: Proceedings of storage and retrieval methods and applications for multimedia, vol 5682
9. Wang L, Liu X, Lin S, Xu G, Shum H (2004) Generic slow-motion replay detection in sports video. In: ICIP, pp 1585–1588
10. Jinjun W, Engsiong C, Changsheng X (2005) Soccer replay detection using scene transition structure analysis. In: Acoustics, speech, and signal processing, proceedings (ICASSP'05)
11. Zhao Z, Shuqiang J, Qingming H, Guangyu Z (2006) Highlight summarization in sports video based on replay detection. In: 2006 IEEE international conference on multimedia and expo, pp 1613–1616. doi:10.1109/ICME.2006.262855
12. Lanagan J, Smeaton FA (2011) Using Twitter to detect and tag important events in live sports. In: Proceedings of the fifth international AAAI conference on weblogs and social media, pp 542–545
13. Changsheng X, Zhang Y, Guangyu Z, Rui Y, Hanqing L, Qingming H (2008) Using webcast text for semantic event detection in broadcast sports video. IEEE Trans Multimed 10(7):1342–1355. doi:10.1109/TMM.2008.2004912
14. Kapela R, McGuinness K, O'Connor NE, Real-time field sports scene classification using colour and frequency space decompositions. J Real-Time Image Process (In review)
15. Lowe DG (1999) Object recognition from local scale-invariant features. In: IEEE international conference on computer vision, pp 1150–1157
16. Dalal N, Triggs B (2005) Histograms of oriented gradients for human detection. In: Proceedings of the 2005 IEEE conference on computer vision and pattern recognition (CVPR 2005), vol 1, pp 886–893
17. Calonder M, Lepetit V, Strecha C, Fua P (2010) BRIEF: binary Robust independent elementary features. Lecture Notes in Computer Science, pp 778–792
18. Alahi A, Ortiz R, Vandergheynst P (2012) In: IEEE conference on computer vision and pattern recognition, Rhode Island, Providence, USA, 16–21 June
19. Leutenegger S, Chli M, Siegwart RY (2011) BRISK: binary robust invariant scalable keypoints. In: 2011 IEEE international conference on Computer vision (ICCV), pp 2548–2555. doi:10.1109/ICCV.2011.6126542
20. Tola E, Lepetit V, Fua P (2010) An efficient dense descriptor applied to wide baseline stereo. IEEE Trans Pattern Anal Mach Intell 32(5):815–830
21. Mikolajczyk K, Schmid C (2005) A performance evaluation of local descriptors. Pattern Anal Mach Intell IEEE Trans 27(10):1615–1630. doi:10.1109/TPAMI.2005.188
22. Khvedchenia I, A battle of three descriptors: SURF, FREAK and BRISK. http://computer-vision-talks.com/2012/08/a-battle-of-three-descriptors-surf-freak-and-brisk/
23. Perronnin F, Dance C (2007) Fisher Kernels on visual vocabularies for image categorization. In: Proceedings of the IEEE conference on computer vision and pattern recognition, vol 1–8
24. Hervè J, Douze M, Schmid C, Perez P (2010) Aggregating local descriptors into a compact image representation. In: IEEE conference on computer vision and pattern recognition, pp 3304–3311

25. Ordonez C (2003) Clustering binary data streams with K-means. In: Proceedings of the 8th ACM SIGMOD workshop on research issues in data mining and knowledge discovery DMKD'03, pp 12–19
26. Coppersmith D, Hong SJ, Hosking JRM (1999) Partitioning nominal attributes in decision trees. Data Min Knowl Discov 3:197–217
27. Levenberg K (1944) A method for the solution of certain problems in least squares. Q Appl Math 5:164–168
28. Marquardt D (1963) An algorithm for least-squares estimation of nonlinear parameters. SIAM J Appl Math 11(2):431–441
29. Hammer B (1997) Generalization of Elman networks. In: Artificial neural networks—ICANN'97, pp 409–414
30. Shivakumara P, Weihua H, Tan CL (2008) Efficient video text detection using edge features. In: 19th International conference on pattern recognition, 2008. ICPR 2008. December 2008, vol 1, no 4, pp 8–11
31. Baggio DL, Emami S, Escriva DM, Khvedchenia I, Mahmood N, Saragih J, Shilkrot R (2012) Mastering OpenCV with practical computer vision projects, Pact Publishing
32. Binary decision tree for classification, MathWorks Documentation. http://www.mathworks.com/help/stats/classificationtreeclass.html

Index

T.B. Moeslund et al. (eds.), *Computer Vision in Sports*,
Advances in Computer Vision and Pattern Recognition,
DOI 10.1007/978-3-319-09396-3